MW00615798

# SYMBOLS & SHADOWS

*Unlocking a Deeper Understanding of the Atonement*

## DONALD W. PARRY
## JAY A. PARRY

DESERET
BOOK

SALT LAKE CITY, UTAH

**Library of Congress Cataloging-in-Publication Data**

Parry, Donald W.
   Symbols and shadows : unlocking a deeper understanding of the atonement / Donald W. Parry and Jay A. Parry.
     p. cm.
   Includes bibliographical references and index.
   ISBN 978-1-60641-129-2 (hardbound : alk. paper)
  1. Atonement.   2. Symbolism.   3. Church of Jesus Christ of Latter-day Saints—Doctrines.   4. Mormon Church—Doctrines.   I. Parry, Jay A.   II. Title.
   BX8643.A85P38 2009
   234'.3—dc22                                    2009012112

Printed in the United States of America
Sheridan Books, Chelsea, MI

10  9  8  7  6  5  4  3  2

# CONTENTS

# CONTENTS

# CONTENTS

## PART 3. THE INFINITE ATONEMENT

# THE ATONEMENT, HINGE POINT OF GOD'S PLAN

THE ATONEMENT OF JESUS CHRIST is the hinge point of all eternity. Because of it the Father's plan is able to come to fruition even when we, his children, wander from the true path.

Without the atonement, we would come to earth, sin, die—and suffer endless woe, becoming angels to the devil and devils ourselves.

With the atonement, if we come unto Christ and partake of those great things he offers us, we can repent of our sins and be purified and renewed, and when we rise in the resurrection, we will rise to glory.

Without the atonement, the Father's plan would come to naught, and the earth would be wasted.

With the atonement, we can become as he is, and the plan continues in an endless cycle of love and power from eternity to eternity.

These truths have been part of the gospel message from the beginning. Adam received a witness of the Redeemer from an angelic messenger, as well as from the voice of God himself. Enoch, Noah, Abraham, Moses, and Isaiah all knew about the essential nature of the atonement of Christ, as did such Book of Mormon witnesses as Lehi, Nephi, Benjamin, Alma, Helaman, Mormon, and Moroni.

In our day, as part of the restoration of all things, we have a sure knowledge of the atonement of Christ. We understand that the Savior and the atonement he performed are the central core of all we are and all we believe. Joseph Smith, the prophet of the Restoration, taught this clearly: "The fundamental principles of our religion are the testimony of the Apostles and Prophets, concerning Jesus Christ, that He died, was buried, and rose again the third day, and ascended into heaven; and all other things which pertain to our religion are only appendages to it."[1]

"The atonement of the Master is the central point of world history," added President Marion G. Romney. "Without it the whole purpose for the creation of earth and our living upon it would fail."[2]

In characteristically bold language, Elder Bruce R. McConkie said, "All things center in, revolve around, are anchored to, and are built upon the atoning sacrifice of the Lord Jesus Christ."[3]

To these prophetic witnesses could be added countless additional testimonies of apostles and prophets and local leaders, teachers, and members of the Church who have stood at pulpits and sat in living rooms bearing testimony that Jesus is the Christ and that without his atonement all is lost—and that with his atonement all is possible.

But there is another form of witness the Lord has given us, one that reaches far beyond the written or spoken word.

## A THOUSAND SYMBOLS, SHADOWS, AND WITNESSES OF THE ATONEMENT

Because of the absolute centrality of Jesus Christ and his atonement to God's perfect plan, our Heavenly Father has given us a "great . . . cloud of witnesses" (Heb. 12:1) of his Son's atonement—a thousand witnesses, ten thousand witnesses, or more. These symbols, shadows, and witnesses are all around us—in the skies, on the earth, and in the earth.

The Lord through his prophets used a great number of symbols, types, and shadows to provide insight into the atonement. The prophets drew on the natural world, including things in the heavens, geographical sites, and the plant and animal kingdom; everyday clothing and sacred vestments; civil and religious positions; building and architectural components; common women and men, as well as prophets, priests, and kings; ordinances, both ancient and modern; historical events;

2

cities; such ordinary things as colors, liquids, numbers, and foods; and many other things. In addition, all parts of the law of Moses—every particle—testified of Jesus and his sacrifice, including the temple rituals, the system of sacrifices, and the annual feasts and festivals. And, of course, the scriptures are filled with overt, direct testimonies, inspired words about the atoning work of the Word.

Almost in the very beginning, Father Adam learned directly from the Savior that "*all things* have their likeness, and *all things* are created and made to bear record of me, both things which are temporal, and things which are spiritual; things which are in the heavens above, and things which are on the earth, and things which are in the earth, and things which are under the earth, . . . *all things* bear record of me" (Moses 6:63; emphasis added).

Nephi learned the same truth: "*All things* which have been given of God from the beginning of the world, unto man, are the typifying of him [Christ]" (2 Ne. 11:4; emphasis added; see also Alma 34:14).

And President John Taylor wrote, "There were so many types, shadows and forms of which [Jesus] was the great prototype."[4]

Why are the types and symbols of the atonement ever present? Because the Father wanted to manifest his Son's atonement clearly and time and again to his children who seek to know him. But whether or not God's children are aware of these types and shadows, the atonement's impact is yet ever present. Hugh Nibley compared it to gravity or the speed of light, calling it "one of the grand constants in nature." It is "omnipresent [and] unalterable. . . . Like gravity, though we are rarely aware of it, it is at work every moment of our lives, and to ignore it can be fatal."[5]

The many witnesses of the atonement are woven together like the threads in a tapestry. Here is the thread of physical objects that symbolize Christ's offering; here is the thread of witnesses in the earth and stars; here is the thread of righteous individuals whose very lives predicted Jesus' sufferings and sacrifice. Also in the pattern are threads representing the law of Moses, the modern ordinances, parables that reveal Christ's divine redemption, symbols from the animal kingdom, and much, much more. And the tapestry as a whole? It depicts the story of

God who became man, condescending to descend to an earth of pain and trouble and taking upon himself the sins and sicknesses of his people.

This book attempts to isolate some of these threads:

Part 1 focuses on types and shadows of the atonement.

Part 2 looks at witnesses and fulfillment of the atonement in Christ's mortal life and sacrifice.

Part 3 testifies of the infinite atonement and the blessings of grace.

Because of the interweaving of the threads, individual symbols often appear in more than one context in the overall tapestry. To a limited degree, this is reflected in the present volume. For example, the symbol of living water, which flows from the Savior, is noted (often briefly) in discussions on symbolisms found in the natural world, the sacrament, and the incidents on the cross. Each mention, however, appears in a different context and provides a new insight into that marvelous symbol. As we see and better understand the threads of the tapestry, the overall picture comes more clearly into focus, and our hearts become filled with praise and gratitude for the goodness and mercy of our God.

At the end of his testimony of Christ, the apostle John wrote, "There are also many other things which Jesus did, the which, if they should be written every one, I suppose that even the world itself could not contain the books that should be written" (John 21:25). The same could be said of the types and shadows that pertain to Christ and his atonement. Since "all things" bear record of Christ and since "all things" typify him, an exhaustive and complete view of this subject is not possible. This volume provides an in-depth introduction, however, that we hope will open eyes and minds to the multitude of witnesses the Lord has given of himself.

## "Always Remember"

President Spencer W. Kimball once said: "When you look in the dictionary for the most important word, do you know what it is[?] It could be 'remember.' Because all of [us] have made covenants . . . our greatest need is to remember. . . . 'Remember' is the word."[6]

Remembering the Savior is so important that we recommit ourselves every week (twice—once with the bread and again with the water) as we take the sacrament to "*always* remember him" (D&C 20:77, 79; emphasis added). Remembering him means that we keep in our minds his singular life and his infinite atonement. It means that we align our will with his and that we seek to obey him in all things.

But in this world, filled with sin and distraction, how do we always *remember?*

Part of the answer lies in the gift our Heavenly Father has given us: a myriad of symbols, types, and shadows that serve as witnesses of Christ. If we can recognize the witnesses of the atonement that God has placed all around us, if we can see the types and shadows and symbols both in the word and in the world, we can be bolstered in our ability to keep our promise to remember—and we will be immeasurably strengthened in the process.

## DEEPENING OUR UNDERSTANDING

Seeking to deepen our understanding of the atonement should be one of the highest priorities of our lives. Elder Richard G. Scott taught persuasively:

> I realize that no mortal mind can adequately conceive, nor can human tongue appropriately express, the full significance of all that Jesus Christ has done for our Heavenly Father's children through His Atonement. Yet it is vital that we each learn what we can about it. The Atonement is that essential ingredient of our Father in Heaven's plan of happiness without which that plan would have no significant meaning.
>
> I strongly believe that there is an imperative need for you to strengthen your understanding of the significance of the Atonement of Jesus Christ so that it will become the secure foundation upon which to build the balance of your life. . . . Your understanding of and faith in the Atonement of Jesus Christ will provide much-needed strength and capacity in your life. It will

also bring confidence in times of trial and peace in moments of turmoil.

I energetically encourage you to establish a personal plan to better understand and appreciate the incomparable, eternal, infinite consequences of the perfect fulfillment by Jesus Christ of His divinely appointed calling as our Savior and Redeemer. . . . Please establish for yourself a must-be-accomplished goal to acquire a better understanding of the Atonement. . . .

. . . As an Apostle of the Lord Jesus Christ—and I do not use those words lightly—I testify that your understanding of the Atonement and the insight it provides for your life will greatly enhance your productive use of all of the [other] knowledge, experience, and skills you acquire.[7]

As we follow the counsel of Elder Scott, we will more fully come to the point where our lives will have the focus Nephi wrote of: "We talk of Christ, we rejoice in Christ, we preach of Christ, we prophesy of Christ, and we write according to our prophecies, that our children may know to what source they may look for a remission of their sins" (2 Ne. 25:26).

## CHAPTER 1

# FROM FONT TO TEMPLE: MODERN ORDINANCES AND THE ATONEMENT

SOME OF THE MOST REMARKABLE WITNESSES of the atonement the Lord has given us are the ordinances of the gospel.

The ordinances receive their very efficacy from the atonement. If there had been no atonement, the ordinances would have no power; they would have no saving purpose whatsoever. The natural man—one who has not been changed by submitting his heart to God and receiving of the powers of the atonement—is an enemy to God (Mosiah 3:19). Without the atonement, we have no way to bridge the gap between being natural, "carnal, sensual, and devilish" (Moses 5:13) and becoming a "saint" (Mosiah 3:19). As long as we remain in that lost and forsaken state without a redeemer, none of our faithfulness or obedience will take us toward eternal life—including the ordinances we participate in.

But with the atonement in place, Christ has *ordained* certain acts that will bind us to him and to the Father by covenant. Through these acts, the *ordinances,* we partake of the promise the Lord gave to Adam after he was baptized with water and fire: "Behold, thou art one in me, a son of God; and thus may all become my sons" (Moses 6:68). Oneness with God is the ultimate purpose of the at-one-ment performed by Christ. Thus the ordinances are keys in that process.

The essential ordinances help to literally fulfill the purposes of the atonement. (The essential ordinances are those that are absolutely necessary for exaltation; they include baptism, confirmation, priesthood ordination for men, and the temple endowment and sealing.) Those purposes include cleansing us of sin, bringing us into the family of Christ, giving us power and authority like those held by Christ, helping us to be strengthened by the accompanying covenants, and (as just noted) bringing us into oneness with God.

There are several other ways the ordinances stand as witnesses of Christ and his atonement:

- *Every ordinance is performed by the authority of the priesthood.* The priesthood itself flows from God. The full, formal name of the Melchizedek Priesthood is "the Holy Priesthood, after the Order of the Son of God" (D&C 107:3). Christ himself is the "priest for ever after the order of Melchizedek" (Ps. 110:4; Heb. 7:17). It is because he is the Atoner that the priesthood has power to bless.

- *The priesthood holder acts for Christ, with his authority.* The priesthood holder acts in Christ's stead, doing the things the Lord would do if he were here. In that process, the priesthood holder is an agent and representative of the Savior himself. This truth is underscored in a principle the Lord expressed to Edward Partridge: "I will lay my hand upon you by the hand of my servant Sidney Rigdon, and you shall receive my Spirit, the Holy Ghost, even the Comforter, which shall teach you the peaceable things of the kingdom" (D&C 36:2). The Lord did not actually place his hands upon Edward Partridge's head. Instead, he commissioned Sidney Rigdon to perform the confirmation of Brother Partridge. In the process, though, it was truly as though the Lord himself were laying his hands on Brother Partridge's head, because Sidney Rigdon had been empowered and sent with full authority to represent God.

- *Every ordinance requires faith in Christ, and every essential ordinance requires repentance, made possible through Christ because of his atonement.* The first principles of the gospel—faith in the Lord

Jesus Christ and repentance through the power of his atonement—accompany not only baptism and the reception of the Holy Ghost but also every ordinance in which we participate. And of course, mankind's ability to exercise faith in Christ and to repent rests on the fact that Christ took upon himself our sins.

- *Every ordinance is done in the name of Christ, because he is the Savior, Redeemer, Mediator, and Atoner.* The Lord taught Adam this principle almost in the beginning. When Adam was offering sacrifices without understanding, the Lord sent an angel to instruct him. What the angel said about sacrifices in some ways is true of every ordinance: "This thing is a similitude of the sacrifice of the Only Begotten of the Father, which is full of grace and truth. Wherefore, thou shalt do all that thou doest in the name of the Son, and thou shalt repent and call upon God in the name of the Son forevermore" (Moses 5:7–8).

  Because our sins separate us from God, we cannot act in our own names and have our acts be recognized by God. We must have a mediator, a savior, whose power of redemption will validate our righteous acts. We need One who is not separated from God to stand between us and God. Hence, all of our righteous acts, all of our testimonies and teachings—and all ordinances—must be done in the name of Jesus Christ, that perfect Redeemer.

- *We follow Christ as we perform priesthood ordinances—and we serve as types of Christ, who also performed the ordinances.* When he was on the earth, the Savior performed blessings of babies, baptisms, confirmations, priesthood ordinations, and healings of the sick. He administered the sacrament. Priesthood holders are doing as he did in these very important events in a person's life. We are types or shadows of the great High Priest.

- *We follow Christ as we receive priesthood ordinances and thereby serve as types of Christ, who also received the ordinances.* When he walked the mortal earth, Jesus Christ received a blessing as a baby, baptism, a form of confirmation, and perhaps other ordinances.

Nephi emphasized that we must follow Christ in receiving the ordinances. After telling us of the baptism of Christ, he quoted the Savior as saying, "Follow thou me" (2 Ne. 31:10; see also vv. 12–13, 16–17). Following Christ in receiving the ordinances not only helps to prepare and qualify us for a celestial reward, but it also enables us to stand as types of Christ. In the process we partake of blessings of his atonement.

• *The presence of the Spirit during ordinances is a witness of the atonement.* During ordinances we often feel the presence of the Spirit and the power of God. To enter into God's presence—or to have him come into ours through his Spirit—is a witness of the atonement of Christ. Without the atonement we are separated from God, with no chance of a re-union. But with the atonement, we are able to be restored to his presence. Our experience with the Spirit during ordinances (both as administrator and as recipient) is a manifestation of Christ's power and demonstrates that his atonement and our obedience in receiving the ordinance work together to help accomplish the re-union we desire.

In addition, the Holy Ghost is the conveyor of all the other godly gifts—gifts of the Spirit, cleansing from sin, strength, comfort, and so on. The gifts are delivered or administered by the Spirit, but the source of the gifts is our Father in Heaven, made possible through the atonement of Christ.

• *Receiving and obeying ordinances is part of what it means to "come unto Christ"* (Moro. 10:32). To come unto Christ and partake of his atonement, we have to meet his requirements: having a broken heart and a contrite spirit, receiving all the prescribed ordinances, and living "by every word that proceedeth forth from the mouth of God" (D&C 84:44). Partaking of the ordinances is not a mere form; it is an essential part of the process of receiving the atonement into our lives.

President Boyd K. Packer has repeatedly taught the crucial importance of ordinances. In instructing leaders of the Church, he said:

You may wonder how to proceed to implement the mission of the Church in the lives of your members. Where should you focus your attention and energy? . . .

We are to bring to pass the immortality and eternal life of man by concentrating on *ordinances* and on the *covenants* associated with them. . . . That is written there in the mission statement of the Church.

A good and useful and true test of every major decision made by a leader in the Church is whether a given course leads toward or away from the making and keeping of covenants. . . . Centering your mind on ordinances and covenants gives purpose to all the many things we do in preaching the gospel and perfecting the Saints.[1]

It is clear that all ordinances point us to our Savior and serve as visible, physical reminders of his atonement. As a group, ordinances are filled with meaning that points us directly to the source that gives them efficacy and power.

In addition, each of the individual ordinances is rich with symbolism pertaining to the Savior. Joseph Smith said, "The ordinances of the Gospel . . . were laid out before the foundations of the world" and "are not to be altered or changed."[2] God has ordained a very particular way that man should perform and receive ordinances, and man has neither the authority nor the wisdom to change those divinely inspired procedures. Further, if we were to change the ordinances, we would surely lose essential, God-designed symbolism. It is not incidental that one of the accusations the Lord made against ancient, apostate man—and repeated in this dispensation—was that he had changed the ordinances and broken the everlasting covenant of the gospel (see Isa. 24:5; D&C 1:15).

Let's look at some individual ordinances and consider some of their specific symbolisms.

## ORDINANCES INVOLVING THE LAYING ON OF HANDS

Joseph Smith learned by revelation that "from the [higher priesthood] comes the administering of ordinances and blessings upon the church, by the laying on of the hands" (D&C 107:67). Laying on of hands is used in priesthood ordinations, confirmations, priesthood blessings, settings apart, patriarchal blessings, fathers' blessings, and blessings of the sick. Important elements of the laying on of hands, all of which have symbolism relating to Christ and his atonement, include the following:

*Hands.* Hands symbolize the power to do, to minister, to bless. Hands can symbolize that the recipient has been touched by the hand of God, conveying the idea of transmission of power from on high (D&C 36:2).

*Head.* The head is the seat of thought, the will, and the five senses. The head represents the entirety of a person. It rules the body and gives it all it needs: food, oxygen, information, and so forth. As the head is the ruling part of the body, Christ is the head or ruling part of each of us. He gives us all we need, both temporally and spiritually. To have hands laid on our head signifies that the ruling portion of the body is fully participating and receiving the blessing. It also signifies that we yield ourselves to Christ, who is our head and the head of the priesthood.

*The circle.* Ann N. Madsen wrote, "The circle of priesthood that had surrounded that infant [in a blessing] symbolically formed a circle of protection against evil throughout that child's life."[3] A circle can represent the protection of priesthood and righteous loved ones—as well as the protection we receive when we submit ourselves to Christ and his plan for us.

A circle also symbolizes completeness and sufficiency. When we are surrounded by a circle of priesthood holders, we are receiving a priesthood action that is sufficient and complete for our need. Further, a circle can symbolize perfection. In a priesthood ordinance involving a circle of hands and priesthood brethren, we are promised a sufficiency of blessings of the atonement of Christ.

*Pronouncement of blessings.* We often speak of receiving blessings from the Lord. When we bless a baby (or anyone) by the power of the priesthood, the ordinance represents an immediate *pronouncement* of a blessing, or the *promise* of a blessing. That blessing is usually conditional and often will be fulfilled sometime in the future. When the blessing is fulfilled, it comes in the form of a gift from God called, again, a blessing.

Blessings are representations of the grace of God, which is given to man because of Christ's atonement. Because the Savior has bridged the gap between God and man, man can once again receive all that God would give him, all in the form of blessings.

All pronouncements of blessings are properly made by *revelation*. Revelation itself is a sign of the atonement. As long as we are enemies to God, we are estranged from him and are not able to receive his guidance and direction. But when we are reconnected to him through the atoning power of Christ, we can receive communication that is both direct and clear. The reality of revelation is a testimony of the reality of the atonement.

## HEALING OF THE SICK

All healing is made possible because of the atonement. "O all ye that are spared," Jesus cried to the survivors of the Nephite devastations, "will ye not now return unto me, and repent of your sins, and be converted, that I may heal you?" (3 Ne. 9:13).

He can heal us of both our spiritual and our physical sicknesses. He has power to do this because, as Alma taught, "he will take upon him the pains and the sicknesses of his people" (Alma 7:11).

Healing the physically sick is a type of spiritual healing. It is a physical manifestation of the power of the atonement, of the power of God's love, sent by way of great blessing unto his children.

*Anointing with consecrated olive oil.* When priesthood brethren use their hands to anoint someone's head with consecrated oil, many symbolisms are occurring at once. Their hands represent God's hands. The recipient's head represents the whole of his or her being. The olive oil represents the Holy Ghost (D&C 45:56–57). The oil also suggests the oil that came forth from the olive press at the olive garden at Gethsemane, which in turn represents the Savior's suffering there.

## CONFIRMATION

One of the great purposes of the laying on of hands is to confirm a person a member of the Church and to invite him or her to receive the Holy

Ghost. Confirmation can therefore help bring a literal fulfillment of one of the great purposes of the atonement: the gift of reconciliation, where we receive the actual, immediate presence of a member of the Godhead.

As noted above, when we receive the Spirit's presence we come, at least to a degree, to a state of at-one-ment with God, through the Spirit. That blessing of at-one-ment is made possible because of the atoning sacrifice of Christ, which we receive as we receive the ordinance and qualify our hearts.

## Baptism

Baptism is one of the most richly symbolic ordinances in the Church. Consider some of the elements in baptism that point us to Christ:

The *white clothing* symbolizes purity, which is possible only through the atonement of Christ.

The *water* has several meanings. It stands for literal water, which can wash, refresh, and renew. It stands for the blood of Christ and for the way in which we can wash our garments, and our bodies, in his blood. And it symbolizes living water, which flows from Christ to constantly strengthen and replenish our souls. Immersion in the water symbolizes fully being washed, fully entering into the covenant, and fully being covered by that living water.

*The right hand raised to the square* symbolizes reaching up to heaven, making a sign of a covenant between God and man. The square in the carpenter's toolbox (remember who the Carpenter is) represents exactness in all we do. Christ, as the only person who was perfectly exact in his mortal life, could himself be symbolized as a square. When we participate in covenants involving the symbol of the square, we are reaching up to God in a way that reminds us of Christ, in whose name the covenants are made.

*The font.* The font is symbolic of the grave. It symbolizes the death of each one of us and our individual resurrection through the power of Christ, as well as the death and resurrection of Christ himself (D&C 128:12–13).

Baptism is also symbolic of us giving the old man to God, of the old man being washed clean, of letting the old man die, and of then being born again, a "new creature" in Christ (2 Cor. 5:17; Eph. 4:20–24). Thus, the font—and baptism by immersion—is symbolic not only of the tomb but also of the womb. But it is not only symbolic—we also literally are made new when we are baptized of the water and the Spirit with pure hearts, with real intent, having faith in Christ. Paul wrote: As the body of Jesus was buried in the tomb, "we are buried with him by baptism into death: that like as Christ was raised up from the dead by the glory of the Father, even so we also should walk in newness of life" (Rom. 6:4).

In our rebirth, we are born into the family of Christ. We take upon ourselves his name and become his sons and daughters (Mosiah 5:7; 27:25; Ether 3:14).

In all births, three elements are present: water, blood, and spirit (Moses 6:59–60). These same three elements were present at the atonement of Christ: water (from his side), blood (from his sufferings), and spirit (the Father's presence, the Son's own spirit, and the Holy Ghost). These three elements are present at our spiritual rebirth: the water of baptism, the blood of Christ through the atonement, and the Spirit of God. And they are also present, or represented, as we remember Christ and our covenant to him in the sacrament.

*Immersion* in the water symbolizes the total commitment of our whole being, fully entering into covenant, fully being washed, fully being covered by the living water that is Christ. With immersion we follow Christ into a new birth. We follow him into the grave and then to resurrection. We follow him with all our being. In sum, immersion in baptism represents both our physical and spiritual death and our being made alive again in Christ.

## SACRAMENT

Of all the ordinances, the sacrament has the most obvious symbolism of the atonement. When Jesus introduced the sacrament to his apostles at the Last Supper, he said regarding the bread, "Take, eat; this is in remembrance of my body which I give a ransom for you." And regarding the wine, he said, "This is in remembrance of my blood of the new testament, which is shed for as many as shall believe on my name, for the remission of their sins" (JST Matt. 26:22, 24).

When he visited the Nephites, he said after providing the sacrament to them, "He that eateth this bread eateth of my body to his soul; and he that drinketh of this wine drinketh of my blood to his soul; and his soul shall never hunger nor thirst, but shall be filled" (3 Ne. 20:8).

The emblems (the word *emblem* means "symbol") of the sacrament point clearly and directly to the atoning sacrifice of Christ in the Garden of Gethsemane and on the cross. As we partake, we have the remarkable opportunity of taking into ourselves symbolic food and drink that represent the very atonement of Jesus Christ—and by taking it into ourselves, we signify that we make that atonement part of us.

The sacrament also has several other symbolisms:

- Ancient sacrifices were performed in "similitude of the sacrifice of the Only Begotten of the Father" (Moses 5:7). The sacramental sacrifice is performed in remembrance of that sacrifice.

- The offering is made by priesthood officiators, who act in behalf of Christ and follow him in breaking the bread and blessing the bread and water.

- Those making the offering kneel and offer a prayer at a table that represents an altar of sacrifice.

- The recipient of the sacrament makes his own sacrifice of a broken heart and a contrite spirit. The words *sacrament, sacrifice,* and *sacred* all come from the same Latin root. Christ made his sacred and holy sacrifice for us so that we could partake of the sacrament, during which we make our own sacred offering, or sacrifice.

- The bread is broken as a reminder that Christ's flesh was broken in the performance of the atonement.

- The bread also represents the bread of life, which also is Christ. Jesus said, "I am the living bread which came down from heaven: if any man eat of this bread he shall live for ever" (John 6:51).

- In addition to representing the blood shed by Christ in the atonement, the water also represents the living water, which flows from Christ.

- The bread and water are covered by a white cloth, like a shroud, just as Christ's body was covered by a shroud.

- The sacramental prayers, which must be offered with exact wording, are Christ-centered: the prayers are offered in the name of Christ and focus on eating and drinking "in remembrance" of the body and blood of Christ; they indicate the participants' willingness to "take upon them the name of thy Son, and always remember him and keep his commandments which he has given them" (D&C 20:77, 79).

- When we keep the covenant to always remember him, the Lord said, "Ye shall have my Spirit to be with you" (3 Ne. 18:7). To have the Spirit with us is a tangible manifestation of oneness with God—and that oneness is a measure of the fulfillment of at-one-ment in our lives.

Finally, Latter-day Saint scholar John A. Tvedtnes has given us this insight:

> [One of] the native Hebrew terms for wine literally means "blood of the grape" (Genesis 49:11; Deuteronomy 32:14 . . . ). . . .
>
> The Hebrew word for "bread" is *lehem,* though its original meaning was "flesh," as we learn from the Arabic cognate, *lahm.* It is the second element in the name of Jesus' birthplace, Beth-lehem, "house of bread." Consequently, bread was a fitting symbol for the flesh of the Savior, who declared himself to be "the true bread from heaven" (see John 6:32–58).[4]

No wonder the sacrament is so important that the entire meeting is named after it. Partaking of the sacrament is the most important thing we'll do at a meeting all week.

## PRIESTHOOD ORDINATION

Priesthood ordinations also point both literally and symbolically to Christ. The elements of the ordinance—priesthood, hands, circle, Spirit, revelation, the name of Christ—were reviewed in our discussion above. When a man receives the Melchizedek Priesthood, he is receiving the priesthood of Christ (D&C 107:3; see also Heb. 2:17; 3:1; 4:14–15; 5:5–10). The priesthood is made available to us as mortals because of the atonement. As Alma taught, "This holy calling [was] prepared from the foundation of the world for such as would not harden their hearts, being in and through the atonement of the Only Begotten Son" (Alma 13:5).

The oath and covenant of the priesthood also points to a union with Christ through the atonement. We read in Doctrine and Covenants 84: "And also all they who receive this priesthood receive me, saith the Lord; . . . and he that receiveth me receiveth my Father; and he that receiveth my Father receiveth my Father's kingdom; therefore all that my Father hath shall be given unto him. And this is according to the oath and covenant which belongeth to the priesthood" (vv. 35–39).

When we do the work of the priesthood in righteousness, we become ministers of the atonement to our brothers and sisters on the earth. The Lord declared this marvelous truth in December 1832, less than three months after revealing the oath and covenant of the priesthood. Said he, "Blessed are ye if ye continue in my goodness, a light unto the Gentiles, and through this priesthood, a savior unto my people Israel" (D&C 86:11; see also D&C 103:9).

## TEMPLE

The temple is distinctly a place of at-one-ment. It is the Lord's house, and it is there that we can often feel his Spirit most strongly. When we enter the doors of the temple, we are walking into sacred space, a place that has been cleansed both physically and spiritually; we thereby enter, in a sense, into the presence of the Lord. The work of at-one-ment, or *re-union,* with God is brought to partial fruition in the temple. As Elder John A. Widtsoe put it, in the temple we may "always have a wonderfully rich communion with God."[5]

The structure, the clothing, the ceremonies of the temple ordinances are all freighted with great symbolism.[6] That symbolism points us to various elements of the plan of salvation; but, significantly, it particularly points to Jesus Christ, his atonement, and his role in bringing to pass the immortality and eternal life of the family of man.

Jesus Christ is so much a focal point of the temple that we are commanded upon entering the temple to see "that all [your] incomings . . . into this house, may be in the name of the Lord; that all [your] outgoings from this house may be in the name of the Lord; that all [your] salutations may be in the name of the Lord, with holy hands, uplifted unto the Most High" (D&C 109:17–19).

Brigham Young University professor Andrew Skinner has written:

> All of the foreordained principles and ordinances of the Father's plan, especially those received in the temple, are intricately tied to the Atonement of Jesus Christ. . . .
>
> The teachings found in the temple are like a funnel. They begin broadly, focusing our attention ever more narrowly on the Son of God and his atoning activities in mortality. Temple teachings also pull together principles from different dispensations in a dramatized, step-by-step ascent to godhood, always with the Atonement in mind.[7]

Elder Marion D. Hanks expressed how thoroughly the temple teaches us of Jesus Christ and his atonement:

> My testimony [is] that for me *everything* in the temple points ultimately to Christ and to our Father. The efficacy of the ordinances and covenants is in his atoning love and delegated authority. . . . *Temple worship can become a critical key to knowing the Lord.* . . .
>
> . . . In learning and appreciating the principles upon which his holy life was based, . . . we can truly appreciate his sacred gift, his atoning death, and the pattern of his holy life. . . .
>
> Ultimately in a temple we kneel at a sacred altar and there covenant and, in the manner of temple symbolism, once more have

our attention pointed toward him and how he died, how much he had to love God's children to suffer what he suffered for us. . . .

. . . The temple should strengthen our preparation to receive the gifts of his atoning love (see D&C 88:32, 33) and to follow his example.[8]

The temple experience may be the epitome of atonement work on the earth. Not only do the ordinances point to the atonement of Christ, not only do the ordinances depend on the atonement for their power and efficacy, but also the overwhelming majority of the ordinances that take place in the temple are performed by people who are functioning as saviors themselves, "saviours . . . on mount Zion" (Obad. 1:21).

## "A Symbolic Linkage"

Speaking of ordinances in general, Latter-day Saint author Lenet Hadley Read has written: "Every revealed ordinance exhibits a symbolic linkage to one element or another of Jesus' ministry. For example, just as the daily sacrifices of Jerusalem's temple foreshadowed Christ's sacrifice (Heb. 7:26–28), so Latter-day Saints see gospel ordinances as pointing to him and to the way back into his presence."[9]

The ordinances of the gospel are marvelous blessings to help us progress along the strait and narrow path to eternal life. They also point us toward Christ and his atonement, both overtly and through divine symbolism. Without the ordinances we would not be able to return to the Father. Without Christ the ordinances would have no efficacy. Elder George F. Richards, a longtime president of the Quorum of the Twelve Apostles, said: "We realize that there is no virtue for salvation and exaltation outside of the atoning blood of Jesus Christ, our Savior. . . . The ordinances of the Gospel have virtue in them by reason of the atoning blood of Jesus Christ, and without it there would be no virtue in them for salvation."[10]

How grateful we are for the gift of the ordinances—and for the power of the atonement of our Savior that gives them "virtue."

## CHAPTER 2

# From Water Cleansings to the Veil: Ancient Ordinances and the Atonement

Each of the modern ordinances—including baptism, the sacrament, administering to the sick, and others (see chapter 1)—has symbolic elements that focus on Jesus Christ and his atoning sacrifice. Correspondingly, ancient ordinances and rituals also consist of types and symbols that center on Jesus' atonement.

Amulek taught that every whit, or even the smallest parts, of the Mosaic law focused on Christ's atonement: "And behold, this is the whole meaning of the law, every whit pointing to that great and last sacrifice; and that great and last sacrifice will be the Son of God, yea, infinite and eternal" (Alma 34:14). Elder Bruce R. McConkie similarly wrote: "Every divine ordinance or performance ordained of God, every sacrifice, symbolism, and similitude; all that God ever gave to his people—all was ordained and established in such a way as to testify of his Son and center the faith of believing people in him and in the redemption he was foreordained to make."[1] Elder Russell M. Nelson's words regarding our modern temples also apply to ancient Israelite temples: "The basis for every temple ordinance and covenant—the heart of the plan of salvation—is the Atonement of Jesus Christ."[2]

We can better understand ordinances and rituals as testimonies of

Christ when we understand the words *ordinance* and *ritual.* The word *ordinance* comes from the Latin *ordinare,* "to put in order or sequence." It follows, then, that the ancient and modern temple, which is a house of ordinances, is also a "house of order" (D&C 109:8). Religious rituals (or rites) are sacred actions or "ceremonial movements."[3] Some scholars refer to these rites of transition as "gestures of approach"[4] because they are religious gestures (or acts or movements) that worshippers make as they approach God during sacred worship. The ancient temple, especially, included sacred gestures that enabled and empowered worshippers to move from the outer gate inward to the most holy place of all, the holy of holies. The gestures of approach are vital to a temple society because they symbolically cleanse and prepare worshippers for entry into and movement through sacred space as they transition from the profane world into the sacred temple.

This chapter will review several ancient ordinances and rituals (gestures of approach): ritual ablutions (washings with water), anointings with olive oil, the laying on of hands on the heads of the Levites, putting on sacred vestments, filling the hands, the law of sacrifice, the laying on of hands on sacrificial animals, eating the shewbread, praying with uplifted hands, and entering the veil. These rituals are not necessarily listed in order or sequence, nor do they represent all of the rituals associated with the ancient temples. Our discussion will focus on the specific elements that symbolize Jesus Christ and the atonement.

## RITUAL ABLUTIONS OR WASHINGS WITH WATER

Ritual ablutions, or washings with water, are directly connected to the atonement, for they symbolically cleanse us from sin and iniquity, just as the atonement literally cleanses us from sin and iniquity. Connecting washings with salvation from sin, the Psalmist wrote: "Wash me throughly from mine iniquity, and cleanse me from my sin. . . . Purge me with hyssop, and I shall be clean: wash me, and I shall be whiter than snow" (Ps. 51:2, 7; see also Ps. 26:6). Similarly, Titus 3:5 links salvation and washings: "He *saved us,* by the washing of regeneration, and renewing of the Holy Ghost" (emphasis added). Revelation 1:5 also makes a connection to ritual washings with the doctrine that Jesus Christ "washed us from our sins in his own blood." The washing with water points to Jesus' atoning blood, which serves as a cleansing agent from sin.

The law of Moses required various ritual washings in connection with the temple and its services, all of which are associated with the atonement.

1. The priests were washed in preparation for serving in the temple. The Lord commanded Moses, "And thou shalt bring Aaron and his sons unto the door of the tabernacle of the congregation, and wash them with water" (Ex. 40:12; 29:4; see also D&C 124:39). This ablution took place before the anointing and the putting on of sacred clothing. It was incumbent upon a priest to ritually wash his hands and feet; failure to do so put him at risk of a divinely decreed death penalty: "For Aaron and his sons shall wash their hands and their feet thereat: When they go into the tabernacle of the congregation, they shall wash with water, that they die not" (Ex. 30:19–20).

2. The high priest washed with water in preparation for making atonement on the Day of Atonement. "And he shall wash his flesh with water in the holy place, and put on his garments, and come forth, and offer his burnt offering" (Lev. 16:24). Later in Israelite history, the high priest prepared himself for entry into the inner sanctum on the Day of Atonement by immersing himself five times.

3. The person who let the scapegoat go in the wilderness on the Day of Atonement was required to "wash his clothes, and bathe his flesh in water" (Lev. 16:26).

4. On the Day of Atonement, the skins, flesh, and dung of the sacrificial bullock and goat were taken outside of the temple area and camp of Israel and burned. The man who burned these animal parts was required to "wash his clothes, and bathe his flesh in water" (Lev. 16:27–28).

## ANOINTINGS WITH OLIVE OIL

In ancient times, both objects and certain persons were anointed with holy oil in order to sanctify them. The Lord commanded Moses to anoint all the vessels, appurtenances, and items that belonged to the tabernacle (Lev. 8:10–11; Num. 7:1), including the ark of the covenant, the work table with its vessels, the seven-branched lampstand, the altars of incense and burnt offering, the wash basin, and other temple instruments (Ex. 30:26–33; 40:9–10; see also Gen. 28:11–18; 31:13). On a regular basis, unleavened wafers were also anointed with oil (Ex. 29:2; Lev. 2:4; 7:12; Num. 6:15).

Priests, kings (1 Sam. 10:1, 24; 15:1; 2 Sam. 2:4; 16:16; 19:11, and so forth), and certain prophets (1 Kgs. 19:16; 1 Chr. 16:22; see also Ps. 105:15; D&C 124:57) were also ceremonially anointed with olive oil for sanctification. Priests were anointed with olive oil in an elaborate ceremony that took place at the "door of the tabernacle of the congregation" (Ex. 40:12–15; 29:4–7).

The following scriptures indicate the purpose of anointing objects or priests for divine service unto the Lord (emphasis added):

"Thou shalt *anoint* it [the altar], to *sanctify* it" (Ex. 29:36; 40:10).

"Thou shalt *anoint* the laver . . . and *sanctify* it" (Ex. 40:11; Lev. 8:11).

Moses "*anointed* it [the tabernacle], and *sanctified* it" (Num. 7:1).

Moses "*anointed* them [the altar and vessels], and *sanctified* them" (Num. 7:1).

Moses "*anointed* the tabernacle and all that was therein, and *sanctified* them" (Lev. 8:10).

Moses "poured of the anointing oil upon Aaron's head, and *anointed* him, to *sanctify* him" (Lev. 8:12; Ex. 40:13).

"*Anoint* them [Aaron's sons], and consecrate them, and *sanctify* them" (Ex. 28:40–41).

Hence, the object of anointing with olive oil was to sanctify objects or people, meaning to declare them to be in a state of holiness. That is to say that the recipient of the anointing became worthy to stand before God in sacred places and to interact with the other sacred persons and objects in a temple setting. The recipient, like the temple itself, was "set apart" and "wholly other"[5] from the profaneness of the world.

Naturally, if the consecrated oil possesses (symbolical) powers to create a uniquely holy (sanctified and set apart) individual, it too must be holy. Repeatedly the oil is called holy. It shall be a "holy anointing oil. . . . It is holy, and it shall be holy unto you. . . . It shall be unto you most holy. . . . It shall be unto thee holy for the Lord" (Ex. 30:31–32, 36–37). So uniquely powerful was the anointing with the consecrated oil that even the objects or people who received the smearing of oil were able to communicate holiness to others. This concept, recorded in Exodus 30:29, states that whosoever or whatsoever thing touched an anointed thing would also become holy.

Those who received the anointing were sanctified and set apart from the profane world and were thus required to adhere to certain responsibilities (Lev. 21:10–12), but they were also offered special privileges (Lev. 4:3–12; 6:20–22; 16:32–34; Num. 4:16; 18:8). For instance, those who received the anointing were protected by God (1 Chr. 6:22; Ps. 105:15; 89:20–23; D&C 121:16), taught from on high (1 John 2:27), gained salvation (Ps. 20:6; 28:8; D&C 109:80), and received mercy from the Lord (2 Sam. 22:51; Ps. 18:50). Additionally, it was forbidden to speak out against the anointed of the Lord (2 Sam. 19:21; see also 1 Sam. 24:6, 10; 26:9, 11, 23).

The anointing rite is Christ-centered because Jesus Christ himself received the sacred anointing. In Psalm 45:7 (a royal wedding hymn written by an anonymous poet) God anoints the Lord with oil: "Therefore God, thy God, hath anointed thee with the oil of gladness above thy fellows." Paul, speaking about the Father and the Son, quoted the same scripture in his epistle to the Hebrews (Heb. 1:9). Two citations in the Acts of the Apostles further indicate God's divine anointing of Christ: "God anointed Jesus of Nazareth" (Acts 10:38; 4:27; see also Isa. 61:1; Luke 4:18, 21). According to William W. Phelps, "Christ . . . was anointed with holy oil in heaven, and crowned in the midst of brothers and sisters."[6]

Even specific titles of Jesus point to his being anointed with oil: *Messiah* is a transliteration of the Hebrew *meshiach,* a term meaning "anointed one," and *Christ* is a transliteration of the Greek *christos,* which also denotes "anointed one." The names clearly attest to the fact that Jesus was the Anointed One who was set apart to perform the service of the Father in the temple. Jesus was a "high priest . . . a minister of the sanctuary, and of the true tabernacle" (Heb. 8:1–2; 9:24).

## LAYING OF HANDS UPON THE LEVITES

The consecration and setting apart ceremony for the Levites comprised several steps, including the laying on of hands (Num. 8:6–10). Concerning this ritual, Numbers 8:10 states, "And thou [Moses] shalt bring the Levites before the Lord: and the children of Israel shall put their hands upon the Levites" (Num. 8:10; cf. Num. 27:22–23). Just as Church members are often set apart by the laying on of hands to perform certain responsibilities and callings, the Levites were set apart by the laying on of hands to carry on the work of the atonement (or the work of offering atonement-related sacrifices) in the ancient Israelite temples.[7]

## PUTTING ON SACRED VESTMENTS

When high priests and priests served in the temple, they wore sacred clothing, which was an integral part of the temple setting. A priest's vestments consisted of four parts—headpiece, sash, tunic, and "undergarments of plain linen."[8] The high priest's vestments consisted of eight pieces—the four belonging to the priest plus an ephod, a robe of the ephod, a breastplate, and a golden plate of the headpiece (Ex. 29:5–6). On the Day of Atonement, which occurred once a year, the high priest dressed in white and wore the girdle, tunic, mitre, and breeches. Inasmuch as the clothing was holy (Ex. 28:2–3), priests and high priests were vested with the sacred clothing in a sacred ceremony. In fact, if the priests failed to wear the linen breeches (and possibly other sacred vestments) while administering in the temple, they were subject to death (Ex. 28:42–43).

Sacred vestments served a number of purposes:

1. Putting on sacred vestments is related to putting on Christ and his holiness. The verbal expression "put on" (getting dressed in clothing) is sometimes related to Jesus Christ and his atonement. The apostle

26

Paul, especially, used "put on" to express sacred doctrines about the Lord: "*put ye on* the Lord Jesus Christ" (Rom. 13:14; emphasis added); "for as many of you as have been baptized into Christ have *put on* Christ" (Gal. 3:27; emphasis added); "ye have *put off* the old man. . . . and have *put on* the new man, which is renewed in knowledge after the image of him that created him" (Col. 3:10; emphasis added); "let us *put on* the armour of light" (Rom. 13:12; emphasis added); "*put on* the whole armour of God" (Eph. 6:11; emphasis added). When we *put on* Jesus Christ we accept him and his atonement, and we become like him.

2. Sacred vestments carry with them symbolisms that point to the blessings of the atonement, as the following examples illustrate:

Enoch said, "I was clothed upon with glory; and I saw the Lord . . . , face to face" (Moses 7:3–4).

"They shall see me . . . , clothed with power and great glory" (D&C 45:44).

"The marriage of the Lamb is come, and his wife hath made herself ready. And to her was granted that she should be arrayed in fine linen, clean and white: for the fine linen is the righteousness of saints" (Rev. 19:7–8).

"He hath clothed me with the garments of salvation, he hath covered me with the robe of righteousness" (Isa. 61:10).

"Clothed in the brightness of his glory" (D&C 65:5).

"Thou shalt make holy garments for Aaron thy brother for glory and for beauty" (Ex. 28:2; see also verse 40).

"Let thy priests be clothed with righteousness" (Ps. 132:9).

"I will also clothe her priests with salvation" (Ps. 132:16).

In these passages the words *glory, salvation, righteousness,* and *holy,* all associated with blessings of the atonement, are positioned with the words *clothed, linen,* and *garments.*

3. Sacred vestments represent the person who wears them. The expression "keep your garments spotless" (Alma 7:25) means to keep yourself spotless, and the person who is "clothed with purity" and who wears "the robe of righteousness" (2 Ne. 9:14) is the one who is pure and righteous. *Garments* in the following passage symbolically refers to

the person who wears them: "For there can no man be saved except his garments are washed white; yea, his garments must be purified until they are cleansed from all stain, through the blood of him of whom it has been spoken by our fathers, who should come to redeem his people from their sins" (Alma 5:21). In other words, the redeemed person has to be washed, purified, and cleansed from all stain by the blood of Jesus Christ.

4. When mortal worshippers wear sacred vestments, they are imitating celestial beings, including God, angels, and redeemed souls, who all wear sacred clothing. When the resurrected Jesus descended from heaven and showed himself to the Nephites in the land of Bountiful, he was "clothed in a white robe" (3 Ne. 11:8). And at the Second Coming, Jesus Christ will be "clothed in his glorious apparel" and "traveling in the greatness of his strength." So great will be his glory that "the sun shall hide his face in shame, and the moon shall withhold its light." His apparel will be red, made so by his treading grapes with anger and fury (D&C 133:46, 49; for the symbolism of treading the grapes, see chapter 16).

God's angels also wear sacred clothing, which has been made white through the atonement; the seven angels who will come out of the temple in heaven will be "clothed in pure and white linen, and having their breasts girded with golden girdles" (Rev. 15:6). The two angels that attended the sepulcher where Jesus was buried were dressed "in shining garments" (Luke 24:4), and Joseph Smith was ministered to "by an holy angel, whose countenance was as lightning, and whose garments were pure and white above all other whiteness" (D&C 20:6; see also JS–H 1:31).

Through the atonement, we also can wear celestial sacred vestments. The saints who go to heaven are "arrayed in white robes," for they "have washed their robes, and made them white in the blood of the Lamb" (Rev. 7:13–14); also, "he that overcometh, the same shall be clothed in white raiment" (Rev. 3:5). In addition to being "clothed with white robes," they have "palms in their hands" (Rev. 7:9; 6:11). At the resurrection, "we shall be caught up in the cloud to meet [the Lord], that we may ever be with the Lord; that our garments may be pure, that we may be clothed upon with robes of righteousness, with palms in our hands, and crowns of glory upon our heads" (D&C 109:75–76; see also Rev. 19:14).

5. Sacred vestments anticipate the resurrection, when we will be clothed with an immortal body.[9] To make this connection, the apostle Paul used language that suggests that at the resurrection we will *put on* immortality as if we are *putting on* clothing: "So when this corruptible *shall have put on* incorruption, and this mortal *shall have put on* immortality, then shall be brought to pass the saying that is written, Death is swallowed up in victory" (1 Cor. 15:54; emphasis added). Elsewhere Paul compared the resurrection to being "clothed upon with our house which is from heaven," referring to our resurrected tabernacles: "For we know that if our earthly house of this tabernacle were dissolved, we have a building of God, an house not made with hands, eternal in the heavens. For in this we groan, earnestly desiring to be clothed upon with our house which is in heaven: If so be that being clothed we shall not be found naked" (2 Cor. 5:1–3). The atonement provides the power of the resurrection so that we can put on incorruption and immortality.

The Book of Mormon also explicitly links the atonement and the resurrection with putting on incorruption: "Wherefore, it must needs be an infinite atonement—save it should be an infinite atonement this corruption could not *put on* incorruption" (2 Ne. 9:7; emphasis added; see also Enos 1:27). And a passage in the Doctrine and Covenants refers to human "bones, which were to be *clothed upon* with flesh, to come forth again in the resurrection of the dead" (D&C 138:43; emphasis added).

The Hebrew root *kpr* not only means "to atone" but it also denotes "to cover."[10] This denotation can pertain to covering temple worshippers of ancient Israel with sacred vestments; *kpr* can also pertain to covering or clothing our spirits with perfect, immortal bodies at the resurrection. That is to say, the atonement takes a broken, torn, or disintegrated body and repairs it into a perfect, resurrected body.

## FILLING THE HANDS

The Bible Dictionary in the Latter-day Saint edition of the Bible refers to an ancient ritual relating to consecrating the priests who

29

administered in the temple; this ritual included filling of the hands of the priest with a portion of the offerings. "The priest's hands were filled . . . with the fat, the kidneys, the right thigh or shoulder, and part of the meal offering."[11] In addition to these animal parts and the meal offering, the priest's left hand was sometimes filled with olive oil. Leviticus says: "And the priest shall take some of the log of oil, and pour it into the palm of his own left hand. . . . And the remnant of the oil that is in the priest's hand he shall pour upon the head of him that is to be cleansed: and the priest shall make an atonement for him before the Lord" (Lev. 14:15, 18). Each of the items that fill the priest's hands—the meal offering, sacrificial victim's parts, and olive oil—relate to Jesus Christ's sacred sacrifice (this relation is explained elsewhere in this chapter).

Scriptural passages refer to the "filling of the hands" ceremony a number of times, but the King James translators translated "filling the hands" as "consecrated." For example, where the King James Version reads "for seven days shall he consecrate you" (Lev. 8:33), the Hebrew has "for seven days he shall fill your hands." And where the King James Version reads "For Moses had said, Consecrate yourselves to day to the Lord" (Ex. 32:29), the Hebrew reads "For Moses had said, Fill your hand today to the Lord." (Other passages that refer to the "filling the hands" ceremony include Ex. 29:29, 33; 32:29; Lev. 16:32; 21:10; Num. 3:3; Judg. 17:5, 12; and 1 Kgs. 13:33.)

## THE LAW OF SACRIFICE

Various animal sacrifices incorporated gestures of approach. Each person who wished to enter God's presence in the temple was required to obey God's law of sacrifice. Adam, Noah, Abraham, and others offered up sacrifices. During the Mosaic period, sacrifices included burnt offerings (Lev. 1:3–17; 6:8–13), grain offerings (Lev. 2:1–16), peace offerings (Lev. 3:1–17), sin offerings (Lev. 4:1–5:13), and trespass or guilt offerings (Lev. 5:14–6:7). All sacrifices focused on Jesus Christ and his atonement (this is explained in chapter 4).

## Laying of Hands on Sacrificial Animals

The laying of hands on the head of certain sacrificial animals was a significant part of the ancient sacrificial system. Various people participated in the laying on of hands, including individual Israelites: "If any man of you bring an offering unto the Lord, . . . he shall put his hand upon the head of the burnt offering; and it shall be accepted for him to make atonement for him" (Lev. 1:2, 4; see also Lev. 3:2, 8, 13); Levites: "And the Levites shall lay their hands upon the heads of the bullocks . . . to make an atonement for the Levites" (Num. 8:12); elders: "And the elders of the congregation shall lay their hands upon the head of the bullock before the Lord" (Lev. 4:15); rulers: and the ruler "shall lay his hand upon the head of the goat" (Lev. 4:24); community members: "one of the common people . . . shall lay his hand upon the head of the sin offering" (Lev. 4:27, 29); and the high priest (Lev. 16:21). The Lord commanded the laying on of hands for various sacrificial offerings, including burnt offerings, peace offerings, sin offerings, and others (Lev. 1:4; 3:1–2; 4:3–4; see also Lev. 24:10–16).

The act of laying hands on sacrificial animals teaches the law of proxy, or the power for one to act as a substitute for another. Specifically, it symbolically transmits the sins of the human(s) onto the animal's head. Or, as one biblical scholar has stated, the laying on of hands "identifies the sinner with the sacrificial victim to be slain and symbolizes the offering of his own life."[12] The symbolism of the laying on of hands is expressed in Leviticus 16:21–22, where the high priest transmitted Israel's sins and iniquities upon the goat's head: "And Aaron shall lay both his hands upon the head of the live goat, and confess over him all the iniquities of the children of Israel, and all their transgressions in all their sins, putting them upon the head of the goat, and . . . the goat shall bear upon him all their iniquities." The sacrificial animals, of course, were types and shadows of Jesus Christ, who bore our sins and iniquities before his death on the cross.

## EATING THE SHEWBREAD

Shewbread literally means "bread of the face" or "bread of the presence," referring to God's face or presence. Perhaps the bread was called such because the priests ate it in the temple, which was God's house, or the place of his presence. This bread was set in two rows, six loaves to a row, upon a table (called the "pure table"; Lev. 24:6) located in the holy place of the temple, north of the altar of incense. The table was made of shittim wood, overlaid with pure gold, and covered with a blue cloth (Lev. 24:5–9; Ex. 25:23–30; Num. 4:7). The priests ate the bread, which was called "most holy," in the holy place (Lev. 24:9). The shewbread possessed sacramental qualities, and eating of it anticipated the emblems of the Lord's sacrament; the table suggested the sacramental table.

## PRAYER WITH UPLIFTED HANDS

In the setting of the ancient tabernacle and temple, the sacred gesture of lifting up the hands often accompanied the act of prayer. When Solomon dedicated the Jerusalem temple, he "stood before the altar of the Lord in the presence of all the congregation of Israel, and spread forth his hands toward heaven and he said, Lord God of Israel" (1 Kgs. 8:22–23; see also D&C 109:8). He then uttered the dedicatory prayer. Other passages also refer to prayer with uplifted hands. The Psalmist wrote, "Hear the voice of my supplications, when I cry unto thee, when I lift up my hands toward thy holy oracle" (Ps. 28:2). Also, "Let my prayer be set forth before thee as incense; and the lifting up of my hands as the evening sacrifice" (Ps. 141:2). Lifting up the hands is a sacred gesture associated with the atonement—those who are truly righteous may at times lift their hands to heaven and show God that their hands are pure (Ps. 24:4), that is, made pure through the atonement, and they expect an answer to their prayers.

## ENTERING THE VEIL,
## WHICH REPRESENTS CHRIST'S FLESH

Entering the veil of the tabernacle or the temple veil that divided the holy of holies from the holy place is a ritual that also teaches us of Jesus' atonement. The veil that separated humankind from God's presence hung in the holy of holies. Artisans and craftsmen created an exceptionally beautiful veil; it was colorful—blue, purple, scarlet—and included images of cherubim (Ex. 26:31–32). This veil, explained Paul, symbolizes Jesus Christ's flesh (Heb. 9:3; 10:19–20). The temple veil stood between humans and their entrance into the temple's holiest place; in the same way, the Savior stands between the celestial kingdom and us. "No man cometh unto the Father, but by me," Jesus declared (John 14:6).

## CHAPTER 3

# PRIESTS AND PURITY:
# THE LAW OF MOSES

IN OLD TESTAMENT TIMES, the law of Moses helped focus the Israelites' attention on Jesus Christ and his atonement. The law of Moses was a set of regulations, directives, and ordinances that encouraged the Israelites to "*look forward* to the coming of Christ, considering that the law of Moses was a type of his coming" (Alma 25:15; emphasis added), and its intent was to persuade them "to look forward unto the Messiah, and believe in him to come as though he already was" (Jarom 1:11). Alma taught that the "ordinances were given after this manner, that thereby the people might *look forward* on the Son of God, it being a type of his order, or it being his order, and this that they might *look forward* to him for a remission of their sins" (Alma 13:16; emphasis added). Paul emphasized that the law of Moses was "our schoolmaster to bring us unto Christ" (Gal. 3:24). And the book of Alma recorded that the righteous Lamanites "did not suppose that salvation came by the law of Moses; but the law of Moses did serve to strengthen their faith in Christ" (Alma 25:16).

Although the law of Moses was instituted long after the practice of animal sacrifice, sacrifice was an integral part of the law and was done away with at the same time as the law of Moses—at the time of Christ's death and resurrection. In the ritual of animal sacrifice, the sacrificial animal would be "dedicated . . . to God and made . . . the sacrificer's representative and substitute" before being slain.[1] In this way, the animal took on the sins of the sacrificer and could be killed so the sacrificer might be made clean. In other words, the process of sacrifice made atonement, symbolically allowing the unblemished animal to pay the price for the sacrificer's sins.

According to various laws revealed to Moses, the atonement affords a wide range of blessings for all of humankind. The atonement halts and prevents plagues, a fact that may benefit us in the last days; the atonement eliminates the defilement of temples, homes, land, and clothing so that the overall environment will be cleansed from corruption; the atonement removes defilement of both intentional and unintentional sins, enabling all of us to become one (or *at one*) with God; and the atonement repairs defective, diseased physical bodies, thus anticipating wholeness in immortality.

All of these items have relevance to us today in one way or another, and each directly parallels the blessings that come through Jesus Christ and his atonement. (Other aspects of the law of Moses and the atonement are dealt with in chapters 2, 4, and 5.)

## THE ATONEMENT HALTS AND PREVENTS PLAGUES

The atonement had power to protect the Israelites from plagues. According to scripture, the Lord gave the Levites "to make an atonement for the children of Israel: that there be no plague among the children of Israel, when the children of Israel come nigh unto the sanctuary" (Num. 8:19). In order to play a role in the atonements made by the Levites, adult Israelite males were required to pay "atonement money"; this money would assure the Israelites "that there be no plague among them," as well as support "the service of the tabernacle" (Ex. 30:11–16). This act of paying atonement money has particular significance for the latter days: just as the Israelites were commanded to offer atonement money to avert plagues, we are commanded to pay tithing so that we are not burned at Jesus' coming (D&C 64:23).

The Lord often used plagues as punishment for immorality and sin during Old Testament times. For example, a great plague occurred when the Israelites committed sexual sins with non-Israelites and worshipped their false gods. In fact, an Israelite male brazenly brought a Midianite woman into the Israelite camp for immoral purposes. His and others' sexual sins and idolatrous practices resulted in a plague that killed 24,000 Israelites (Num. 25:1–14). To halt the plague and the resulting deaths, the priest Phinehas, Aaron's grandson, "made an atonement for the children of Israel" (Num. 25:13). Because Phinehas did this, the Lord blessed him and his posterity.

As a God who renders judgment, the Lord sends plagues upon the disobedient (Ex. 7–12; Lev. 26:21; Deut. 28:58–59; Mosiah 12:6–7). But as a God of mercy, the Lord "plagues," or destroys, death, meaning that through his atonement he overcomes death for all humankind. Note the words of Hosea that God will be death's plagues: "I will ransom them from the power of the grave; I will redeem them from death: *O death, I will be thy plagues;* O grave, I will be thy destruction" (Hosea 13:14; emphasis added). In this way, the atonement of the Lord Jesus Christ can both save the children of God from plagues and act as a plague to death, thereby saving the children of God from death as well.

## THE ATONEMENT RESTORES PURITY BY ELIMINATING DEFILEMENT: TEMPLES, HOMES, LAND, AND CLOTHING

Another of the great blessings that the atonement affords is its ability to cleanse or eliminate defilement from all aspects of our lives. Similarly, atonements made in Old Testament times eliminated defilement from physical things, such as temples, homes, land, and clothing.

*Atonement for the temple.* On the Day of Atonement, while wearing white "linen clothes, even the holy garments," the anointed high priest offered sacrifices to make atonement for the temple itself: "And he shall make an atonement for the holy sanctuary, and he shall make an atonement for the tabernacle of the congregation, and for the altar, and he shall make an atonement for the priests, and for all the people of the congregation" (Lev. 16:32–33). Atonement was made for the temple because of the uncleanness and sins of the children of Israel. The temple must remain holy because it is the Lord's house, the place where Jehovah dwells.

Additionally, atonement was also made specifically for the altar within the temple on the Day of Atonement. The high priest would make "an atonement upon the horns of [the altar] once in a year with the blood of the sin offering" (Ex. 30:10). The high priest placed the blood of the bullock and goat upon the altar's horns "to make an atonement for the holy place" because of Israel's uncleanness (Lev. 16:15–19; 27, 33) and because Israel's sins were symbolically written or engraven on the altar's horns (Jer. 17:1). This act of atonement was so powerful that it rendered the altar "most holy," to the point that the altar itself could convey holiness to whatever or whoever touched it. For according to the scriptures, "whatsoever toucheth the altar shall be holy" (Ex. 29:36–37).[2] In the last days, after a temple has been built in Jerusalem, an atonement will also be made for the temple there and its altar, as recorded in Ezekiel (Ezek. 43:20; 45:20).

*Atonement for homes.* Just as atonement can cleanse temples and altars, atonement can also cleanse homes. An example of this comes in Leviticus 14:33–57, which discusses a house that has been contaminated by leprosy or another skin disease and gives direction for its purification through the atonement. In these verses from Leviticus, the priest is commanded to make a diagnosis, pronounce the home "clean" or "unclean" from contamination, and subsequently have it destroyed or purified. For such a house that the priest pronounces clean, purification rites include the sacrifice of a bird; then, as the scriptures say, the priest "shall make an atonement for the house" (Lev. 14:53). The contaminated house may symbolize a place of spiritual contamination that must be purified through the atonement in order to become a suitable dwelling place for a God-fearing family.

*Atonement for the land.* The Mosaic law regarding the atonement for the land is detailed in the book of Numbers. The scriptures read, "Bloodshed pollutes the land, and atonement cannot be made for the land on which blood has been shed, except by the blood of the one who shed it" (NIV Num. 35:33). In other words, after land has been defiled by bloodshed, that land and those who dwell thereon cannot be one with God unless the one who shed blood atones for the bloodshed with his own life. Following that scripture in the book of Numbers, the Lord continues by explaining the importance of having an undefiled land: "Defile not therefore the land which ye shall inhabit, wherein I dwell: for I the Lord dwell among the children of Israel" (Num. 35:34).

*Atonement for clothing.* Leviticus (13:47–59; 14:54–57)[3] deals with clothing that has mildew or that has been contaminated by a skin disease or plague, the priest's diagnosis of that clothing, his pronouncement of "clean" or "unclean," and the subsequent washing or burning of the clothing. Why so much attention to one's contaminated clothing? Clothing is an outward symbol of the person who wears it, and a tainted garment seems to symbolize the uncleanness and defilement of that person. The Mosaic law required the destruction of the clothing or its restoration to a state of ritual purity.

## The Atonement Cleanses Sinners from Both Intentional and Unintentional Sins

The law of Moses dealt with two categories of sins: (1) willful sins, or those of an intentional, premeditated, or rebellious nature; and (2) inadvertent or unintentional sins. All sins—minor or major, willful or unintentional—separate sinners from God and his glory and excellence because all sins, even those deemed inconsequential to some individuals, represent an infraction of one of God's laws. Therefore, atonement must be made for both willful and unintentional sins. The law of Moses expressed means and ways of atoning for both types of sins:

*Intentional sins.* Intentional sins include profaning the Lord's name, committing immoral acts, worshipping idols, breaking the Sabbath, bearing false witness, taking improper oaths, touching unclean things (Lev. 5:1–13; 6:1–7; and other passages), and numerous other sins. In order to remove the separation between God and humans that is caused by willful sins, God established the law of sacrifice. Priests, representing the Lord himself, regularly made atonement for "any sin that men commit, to do a trespass against the Lord, and that person be guilty" (Num. 5:6). After the sinner confessed a sin, the priest offered up a ram, "whereby an atonement shall be made for him" (Num. 5:6–8). The scriptures include numerous examples of priests making atonements for sin. For example, Moses offered atonement for the Israelites who had committed the great sin of making and worshipping the golden calf (Ex. 32:30).

As a payment for all other sins for which the priests did not make a special atonement, the high priest, also representing the Lord, would offer burnt offerings once a year on the Day of Atonement, making atonement for himself and his family (Lev. 16:6, 11), the priests, and the rest of the people. "For on that day shall the priest make an atonement for you, to cleanse you, that ye may be clean from all your sins before the Lord" (Lev. 16:30). On this holy day, a scapegoat is presented to the Lord, the sins of the people are conferred upon its head, and then the animal is let loose in the wilderness. Although the scapegoat is not slaughtered, it too makes atonement for the people (Lev. 16:10).

*Unintentional sins.* Unintentional sins are sins that are committed through ignorance, thoughtlessness, or carelessness. For example, if a man borrowed a tool from his neighbor and forgot to return it, that man has committed an unintentional sin. Or, if a person failed to properly enclose his ox and it gored a neighbor, then the ox's owner has sinned through carelessness. In these cases, atonement must be made to maintain order in the community.

In the Lord's laws regarding unintentional sins, which laws pertained to individuals, priests, rulers, and the entire congregation of Israel, each law follows a particular pattern: formula ("if _____ shall sin through ignorance"), identification of the animal to be sacrificed, transference of sins by the laying on of hands, the command to sacrifice the animal, a ritual involving the placement of the victim's blood on the altar's horns, and a statement regarding the atonement and forgiveness. The following table sets forth this pattern of atonement for unintentional sins.

| Commission of unintentional sins | Priests | Entire community of Israel | Rulers | Individuals |
|---|---|---|---|---|
| Formula | "if a [priest] shall sin through ignorance" | "if the whole congregation of Israel sin through ignorance" | "when a ruler hath sinned . . . through ignorance" | "if any one of the common people sin through ignorance" |
| Sacrificial victim | young bullock without blemish | young bullock | kid goat without blemish | female kid goat without blemish |
| Transference of sins to victim | priest "shall lay his hand upon the bullock's head" | elders "shall lay their hands upon the head of the bullock" | ruler "shall lay his hand upon the head of the goat" | "he shall lay his hand upon the head of the sin offering" |
| Sacrifice | "kill the bullock before the Lord" | "bullock shall be killed before the Lord" | "kill it . . . before the Lord" | kill offering |
| Ritual | priest puts blood on altar's horns, etc. | priest puts blood on altar's horns, etc. | priest puts blood on altar's horns, etc. | priest puts blood on altar's horns, etc. |
| Atonement and forgiveness | | "priest shall make an atonement . . . it shall be forgiven them" | "priest shall make an atonement . . . it shall be forgiven him" | "priest shall make an atonement . . . it shall be forgiven him" |
| Reference | Lev. 4:1–12, 20 | Lev. 4:13–21; Num. 15:22–26 | Lev. 4:22–26 | Lev. 4:27–35; 5:14–19; Num. 15:27–29 |

Through these atonement rituals, the Lord afforded the Israelites the opportunity to be cleansed from unintentional sin, just as the priests could make animal sacrifices to atone for intentional sin. We can look at these atonement sacrifices as a means of understanding Christ's great and last sacrifice for *our* sin, recognizing that his atonement paid the price for both our intentional sins and our unintentional sins.

## ATONEMENT AND THE PHYSICAL BODY

In the law of Moses, the Lord revealed various laws pertaining to the atonement and its role in healing ruptured, defective, or diseased physical bodies. The problems with the physical body could include those who have a "running issue from the flesh" (Lev. 15:2), individuals with leprosy or skin diseases, women after childbirth, and priests with blemishes. People with these problems are said to have defective coverings, meaning that their bodies' outer protective layers (their integument, primarily skin) are flawed in a manner that requires the atonement. The Mosaic laws requiring atonement for physical diseases may trouble some in modern times because of our understanding that God does not judge people based on their bodily defects or diseases; however, the ability of the atonement to overcome and heal physical imperfections symbolizes Jesus Christ's power to overcome sins or spiritual uncleanness and shortcomings. As we ponder these sacred truths, we realize just how completely the law of Moses is able to teach the atonement.

We can gain additional insight into the treatment of imperfect bodies under the Mosaic law by examining the original Hebrew text. The Hebrew root *kpr* (usually translated as *atone* or *atonement* in the King James Version) often means "to cover." In our present discussion of defective coverings (the body's ruptured, defective, or diseased integument), the atonement ("to cover") conveys the idea of covering these ruptured bodies with a new protective layer. Biblical scholar Mary Douglas explains: "According to the illustrative cases from Leviticus, to atone means to cover, or recover, cover again, to repair a hole, cure a sickness, mend a rift, make good a torn or broken covering. As a noun, what is translated atonement, expiation, or purgation means integument made good; conversely, the examples in the book indicate that defilement means integument torn. Atonement does not mean covering a sin so as to hide it from the sight of God; it means making good an outer layer which has rotted or been pierced."[4] Clearly there is more to the atonement than redemption from sin: the atonement completes and perfects physical things, including the human body, and each example of ruptured, defective, or diseased physical bodies is symbolic and points, to a greater or lesser extent, to Jesus Christ and his atonement.

Leviticus presents the following examples of ruptured or defective physical bodies, each of which requires ceremonial purification and atonement:

*Leprosy or persons with other diseases or sicknesses* (Lev. 13–14).[5] Leprosy was "the disease [that] was regarded as a living death."[6] This can be seen from Aaron's description of his sister, Miriam, when she became leprous: "Let her not be as one dead, of whom the flesh is half consumed when he cometh out of his mother's womb" (Num. 12:12). Throughout the scriptures, leprosy is symbolically linked to sins and transgressions—those things that lead us to spiritual death. As one scholar summarizes, "Leprosy is always taken as a type of sin."[7] According to Douglas, "A settled state of leprosy is a chronic failure of the body's covering to contain its fluids and flesh. This is the bad pollution which is a figure for idolatry, lies, deceit, and all forms of unrighteousness. Leprosies need atonement by the priest."[8]

Leviticus describes the leper's awful state: "He is a leprous man, he is unclean: the priest shall pronounce him utterly unclean; his plague is in his head. And the leper in whom the plague is, his clothes shall be rent, and his head bare, and he shall put a covering upon his upper lip, and shall cry, Unclean, unclean. All the days wherein the plague shall be in him he shall be defiled; he is unclean: he shall dwell alone; without the camp shall his habitation be" (Lev. 13:44–46). In this passage, the term *unclean* is repeated five times and refers to ceremonial or ritual uncleanness, not to physical uncleanness. Great sinners are also unclean, defiled, and alone (without the Spirit) until they apply the atonement in their lives. Correspondingly, those of us who commit certain sins are not permitted to attend the temple until we are ceremonially cleansed by partaking of the sacrament after sincere repentance, just as the leper was not allowed to dwell among the rest of the Israelites until his leprosy was ceremonially cleansed. Leprosy is sometimes a contagious disease, and this contagiousness may have a parallel in that those who have a rebellious or sinful nature may influence others to join in their sins.

Beyond the above statements regarding leprosy and sin, a number of scriptures associate diseases with sin, as the following four cases illustrate.

1. In a poetic parallelism in Psalms, *iniquities* parallels *diseases:* "Who forgiveth all thine iniquities; who healeth all thy diseases" (Ps. 103:3; Ecc. 6:2).

2. In Deuteronomy, the Lord warned the Israelites of the consequences of choosing disobedience, saying: "If thou wilt not observe to do all the words of this law that are written in this book, that thou mayest fear this glorious and fearful name, the Lord thy God; then the Lord will make thy plagues wonderful, and the plagues of thy seed, even great plagues, and of long continuance, and sore sicknesses, and of long continuance. Moreover he will bring upon thee all the diseases of Egypt, which thou wast afraid of; and they shall cleave unto thee" (Deut. 28:58–60). But if Israel chose obedience, the Lord would protect them from the diseases that he sent upon the Egyptians: "If thou wilt diligently hearken to the voice of the Lord thy God, and wilt do that which is right in his sight, and wilt give ear to his commandments, and keep all his statutes, I will put none of these diseases upon thee, which I have brought upon the Egyptians: for I am the Lord that healeth thee" (Ex. 15:26; Deut. 7:15).

3. Miriam, Moses and Aaron's sister, became leprous for seven days when she sinned by speaking out against the prophet Moses (Num. 12:1–15; see also Deut. 24:9). Uzziah, the king of Judah, also became leprous when he sinned by attempting to burn incense upon the temple's altar without having the authority to do so. As a consequence, Uzziah gave up his kingship, lived in separation, and "was cut off from the house of the Lord" (2 Chr. 26:16–21).

4. There is a correspondence, as Paul explained in his letter to the Corinthians, between partaking of the sacrament unworthily and

sicknesses: "For he that eateth and drinketh unworthily, eateth and drinketh damnation to himself, not discerning the Lord's body. For this cause many are weak and sickly among you, and many sleep" (1 Cor. 11:29–30).

*An important word of caution:* The passages presented in these four illustrative cases and other scriptures do not suggest, nor is it true, that all or most people who have diseases or sicknesses have committed sins. Sicknesses and diseases come through the normal processes of mortality upon the innocent and the guilty, the repentant and the rebellious, infants and the elderly, saints and sinners, and everyone in between. Sicknesses are a significant part of our mortal experience and training. But when we are made whole (whether in this life or in the resurrection), we can know that the blessing comes through the grace of Christ, made possible through his atonement.

Lepers were allowed to return to both the temple and the Israelite community when they had been physically healed, had been ceremonially cleansed, and the priest had made atonement for them. The ceremonial cleansing of the physically healed leper focused on Jesus Christ and his atonement, for the cleansing required temple rituals and sacrificial offerings. In these rituals, the priest (symbolizing Jesus Christ) diagnosed the one with a skin disease (Lev. 13:1–46) and then pronounced that person "clean" or "unclean" (Lev. 13:8–18). If that person was unclean, then he or she was excluded from the community and the temple (Lev. 13:46; see also 2 Chr. 26:21; Ps. 51:7, 11), but if clean, then that person was qualified to prepare to return to the temple. All of this was symbolic of Jesus Christ, who is the one who pronounces us "clean" or "unclean"; if unclean, we belong outside of the temple, but if "clean," we are blessed to live with the righteous and to enter God's holy house.

The cleansing ritual required two birds, cedar wood, scarlet, hyssop, and blood of a sacrificial animal (Lev. 14:4–6, 49–52).[9] Each of these items pertained to Jesus Christ and his atonement. For example, after the priest killed one of the two birds, he took the other bird and dipped it in the blood of the sacrificed bird; then he let the living bird loose in an open field (Lev. 14:4–7). The sacrificed bird symbolized Jesus' death, and the bird that was freed (after being dipped in the blood of the sacrificed bird) perhaps represented the freedom that we receive

44

because of Jesus' death—freedom from sin and death. The following statement sums up all of the rituals connected to the cleansing of the leper: "The priest shall make an atonement for him, and he shall be clean" (Lev. 14:20; see also vv. 18–19, 29, 31).

*Male or female with an issue from the flesh.* A male or female who had an issue from his or her flesh was ritually unclean, meaning that such a person required atonement (Lev. 15:1–30). Scholars are divided as to what it meant to have a running issue—was it secretions from the sexual organs, bodily or social diseases with discharges, menstrual bleeding, blood flows caused by a wound, or something else? Lamentations 4:9 uses the same verb found in Leviticus 15 (referring to an issue) and applies it to blood from a sword injury. If blood was meant as the discharge, then that indicates the initial stages of loss of life because sufficient blood flow results in loss of life. Regardless of what type of bodily discharge was meant, bodily discharges indicate that our bodies are imperfect and mortal.

For the person with the running issue to be cleansed, after the issue has stopped, the Mosaic law required the subject to wash his or her clothes (this had both social and spiritual implications), bathe (possibly a ritual immersion) in running water (a physical and spiritual cleansing agent), and give two doves or pigeons to the priest to be sacrificed. The priest then offered the birds, "one for a sin offering, and the other for a burnt offering," and "the priest [would] make an atonement" for that man or woman who had an issue (Lev. 15:15). As in many other sacrifice rituals, the priest symbolizes Jesus Christ, who offered himself as a sacrificial offering and made atonement for each of us.

*A woman after childbirth.* A woman was considered ritually unclean after her issue of blood following childbirth, and the law required a period of purification followed by temple rituals and animal sacrifices on her behalf. The scriptures tell us that Mary, the mother of Jesus, adhered to these purification rites after Jesus' birth: "And when the days of her purification according to the law of Moses were accomplished" (Luke 2:22), Joseph, Mary, and Jesus went to Jerusalem's temple. The cleansing rituals for a woman after giving birth included a burnt offering of a lamb and a sin offering of a dove or pigeon; then "the priest [would] make an atonement for her, and she [would] be clean" (Lev. 12:1–8).

Why would atonement be required for a woman who had just suffered great pains in order to bring new life into the world? To cite Douglas once more, to atone means to "to repair a hole, cure a sickness, mend a rift, make good a torn or broken covering. . . . Atonement . . . means making good an outer layer which has rotted or been pierced."[10] In other words, a mother needed an atonement sacrifice in order to "make good [her] torn or broken covering," caused when she gave new physical life. In this there is a symbol of Jesus Christ, whose covering was torn and broken in order to give us spiritual life.

*Priests with physical blemishes,* such as blindness, lameness, dwarfism, a hunched back, crippled feet or hands, or other deformities or disfigurements could not participate in sacrificial offerings (could not "come nigh unto the altar") or partake of the holy food (Lev. 21:16–23). Furthermore, priests who had certain skin diseases (possibly leprosy), had an issue from their flesh, had touched unclean things (corpse, creeping things), or had eaten unclean things ("that which dieth of itself, or is torn with beasts" [Lev. 22:8]), were not allowed to deal with sacred things or eat the sacred food until they had completed a ritual purification. Priests who violated these commandments were subject to excommunication or even death (Lev. 22:1–9). On the one hand, a priest with blemishes can represent one who has spiritual imperfections, or one who is unworthy to perform sacred rituals, such as temple services. On the other hand, a righteous priest without physical blemishes can symbolize Jesus Christ, who was a priest "without blemish and without spot" (1 Pet. 1:19; see also Eph. 5:25–27).

*Summary on the atonement and the physical body.* From the scriptures, we learn the following spiritual truths about the Mosaic laws regarding the atonement and defective bodies:

1. The souls of men and women constitute a temple of God. On May 6, 1833, the Lord revealed to Joseph Smith, "The elements are the tabernacle of God; yea, man is the tabernacle of God, even temples; and whatsoever temple is defiled, God shall destroy that temple" (D&C 93:35; see also 1 Cor. 3:16–17; 2 Cor. 5:2; 6:16–7:1). Helaman 4:24

informs us that the individual who defiles his or her temple causes the Spirit of God to depart, and that temple becomes an "unholy temple": "And they saw that they had become weak, like unto their brethren, the Lamanites, and that the Spirit of the Lord did no more preserve them; yea, it had withdrawn from them because the Spirit of the Lord doth not dwell in unholy temples" (cf. Mosiah 2:36–37). Just as the atonement cleanses and sanctifies temples that are constructed by human builders (such as the temple of Solomon), even so the atonement cleanses and sanctifies us so that we will not remain unholy temples.

2. The Mosaic laws regarding the atonement and the physical body anticipate the resurrection: just as the Mosaic laws regarding the atonement and the physical body make those with defective bodies ritually clean, even so the atonement will make our bodies eternally clean from mortal defects and deficiencies at the resurrection. Any defects that we have during mortality or at death—including imperfect vital organs, blindness, scars, missing limbs, physical deficiencies, cancerous parts, and so forth—will be fully repaired at the resurrection. Furthermore, all bodies that have lain down to rest in death will be restored at the resurrection. In fact, the atonement is so all encompassing in its power through Jesus Christ that he will restore us to perfect, immortal, and indestructible bodies. Jesus, of course, was the first to be resurrected, and the atonement restored Jesus' own physical body to wholeness after his sufferings, crucifixion, and consequent death. Though he was beaten, disfigured, and pierced, and though he bled profusely, he was wholly restored at his resurrection. From this we learn that no matter what kind of abuse our mortal bodies endure, they too can be made perfect at the resurrection.

3. The laws regarding broken bodies point to Jesus Christ, who during the final hours of mortality experienced a ruptured outer covering. He was beaten, whipped, crowned with piercing thorns, pierced with nails in six places, and wounded with a spear in a seventh place. The whipping, nail and spear piercing, and thorns all caused bleeding, fitting the description in Mosaic law regarding one who has a running issue from his flesh. But beyond all that, he experienced a form of suffering that was distinct from all others who had or who would ever live: he bled from every pore, the epitome of one with a running issue.

CHAPTER 4

# PIERCED BREAD AND BLOOD: THE LAW OF SACRIFICE

FROM THE TIME OF ADAM AND EVE to the time of Christ's death and resurrection, the children of God were commanded to offer animal sacrifice. In the very beginning, the Lord "gave unto [Adam and Eve] commandments, that they should worship the Lord their God, and should offer the firstlings of their flocks, for an offering unto the Lord. And Adam was obedient unto the commandments of the Lord" (Moses 5:5). Sometime later an angel appeared to Adam and asked, "Why dost thou offer sacrifices unto the Lord? And Adam said unto him: I know not, save the Lord commanded me." The angel proceeded to teach Adam the meaning of sacrifices, saying, "This thing is a similitude of the sacrifice of the Only Begotten of the Father, which is full of grace and truth" (Moses 5:6–7).

Sacrifices, then, are *similitudes* of the sacrifice of Jesus Christ. Joseph Smith taught that "sacrifice was instituted for a type, by which man was to discern the great Sacrifice which God had prepared."[1] And President Joseph Fielding Smith provided this summary statement: "All the sacrifices of old, from the days of Adam to the atonement of Jesus Christ by blood were in the similitude of and a reminder of the great sacrifice, and pointed forward to its fulfillment by Jesus upon the cross."[2]

Clearly, the view that sacrifices were a similitude of the great and last sacrifice is and always has been the testimony of God's prophets and apostles. This chapter will examine several specific aspects of the law of sacrifice, focusing on their roles as types and shadows of Jesus Christ.

## THREE OBJECTS OF THE SACRIFICES TESTIFY OF JESUS AND HIS SACRIFICE FOR US

Three specific objects in the sacrifices—the offering, the priest, and the offerer—testify of Jesus and his atonement. Biblical scholar Andrew Jukes has written that in every sacrificial offering,

> There are at least three distinct objects presented. . . . There is the *offering*, the *priest*, the *offerer*.
> What, then is *the offering*? what *the priest*? what *the offerer*? Christ is the offering, Christ is the priest, Christ is the offerer. As *offerer*, we see Him *man under the law*, standing our substitute, for us to fulfil all righteousness. As *priest*, we have Him presented as *the mediator*, God's messenger between Himself and Israel. While as *the offering* He is seen *the innocent victim*, a sweet savour to God, yet bearing the sin and dying for it.[3]

It is evident that every aspect of the ritual of sacrifice points toward Christ and his ultimate sacrifice for the sins of the world.

## THE SIX ACTS OF THE SACRIFICES TESTIFY OF JESUS AND HIS SACRIFICE FOR US

According to the LDS Bible Dictionary, "under the law of Moses, sacrifices were varied and complex, and a multitude of rules were given to govern the procedure, in keeping with the general character and purpose of the Mosaic law. . . . In all the animal sacrifices of the Mosaic law there were six important acts." The six acts were "the presentation of the sacrifice," "the laying on of hands," "the slaughtering of the animal," "the pouring out or sprinkling of the blood," the burning of the sacrifice, and the partaking of the sacrificial meal.[4] The accompanying chart provides a brief explanation of each of these six events.

| Action number | Action | Three acts conducted by the worshipper |
|---|---|---|
| Act 1 | Presentation of the sacrifice | The worshipper presented the sacrifice at the door of temple or on the north side of the altar (Lev. 1:3; 3:2). |
| Act 2 | Laying on of hands | The worshipper laid his hands on the sacrifice to consecrate the offering to God and to make the sacrifice a substitute for the offerer (Lev. 1:4; 16:21; see also Num. 8:10; 27:18, 20). |
| Act 3 | Slaughtering of the animal | The worshipper slaughtered the animal, an act that pointed to Jesus' sacrifice; later in history the priests performed the sacrifice. |
| **Action number** | **Action** | **Three acts conducted by the priests** |
| Act 4 | Sprinkling or pouring of the blood | For most animal sacrifices, the priest collected the victim's blood and sprinkled a portion of it on the sides of the altar and poured the remainder at the altar's base (Ex. 29:12; Lev. 1:5; 3:2; 4:7; Lev. 8:15; Num. 18:17; see also Lev. 17:11). |
| Act 5 | Burning of the sacrifice | Depending on the sacrifice, the priest burned all or part of the animal on the altar. |
| Act 6 | Partaking of the sacrificial meal | Participants of the sacrificial meal included (depending on the type of sacrifice):<br>a. Worshippers and priests (in the case of the peace offerings) (Lev. 7:11–36)<br>b. Only the priests and their families (Lev. 10:14; 22:10–12; Num. 18:14)<br>c. Only the priests (Lev. 6:16, 26; 7:6; 24:9) |

Note that the worshippers conducted acts one through three, and acts four and five pertained to the priests. The sixth act, partaking of the sacrificial meal, could pertain to priests only, to priests and worshippers, or to priests and their families.

Because sacrifices were offered as a "similitude of the sacrifice of the Only Begotten of the Father" (Moses 5:7), the entire six-part process of the animal sacrifices focused on Jesus Christ and his atonement. In act number two, for example, when the offerer laid his hands on the animal's head, this served to transfer the offerer's sins to the animal. The symbolism of laying on of hands in sacrifices is explained in Leviticus 16:21, where Aaron lays his hands on the scapegoat: "And Aaron shall lay both his hands upon the head of the live goat, and confess over him all the iniquities of the children of Israel, and all their transgressions in all their sins, putting them upon the head of the goat."

More should be said about the sixth act—the partaking of the sacrificial meal—which anticipated our modern sacrament. Specific directions were given as to who would partake of the sacrificial meal: under the law of Moses, the priests, their families, and worshippers would partake of sacrificial meals, which consisted of both meat from the offerings and consecrated bread. The direction given in the scriptures says that for this act in an animal sacrifice, the priests "shall eat the flesh of the ram, and the bread that is in the basket, by the door of the tabernacle of the congregation. And they shall eat those things wherewith the atonement was made, to consecrate and to sanctify them" (Ex. 29:32–33; Lev. 7:31–33; 8:31–36; 10:12–18).

All priests were told to eat "one as much as another" (Lev. 7:10), and it seems that there was plenty of food (2 Chr. 31:10). Nonpriestly families who offered the sacrificial animals to the Lord in the temple also partook of the sacrificial meals (Lev. 7:11–36), and this allowed for social and spiritual communion between priests and Israelite families who offered sacrifices. Strangers, sojourners, and hired servants in the priest's household were not permitted to eat the sacred meal (Lev. 22:10; Ex. 29:33), and those who were defiled and unclean were not permitted to partake of the holy food until they had participated in sacred rituals (Lev. 22:1–6). These directions for the last act in the ritual of sacrifice were so important to the Lord that certain unclean persons who partook of the sacred food were subject to excommunication (Lev. 7:20–21; 22:1–2).[5]

Most important, the ancient sacrificial meal was Christ-centered. It is analogous to a sacred meal of our own dispensation: the sacrament of bread and water. Once again, we see that the sacrificial meal *looked forward* to Jesus' sacrifice; the sacrament *remembers* his sacrifice. Both meals—the one from the old law and the other from the new gospel—signify Jesus' broken body and atoning blood.

Several specific sacrificial offerings, including burnt (Lev. 1:3–17; 6:8–13), grain (Lev. 2:1–16), peace (Lev. 3:1–17), sin (Lev. 4:1–5:13), and trespass, or guilt, offerings (Lev. 5:14–6:7), provide fascinating details into the meaning of Jesus' divine atonement, and a study of them reveals a number of symbols and spiritual meanings.

## Flaying the Sacrifice, Pierced Bread, and Beaten Oil

Beyond the six chief acts associated with the sacrificial offerings, numerous other aspects of the sacrificial system testify of Jesus Christ and his sacrifice. This section will deal with three: flaying the sacrificial victim, pierced bread, and beaten oil.

1. *Flaying the sacrificial victim.* Leviticus refers to the flaying of the bullock after it was slaughtered: "And he shall kill the bullock before the Lord. . . . And he shall flay the burnt offering" (Lev. 1:5–6). Another passage suggests that the task of flaying required much work and that the Levites assisted the priests as they flayed the burnt offerings: "But the priests were too few, so that they could not flay all the burnt offerings: wherefore their brethren the Levites did help them, till the work was ended" (2 Chr. 29:34; see also 2 Chr. 35:11). To flay here apparently means to skin the animal. After killing the sacrificial victim, the offerer or member of the priesthood would skin the animal. The Hebrew word *psht,* which the King James translators rendered as "to flay," usually means "to strip off clothing" or "to strip naked" (Gen. 37:23; Job 22:6; 1 Sam. 19:24; Ezek. 16:39; 26:16; 44:19; Hosea 2:3).

Flayed sacrificial victims were symbols of Jesus Christ. Jesus was unceremoniously stripped of clothing—his garments and "coat"—before his crucifixion. "Then the soldiers, when they had crucified Jesus, took his garments, and made four parts, to every soldier a part; and also his coat: now the coat was without seam, woven from the top throughout. They said therefore among themselves, Let us not rend it, but cast lots for it, whose it shall be: that the scripture might be fulfilled, which saith, They parted my raiment among them, and for my vesture they did cast lots" (John 19:23–24). President Spencer W. Kimball wrote, "How he must have suffered when [the soldiers] violated his privacy by stripping off his clothes and then putting on him the scarlet robe!"[6]

The flaying of the sacrificial victims also looked forward to the scourging of Jesus, when he was stripped of parts of his skin. During his trial, when he appeared before the Roman governor Pontius Pilate, he was scourged before his crucifixion (Matt. 27:26). Perhaps Peter referred to this scourging when he wrote that Jesus "[bore] our sins in his own body" (1 Pet. 2:24). Isaiah had prophesied of the scourging more than seven centuries earlier with these words: "I gave my back to the smiters" (Isa. 50:6).

2. *The pierced bread.* Several Old Testament passages refer to a special bread-like food that was eaten by temple worshippers or burned on the altar with sacrificial offerings (Ex. 29:2, 25; Lev. 2:4; 7:12; 8:26; 24:5; Num. 6:15, 19). This bread is called *halah* (Hebrew, plural *halot*), which suggests "pierced" bread (from the Hebrew root *hll*, "to pierce").[7] Elsewhere in the scriptures the Hebrew root (*hll*) refers to *piercing,* specifically to one who is pierced by the sword or by an arrow (1 Sam. 31:3; Lam. 4:9). We do not know exactly why this bread was called *halah,* but perhaps the dough was pierced or perforated before it was placed in the oven. The "pierced" bread seems to typify Jesus Christ, who is called the "bread of life" and who was pierced while on the cross. Both Isaiah and the Psalmist prophesied of Jesus' piercing as part of the atonement: "He was pierced for our transgressions" (NIV Isa. 53:5; here Isaiah uses the same root used for *halah*); "They pierced my hands and my feet" (Ps. 22:16).

Just as *pierced bread* was a significant part of the ancient sacrificial system, *broken bread* was used by Church members during the early

Christian era and is used again during our own dispensation as a reminder of Christ's sacrifice. We remember that Jesus himself broke the sacramental bread in anticipation of his broken body. Matthew recorded, "And as they were eating, Jesus took bread, and blessed it, and brake it, and gave it to the disciples, and said, Take, eat; this is my body" (Matt. 26:26). During our sacrament meetings today, priests also break the bread. That the broken bread is an emblem of Jesus' broken body is clear from a statement made by President John Taylor: "I take pleasure in meeting with the Saints. I like to break bread with them in commemoration of the broken body of our Lord and Savior Jesus Christ, and also to partake of the cup in remembrance of his shed blood."[8] In all likelihood, the Israelites used the pierced bread in the same way we use the broken bread—to draw their minds toward the ultimate sacrifice, during which the body of the sacrificial victim would be both pierced and broken.

3. *Beaten oil.* The ancient sacrificial system included several regulations that pertained to beaten olive oil, or "oil made by beating or pounding the olives in a mortar."[9] For example, the daily offering at the temple included two lambs, a drink offering, and flour mixed with olive oil. The flour and olive oil mixture consisted of a tenth part of an ephah (about two quarts) of fine flour and a fourth part of a hin (about a quart) of beaten oil (Ex. 29:40; Num. 28:5–7). These three offerings—the lambs, the drink offering, and the flour and oil mixture—were offered "day by day, for a continual burnt offering" (Num. 28:3). Beaten oil was also used for the temple lampstand to provide light for those who worked in the temple. God commanded Moses, "Thou shalt command the children of Israel, that they bring thee pure oil olive beaten for the light, to cause the lamp to burn always" (Ex. 27:20).

Beaten oil has been described as "fine and costly"[10] and was highly prized, more so than olive oil that was prepared through other methods, such as an olive press. Why, then, was beaten oil utilized as an offering to the Lord in his temple as part of the daily offering, and why was it used for the lampstand to illuminate the temple? The beaten oil was used because it symbolizes Jesus in two important ways. First, he is the Anointed One, or the one who has been anointed with olive oil. He is called *Christ* and *Messiah,* which mean the anointed one in Greek and Hebrew, respectively.

Second, the beaten oil anticipates the experience of Jesus Christ just hours before his death on the cross: he too was beaten. Matthew, Mark, and Luke provided these testimonies: "Then did they spit in his face, and buffeted him; and others smote him with the palms of their hands" (Matt. 26:67); "And some began to spit on him, and to cover his face, and to buffet him . . . and the servants did strike him with the palms of their hands" (Mark 14:65); "And the men that held Jesus mocked him, and smote him. And when they had blindfolded him, they struck him on the face, and asked him, saying, Prophesy, who is it that smote thee?" (Luke 22:63–64). President Kimball wrote of this account: "In quiet, restrained, divine dignity he stood when they cast their spittle in his face. He remained composed. Not an angry word escaped his lips. They slapped his face and beat his body. Yet he stood resolute, unintimidated."[11] Isaiah had prophesied this evil treatment of Jesus Christ seven centuries earlier: "I gave my back to the smiters, and my cheeks to them that plucked off the hair: I hid not my face from shame and spitting" (Isa. 50:6).

Since the beaten oil represents Christ, it was used in the lampstand to illuminate the temple because Christ is the light of the world. In the Book of Mormon, Mosiah declares, "He is the light and the life of the world; yea, a light that is endless, that can never be darkened" (Mosiah 16:9). It is only fitting, then, that the beaten oil be used to give light in the temple, just as Christ gives light to all the world.

## THE LOCATION OF SACRIFICES BASED ON THE NATURE OF THE SINS AND OFFENSES

The law of Moses taught wonderful truths regarding the significance of the location of sacrifices in the temple precinct. Lesser unintentional transgressions (transgressions that came as a result of ignorance or accident), such as those committed by only one person, were atoned for in the tabernacle or temple courtyard, a short distance from the holy of holies. Greater unintentional transgressions, such as those committed by the entire congregation, were atoned for in the holy place, which was adjacent to the holy of holies. The greatest sins, those that were willful or deliberate (conducted with full knowledge of the commission of sin), were atoned for in the holy of holies. The principle underlying the various locations of the atonement sacrifices is that the greater the offense against God, the more that offense penetrates into the temple precinct; also, the greater the offense, the more the atonement for that offense needs to be made in the holy of holies, or the place closest to God. The accompanying chart illustrates these ideas.

Latter-day Saint professor Stephen D. Ricks summarizes the concept of the magnitude of sins and the location of the sacrifices: "In Leviticus the sacrificial offerings for sin fall into two categories, those designed to atone for *unintentional transgressions* and those that atoned for *willful sins.* The former included the burnt offering (see Lev. 1:1–17; Lev. 6:8–13), the sin (purification) offering (see Lev. 4:1–5:13; Lev. 6:24–30), and the guilt (trespass) offering (see Lev. 5:14–6:7). Each of these sacrifices was performed by the transgressor himself in the tabernacle or temple anytime during the year. . . .

"Sacrifices for intentional sins, however, could be offered only by the high priest, and on only one day of each year—the Day of Atonement."[12]

## LOCATIONS OF SACRIFICES
## BASED ON THE NATURE OF THE OFFENSE

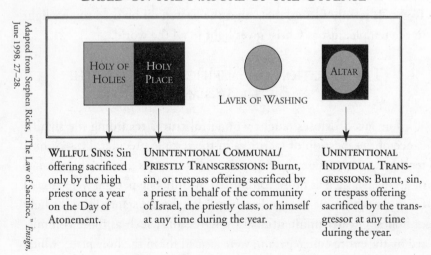

Adapted from Stephen Ricks, "The Law of Sacrifice," *Ensign,* June 1998, 27–28.

| HOLY OF HOLIES | HOLY PLACE | | ALTAR |

LAVER OF WASHING

**WILLFUL SINS:** Sin offering sacrificed only by the high priest once a year on the Day of Atonement.

**UNINTENTIONAL COMMUNAL/ PRIESTLY TRANSGRESSIONS:** Burnt, sin, or trespass offering sacrificed by a priest in behalf of the community of Israel, the priestly class, or himself at any time during the year.

**UNINTENTIONAL INDIVIDUAL TRANSGRESSIONS:** Burnt, sin, or trespass offering sacrificed by the transgressor at any time during the year.

## JESUS CHRIST AND SUBSTITUTION, PERFECTION, FAITH, AND GOD'S ACCEPTANCE

*Substitution, perfection, faith,* and *God's acceptance* and *forgiveness* are four important concepts that deal with the ancient sacrificial offerings and their fulfillment in Jesus Christ. Understanding these four concepts assists us in gaining a greater appreciation for Jesus Christ and the atonement.

*Substitution.* During the Old Testament period, people's sins were symbolically transferred to animals, and the animals were sacrificed vicariously for the persons. The transference of sins from humans to sacrificial animals usually occurred by the laying on of hands, wherein human sin was symbolically transferred through the offerer's hands to the head of the animal. The animal was then sacrificed in an act of atonement as a substitution for the offerer. In a much more significant, substantial, and perfect way, substitution, or vicarious sacrifice, points to Jesus Christ, who was sacrificed in an infinite atonement for all sinners. President Joseph Fielding Smith taught that "the whole plan of redemption is based on vicarious sacrifice, One without sin standing for the whole human family, all of whom were under the curse."[13]

*Perfection.* The sacrificial animal's *perfection* was a vital aspect of the ancient order of sacrifices. The expression "without blemish" occurs more than three dozen times in the Old Testament, and this high frequency underscores its importance in the sacrificial system. The Lord required that sacrificial animals have no blemishes, instructing his people: "Ye shall offer at your own will a male without blemish, of the beeves, of the sheep, or of the goats. But whatsoever hath a blemish, that shall ye not offer: for it shall not be acceptable for you . . . it shall be perfect to be accepted; there shall be no blemish therein" (Lev. 22:19–21; see also Ex. 12:5). The Lord then defined what it meant to have a blemish: "Blind, or broken, or maimed, or having a wen [wart], or scurvy, or scabbed, ye shall not offer these unto the Lord, nor make an offering by fire of them upon the altar unto the Lord. Either a bullock or a lamb that hath any thing superfluous or lacking in his parts, that mayest thou offer for a freewill offering; but for a vow it shall not be accepted. Ye shall not offer unto the Lord that which is bruised, or crushed, or broken, or cut; neither shall ye make any offering thereof in your land" (Lev. 22:22–24).

In addition to the law regarding blemished animals, the Lord also gave a law regarding blemished priests. If the priests had certain physical deformities or disfigurements, they were not permitted to participate in sacrificial offerings or to partake of holy food (Lev. 21:16–23). In this way, the priest's body, like the animal's body, became a symbol for Christ's sacrifice. As biblical scholar Mary Douglas has written, "We know that the priest's body is an analogy for the sacrificial offering" because both the priest's body and the animal's body had to be without blemishes.[14] Apostles in the New Testament also testified that the priest's physical blemishes symbolized spiritual imperfections or iniquities. Peter used terminology associated with blemished priests when he referred to certain iniquities as "spots" and "blemishes" (2 Pet. 2:13). Later, Peter used the same terminology, urging the Saints to "be diligent that ye may be found of him in peace, without spot, and blameless" (2 Pet. 3:14; see also Jude 1:7–12). Paul again used such terminology when he taught that Christ would "sanctify and cleanse" the church "with the washing of water by the word, that he might present it to himself a glorious church, not having spot, or wrinkle, or any such thing; but that it should be holy and without blemish" (Eph. 5:26–27; see also D&C 36:6; 38:31).

The perfection of the sacrificial animal's body and the priest's body symbolized Jesus' perfection. Jesus was perfect in all ways, and prophets and apostles have always testified of this. Paul wrote that Jesus Christ "offered himself without spot to God" (Heb. 9:14), and Peter explained that Jesus Christ was like a "lamb without blemish and without spot" (1 Pet. 1:19). Elder Anthon H. Lund made this truth clear when he wrote that Jesus was "without blemish or fault. No sin was found in Him, and as such He was a proper subject for the sacrifice."[15] Jesus' sinlessness empowered him to be our Savior and Redeemer, as President Taylor explained: "And being Himself without sin (which no other mortal was), He took the position of Savior and Redeemer, which by right belonged to Him as the first born."[16]

*Faith.* Faith is a vital part of the sacrificial system because all sacrifices must be offered in faith (Heb. 11:4). Abel serves as a historical example of one who offered his sacrifice in faith, just as Cain serves as an example of one who did not. As Joseph Smith said: "By faith in this atonement or plan of redemption, Abel offered to God a sacrifice that was accepted, which was the firstlings of the flock. Cain offered of the fruit of the ground, and was not accepted, because he could not do it in faith, he could have no faith, or could not exercise faith contrary to the plan of heaven. It must be shedding the blood of the Only Begotten to atone for man; for this was the plan of redemption; and without the shedding of blood was no remission; . . . to offer a sacrifice contrary to that, no faith could be exercised, because redemption was not purchased in that way, nor the power of atonement instituted after that order."[17]

*God's acceptance and forgiveness.* The final, central part of the sacrificial system pertains to God's recognition of the sacrifice, which served as a prerequisite for obtaining God's forgiveness of the sins of the sacrificial offerer. Regarding God's acceptance, a formulaic expression reads, "And the priest shall make an atonement for him for his sin which he hath sinned, and it shall be forgiven him" (Lev. 5:10). This phrase is repeated many times throughout Leviticus and Numbers, although with slightly different wording (Lev. 4:20, 26, 31, 35; 5:10, 13, 16, 18, 26; 6:7; 19:22; Num. 15:25, 28; and so forth).

## JESUS CHRIST'S BLOOD—AN ESSENTIAL COMPONENT OF THE ATONEMENT

One of the most crucial aspects of animal sacrifices was the blood of the sacrificed animal, which symbolizes the vital role that the blood of Jesus Christ played in the atonement. Many prophets and apostles have taught the following truths concerning his blood and its significance:

1. *The atonement required the shedding of Christ's blood.* God's eternal plan of redemption required Christ's blood, and ultimately his death, in order to bring about the atonement. "There could be no redemption for mankind save it were through the death and sufferings of Christ, and the atonement of his blood" (Alma 21:9; see also Alma 24:13).

Also, the "law of Moses availeth nothing except it were through the atonement of [Christ's] blood" (Mosiah 3:15). The prophet Amulek explained that the atonement could only be fulfilled through the blood of Christ: "For it is expedient that there should be a great and last sacrifice; yea, not a sacrifice of man, neither of beast, neither of any manner of fowl; for it shall not be a human sacrifice; but it must be an infinite and eternal sacrifice. Now there is not any man that can sacrifice his own blood which will atone for the sins of another" (Alma 34:10–11). From these words, we see that God's plan for salvation could not have been fulfilled through the shedding of the blood of just anyone or anything. Only the blood of Christ, who was a God, could atone for humankind; human blood would have been wholly ineffective.

2. *Jesus Christ's blood sanctifies us.* Paul presented the doctrine of sanctification through the blood of Christ in an unmistakable manner: "Wherefore Jesus also, that he might *sanctify the people* with his own blood, suffered without the gate" (Heb. 13:12; emphasis added). The Lord taught Adam that those who would return to be with God would need to "be cleansed by blood, even the blood of mine Only Begotten; that ye might be *sanctified* from all sin" (Moses 6:59; emphasis added).

These teachings regarding the sanctifying power of blood were represented and foreshadowed in the ancient temples that operated under the law of Moses. The law made it clear that the blood of sacrificial animals sanctified temple priests (Lev. 8:23, 30), cleansed lepers from their leprosy (Lev. 14:6–7), and purified and sanctified the temple's altar (Lev. 8:15). Through these examples, we see that in the law of sacrifice, which law served to anticipate Christ's sacrifice, the blood from sacrificial animals was required to sanctify priests and lepers in the same way that Christ's blood is required to sanctify sinners.

3. *Only Christ's blood brings remission.* Joseph Smith taught a powerful truth when he said, "It must be shedding the blood of the Only Begotten to atone for man; for this was the plan of redemption; and without the shedding of blood was no remission."[18]

4. *Our garments are washed white in Jesus' blood.* Sacrificial law required priestly officiators to sprinkle the blood of certain sacrificial animals onto the temple's altar or before the veil (Ex. 24:6; Lev. 4:6, 17;

and so forth). As the priest sprinkled the blood, it occasionally splattered onto his temple clothing. The law anticipated and provided for such splatterings with these words: "When there is sprinkled of the blood thereof upon any garment, thou shalt wash that whereon it was sprinkled in the holy place" (Lev. 6:27). The stained garments and subsequent cleansing symbolizes each of us repenting, coming unto Christ, and washing our own garments "white through the blood of the Lamb" (Alma 13:11).

Cleansing our garments (or our souls) is crucial for those of us who wish to be saved and to enter God's kingdom: "There can no man be saved except his garments are washed white; yea, his garments must be purified until they are cleansed from all stain, through the blood of him . . . who should come to redeem his people from their sins" (Alma 5:21). So how does one wash his or her garments in Christ's blood? Jesus Christ himself provided the answer when he spoke of *faith, repentance,* and *faithfulness:* "And no unclean thing can enter into his kingdom . . . save it be those who have washed their garments in my blood, because of their faith, and the repentance of all their sins, and their faithfulness unto the end" (3 Ne. 27:19).

5. *Christ's blood signifies spiritual life.* Blood is the common element in both mortal life and spiritual life. With regard to mortal blood signifying physical life, the scriptures reveal that for humans "blood is the life" (Deut. 12:23), and blood "is the life of all flesh" (Lev. 17:14). Correspondingly, "flesh" and "blood" pertain to mortals (Deut. 12:23; Matt. 16:17; 1 Cor. 15:50; Gal. 1:16; Heb. 2:14). Scientifically, there is a tangible connection between blood and mortality, as the following statements indicate:

*Blood and nourishment.* "Blood nourishes the body. Much like a trucker, it carries nutrition and oxygen to the cells and carries waste products away to be processed by the lungs, liver, and kidneys. . . . Blood has to be moving to perform these functions."[19]

*Blood and mortal vitality.* "Without blood we have the gray color of the dead," rather than the look of vitality.[20]

*Blood and the heart.* Blood flows through the heart to give us life.

"Just like a truck or train gives life to a city, i.e., bringing the products we need for daily living."[21]

*Blood, muscles, and nerves.* "The salts in the plasma play a key role in the electrical depolarizations used by the muscles and nerves to initiate their deployment."[22]

*Blood and temperature control.* "The blood has a major role in keeping the body at a constant temperature."[23]

*Blood and the purification cycle.* Our blood, lungs, liver, and kidneys work together to purify the body: "The lungs (removing carbon dioxide and maintaining the proper pH), liver (removing toxic chemicals) and kidneys (removing toxic chemicals and restoring the proper pH)."[24]

*Blood and healing.* "When an injury occurs, the blood, by way of its clotting properties, provides for immediate hemostasis wherein a clot can form and blood loss stops. The blood may then carry molecules (cytokines) to signal the body to send inflammatory cells (white blood cells) to go to the area and begin the cleanup process. The white blood cells obviously are transferred in the blood. The cytokines also mobilize fibroblasts and other structural tissues to rebuild the damaged tissues."[25]

In sum, blood is part of our divine creation, and no artificial or man-made fluid can permanently serve as its substitute. The significance of blood as a life-giving force to mortals and the atonement is found in Leviticus 17:11: "For the life of the flesh is in the blood: and I have given it to you upon the altar to make an atonement for your souls: for it is the blood that maketh an atonement for the soul."

Just as our own blood gives us physical life, so does Christ's blood signify spiritual life. Jesus taught this truth when he stated, "Whoso . . . drinketh my blood, hath eternal life; and I will raise him up at the last day" (John 6:54). Also, the Lord taught that mortal blood (together with water and spirit) makes one into a "living soul," and Jesus' blood (coupled with baptismal water and the Spirit) gives one eternal life and glory (Moses 6:59).

6. *The blood of the sacrificial animal anticipates Jesus Christ's atoning blood.* The shedding of blood in animal sacrifices pointed to Christ's "atoning blood" (Mosiah 4:2; Lev. 1–6). The sacrificial blood of animals was a type and shadow of Christ's blood but held no eternal

efficacy alone. Animals' blood could never remove our sins; only Christ's blood has the power to do that. As Paul wrote, "It is not possible that the blood of bulls and of goats should take away sins," but Jesus Christ "had offered one sacrifice for sins for ever" (Heb. 10:4, 12).

7. *Jesus' blood has relevance to the doctrines of faith, justification, becoming clean, and obtaining forgiveness.* Core doctrines relating to faith, justification, becoming clean, and obtaining forgiveness are associated with the blood of Jesus Christ. For example, John wrote that "the blood of Jesus Christ . . . cleanseth us from all sin" (1 John 1:7); correspondingly, Paul wrote of "faith in his blood" (Rom. 3:25) and "being now justified by his blood" (Rom. 5:9), and he explained that the blood of Christ could "purge your conscience" (Heb. 9:14). A final passage demonstrates the reciprocal nature of Christ's blood and forgiveness: at the end of Benjamin's speech in the Book of Mormon, the people reacted by falling to the earth and crying out, "O have mercy, and apply the atoning blood of Christ that we may receive forgiveness of our sins" (Mosiah 4:2).

8. *Christ's blood protects us from the destroying angel.* On the night of the first Passover, Israelites ensured that the destroying angel would pass over them by placing the Passover lamb's blood on their doorposts before the destruction of firstborn males (Ex. 12:22). The Passover lamb's blood symbolizes Jesus' blood, which saves us from everlasting destruction.

CHAPTER 5

# FEASTS, FASTS, AND FESTIVALS: HOLY DAYS ANTICIPATE JESUS' ATONEMENT

ANCIENT ISRAELITES COMMEMORATED a number of sacred feasts that focused on Jesus and his atonement. These feasts included the Passover and the Feast of Unleavened Bread, Firstfruits, Feast of Trumpets, Day of Atonement, and Feast of Tabernacles (Lev. 23; Num. 28–29). The feasts were established and authorized by the Lord (Lev. 23:1, 9, 23, 26, 33). Each was called a "holy convocation," or holy assembly (Lev. 23:3, 4, 8, 21, 24, 27, 35, 36), each involved an offering or sacrifice (Lev. 23:8, 12, 16, 25, 27, 36), and, most important, each focused on the atonement of Jesus Christ. This chapter will focus primarily on the Passover and the Day of Atonement.

## MESSIANIC SYMBOLISM IN THE PASSOVER

Enacted annually during the Jewish month of Abib (which occurs around March or April), the Passover recalls the occasion when God's destroying angel "passed over" the obedient of Israel. This feast, as prescribed in Exodus 12, points to Jesus Christ's atoning sacrifice.[1] The sacrificed Passover lamb (Ex. 12:3–6, 46) prefigured Jesus Christ, who became the Lamb sacrificed for the sins of the world. The Passover lamb was to be without blemish (Ex. 12:5), just as Jesus Christ would be

64

without blemish (1 Pet. 1:18–19), and the lamb had to be a male (Ex. 12:5), perhaps prefiguring Jesus' gender. Further, the feast encompassed rituals and commandments that anticipated Jesus' death on the cross—his blood would spill on the cross, he would be killed after noon, and a large assembly would kill him. In fact, the correspondences between the Passover and Jesus Christ's death are so notable that Paul named Jesus "Our Passover" (1 Cor. 5:7), Nephi called him "Lamb" and "Lamb of God" (1 Ne. 13:35; 10:10), and John the Baptist proclaimed him to be "the Lamb of God, which taketh away the sin of the world" (John 1:29).

The Passover teaches us the law of proxy, or the capacity or power for one to act as a substitute for another. In the Passover, the lamb served as a proxy for the Israelite family so that the destroying angel would pass over them. In other words, God did not require human blood from family members, such as the firstborn son; instead, the lamb's blood, which was smeared on the doorposts on the night of the Passover, served as a proxy, similar to the way that Jesus Christ's blood saves us from the destructive elements of death and sin. Of course, those who failed to smear the doorposts, such as the Egyptians or perhaps negligent or disobedient Israelites, were not protected from death because the lamb's blood did not deliver them from the destroying angel.

Although we do not continue the practice of the Passover today, Jesus Christ used two symbols from the Passover—bread and wine—when he instituted the sacrament (Matt. 26:17–28) at the Last Supper, a Passover meal, saying, "Take, eat; this is my body," and "this is my blood of the new testament, which is shed for many for the remission of sins" (Matt. 26:26–28). The bread and wine used in the Passover ceremony looked forward to Jesus' sacrifice as the Passover Lamb; the bread and water used in the sacrament ceremony look backward to Jesus' broken body and the blood that he shed. In our sacrament prayers we are reminded to partake of the sacramental bread "in remembrance of the body" of Jesus and the sacramental water "in remembrance of the blood" of Jesus (D&C 20:77, 79).

Examples of correspondences between the Passover and Jesus can be seen in the accompanying table. Many are straightforward, such as the command in Exodus 12:46 concerning the Passover lamb—"neither shall ye break a bone thereof"—which has an unambiguous fulfillment in Jesus Christ, as recorded in John: "But when [the soldiers] came to Jesus and saw that he was dead already, they brake not his legs. . . . For these things were done, that the scripture should be fulfilled, A bone of him shall not be broken" (John 19:33, 36).

Other correspondences are of a more subtle nature. For example, the commandment to smear the blood on the doorposts may have been given to teach the ancient Israelites to remember that their incomings and outgoings through that door should be in the name of the Lord (see also D&C 109:17–18), or it may have been given to remind them that it is only through the blood of the Lamb of God that we may enter through the door (or gate or veil) that leads to heaven.

| Passover | Jesus Christ |
| --- | --- |
| The Passover offering was a lamb (Ex. 12:3). | Jesus is "the Lamb of God" (John 1:29). |
| The lamb was called "the Lord's Passover" (Ex. 12:11). | Jesus was called "Passover" (1 Cor. 5:7). |
| The Passover lamb needed to be a male (Ex. 12:5, 46). | Jesus is male. |
| The Passover lamb needed to be without blemish (Ex. 12:5). | Christ was "without blemish and without spot" (1 Pet. 1:18–19). |
| The lamb was sacrificed at Passover (Ex. 12:6). | Jesus was sacrificed at Passover (John 19:14). |
| The Passover lamb was killed after noon (Ex. 12:6). | Jesus was killed after noon (Matt. 27:46). |
| Israel ate bitter herbs (Ex. 12:8). | Jesus drank from the bitter cup (D&C 19:18). |
| The token of the lamb's blood saved ancient Israel from death (Ex. 12:13). | Christ's atoning blood saves souls from the grave and from spiritual death (Hel. 5:9). |

| Passover | Jesus Christ |
|---|---|
| Lamb's blood was struck on the door's vertical posts and horizontal beam (Ex. 12:7). | Christ's blood fell on the cross's vertical post and horizontal beam. |
| The remainder of the lamb needed to be consumed by fire (Ex. 12:10). | The Lord gave himself entirely to sacrifice—body and spirit. |
| Israel ate the "flesh" of the lamb (Ex. 12:8). | Sacramental bread, which is eaten, represents Christ's body (Matt. 26:26). |
| Firstborn males of Egypt died (Ex. 12:29). | Christ was the firstborn of the Father and is firstborn of the dead (D&C 93:21; Col. 1:18). |
| The whole assembly killed the Passover lamb (Ex. 12:6). | The entire nation slew Jesus (Matt. 27:20–23; Luke 23:1, 10, 13, 23, 35). |
| Strangers were forbidden to eat of the feast until they were circumcised (Ex. 12:43, 48). | Only those who enter into a covenant with Christ are saved (D&C 52:2). |
| No bones of the sacrificial lamb were to be broken (Ex. 12:46). | Christ's bones were not broken on the cross (John 19:33). |
| The Passover released Israel from bondage (Ex. 12:31). | The atonement releases mortals from the bondage of sin and death (D&C 84:49; 2 Ne. 9:12). |
| The Passover provided temporal deliverance to those who smeared the lamb's blood on their door posts (Ex. 12:7, 12). | Jesus provides spiritual deliverance to those who accept his blood (Matt. 1:21; Luke 4:18). |
| The Israelite calendar restarted at Passover (Ex. 12:2). | The world reckons time from the coming of the Savior. |
| Those who did not observe the Passover were "cut off" (Ex. 12:15; Num. 9:10–13). | Those who do not accept Jesus, the Passover, are cut off. |

## Messianic Foreshadowing in the Day of Atonement

The Day of Atonement, held on the tenth day of the seventh month of the year, was an exceptionally hallowed ancient Israelite festival. It was during the Day of Atonement that the high priest made atonement for the tabernacle and the altar, for the priests, and for the people. "And this shall be an everlasting statute unto you, to make an atonement for the children of Israel for all their sins once a year" (Lev. 16:34). The Day of Atonement focused on a number of rituals that pertained to the atonement, such as the sacrifice of a bull and a goat, the sprinkling of blood on the altar, the confession of sins on the head of a second goat (the scapegoat) by the laying on of hands, and the high priest's entrance into the temple's holy of holies. The sole purpose of these rituals was to be perfect symbols for the great and last sacrifice: Christ's infinite atonement. In *The Promised Messiah,* under the heading "The Day of Atonement—A Type of Christ," Elder Bruce R. McConkie wrote: "Now we come to the heart and core and center of the whole Mosaic structure, namely, the atonement of the Lord Jesus Christ. This is what the Law of Moses is all about. . . . The chief symbolisms, the most perfect similitudes, the types and shadows without peer, were displayed before all the people once each year, on the Day of Atonement."[2]

| Day of Atonement | | Jesus Christ |
|---|---|---|
| Atonement was made for all Israelites (Lev. 23:27–28). | Atonement | Jesus Christ worked out the atonement for all. |
| The high priest officiated on the Day of Atonement (Lev. 16). | High priest | As the "high priest of good things to come" (Heb 9:11), Jesus provides the infinite atonement. |

| Day of Atonement | | Jesus Christ |
|---|---|---|
| The high priest wore holy, white, linen vestments (Lev. 16:4). | White vestments | The "clean and white . . . linen" represents "the righteousness of the saints" (Rev. 19:8); their garments are made white through Jesus' atoning blood (1 Ne. 12:10). |
| The high priest sacrificed animals to make atonement for Israel's uncleanness, transgressions, and sins (Lev. 16:6, 11, 15–20). | Sacrifices for sins | Jesus offered himself as a sacrifice for the sins of the world (Heb. 7:27; Alma 34:8). His sacrifice was "neither by the blood of goats and calves, but by his own blood" (Heb. 9:12). |
| No one accompanied the high priest to the Holy of Holies, where he made an atonement for the people (Lev. 16:15–17, 34). | Unaccompanied in sacred work | Jesus trod the winepress alone (Isa. 63:1–3; D&C 88:106) when he atoned for our sins. |
| The high priest represented Israel before God (Lev. 16:3, 6, 11). | Mediator | Christ the high priest represents us before God (D&C 45:3–4; Heb. 7:26–27; 9:11; 1 Tim. 2:5). |

## OTHER ISRAELITE FEASTS ANTICIPATING JESUS' WORK OF REDEMPTION

In addition to those feasts discussed above, Leviticus 23 lists other feasts that also prophesied of Jesus' redemptive work.

1. *The Jubilee Year.* After seven cycles of seven years, or every fiftieth year, the Israelites celebrated the Jubilee Year (the name "Jubilee" comes from the Hebrew name for the ram's horn, *yobel,* which was used to announce the jubilee). During the year, liberty was celebrated, lands that

had changed hands reverted back to the original owner, and all bond-men of Israelite birth were set free. Cultivated lands were allowed one year of rest, and the spontaneous growth of produce was left for the poor. Finally, all debts owed were to be released (Lev. 25:8–55; 27:16–25; Num. 36:4; Neh. 5:1–13).

The Jubilee Year was also known as the "year of redemption," and many aspects of that year pertain to Jesus' work of redemption. The focus on liberty and the setting free of the bondmen, for example, bring to mind the concept that all of us are freed from our sins and from death because of Jesus' atonement.

2. *Feast of Trumpets.* The feast of trumpets was also established "to make an atonement" (Num. 29:5) for the Israelites. This feast prophe-sied of Jesus' redemptive work, pointing forward to the time when a trump will announce Jesus' second coming—for he will "descend from heaven with a shout, with the voice of the archangel, and with the trump of God" (1 Thes. 4:16; Matt. 24:31). In addition, a trump will announce the resurrection (1 Cor. 15:52; D&C 29:26), which is brought to pass because of the atonement.

3. *Feast of Unleavened Bread.* Unleavened bread signifies Jesus Christ, who is "the bread of life" (John 6:35); unleavened bread also sig-nifies the Saints of God who are commanded to "purge out . . . the old leaven, that ye may be a new lump, as ye are unleavened" (1 Cor. 5:7), which we are enabled to do through Christ's atonement.

4. *Firstfruits.* In the early spring, the ancient Israelites had a feast celebrating the firstfruits, or the first crops gathered in the season. For this feast, a sheaf of barley was harvested and then presented in the temple to the priest, who waved it before the Lord. In addition to the firstfruits, many symbolic offerings were presented for this feast, in-cluding an unblemished male lamb; fine flour mixed with olive oil; and a drink offering of wine (Lev. 23:9–14). The firstfruits themselves sig-nify Jesus Christ, who was the first to be resurrected. He is "the first-fruits of them that slept" and is referred to as "Christ the firstfruits" (1 Cor. 15:20–23; see also 2 Ne. 2:8–9). And just as the firstfruits were waved on Sunday, even so Jesus was resurrected on a Sunday.

## CHAPTER 6

# FROM ADAM TO JONAH: PEOPLE AS TYPES AND SHADOWS

A GREAT NUMBER OF RIGHTEOUS men and women from the Old Testament and Book of Mormon, including prophets, priests, kings, and others, served as types and shadows of Jesus Christ. Their personal purity and righteousness, as well as events in their lives, foreshadowed Jesus' righteousness and his works. The parallels between these individuals and Christ are so striking that these persons "were types and shadows of our Lord's coming; they were living, walking, breathing Messianic prophecies."[1] Elder Jeffrey R. Holland wrote: "Jehovah used an abundance of archetypes and symbols. Indeed, these have always been a conspicuous characteristic of the Lord's instruction to his children. Examples of those figures—especially prefigurations of Christ—are present throughout the pre-Messianic record. . . .

". . . Moses (like Isaac, Joseph, and so many others in the Old Testament) was himself a prophetic symbol of the Christ who was to come."[2] And according to LDS scholar Andrew C. Skinner, "The very lives of Old Testament personalities—prophets, priests, and kings—are similitudes of the life of the great Prophet, Priest, and King, the Anointed One of the Father, the Holy One of Israel."[3]

For instance, consider these brief examples:

*Melchizedek,* whose name means "my king is righteous" or "king of righteousness," was a type of Jesus Christ, the righteous "King of kings"

(Rev. 19:16; see Heb. 7:15; JST Gen. 14:17). Melchizedek was the king of Salem (or king of Peace); Jesus Christ is the Prince of Peace. Melchizedek's priesthood, faith, and power (JST Gen. 14:25–31) anticipated Christ's priesthood, faith, and power.

*Abinadi's life* foreshadowed Jesus' ministry and sacrifice in a number of ways. Both Abinadi and Jesus were bound and judged by rulers and priests, both were imprisoned for three days, both were innocent of any crimes, both were protected until their mission was complete, and both suffered humiliating deaths.[4]

*Gardeners* can be types of Jesus Christ. "On that first Resurrection Sunday, Mary Magdalene first thought she saw a gardener. Well, she did—the Gardener who cultivated Eden and who endured Gethsemane. The Gardener who gave us the rose of Sharon, the lily of the valley, the cedars of Lebanon, the tree of life."[5]

Jesus is the *Physician* who took "upon him the pains and the sicknesses of his people" (Matt. 9:12; Alma 7:11–12), and "with his stripes we are healed" (Isa. 53:5).

*Worthy high priests* can symbolize Jesus. Christ is the "faithful high priest" (Heb. 2:17; 5:10); like the high priests of the Mosaic order who were required to be holy and undefiled (Lev. 21:1), Christ was "an high priest . . . who is holy, harmless, undefiled, separate from sinners" (Heb. 7:26).

## EVE, A TYPE OF CHRIST

From the Garden of Eden to their exaltation, and beyond, Adam and Eve share equal status. God created both Adam and Eve, he made both of them in his image, both partook of the fruit, and both were exiled from the garden. Christ's atonement covered both equally, and he made garments of skin for both of them. Together, as mortals, they multiplied and replenished the earth. As exalted personages, Eve and Adam share a "golden throne" that is set on a "circular foundation." They, equally and without variation, are described by Joseph Smith as being "clothed in white garments . . . and their faces shone with immortal youth. They were the two most beautiful and perfect specimens of mankind I ever saw."[6] Eve, like Adam, is a type and shadow of Jesus Christ; but Eve typifies the Lord differently, reflecting her different and unique callings.

*Eve is named Life; Jesus is Life.* The name *Eve* signifies life and refers to Eve as a bringer of life to her great posterity. "And Adam called his wife's name Eve." Genesis gives an explanation of Eve's name, noting, "Adam called his wife's name Eve; because she was the mother of all living" (Gen. 3:20). Although non-English words are used elsewhere in the story (*Adam, cherubim, Eden, Pison, Havilah,* and so forth), only with Eve's name is an explanation attached—an emphasis on Eve's significance in the story. Moses 4:26 provides additional information regarding Eve's name: "And Adam called his wife's name Eve, because she was the mother of all living; for thus have I, the Lord God, called the first of all women, which are many."

In Genesis 4:1–2 the author shows the appropriateness of Eve's name by recounting that Eve gave birth: "Adam knew Eve his wife; and she conceived, and bare Cain. . . . And she again bare his brother Abel" (Gen. 4:1–2). These verses show that Eve, in accordance with her name, is a life-giving entity. But Eve as *life* is not limited merely to biological considerations. God's cursing of the serpent includes the promise that Eve's seed would crush the serpent's head (Gen. 3:15); this seed is none other than Jesus (Rom. 16:20; Heb. 2:14), who will destroy both the serpent and death. In other words, Eve the *life* brought forth Jesus the *Life,* and it is Jesus who brings spiritual life to humankind and who subdues Satan.

Eve as *life* is a type of Jesus Christ, who is the "light and life of the world" (D&C 12:9; 10:70; 3 Ne. 11:11), the "Word of life" (1 John 1:1), and the "Prince of Life" (Acts 3:15). He is the "light which is in all things, which giveth life to all things" (D&C 88:13). He "giveth life unto the world" (John 6:33). Jesus through his atoning sacrifice provides eternal life to those who repent and keep the commandments. "He that believeth on the Son hath everlasting life: and he that believeth not the Son shall not see life" (John 3:36). Stated differently, "He that hath the Son hath life; and he that hath not the Son of God hath not life" (1 John 5:12). Jesus taught Martha, "I am the resurrection, and the life: he that believeth in me, though he were dead, yet shall he live" (John 11:25). Then, as proof of his great power to restore life, Jesus Christ raised Martha's brother, Lazarus, from the dead. As Paul stated, "The gift of God is eternal life through Jesus Christ our Lord" (Rom. 6:23). Just as Eve has given physical life to all God's children on this earth, Christ both extends eternal life to the obedient and faithful and gives immortality through the resurrection to all of earth's inhabitants.

*Eve is a help; the Lord is a help.* Only two individuals in the Bible are explicitly identified as *help* (Hebrew *'ezer*): Eve (twice) and God (sixteen times).[7] No others—including kings, queens, ranking military officers, prophets, or priests—are presented as *help*.[8] Moreover, the vastly powerful and commanding pharaoh of Egypt, together with his officials and representatives, is specifically depicted as not being a help (Isa. 30:1–5). The fact that God is called a *help* provides insights into why Eve is called a help. In what manner is God a help? The prophets reveal that God is a help because he sustains and preserves the lives of all his people. The following five examples (out of the sixteen passages that identify God as help) demonstrate this idea.

1. God is first called *help* in Exodus 18, where an explanation is provided for the naming of Eliezer, Moses and Zipporah's son. Eliezer, meaning *God Is a Help* (or *My God Is a Help*), was so named because God "was mine help ['*ezer*], and delivered me from the sword of Pharaoh" (Ex. 18:4). In this passage God is a help by preserving the life of Moses from his archenemy, the pharaoh.

2. Deuteronomy 33 consists of the words that Moses spoke as he blessed the tribes of Israel shortly before his death. At the conclusion of these blessings, Moses praised God with praises set forth in poetic verse (Deut. 33:26–29). Twice he referred to God as a help who would "thrust out the enemy from before [Israel]." The three occasions in Deuteronomy 33 when God is called a help (see also verse 7) are associated with Israel's enemies because God helps his people by saving them from destruction by their enemies.

3. In Psalm 33 the Lord is called a help who delivers humans from death and preserves them during famine. "The eye of the Lord is upon them that fear him, upon them that hope in his mercy; to deliver their

soul from death, and to keep them alive in famine. Our soul waiteth for the Lord: he is our help ['*ezer*] and our shield." (Ps. 33:18–20).

4. Psalm 121 opens with, "I will lift up mine eyes unto the hills, from whence cometh my help ['*ezer*]. My help ['*ezer*] cometh from the Lord, which made heaven and earth" (vv. 1–2). In the succeeding six verses, the author emphasizes the Lord's preservation of life. Six times the Psalmist uses the Hebrew root *shmr,* which has the sense of to keep or preserve. The Lord "shall preserve thee from all evil: he shall preserve thy soul. The Lord shall preserve thy going out and thy coming in from this time forth, and even for evermore" (vv. 7–8).

5. A passage in Hosea identifies the Lord's kingship and redemptive powers and establishes him as a help. The Lord addresses members of the house of Israel: "O Israel, thou hast destroyed thyself; but in me is thine help. I will be thy king: where is any other that may save thee. . . . I will ransom them from the power of the grave; I will redeem them from death" (Hosea 13:9–10, 14). How is God a help to the house of Israel? He ransoms them from the grave's control and redeems them from death.

All sixteen scriptural passages that establish that the Lord is a help are connected, implicitly or explicitly, to God's sustaining the life of his human creations. He is a help because he protects his creative works from mortal destruction, death, and the grave. He preserves them during periods of trouble and keeps them alive during famines. He crushes their foes and strikes down their adversaries. He increases them and their children. Unlike mortals "in whom there is no help" (Ps. 146:3), the Lord is a help who preserves needy mortals, the bowed-down old man, the stranger, the widow, and the fatherless. The Lord is a help who ransoms his mortals from the power of the grave and redeems them from death.

In sum, twice Eve is called a help (Gen. 2:18, 20), and as such she, like the Lord himself, served to sustain life. She was no more a subordinate to Adam than the Lord is a subordinate to the mortals for whom he is a help.

## MICHAEL, "THE FIRST ADAM"; JESUS CHRIST, THE "LAST ADAM"

Both Adam and Jesus had vital roles in the plan of salvation. Both participated in the creation; subsequently Adam caused the fall, and later Jesus brought about the atonement. Consequently, there are many parallels between what Adam did that caused the fall and what Christ did to save us from the fall. In fact, the correspondences and parallels between Adam and Jesus are so considerable that Paul named Adam "the first Adam," and he designated Jesus the "last Adam" (1 Cor. 15:45–47). Paul also wrote that Adam was "the figure of him that was to come" (Rom. 5:14), a reference to Jesus Christ.

The location of the fall is noteworthy: a garden "eastward in Eden," wherein were a great number of symbols of life, including beautiful trees with fruits that were "good for food" (Gen. 2:8–9). Life prevailed in this garden until the fall, which brought about mortal and spiritual death. The location of the atonement was also a garden, one named Gethsemane. Life prevailed in this garden too, but in significantly different ways: Jesus' atonement brought about immortality (life forever) and eternal life (life with God).

Two different trees, one associated with Adam and the other with Jesus, correspond to each other. Adam's eating of the fruit of the tree of the knowledge of good and evil brought about the fall and subsequently death. Jesus was crucified on a tree to complete the atonement and provide us with life. Peter testified that Jesus "bare our sins in his own body on the tree, that we, being dead to sins, should live unto righteousness" (1 Pet. 2:24). Christ's atoning sacrifice enabled and empowered each of us to "be partakers of the fruit of the tree of life" (Alma 5:62), which fruit consists of sacramental emblems: "Come unto me and ye shall partake of the fruit of the tree of life; yea, ye shall eat and drink of the bread and the waters of life freely" (Alma 5:34).

Two different garments, one associated with Adam and the other with Christ, correspond to each other and have defining roles in the fall and the atonement. Adam and Eve's nakedness is emphasized in Genesis 2–3: "and they were both naked," "they knew that they were naked," "I

76

was afraid, because I was naked," "who told thee that thou wast naked?" (Gen. 2:25; 3:7, 10–11). A crucial point in the story, however, took place when the Lord made "coats of skins, and clothed them" (Gen. 3:21). The coats of skins were likely made from lambskins, anticipating Jesus Christ, the Lamb of God. That the Lord himself attended to the making of coats of skins to clothe the couple prophesies of the time when the Lord, because of the atonement, will clothe each of us with immortal skins at the resurrection. This act of covering the couple was an act associated with the atonement, for the Hebrew word *kpr* means both "to atone" and "to cover." See also Paul's second letter to the Corinthians, where he likens the resurrection to "being clothed" and "clothed upon" and to the spirit without the body as being "naked" and "unclothed" (2 Cor. 5:1–4).

There are several other important parallels between Adam and Jesus Christ. First, Adam brought forth physical death; Jesus gave us the resurrection. "For since by man [Adam] came death, by man [Christ] came also the resurrection of the dead. For as in Adam all die, even so in Christ shall all be made alive" (1 Cor. 15:21–22). Linked to this, Adam and Eve, as the father and mother of the mortal race, provided physical bodies for our spirits; Christ provides immortal bodies for our spirits at the resurrection. Finally, Adam was the first in mortality to offer sacrifices, but Christ signified the last sacrifice: "That great and last sacrifice will be the Son of God, yea, infinite and eternal" (Alma 34:14).

## ABEL, THE FIRST MARTYR

Abel was, in a number of ways, a remarkable type of Christ. Abel's occupation as a shepherd looked forward to Jesus, who was "the good shepherd [who] giveth his life for the sheep" (Moses 5:17; John 10:11). Abel possessed spiritual qualities that anticipated Jesus' spiritual perfections. Just as "Abel hearkened unto the voice of the Lord" (Moses 5:17), Jesus hearkened unto his Father's voice. Abel was gifted with faith (Heb. 11:4), by which he "brought of the firstlings of his flock and of the fat thereof. And the Lord had respect unto Abel and to his offering" (Gen. 4:4). Paul called Abel's offering "a more excellent sacrifice" (Heb.

11:4), and yet his excellent offering was but a shadow of the time when Jesus came "to put away sin by the sacrifice of himself" (Heb. 9:26). Joseph Smith said of Abel: "Abel offered to God a sacrifice that was accepted, which was the firstlings of the flock. . . . Abel offered an acceptable sacrifice, by which he obtained witness that he was righteous, God Himself testifying of his gifts."[9]

Eventually Satan convinced Cain to murder Abel to get gain, saying, "This day I will deliver thy brother Abel into thine hands." Cain rejoiced in the fact that he could "murder and get gain" by killing Abel and obtaining his flocks (Moses 5:29–33). Millennia later, history repeated itself when Satan tempted Judas to conspire against Jesus in order to obtain thirty pieces of silver. Ultimately, then, Abel's murder presaged Jesus' death on the cross.

## ABRAHAM OFFERS ISAAC AS A SACRIFICE

Abraham's willingness to sacrifice his beloved son, Isaac, parallels God's offering of his beloved son, Jesus. Jacob 4:5 explicitly states that Abraham's obedience in "offering up his son Isaac" is a "similitude of God and his Only Begotten Son." Paul also wrote that Abraham's offering of Isaac was symbolic ("a figure") of God's gift of Jesus. "By faith Abraham, when he was tried, offered up Isaac: and he that had received the promises offered up his only begotten son, of whom it was said, That in Isaac shall thy seed be called: Accounting that God was able to raise him up, even from the dead; from whence also he received him in a figure" (Heb. 11:17–19; see also Gal. 3:16). This passage explains why Abraham may have been willing to offer his son—Abraham believed that if he sacrificed him God would raise him from the dead.

There are a number of striking and significant parallels between Isaac and Jesus that demonstrate that Isaac was a type of Jesus Christ and his sacrifice. These parallels include the following:

*Prophecy of birth.* Isaac's birth was prophesied (Gen. 17:16); Christ's birth was prophesied (Isa. 7:14; Luke 1:31).

*Miraculous birth.* Isaac was born of aged parents (Gen. 17:17; 18:10–15; 21:1–2); Christ was miraculously born of a virgin (Luke 1:30–35; 1 Ne. 11:19–20).

*The Father and the Son.* Genesis 22:1–13 emphasizes that Isaac is a *son,* calling him "son" eight times and "only son" twice (although Abraham and Hagar already had Ishmael). Jesus is the "only begotten of the Father" (John 1:14; see also v. 18). Both Isaac and Jesus are called "son of promise" (see Gal. 4:22–26; Acts 13:32–33). Genesis 22 also emphasizes the role of the father, where Abraham is the father. *Father* is found more than a dozen times in the text; further, *Ab* in the name *Abraham* means *father.*

*Burnt offering.* Genesis 22 (vv. 2–3, 6–8, 13) used the expression "burnt offering" six times in referring to the type of sacrifice Isaac was to become; the burnt offerings of the Old Testament looked forward to Jesus' sacrifice.

*Submission.* Both Isaac and Jesus Christ willingly submitted to the sacrifice (Gen. 22:6–9; Luke 22:42).

*Carried the wood.* Isaac bore the wood for his sacrifice (Gen. 22:6), and Christ carried the cross to his sacrifice (John 19:17).

*Bound.* Abraham bound Isaac to the altar (Gen. 22:9); Jesus was bound before he was "delivered . . . to Pontius Pilate the governor" (Matt. 27:2).

*Substitute sacrifice.* God provided a lamb as a substitute sacrifice for Isaac (Gen. 22:7–8, 13); Christ the Lamb is the substitute sacrifice for all of us (D&C 19:16).

*Moriah.* Isaac traveled to the land of Moriah for sacrifice (Gen. 22:2), the very site where Solomon would build his temple (2 Chr. 3:1) and where thousands of sacrifices would be offered for several centuries in anticipation of Jesus' sacrifice; Christ was crucified on Moriah at Golgotha, a short distance north of the altar (John 19:17–18).

*Three days.* For Isaac, it was a three-day journey home from the place of sacrifice (Gen. 22:4); Christ was in the spirit world three days after his sacrifice (Mosiah 3:10).

## Joseph of Egypt Foreshadowed Christ

Much of Genesis 37–50 is dedicated to the narrative of Joseph of Egypt; in fact, more chapters and verses in Genesis pertain to Joseph than to any other character in that book, including such prominent figures as Adam, Eve, Abraham, and Sarah. These chapters reveal specific incidents in Joseph's life, beginning with Joseph as a seventeen-year-old tending flocks with his brothers. At about this time Israel "made him a coat of many colours," and his brothers "hated him" (Gen. 37:3–4). So great was their hatred that they devised a plan wherein Joseph was stripped of this special garment and sold as a common slave for twenty pieces of silver (Gen. 37:28). His purchasers then took him to Egypt, where his experiences continued. Years passed, and eventually Joseph turned thirty years old, a pivotal time in the life of this prophet.

These experiences and many others paralleled similar instances in the life of Jesus Christ, making Joseph a type and shadow, or a similitude of Jesus Christ. Jesus too was a good shepherd who cared for his Father's sheep. Jesus, at thirty years of age, began his ministry. Jesus' brethren and fellow mortals hated and persecuted him. They devised evil plans against him, and eventually he too, like Joseph of old, was sold for the price of a slave. Shortly before Jesus' death, he was stripped of his garment.

The list of parallels between the lives of Joseph and Jesus is both extensive and significant. Joseph served as a type for Christ in the following ways: Both were good shepherds (Gen. 37:12–16; John 10:11–15). Both were clothed in authority and power of their father. Joseph, for instance, was given the "coat of many colours" (Gen. 37:3), a symbol of priesthood authority. Both were revelators who revealed things pertaining to the future (JST Gen. 50:24–38; Matt. 24). Both were fully obedient to the will and wishes of their fathers and responded to their calls to serve, saying, "Here am I" (Gen. 37:13; Abr. 3:27). Both blessed those with whom they labored in prison (Gen. 39:21–23; D&C 138). Both were tempted with great sin but refused its enticements (Gen. 39:7–12; Matt. 4:1–11). As Joseph's brothers bowed to him in fulfillment of prophecy, so all will yet bow the knee to Christ (Gen.

43:26–28; D&C 76:110). Through both, mercy is granted to a repentant people. As Joseph's brothers sought forgiveness of him, so Christ's brothers will eventually seek forgiveness of him. Both were thirty years old when they began their life's work (Gen. 41:38–46; Luke 3:23).

Joseph was also a type of Jesus Christ with regard to Jesus' trials, sufferings, and crucifixion. Both Joseph and Christ were sold; it was Judah who sold Joseph for twenty pieces of silver (Gen. 37:26–28), and it was Judas (Greek for Judah) who sold Jesus for thirty pieces of silver (Matt. 26:15). Both were falsely accused—Joseph by Potiphar's wife (Gen. 39:13–19), Christ by false witnesses (Matt. 26:59–61). Wicked men conspired to kill both Joseph and Jesus (Gen. 37:18–20; Matt. 26:3–4; John 11:49–53). Men stripped them of their special garments (Gen. 37:3, 23; John 19:23–24). Both were cast into a pit—Christ to the world of spirits, Joseph into an empty cistern (Gen. 37:20–24; 1 Pet. 3:18–19). Both were betrayed with great duplicity (Gen. 37:27; John 18:31). Both were saviors to their people, giving them the bread of life. Joseph saved his family with a temporal salvation (Gen. 45:11; 47:12–13). Christ as the Bread of Life saves the family of mankind with a spiritual salvation (Matt. 14:15–21; 15:32–38; John 6:32–35).[10]

## MOSES, A SIMILITUDE OF JESUS CHRIST

Moses' life and mission paralleled the future life and mission of Jesus Christ, so much so that God revealed to Moses that "thou art in the similitude of mine only Begotten" (Moses 1:6). In fact, "in no ministry did [the Lord] use similitudes more than in that of Moses. . . . Moses (like Isaac, Joseph, and so many others in the Old Testament) was himself a prophetic symbol of the Christ who was to come."[11] Moses, in a number of significant ways, was a similitude of Jesus:

*Moses the Begotten.* Moses' name is etymologically related to the Egyptian words *mes* and *mesu,* meaning *child* or *son.*[12] This links Moses to Jesus Christ, who is designated *Son*—son of Abraham, Son of David, Son of God, son of Joseph, Son of Man, son of Mary, Son of Righteousness, Son of the Eternal Father, Son of the Everlasting God, Son of the Highest, Son of the Living God, and Son of the Most High

God.[13] In the language of Adam, God is denominated "Ahman," and Jesus is named "Son Ahman."[14] The Doctrine and Covenants twice refers to Son Ahman: "your Redeemer, even the Son Ahman" (D&C 78:20) and "Son Ahman; or, in other words, Alphus; or in other words, Omegus; even Jesus Christ your Lord" (D&C 95:17).

Moses' name is also linked to Jesus Christ's sonship and his designation as "Only Begotten." In the book of Moses the Lord told Moses, "Thou art my son" (Moses 1:4). And then for emphasis the theme of sonship is repeated: "I have a work for thee, Moses, my son"; "This one thing I show unto thee, Moses, my son" (Moses 1:6–7). After Moses' miraculous conversation with the Lord, Satan attempted to deceive Moses by claiming that he himself was the Only Begotten (Moses 1:19) and commanding Moses to worship him. In response, Moses said: "I am a son of God, in the similitude of his Only Begotten. . . . Get thee hence, Satan; deceive me not; for God said unto me: Thou art after the similitude of mine Only Begotten" (Moses 1:13, 16). Finally, Moses commanded him "in the name of the Only Begotten, depart hence, Satan" (Moses 1:21), and Satan left.

*Moses the Deliverer.* As a type of Jesus Christ, Moses delivered the Israelites from their Egyptian bondage (Ex. 3:1–12). The Lord told Moses: "And the Lord said, I have surely seen the affliction of my people which are in Egypt, and have heard their cry by reason of their taskmasters; for I know their sorrows; and I am come down to deliver them out of the hand of the Egyptians. . . . Come now therefore, and I will send thee unto Pharaoh, that thou mayest bring forth my people the children of Israel out of Egypt" (Ex. 3:7–8, 10). Jesus too is our Deliverer, and as Moses delivered his people with a temporal salvation, Jesus delivers us with an eternal salvation.

*Moses the Mediator.* After God revealed the Ten Commandments to Moses, an awesome display of thunderings, lightnings, and smoke came from God's mountain, Mount Sinai. This display caused the Israelites to fear and to move away from the mountain. They said to Moses: "Speak thou with us, and we will hear: but let not God speak with us, lest we die. . . . And the people stood afar off, and Moses drew near unto the thick darkness where God was. And the Lord said unto Moses,

Thus thou shalt say unto the children of Israel, Ye have seen that I have talked with you from heaven" (Ex. 20:19–22). Moses thus mediated between the Israelites and God, on this occasion as well as on others.

Just as Moses mediated the old covenant, so Christ mediates the new. "Moses . . . was ordained by the hand of angels to be a mediator of this first covenant, (the law). Now this mediator was not a mediator of the new covenant; but there is one mediator of the new covenant, who is Christ. . . . Christ is the mediator of life; for this is the promise which God made unto Abraham" (JST Gal. 3:19–20). Christ became the Mediator of life through the shedding of his blood and through his death (Heb. 9:14–15). Elder Boyd K. Packer explained the purpose of a mediator: "Unless there is a mediator, unless we have a friend, the full weight of justice untempered, unsympathetic, must, positively must fall on us. The full recompense for every transgression, however minor or however deep, will be exacted from us to the uttermost farthing.

"But know this: Truth, glorious truth, proclaims there is such a Mediator."[15]

Beyond the themes of Deliverer and Mediator, Moses' life paralleled Jesus' in a number of other ways. Like the Lord, Moses was a "king (Deut. 33:5; Matt. 21:5), teacher (Deut. 4:5; Matt. 5:2), prophet (Deut. 18:15–19; 1 Ne. 22:21), and lawgiver (John 1:17; Isa. 33:22). Both Jesus and Moses were called 'faithful' (Heb. 3:1–6), were 'mighty in words and deeds' (Acts 7:22; John 1:1), performed signs and miracles (Ex. 4:28–31; John 20:30), fasted forty days (Ex. 34:28; Matt. 4:2), controlled the sea (Ex. 14:21; Matt. 8:26), and were sent from God (Ex. 3:1–12; John 6:57). Both called 'seventy' (Num. 11:16–17; Luke 10:1), and both came forth out of Egypt (JST Gen. 50:29; Matt. 2:15). Finally, miraculous circumstances attended the birth of both Moses and Jesus (Ex. 2:1–6; Luke 1:27–38)."[16]

## BOAZ: REDEEMER AND REDEMPTION

Key parts of the story of Ruth are concerned with redemption, or buying back. The Hebrew root *gaal*, or redeem, is found eighteen times in this short book of four chapters. Boaz, who is called a "redeemer" (from the Hebrew; KJV=kinsman), is a type and shadow of Jesus Christ, the Great Redeemer. A close examination of Ruth (see especially Ruth 2:20; 3:9–13; 4:1–12) reveals much about the meaning of redemption. The book contains a number of significant theological statements, including that Boaz spreads his wing (KJV=skirt) over Ruth (Ruth 3:9), follows the Levirate law of marriage and marries Ruth (Ruth 4:1–10; cf. Deut. 25:1–10), and "purchases" Ruth to "be my wife, to raise up the name of the dead upon his inheritance, that the name of the dead be not cut off from among his brethren" (Ruth 4:10).

## JOB: SUFFERING SERVANT, MAN OF GRIEF

Job, a man from the land of Uz, is described as being "perfect and upright, and one that feared God, and eschewed evil" (Job 1:1). Job's uprightness emulates Jesus Christ's excellence, and Job's blamelessness foresees Jesus' sinlessness. Job offered sacrifices and sanctified his children (Job 1:1, 5), anticipating Jesus' infinite sacrifice and the sanctification of those who will become his sons and daughters. Job served as a mediator between God and his children and friends (Job 1:5; 42:8), "but there is one mediator of the new covenant, who is Christ. . . . Now Christ is the mediator of life" (JST Gal. 3:20).

Job also experienced enormous sufferings, distresses, and anguish, just as the Savior did. While his three daughters and seven sons were eating a meal at Job's oldest son's home, Job's property—7,000 sheep, 3,000 camels, 500 yoke of oxen, and 500 she asses—was stolen or destroyed. Sabeans stole the oxen and asses, fire from heaven burned the sheep, and the Chaldeans carried away the camels. While Job was processing the enormity of these temporal losses, a messenger came to him and reported an appalling tragedy: a powerful wind had pulled down the home upon Job's children while they were enjoying dinner, killing them all (Job 1:2, 14–19). Job responded to these tragedies by rending his mantle, shaving his head, falling to the ground, and worshipping the Lord. "In all this Job sinned not, nor charged God foolishly" (Job 1:22).

Satan "smote Job with sore boils from the sole of his foot unto his crown" (Job 2:7). His physical condition and appearance were so horrific that his wife told him to "curse God, and die" (Job 2:9). When Job's three friends saw his miserable appearance, although they were yet a distance from him, they "knew him not, they lifted up their voice, and wept; and they rent every one his mantle, and sprinkled dust upon their heads." Afterward they "sat down with him upon the ground seven days and seven nights, and none spake a word unto him: for they saw that his grief was very great" (Job 2:12–13).

Job's great sufferings in the flesh—his loss of children and property, and the boils that covered him—anticipated the Suffering Servant and Man of Grief, Jesus Christ (Isa. 53). Jesus descended below all things and yet remained the Sinless One. Jesus suffered bodily pain and affliction beyond mortal comprehension, and yet like Job he never charged his Father foolishly. While experiencing his sufferings, Job even bore a powerful testimony of the Redeemer and the resurrection: "For I know that my redeemer liveth, and that he shall stand at the latter day upon the earth: and though after my skin worms destroy this body, yet in my flesh shall I see God" (Job 19:25–26).

After all of his afflictions Job received a double portion of property—14,000 sheep, 6,000 camels, 1,000 yoke of oxen, and 1,000 she asses (Job 42:12), representing exactly double the numbers of his portion from his earlier days. He also was blessed with ten additional children, who in eternity would be added to the ten children he lost in his troubles (Job 1:2, 18–19; 42:13). In Old Testament times, the firstborn son often received a double portion of his father's inheritance. Therefore, Job's double portion points to Christ, who is the Firstborn (D&C 93:21). Further, Job lived to see his seed until "four generations" (Job 42:16), paralleling Jesus Christ, who was promised that he would "see his seed" (Isa. 53:10), or those who have been spiritually begotten of him and become his sons and daughters (Mosiah 15:5–13).

## JONAH: THE SIGN OF CHRIST'S DEATH, BURIAL, AND RESURRECTION

When certain scribes and Pharisees said to Jesus, "Master, we would see a sign from thee," he responded, "An evil and adulterous generation seeketh after a sign; and there shall no sign be given to it, but the sign of the prophet Jonas [Jonah]" (Matt. 12:38–39). Jesus Christ's comparison to Jonah has three significant aspects: (1) The sign of the prophet Jonah refers to Jesus' "death, burial, and resurrection."[17] (2) Jesus compared Jonah's three days and three nights in the great fish to the three days and nights that he, Jesus, would spend in the spirit world. He declared, "For as Jonas was three days and three nights in the whale's belly; so shall the Son of man be three days and three nights in the heart of the earth" (Matt. 12:39–40; cf. Jonah 1:17: "And Jonah was in the belly of the fish three days and three nights"). (3) Jesus compared himself to Jonah, saying, "And, behold, a greater than Jonas is here"; he then informed his audience that the Ninevites had repented at the preaching of Jonah, but Jesus' audience had failed to repent at his teaching, even though he was greater than Jonah.

There are other ways Jonah served as a type of Jesus Christ. One outstanding example concerns the time that Jonah slept on the ship during the raging storm. The ship's captain came to him and said: "What meanest thou, O sleeper? arise, call upon thy God, if so be that God will think upon us, that we perish not" (Jonah 1:6). This parallels the occurrence when Jesus slept in the ship during a great storm and others awoke him and said, "Master, carest thou not that we perish?" (Mark 4:38–39). In one instance, Jonah's invitation to the sailors to throw him overboard was the cause of the storm's ceasing (Jonah 1:3–12), and in the second, Jesus directly caused the storm to cease.

CHAPTER 7

# FROM NOAH'S ARK TO ABIGAIL'S OFFERING: SCRIPTURAL STORIES AND EVENTS THAT TESTIFY OF CHRIST

ELDER BRUCE R. MCCONKIE WROTE: "No doubt there are many *events* in the lives of many prophets that set those righteous persons apart as types and shadows of their Messiah. It is wholesome and proper to look for similitudes of Christ everywhere and to use them repeatedly in keeping him and his laws uppermost in our minds."[1]

Earlier we looked at specific *people* whose lives stood impressively as types of Christ (see chapter 6). In addition, the scriptures contain many specific *events* that teach us of Jesus Christ and his atonement. As we read the scriptures with this kind of mind-set, our understanding of and appreciation for the infinite atonement of our Savior will measurably deepen.

Interestingly, the Book of Mormon: Another Testament of Jesus Christ gives a more *overt* testimony of the Savior and his mission, while the first testament of Jesus Christ, the Old Testament, seems to give more *types and shadows*. The Book of Mormon may therefore be said to be more direct; the Old Testament, while telling literal stories, appears at the same time to be more symbolic.

This chapter focuses on scriptural stories that testify of Christ and his atonement. Many other stories could also be used, but these will serve to convey the principle that a symbolic truth about Christ lies be-hind many of the literal stories in the scriptures. (Some of the people mentioned in this chapter are treated in chapter 6 as individuals who are types; here we look more narrowly at specific incidents in their lives, rather than at broader patterns.)

## NOAH'S ARK

The story of Noah's ark is well known to children throughout the Jewish and Christian world. It has captured the imagination of count-less artists, who meticulously depict lions and elephants and ostriches and giraffes. But not commonly understood or acknowledged is the fact that Noah is a marvelous type of Christ.

The story begins with a statement of the miserable condition of mankind: "And God saw that the wickedness of man was great in the earth, and that every imagination of the thoughts of his heart was only evil continually. . . . All flesh had corrupted his way upon the earth" (Gen. 6:5, 12). Such is our state in the fallen world. Everyone who ever lives is "carnal, sensual, and devilish" (Alma 42:10; see also Mosiah 16:3) unless and until they come unto Christ and receive of the bless-ings of his atonement.

Standing in contrast to this wickedness is Noah, a man of God. "Noah found grace in the eyes of the Lord," the account says. He "was a just man and perfect in his generations" (Gen. 6:8, 9). As one who had aligned his will with the will of the Lord, Noah was able to prepare a means for the salvation of all who would listen to him. That means was the ark, built according to the specifications of God. Here Noah is a type of the Christ, who was truly "perfect" in the ultimate sense.

The ark was built of gopher wood, referring to a tree biblical schol-ars have not been able to identify. Noah was instructed to "pitch it within and without" (Gen. 6:14). In other words, he was to cover the wood with a waterproofing substance. The Hebrew word (*kpr*), trans-lated *pitch* in this verse, is used many other times in the Bible. The word as used in Genesis 6:14 denotes a protective covering. In every other in-stance where this Hebrew word is found, it refers to the atonement. The atonement of Jesus Christ provides us with a protective covering; it shields us from the power of the adversary, just as the pitch protected the ark from the life-threatening waters.

Noah was told that "everything that is in the earth shall die" (Gen. 6:17), which clearly parallels the state of every living creature on earth as a result of the fall. Later, the account of Noah and the flood continues to parallel the fall by saying that "all flesh died that moved upon the earth, both of fowl, and of cattle, and of beast, and of every creeping thing that creepeth upon the earth, and every man: all in whose nostrils was the breath of life, of all that was in the dry land, died. And every living substance was destroyed which was upon the face of the ground, both man, and cattle, and the creeping things, and the fowl of the heaven; and they were destroyed from the earth" (Gen. 7:21–23). Because of the fall, nothing was spared the fate of death.

The very earth was immersed with water to cleanse it from the sin and corruption that covered it: "And the waters prevailed exceedingly upon the earth; and all the high hills, that were under the whole heaven, were covered . . . ; and the mountains were covered" (Gen. 7:19–20). In the same way, the effects of the fall fully cover the earth—and fully cover each of us until we enter into God's protective care and receive the blessings of Christ's atonement.

Even though Noah understood that the "waters upon the earth [would] destroy all flesh, wherein is the breath of life, from under heaven" (Gen. 6:17), there was a crucial exception: "But with thee will I establish my covenant; and thou shalt come into the ark, thou, and thy sons, and thy wife, and thy sons' wives with thee. And of every living thing of all flesh, two of every sort shalt thou bring into the ark, to keep them alive with thee; they shall be male and female. . . . And Noah only remained alive, and they that were with him in the ark" (Gen. 6:18–19; 7:23). Even though the universal result of the fall is physical death, and even though the inevitable result of our personal sin is spiritual death, when we enter into covenant with God, made possible through Christ and his atonement, we enter a place of safety. Then and only then will we remain alive. The ark was the only means of survival from the flood, and Jesus Christ is the only means of survival from death and sin.

Then, if we continue faithful to that covenant, God will help us through the storms of life. As Noah experienced: "And God remembered Noah, and every living thing, and all the cattle that was with him in the ark: and God made a wind to pass over the earth, and the waters asswaged; the fountains also of the deep and the windows of heaven were stopped, and the rain from heaven was restrained" (Gen. 8:1–2).

The difficulties of life may not pass quickly. Noah and his family were on the ark for a full year (Gen. 7:11; 8:13–16; even though the record seems to indicate that they were on the ark for a year and ten days, the time measures exactly a year when the Hebrew lunar calendar is adjusted to the solar year). During that time they were carried through a storm that lasted nonstop for forty days and nights (Gen. 7:12); they traveled their lonely way across the "great deep" (Gen. 7:11), knowing that every single person and every animal on the earth—except those on the ark—had been slain. Their craft had only one small window (Gen. 6:16), and surely they must have felt closed in and claustrophobic at times. But they were safe, and the Lord preserved and carried them through the trial, just as he promised he would.

When the storm was over and the floods had abated, the Lord made an "everlasting covenant between God and every living creature of all flesh that is upon the earth" (Gen. 9:16) that never again would he bring destruction by flood upon the earth. "I will not again curse the ground any more for man's sake," the Lord said, "neither will I again smite any more every thing living, as I have done" (Gen. 8:21). Noah and his family were safe, and they were commanded to be "fruitful, and multiply; bring forth abundantly in the earth, and multiply therein" (Gen. 9:7). They would become the parents of all the human race, newly placed upon the face of the earth. This points to Christ: he also becomes the Father of all through his atonement. And once he performed the atonement, it was good for all time. The flood occurred only once; Noah's provision of the ark, built under God's instruction, was required only once. Likewise, the fall had occurred only once, and the atonement was required only once. Under the power of the atonement, a new human race, born again unto Christ, will inherit the earth.

## MOSES AND THE ROCK

The book of Exodus includes a stunning and somewhat complex story that presents a type of Christ and his atonement, one that is rich with symbolism. As the children of Israel journeyed in the wilderness, they stopped at a place called Rephidim. They soon learned that there was no water in that part of the desert.

"Wherefore the people did chide with Moses, and said, Give us water that we may drink. And Moses said unto them, Why chide ye with me? wherefore do ye tempt the Lord?" (Ex. 17:2).

The people accused Moses of bringing them "up out of Egypt, to kill us and our children and our cattle with thirst" (Ex. 17:3). It was an outrageous accusation—particularly in light of all the manifestations of power the Lord had given through Moses. Not long before, the Lord had freely provided them with all the food they could eat—a daily supply of manna that was perfectly sufficient.

With the accusation against Moses came a physical threat: "They be almost ready to stone me," Moses said (Ex. 17:4).

The Lord provided the solution: Moses was to take his rod and, accompanied by the elders of Israel, go to the rock in Horeb. "Thou shalt smite the rock, and there shall come water out of it, that the people may drink," the Lord said (Ex. 17:6).

Moses did as he was instructed, and the people had enough to drink and to spare.

Much of the symbolism of this event is apparent: The wilderness represents the challenges of life in this fallen world. Jesus is the rock (Deut. 32:30–31; 1 Cor. 10:4), the source of the living water of life (John 4:14; 7:37–39). Just as he provided water to sustain the physical life of his covenant people in the wilderness, so will he provide the gifts of the Holy Ghost to sustain his children through their mortal lives. This event is a lovely, meaningful symbol.

But the symbolism behind one element in this story is harder to decipher. If the rock represented Christ, why was Moses instructed to strike it?

The meaning of two key words in Exodus 17:2 helps us to understand the context of what is happening. The original Hebrew suggests a change in those two words: "Wherefore the people did [contend] with Moses, and said, Give us water that we may drink. And Moses said unto them, Why [contend] ye with me? wherefore do ye [test or try] the Lord?" The two names Moses gave to the location of the rock of Horeb further underscore the importance of these words. *Meribah* means "contend." And *Massah* means "to test, to try, or to tempt."

The people were contending with Moses in a legal sense; in essence, they were accusing him—and the Lord—of breach of contract. The agreement was that the Lord would deliver them from Egypt and take them to the promised land. The reality seemed to be that they were going to die in the desert.

In response to the accusation, the Lord invited Moses to take his special rod, the one he used to strike the Nile River and turn it to blood, and to strike the rock on which the Lord stood. Striking the rock that represented the Lord was symbolically striking the Lord himself.

In this story, the Lord was falsely accused. The people were rebellious and unrighteous. They were doubting God and ready to stone the prophet. Yet "in all their affliction he was afflicted, and the angel of his presence saved them: in his love and in his pity he redeemed them; and he bare them, and carried them all the days of old" (Isa. 63:9). He "gave [his] back to the smiters" (Isa. 50:6). The rod that had turned water to blood was now used to draw water from rock; it was used to provide the healing, sustaining waters of life from the great Source of such water.

Thus, this story contains another layer of meaning that points to the atonement. Just as Jehovah in the desert, innocent of offense, nevertheless accepted the punishment for sins resulting from the choices of the rebellious people, so did Jesus in the Garden of Gethsemane accept punishment for the sins of the rebellious. And not only was he "smitten [and] . . . bruised" (Isa. 53:4, 5), but then, in his marvelous grace, he provided the ever-flowing waters of life for those who had brought his pains in the first place!

## ELISHA AND THE AX

After Elisha received the calling and mantle of the prophet Elijah, he worked with a group called "the sons of the prophets" (2 Kgs. 6:1). They apparently lived together in a communal setting, but the group grew too large to accommodate them all. Elisha's disciples decided to build a new dwelling place for the group near the Jordan River. Elisha approved of their plan and accompanied them to the construction site. While they were cutting wood, an ax head flew off and went into the river. The man who was using the ax cried out to Elisha, "Alas, master! For it was borrowed." Elisha asked the man to tell him where it fell. The prophet then cut down a stick and cast it into the river at the appropriate place, "and the iron did swim." Then Elisha said to the man, "Take it up to thee," which the man did, and the ax head was restored (2 Kgs. 6:1–7).

This miracle, which actually occurred as described, has seemed strange to readers for many generations. Why did the Lord perform such an impressive miracle for such a seemingly trivial problem?

On one level, this miracle demonstrates that the Lord is concerned with the small details of our lives as well as with the larger ones. He desired to bless the man who had borrowed the ax at a time when iron implements were relatively rare. Though the man lost the ax head in the process of doing a worthy work, he may have had to work off the loss of the ax by becoming a bondservant to the ax's owner.

On another level, this story bears a witness of Christ and his atonement, and it can be read symbolically. Each of us is precious to the Lord, as the ax head was to the man who lost it. Yet we don't own ourselves—we have been bought with a price and belong to God (1 Cor. 6:20; 7:23). By coming to this fallen earth, we inevitably fall ourselves and become lost. We die both spiritually and physically, sinking into the waters of mortality, seemingly lost forever.

But God's servants, the prophets (represented here by Elisha), bring to us the blessings of the atonement of Christ. Elisha cut down a branch, just as another Branch, symbolic of Christ, would be cut down by wicked men in mortality (Zech. 3:8; 6:12). That Branch was also placed in the waters of mortality. But the true Branch never partook of sin, never sank into the murky water. Even though he came to earth, he never fell into sin. Then, by his power, he lifts us up to where he is. He changes our nature—iron cannot float, but wood can. He transforms us so that we become as he is.

It is noteworthy that Jesus Christ was baptized by immersion in this very river. As we follow his example in life, he will bring us forth from the river of death and sin and lift us to a new birth. And, in the end, through a marvelous manifestation of power, he will lift us from the darkness of death to a resurrection of glory.

## ABIGAIL AND DAVID

The book of 1 Samuel 25 contains the impressive story of Abigail, who lived in the time of David. David and his six hundred men were in the wilderness of Paran, seeking refuge from Saul. While there, they offered protection to Nabal, a wealthy sheep rancher. But when David asked for provisions in return, Nabal rudely rebuffed him, refusing him even food and water. (The name *Nabal* in Hebrew literally means "fool.") In response, David took four hundred armed men against Nabal, prepared to kill him and all his men.

Abigail, the wife of Nabal, learned both of the dispute and of David's plan. She hastily prepared food for the army and bravely went out to meet David. "And when Abigail saw David, she hasted, and lighted off the ass, and fell before David on her face, and bowed herself to the ground, and fell at his feet, and said, Upon me, my lord, upon me let this iniquity be. . . . I pray thee, forgive the trespass of thine handmaid" (1 Sam. 25:23–24, 28). She blessed David and his men and prophesied that the Lord would make of David "a sure house," that he would become "ruler over Israel," and that "the soul of my lord shall be bound in the bundle of life with the Lord thy God; and the souls of thine enemies, them shall he sling out, as out of the middle of a sling" (1 Sam. 25:28, 30, 29). These blessings, Abigail said, would come be-cause David hearkened to her voice; in doing so, he did not commit offense before the Lord in the matter of Nabal, and his hands remained unstained from the blood of Abigail's household.

Then David responded: "Blessed be the Lord God of Israel, which sent thee this day to meet me: And blessed be thy advice, and blessed be thou, which hast kept me this day from coming to shed blood, and from avenging myself with mine own hand. . . . So David received of her hand that which she had brought him, and said unto her, Go up in peace to thine house; see, I have hearkened to thy voice, and have accepted thy person" (vv. 32–33, 35).

The offering of Abigail in this account is noteworthy.

- She was sinless in the dispute between David and her husband.

- Yet she took upon herself the sin of her husband to save his life.

- At the same time, she helped turn David from committing mortal sin.

- Though both Nabal and David were undeserving, she made intercession for them both.

- She took gifts to David to help him on his way: bread, wine, and sheep.

In our lives, we also are sometimes unwise, unjust, and sinful, as Nabal was. We are hasty and quick to judge others—and to exact justice, as David was. The atonement is for those who are sinful. It is also for those who are sinned against—and who then respond in a sinful way.

Like Abigail, our Savior pleads with us to make the right choice. Like Abigail, our Savior takes upon himself our sin, hoping we will turn from that sin and choose wisely thereafter. Like Abigail, our Savior brings us every needful thing to help us on our way.

We are undeserving. We are the offenders. As Paul said, "There is none righteous, no, not one" (Rom. 3:10). And yet in his love, Christ chooses to bear our sin; and he seeks in his meekness to help us choose righteously.

As we think of Abigail falling on the ground before David in behalf of Nabal, we can think of our Savior falling on the ground before the Father in our behalf. And as we hear Abigail's pleading to David— "Upon me, my Lord, upon me let this iniquity be. I pray thee, forgive the trespass of thine handmaid"—we can know that in an olive garden in Jerusalem, long ago, our Savior so pleaded for us.

## OTHER EXAMPLES

The Old Testament is filled with stories that bear witness of the atonement of Christ. These stories are both literally true and deeply symbolic. Here are a few additional well-known stories that have such symbolism:

*Jacob's ladder.* Isaac instructed his son Jacob to marry one of the daughters of Laban, who lived a considerable distance away. While Jacob was on his journey, one night as he slept "he dreamed, and behold a ladder set up on the earth, and the top of it reached to heaven: and behold the angels of God ascending and descending on it. And behold, the Lord stood above it" (Gen. 28:12–13). When Jacob awoke, he said: "Surely the Lord is in this place; and I knew it not. . . . How dreadful [awesome] is this place! this is none other but the house of God, and this is the gate of heaven" (Gen. 28:16–17). He named the place Bethel, meaning "House of God."

The ladder obviously is a passageway to heaven, and Jacob was in a place where heaven came down to earth, or where earth reached up to heaven. But the specific meaning of the ladder is obscure. The mortal Jesus, however, gave the interpretation. When he saw Nathaniel for the first time, Jesus prophesied to him, "Verily, verily, I say unto you, Hereafter ye shall see heaven open, and the angels of God ascending and descending *upon the Son of man*" (John 1:51; emphasis added). Jesus himself, through his atonement, is the passageway to heaven, the Way we can walk to regain the presence of God.

*Ruth and Boaz.* In his interactions with Ruth, Boaz is a type of

Christ. He gives her food and drink, comforts her, protects her, "redeems" her from her status of being without husband or family, and receives her as a wife—all things that the Lord does for us spiritually through his atonement (Ruth 2:8–9, 13, 14; 3:9; 4:3–10, 13). Continuing the type, Boaz even purchases Ruth, according to the custom of the time (Ruth 5:10); and Jesus Christ has, as Paul said, "bought [us] with a price" (1 Cor. 6:20)—which price was his suffering in the Garden of Gethsemane and on Golgotha. (For additional commentary on Boaz, see chapter 6.)

*David and Goliath.* David, in his youthful innocence and purity, also stands as a type of Christ. He stood against the Goliath of sin, against which all others were powerless. Refusing earthly means of protection or attack, David relied on the power of God to overcome his enemy, who sought to enslave all of Israel (1 Sam. 17). In the same way, in his perfect purity Christ stands against the monster of sin, which would enslave us all. He conquers that enemy, gaining the victory for all of us. In all this he is supported and enabled and empowered by his Father.

Christ gained the victory over Satan just as David conquered Goliath: "I come to thee in the name of the Lord of hosts, the God of the armies of Israel, whom thou hast defied. This day will the Lord deliver thee into mine hand; and I will smite thee, and take thine head from thee; . . . that all the earth may know that there is a God in Israel. And all this assembly shall know that the Lord saveth not with sword and spear: for the battle is the Lord's, and he will give you into [my] hands" (1 Sam. 17:45–47).

*Jonah and the fish.* Though Jonah was sinful in choosing to flee from the command of God, in some ways his experience is symbolic of Christ's atonement. He chose to die (being thrown overboard into the stormy ocean) to save the lives of his fellows (Jonah 1:1–15), just as the sinless Christ would later do. Further, his three days and nights in the belly of the fish were symbolic of death and going to the spirit world, and his coming forth from the fish represents Christ's resurrection. As Jesus said centuries later, "For as Jonas was three days and three nights in the whale's belly; so shall the Son of man be three days and three nights in the heart of the earth" (Matt. 12:40; for additional commentary on Jonah, see chapter 6).

*Esther and the king.* When all of the Lord's chosen people in Persia and Media were threatened with death, Esther went before the king to plead for mercy, even though she knew her efforts would likely bring her own death. She was innocent of wrongdoing but willingly made the sacrifice. That which she said to the king could be said of all of us in mortality: "For we are sold, I and my people, to be destroyed, to be slain, and to perish" (Esth. 7:4).

So also did Christ offer his own life to save our souls from death and hell. Mordecai, Esther's cousin and foster father, asked her, "Who knoweth whether thou art come to the kingdom for such a time as this?" (Esth. 4:14). The same question could be asked of Christ—and the answer, of course, is *yes.*

*Daniel and the lions' den.* Daniel, who refused to "defile himself" (Dan. 1:8) with food of the Gentiles and who refused to obey a law forbidding prayer to God (Dan. 6:7–10), was cast into a den of lions. But through the power of God he was preserved and miraculously came forth again alive. So also was Jesus Christ, in his purity, threatened with death; and he faced a mortal enemy and descended below all things into the bowels of hell. But through the power of God he prevailed against Satan in the Garden of Gethsemane, and after he had gone into the world of the dead, he came forth again alive, resurrected, never to die again.

This story also describes our ultimate pathway if we choose as Daniel did. Even though we will be cast into the pit of death, yet God will continue with us there, his angels will attend and protect us, and we will finally be brought forth triumphant and eternally alive through the power of Christ.

## CHAPTER 8

# TOUCH AND TESTIMONY: SCRIPTURAL PATTERNS OF THE ATONEMENT

IN ADDITION TO THE VARIOUS TYPES of Christ found in the scriptures, the Lord's word gives us a number of *patterns* that point to his atonement and teach us about it. In this chapter we'll briefly look at seven such patterns: deliverance from bondage, marriage and divorce, barren women giving birth, the personal touch of Jesus Christ, the prayers of Christ, the burden of the prophets, and Jesus' testimonies of himself.

## DELIVERANCE FROM BONDAGE

The theme of bondage and deliverance is found again and again in the scriptures. The Lord said to the children of Israel through Moses: "I have also heard the groaning of the children of Israel, whom the Egyptians keep in bondage; and I have remembered my covenant. Wherefore say unto the children of Israel, I am the Lord, and I will bring you out from under the burdens of the Egyptians, and I will rid you out of their bondage, and I will redeem you with a stretched out arm, and with great judgments" (Ex. 6:5–6).

This great deliverance became a regular form of testimony among the Jews, who often repeated in their oaths and prayers, "The Lord liveth, that brought up the children of Israel out of the land of Egypt" (Jer. 16:14).

Many centuries later, Alma said to his son Helaman: "I would that ye should do as I have done, in remembering the captivity of our fathers; for they were in bondage, and none could deliver them except it was the God of Abraham, and the God of Isaac, and the God of Jacob; and he surely did deliver them in their afflictions. . . . And he has delivered them out of bondage and captivity from time to time" (Alma 36:2, 28).

This theme is frequently repeated in the Book of Mormon. The people were brought into bondage, often as a result of their own sins, and only through the Lord were they delivered (among many examples, see Mosiah 7:15, 20, 33; 11:21–23; 12:2, 15, 34; 24:13–17, 21; 25:8, 10, 16; Alma 5:5; 29:11–12). As we read these accounts, combined with others in the Book of Mormon and the Old Testament, it soon becomes clear that physical bondage of the Lord's people is a type of their spiritual bondage to sin, and that their physical deliverance is a type of the spiritual deliverance that comes through the atonement of Jesus Christ.

Thus we read in latter-day revelation: "The whole world lieth in sin, and groaneth under darkness and under the bondage of sin. . . . For whoso cometh not unto me is under the bondage of sin" (D&C 84:49–51). The bondage comes through sin—and the solution lies in Christ.

We find the same image in the New Testament. In Romans, Paul says that we "shall be delivered from the bondage of corruption into the glorious liberty of the children of God" (Rom. 8:21). Later, he wrote to the Galatians, "Stand fast therefore in the liberty wherewith Christ hath made us free, and be not entangled again with the yoke of bondage" (Gal. 5:1).

The Book of Mormon testifies with great plainness that Christ is the key to our deliverance from bondage:

> But if ye will turn to the Lord with full purpose of heart, and
> put your trust in him, and serve him with all diligence of mind, if

ye do this, he will, according to his own will and pleasure, deliver you out of bondage. (Mosiah 7:33)

Yea, . . . they poured out their thanks to God because he had been merciful unto them, and eased their burdens, and had delivered them out of bondage; for they were in bondage, and none could deliver them except it were the Lord their God. (Mosiah 24:21)

And were it not for the interposition of their all-wise Creator, and this because of their sincere repentance, they must unavoidably remain in bondage until now. But behold, he did deliver them because they did humble themselves before him; and because they cried mightily unto him he did deliver them out of bondage; and thus doth the Lord work with his power in all cases among the children of men, extending the arm of mercy towards them that put their trust in him. (Mosiah 29:19–20)

## Marriage and Divorce

Another recurring scriptural theme that teaches us about the atonement is that of marriage and divorce. The Lord repeatedly uses the metaphor that he is the bridegroom and husband and that we are the bride. We learn in Hosea that the Lord is the one who is betrothed to the covenant people (Hosea 2:19–20); and through other prophets he is called "husband": "for thy Maker is thine husband" (Isa. 54:5); "I am married unto you" (Jer. 3:14); "I was an husband unto them, saith the Lord" (Jer. 31:32). Other scriptures depict him as the bridegroom (Jer. 2:1–4; Matt. 9:15; Rev. 19:7; 21:9; D&C 33:17–18; 65:3; 133:10).

The Lord's bride is the "holy city, new Jerusalem" (Rev. 21:2, 9), Zion (Isa. 54:1–6), and the Church (D&C 109:73–74). His bride is represented by the faithful Saints, "they which are written in the Lamb's book of life" (Rev. 21:27), they who are the wise virgins (Matt. 25:1–13), they who are "holy and without blemish" (Eph. 5:27)—all these are the "Lamb's wife" (Rev. 21:9). "For I am jealous over you with godly jealousy," Paul said, "for I have espoused you to one husband, that

101

I may present you as a chaste virgin to Christ" (2 Cor. 11:2). At the Lord's coming, the Saints will cry out, "Let us be glad and rejoice, and give honour to him: for the marriage of the Lamb is come, and his wife hath made herself ready" (Rev. 19:7).

The marriage of the Bridegroom to his bride is a metaphor for the union between the Lord and his people, made possible through the atonement. Using marriage as a symbol underscores the sweetness and blessing of that union. There is no sweeter or more meaningful relationship on earth than that between a holy husband and a holy wife—and that is the kind of relationship (in terms of depth of feeling and completeness of union) the Lord is inviting us to. That marriage is between Christ and the Church—but the Church is not just an organization on the earth; it is also the individual souls who belong to that organization. Though the Saints are to prepare for the marriage all their lives (Matt. 25:1–13; D&C 45:56–57), it will be brought to its culmination (with the body of the Church) when Christ returns in glory. Of course, as individuals, we are bound to Christ as soon as we are ready. (For other references to the marriage of the Lamb, see Isa. 62:5; Zeph. 1:7–8; JST Matt. 22:14; Eph. 5:23, 32; D&C 58:6–11; 88:92.)

There are times when the Lord's people have turned from him in apostasy or idolatry; continuing the marriage metaphor, the Lord has referred to that apostasy as adultery (Isa. 57:7–8; Jer. 3:20; Hosea 4:6; 9:1). In ancient Israel, when the people turned away from the Lord and would not repent, he finally said, "When for all the causes whereby backsliding Israel committed adultery I had put her away, and given her a bill of divorce" (Jer. 3:8).

But the time will come when the Lord's people, fully repentant and partaking of the blessings of the atonement, will be restored to their position as the Lord's bride. "Fear not," the Lord says to Israel (Isa. 54:4). She will not be confounded; she will not be brought to shame; in her blessings she will even forget the shame of her past. "For a small moment have I forsaken thee; but with great mercies will I gather thee," the Lord says. "In a little wrath I hid my face from thee for a moment; but with everlasting kindness will I have mercy on thee" (Isa. 54:7–8). Though Israel has suffered much as a result of her choices, as she partakes of the atonement the Lord will restore to her all blessings and will bring her unto himself.

## BARREN WOMEN GIVING BIRTH

Another repeated pattern in the scriptures is that of barren women—those who desperately desired to have a child but could not have one. The Old Testament gives the examples of Sarah, Rebekah, Rachel, Hannah, the wife of Manoah (mother of Samson), and the Shunammite woman who helped Elisha; the New Testament gives the example of Elisabeth. In each of these examples, the woman was able to finally become pregnant and have a child because God "opened her womb"; in other words, God performed a miracle whereby life could come where none had before been possible. In at least two of these cases (Sarah and Elisabeth), the new mother was past childbearing years, apparently having gone through menopause and *then* having a child.

Further, God established a bloodline from the beginning through which the Only Begotten Son of the Father would be born. That family line started with Adam, of course, and went down through Noah, Abraham, Isaac, Jacob, Judah, and David. But in several instances the appointed woman through whom the line was to continue (Sarah, Rebekah, and Rachel) was unable to have a child. The bloodline continued only through a marvelous miracle performed by God himself.

In other instances, women in Christ's ancestral line became pregnant through sinful sexual relations (Judah with Tamar and David with Bathsheba). And one of the female ancestors of the Anointed One may have been the harlot Rahab.[1]

In a miraculous reversal, the very mother of Christ was neither barren nor impure. Instead, in the innocence and purity of her youth, she was overshadowed by "the power of the Highest" (Luke 1:35); she "was called a virgin, both before and after she gave birth. (See 1 Ne. 11:20.)"[2]

What does all this tell us about the atonement of Jesus Christ? It teaches that the God of our fathers is all-powerful. He can enable a woman who is past menopause to become pregnant. He can even cause a virgin to become "with child." This same God can apply the powers of the atonement to bring to pass great miracles in our individual lives.

Another lesson: the purposes of God cannot be thwarted. Even though some of Christ's ancestors chose sin, even gross sin, the Lord was still able to sufficiently influence events so that Mary and Joseph were ready and able to do all that was required of them.

A third lesson: There are times in our lives when we are barren. We may be spiritually unfruitful. But Christ has power to engender new life within us. He can bring to pass miracles in lives that seem past their time. He can take us from spiritual sterility to surprising fertility. "In the barren deserts" he can bring forth "pools of living water," and the "parched ground" of our souls "shall no longer be a thirsty land" (D&C 133:29).

Such blessings come through the atonement as we follow the counsel of Alma to those whose "ground is barren": we must "nourish the word, yea, nourish the tree as it beginneth to grow, by your faith with great diligence, and with patience, looking forward to the fruit thereof, it shall take root; and behold it shall be a tree springing up unto everlasting life" (Alma 32:39, 41; see also 2 Peter 1:2–8).

Because of these truths, we can cry out with the Psalmist in saying, gratefully, about our own spiritual lives: "He maketh the barren woman to keep house, and to be a joyful mother of children. Praise ye the Lord" (Ps. 113:9). And we can accept the invitation found in Isaiah 54, wherein we can rejoice at the remarkable blessings the Lord has given us in removing our spiritual barrenness and replacing it with much fruit: "Sing, O barren, thou that didst not bear; break forth into singing, and cry aloud, thou that didst not travail with child: for more are the children of the desolate than the children of the married wife, saith the Lord" (Isa. 54:1).

## PERSONAL TOUCH OF JESUS CHRIST

The patterns of personal touch by the living Christ teach a most valuable lesson about the atonement. The Gospels repeatedly witness that Jesus touched people as he healed them. He touched Peter's mother-in-law, who was sick with fever (Matt. 8:15); Peter, James, and John at the Mount of Transfiguration (Matt. 17:7); the two blind men who were sitting by the wayside (Matt. 20:34); Jairus's daughter, who had died (Mark 5:41); the boy with the "foul spirit" (Mark 9:25); the woman who "had a spirit of infirmity eighteen years" (Luke 13:11–13); and the ear of the servant of the high priest, which had been cut off by Peter (Luke 22:51).

He touched Peter as he sank into the sea after briefly walking on water (Matt. 14:31). He touched the little children when he "took them up in his arms, put his hands upon them, and blessed them" (Mark 10:16). He touched the sick in a multitude, laying "his hands on every one of them, and healed them" (Luke 4:40).

Lepers were not touched because leprosy was thought to be contagious through touch and because in the law of Moses leprosy made one ritually unclean, but Jesus touched even lepers (see, for example, Matt. 8:3). Of Jesus' touch of the leper in Matthew 8, the nineteenth-century cleric George Macdonald wrote:

> Jesus could have cured him with a word. There was no need he should touch him. *No need* did I say? There was every need. For no one else would touch him. The healthy human hand, always more or less healing, was never laid on him; he was despised and rejected. It was a poor thing for the Lord to cure his body; he must comfort and cure his sore heart. Of all men a leper, I say, needed to be touched with the hand of love. . . . It was not for our master, our brother, our ideal man, to draw around him the skirts of his garments and speak a lofty word of healing, that the man might at least be clean before he touched him. The man was his brother, and an evil disease cleaved fast unto him. Out went the loving hand to the ugly skin, and there was his brother as he should be— with the flesh of a child. I thank God that the touch went before the word. Nor do I think it was the touch of a finger, or of the finger-tips. It was a kindly healing touch in its nature as in its power. Oh blessed leper! thou knowest henceforth what kind of a God there is in the earth— . . . a God such as himself only can re-veal to the hearts of his own. That touch was more than the

healing. It was to the leper . . . what the [statement] *Neither do I [condemn thee]* was to the woman [at] the temple.[3]

Poignantly, the Savior personally touched the sacrament, both when he administered it to his apostles and to the Nephites: "And . . . Jesus took bread, and blessed it, and brake it, and gave it to the disciples" (Matt. 26:26; see also 3 Ne. 18:3). Imagine: he personally handled the very emblems of his sacrifice and personally gave them to his followers and invited them to partake. The feelings that the apostles had were likely heightened further among the Nephites, for the hands that broke the bread and gave them the wine bore the marks of his crucifixion— and the people had earlier touched those very hands individually and personally!

Just as Christ reached out in a very personal way and touched and blessed individuals during his ministry, so does he reach out in a very personal way to touch and bless us through his atonement. And just as Christ gave the sacrament in a personal way to his disciples on both sides of the ocean, so he offers the blessings of the atonement in a personal way to each of us.

But it is not enough for us to simply wait for him to touch us. He also invites us to touch him, and in the process increase our union of spirit and love. After Jesus was resurrected, he appeared to the eleven apostles. There, he said, "Behold my hands and my feet, that it is I myself: handle me, and see; for a spirit hath not flesh and bones, as ye see me have" (Luke 24:39). When he visited the Nephites, he again invited personal touch from them, one by one:

> Arise and come forth unto me, that ye may thrust your hands into my side, and also that ye may feel the prints of the nails in my hands and in my feet, that ye may know that I am the God of Israel, and the God of the whole earth, and have been slain for the sins of the world.
>
> And it came to pass that the multitude went forth, and thrust their hands into his side, and did feel the prints of the nails in his hands and in his feet; and this they did do, going forth one by one until they had all gone forth, and did see with their eyes and did

feel with their hands, and did know of a surety and did bear record, that it was he, of whom it was written by the prophets, that should come. (3 Ne. 11:14–15)

If we will receive the Lord's effort to touch each of us personally and individually with the atonement, and if we will reach out to him with all our hearts, we will grow in our union with him and receive ever more marvelous gifts and blessings. The Lord said through Joseph Smith, "Be faithful and diligent in keeping the commandments of God, and I will encircle thee in the arms of my love" (D&C 6:20). And, in time, we will be able to testify as Lehi did: "Behold, the Lord hath redeemed my soul from hell; I have beheld his glory, and I am encircled about eternally in the arms of his love" (2 Ne. 1:15).

## THE PRAYERS OF CHRIST

The prayers of the Savior provide a pattern that points to oneness with the Father, a oneness made possible through Christ himself and the infinite atonement he has wrought.

The prayer of Christ we have the most complete record of was offered shortly before he entered the Garden of Gethsemane. Sometimes called the great Intercessory Prayer, this petition outlines many of the purposes of the atonement that he would shortly perform. It was in this setting that he said, in prayer to the Father, "This is life eternal, that they might know thee the only true God, and Jesus Christ, whom thou hast sent."

Later he prayed: "And now I am no more in the world, but these are in the world, and I come to thee. Holy Father, keep through thine own name those whom thou hast given me, that they may be one, as we are." Then he prayed that his disciples—and those who would believe in all ages of the world—would have a oneness, or union, with God and with one another, which is possible through the atonement.

Neither pray I for these alone, but for them also which shall believe on me through their word; that they all may be one; as thou, Father, art in me, and I in thee, that they also may be one in us: that the world may believe that thou hast sent me. And the glory which thou gavest me I have given them; that they may be one, even as we are one: I in them, and thou in me, that they may be made perfect in one; and that the world may know that thou hast sent me, and hast loved them, as thou hast loved me. . . .

And I have declared unto them thy name, and will declare it: that the love wherewith thou hast loved me may be in them, and I in them. (John 17:3, 11, 20–23, 26)

When the resurrected Christ visited the Nephites, he offered a similar prayer in their presence. Once again he pleaded that his followers would have a union of spirit, purpose, and love among themselves and between them and God. He also asked that the Father would enable them to become purified (3 Ne. 19:23, 28–29). These are among the greatest purposes of the atonement.

Because the Savior prayed with such power before Gethsemane— and with even greater power in the garden itself—the oneness and likeness we desire with God are possible. We can become purified, glorified, and one with God himself. And because of those prayers, offered so long ago, Christ can continue to offer the marvelous prayer recorded in latter-day scripture:

Listen to him who is the advocate with the Father, who is pleading your cause before him—saying: Father, behold the sufferings and death of him who did no sin, in whom thou wast well pleased; behold the blood of thy Son which was shed, the blood of him whom thou gavest that thyself might be glorified; wherefore, Father, spare these my brethren that believe on my name, that they may come unto me and have everlasting life. (D&C 45:3–5)

## THE BURDEN OF THE PROPHETS

The overriding burden, or sacred responsibility, of the prophets was to bear testimony of Jesus Christ. They were to preach, teach, expound, and exhort, seeking to tell the people the various truths they needed to hear. But through it all they were to testify that Christ's atonement provided the answer to the great problems of life, especially the seemingly insurmountable challenges of sin and death.

We have many testimonies—part of what Paul called "so great a cloud of witnesses" (Heb. 12:1)—from individual prophets about the life, mission, and atoning sacrifice of Jesus Christ. These prophets include Adam, Enoch, and Moses in the book of Moses; Moses, Job, David, Isaiah, Ezekiel, Jeremiah, and some of the "minor prophets" in the Old Testament; Peter, James, John, Matthew, and Paul in the New Testament; Lehi, Nephi[1], Jacob, Omni, Benjamin, Mosiah, Alma[1], Alma[2], Helaman[2], Nephi[2], Nephi[3], Mormon, Moroni[2], the brother of Jared, and Ether in the Book of Mormon; and Joseph Smith, Sidney Rigdon, Oliver Cowdery, and Joseph F. Smith in the Doctrine and Covenants.[4]

In addition, the Lord has given a number of witnesses that teach that a testimony of Christ pervades all the scriptures. Here are a few examples:

> God . . . had shewed by the mouth of all his prophets, that Christ should suffer. (Acts 3:18)

> There came many to him [Paul] into his lodging; to whom he expounded and testified the kingdom of God, persuading them concerning Jesus, both out of the law of Moses, and out of the prophets. (Acts 28:23)

> I . . . came not with excellency of speech or of wisdom, declaring unto you the testimony of God. For I determined not to know any thing among you, save Jesus Christ, and him crucified. (1 Cor. 2:1–2)

> We labor diligently to write, to persuade our children, and also our brethren, to believe in Christ, and to be reconciled to God; for we know that it is by grace that we are saved, after all we can do. . . . And we are made alive in Christ because of our faith. . . . And we talk of Christ, we rejoice in Christ, we preach of Christ, we prophesy of Christ, and we write according to our prophecies, that our children may know to what source they may look for a remission of their sins. (2 Ne. 25:23, 25, 26)

We knew of Christ, and we had a hope of his glory many hundred years before his coming; and not only we ourselves had a hope of his glory, but also all the holy prophets which were before us. (Jacob 4:4)

None of the prophets have written, nor prophesied, save they have spoken concerning this Christ. (Jacob 7:11)

Did not Moses prophesy unto them concerning the coming of the Messiah, and that God should redeem his people? Yea, and even all the prophets who have prophesied ever since the world began—have they not spoken more or less concerning these things? (Mosiah 13:33)

Yea, did [Moses] not bear record that the Son of God should come? And as he lifted up the brazen serpent in the wilderness, even so shall he be lifted up who should come. . . . And now behold, Moses did not only testify of these things, but also all the holy prophets, from his days even to the days of Abraham. . . .

And now I would that ye should know, that even since the days of Abraham there have been many prophets that have testified these things. . . . But behold, this is not all—our father Lehi . . . [and] Nephi also testified of these things, and also almost all of our fathers, even down to this time; yea, they have testified of the coming of Christ, and have looked forward, and have rejoiced in his day which is to come. (Hel. 8:14, 16, 19, 21, 22)

All those from the beginning . . . who believed in the words of the holy prophets, who spake as they were inspired by the gift of the Holy Ghost, who truly testified of him in all things, should have eternal life. (D&C 20:26)

Jesus himself bore testimony that the scriptures consistently taught of him and his atonement:

O fools, and slow of heart to believe all that the prophets have spoken: Ought not Christ to have suffered these things, and to enter into his glory?

And beginning at Moses and all the prophets, he expounded

unto them in all the scriptures the things concerning himself. (Luke 24:25–27)

Search the scriptures; for . . . they are they which testify of me. (John 5:39)

Behold, I am Jesus Christ, whom the prophets testified shall come into the world. (3 Ne. 11:9–10)

## Jesus' Testimonies of Himself

Here is a final example of the pattern wherein the scriptures point to the atonement: the mortal Jesus bore plain testimony of himself a number of times. (The resurrected Jesus has likewise borne such a testimony countless times; for examples, see the opening verses of many of the sections of the Doctrine and Covenants.) One powerful form of that testimony comes in the "I am" statements of Jesus, found in the Gospels of John and Mark:

I am the living bread which came down from heaven: if any man eat of this bread, he shall live for ever. (John 6:51)

I am the light of the world: he that followeth me shall not walk in darkness, but shall have the light of life. (John 8:12)

Ye are from beneath; I am from above: ye are of this world; I am not of this world. . . . If ye believe not that I am he, ye shall die in your sins. . . . When ye have lifted up the Son of man, then shall ye know that I am he, and that I do nothing of myself; but as my Father hath taught me, I speak these things. (John 8:23–28)

I am the door: by me if any man enter in, he shall be saved, and shall go in and out, and find pasture. (John 10:9)

I am the good shepherd: the good shepherd giveth his life for the sheep. (John 10:11)

Say ye of him, whom the Father hath sanctified, and sent into the world, Thou blasphemest; because I said, I am the Son of God? (John 10:36)

I am the resurrection, and the life: he that believeth in me, though he were dead, yet shall he live. (John 11:25)

I am the way, the truth, and the life: no man cometh unto the Father, but by me. (John 14:6)

I am the true vine, and my Father is the husbandman. (John 15:1)

Then said the chief priests of the Jews to Pilate . . . that he said, I am King of the Jews. (John 19:21)

The high priest asked him, . . . Art thou the Christ, the Son of the Blessed? And Jesus said, I am: and ye shall see the Son of man sitting on the right hand of power, and coming in the clouds of heaven. (Mark 14:61–62)

Jesus' witnesses of himself clearly point to his atonement: the living bread that enables us to "live for ever"; the one who can help us avoid dying in our sins; the light of the world; the door to salvation; the good shepherd who gives his life for the sheep; the Son of God; the resurrection and the life; the way, the truth, and the life; the true vine; the source of life to the branches; "the Christ, the Son of the Blessed"; the true King of the Jews.

These testimonies reflect the truth of what the Father has proclaimed repeatedly in regard to Jesus Christ: "Behold my Beloved Son, in whom I am well pleased, in whom I have glorified my name" (3 Ne. 11:7; see also Matt. 3:17; 17:5; JS–H 1:17).

## CHAPTER 9

# From the Lost Sheep to the Unmerciful Servant: Parables of the Atonement

Jesus' parables have many levels of meaning. On the surface they often tell a simple story of life in the time of Christ. On the next level many parables encourage us in our relationships with one another. But on the highest level, many parables bear testimony of Jesus Christ as our Savior and Redeemer.

Some of the parables teach important truths about the atonement. These include the parables of the lost sheep, the lost coin, the lost son (typically called the prodigal son), the laborers in the vineyard, the unmerciful servant, the good Samaritan, the wicked husbandmen, the ten virgins, and the wedding supper. As we read these parables with the atonement in mind, our understanding of Christ's love and sacrifice increases, as does our sense of his outreach to those who have fallen far from the Father but can still return by coming unto Christ and partaking of his grace.[1]

The parable of the laborers in the vineyard (Matt. 20:1–16), for example, teaches that the Lord is merciful whenever we come unto him and give ourselves to his service. It also teaches that we receive a full and sufficient reward at the end, not through our efforts but through the goodness of his grace. His mercy and his grace, of course, are available because of the atonement.

The parable of the wicked husbandmen (Matt. 21:33–41) is clearly about the sacrifice Christ would make when he came to earth representing the Father. Knowing what awaited him here, he still came down, where he fell into the hands of wicked men, who "caught him, and cast him out of the vineyard, and slew him" (Matt. 21:39).

The parable of the ten virgins (Matt. 25:1–13), among other things, testifies of our opportunity to be united to Christ, the Bridegroom, through his atonement.

Let's look at four parables in detail to see what they teach us of Jesus Christ and his atonement. (Remember, however, that each parable can have multiple meanings.)

## The Lost Sheep

This well-loved parable was taught twice—in Capernaum (Matt. 18:12–14) and in Perea (Luke 15:3–7). The story is simple: a man had one hundred sheep, but one became lost. The shepherd left the ninety-nine and went into the wilderness to find the single lost sheep (JST Luke 15:4). "And when he hath found it, he layeth it on his shoulders, rejoicing" (Luke 15:5). In giving the moral to the story, Jesus explicitly related it to those who have strayed through sin: "Likewise joy shall be in heaven over one sinner that repenteth" (Luke 15:7).

The metaphor of people as sheep and God as the shepherd would have been familiar to Jesus' listeners. It had been used earlier by Ezekiel: "Thus saith the Lord God; Behold, I, even I, will both search my sheep, and seek them out. As a shepherd seeketh out his flock in the day that he is among his sheep that are scattered; so will I seek out my sheep, and will deliver them out of all places where they have been scattered in the cloudy and dark day. . . . I will seek that which was lost, and bring again that which was driven away" (Ezek. 34:11–13, 16). They also would have known the beautiful psalm, "The Lord is my shepherd; I shall not want. He maketh me to lie down in green pastures: he leadeth me beside the still waters. He restoreth my soul." Twice the Psalmist says, "He leadeth me." And he says of the shepherd, "Thou art with me" (Ps. 23:1–4).

One hundred is a large flock—the loss of one sheep may not be important economically—but each one is important to the shepherd. Since this is a good shepherd, he surely leaves the ninety-nine in a safe condition—in a cave or under the care of another shepherd—and goes out looking. How long does he search? Until he finds the missing sheep. When he finds it, the shepherd physically carries it to safety. As Isaiah wrote, "He shall feed his flock like a shepherd: he shall gather the lambs with his arm, and carry them in his bosom, and shall gently lead those that are with young" (Isa. 40:11).

As we apply this parable to an understanding of the atonement, we can consider that each of us, at times, is the lost sheep, and each of us needs the Good Shepherd. Elder Bruce C. Hafen wrote with powerful insight:

> The lost sheep are not just the people who don't come to church. . . . The lost sheep is a mother who goes down into the valley of the dark shadows to bring forth children. The lost sheep is a young person, far away from home and faced with loneliness and temptation. The lost sheep is a person who has just lost a critically needed job; a business person in financial distress; a new missionary in a foreign culture; a man just called to be bishop; a married couple who are misunderstanding each other; a grandmother whose children are forgetting her. I am the lost sheep. You are the lost sheep. "*All* we like sheep have gone astray." (Isaiah 53:6; emphasis added.)[2]

Jesus often personally sought out the lost sheep, reaching out to those in need of blessing, help, and repentance. The Gospel of Luke records many instances of his selfless ministry (see, for example, Luke 5:29–32; 7:36–50; 17:11–19; 19:1–9). And even now he reaches out to each one of us, never failing in his desire to bless and help each one of us. When we hearken to his voice and turn more fully to him, we can be the fulfillment of what Peter said: "Ye were as sheep going astray; but are now returned unto the Shepherd and Bishop of your souls" (1 Pet. 2:25).

In the Gospel of John, Jesus teaches more about the love of the Good Shepherd for his flock. "I am the good shepherd," he said. "The good shepherd giveth his life for the sheep. . . . I am the good shepherd, and know my sheep, and am known of mine. . . . And I lay down my life for the sheep" (John 10:11–15).

If we are the true flock of Christ, we will know him. We will "follow him," and we will "know his voice" (John 10:4). We will seek with all our hearts to be with him, to set aside our sins and weaknesses, to love him with our whole souls. Then, as members of the true flock, we will receive even greater blessings from the atonement.

## THE PRODIGAL SON

This parable tells about a man who had two sons. The younger of the two asked for his inheritance, which he took and went "into a far country," where he "wasted it" with "riotous living." After his money was gone, a great famine occurred in the land, and the younger son didn't even have enough to eat. He finally got work feeding swine—but he noticed that even the swine had more to eat than he did. "He came to himself" and said, "I will arise and go to my father, and will say unto him, Father, I have sinned against heaven, and before thee, and am no more worthy to be called thy son: make me as one of thy hired servants."

> And he arose, and came to his father. But when he was yet a great way off, his father saw him, and had compassion, and ran, and fell on his neck, and kissed him.
>
> And . . . the father said to his servants, Bring forth the best robe, and put it on him; and put a ring on his hand, and shoes on his feet: and bring hither the fatted calf, and kill it; and let us eat, and be merry: for this my son was dead, and is alive again; he was lost, and is found. (Luke 15:17–24)

We know that in the story the older son became angry at the rejoicing for the return of his wayward brother.

This parable brings together many principles related to the

116

atonement: repentance, confession, forgiveness, and (to a degree) restoration of blessings. President Gordon B. Hinckley, then a member of the Quorum of the Twelve, said of this parable: "I ask you to read that story. . . . It is large enough to encompass . . . all mankind, for are we not all prodigal sons and daughters who need to repent and partake of the forgiving mercy of our Heavenly Father and then follow his counsel?"[3]

In one interpretation, the father in the parable represents our Heavenly Father. The younger son represents each of us when we stray. The older son represents us when we need to set aside our pride and self-righteousness and accept the repentance of others with joy.

Many of the phrases in the parable teach truths about the atonement: the "far country" can signify our distancing ourselves from God; the "mighty famine" can represent a spiritual famine, where we lack the Spirit and the word of God; the confession of sin to the father can represent our confession to God; the return to the father can symbolize our return to the Father; and the father's compassion can teach us of God's pure love for us.

The best robe, the ring, and the shoes also have important symbolism: In a spiritual sense, the best robe can represent the white robe of righteousness through Christ, or the robes of the priesthood. The ring, likely a signet ring, was a sign of authority. Shoes, or sandals, indicated that the wearer was a free man, rather than a slave. Together, the robe, the ring, and the shoes stood as clear symbols of the young man's restored position. The son came home asking to be a lowly servant. In response, the father accepted him fully as a son, as well as an honored guest, one given significant authority.

The father observed, "For this my son was dead, and is alive again; he was lost, and is found" (Luke 15:24). Obviously the son was not physically dead, but he had become dead to Christ. Paul used this image when he wrote to the Ephesians: "And you hath he quickened, who were dead in trespasses and sins. . . . Even when we were dead in sins, [God] hath quickened us together with Christ . . . and hath raised us up together" (Eph. 2:1, 5–6).

Paul is saying here that when we sin, we become dead in the ways that matter most—for the dead in the body can still live in God, but the spiritually dead remain so regardless of what sphere they dwell in. But when we repent, we are renewed and revitalized. It is as though we were raised from the dead, resurrected in our spiritual being. The father of the prodigal son understood these things, and he rejoiced that the son who was dead had come to an awareness of his sins and, repentant, had come home, not only to the father's estate but also to God.

The elder son also was in need of repentance. In his pride and self-righteousness, he became angry and refused to join the group in their rejoicing. He protested that he was without fault and essentially accused his father of ingratitude. Of course, in our relationship with our Heavenly Father, none of us is without sin. President Howard W. Hunter taught that both sons had a lesson to learn: "Both brothers in the parable desperately need the Lord to free them of their burdens. This is the message of the parable.

"We learn from this parable that all of us, regardless of our status or condition, have an absolute need of the Lord's saving grace."[4]

The father's response to his son's appearance on the horizon is a marvelous manifestation of grace, demonstrating the goodness of God toward us. He waits and watches as we walk a path of sin, yearning for us to return. When we do, he sees us even when we are a long ways off, and he meets us with an embrace of pure love (2 Ne. 1:15; Morm. 5:11).

This parable emphasizes the power of God's forgiveness, as well as the joy experienced by God and all those who love him when a sinner repents and returns to the path of righteousness. In all cases, God feels the loss deeply, and when he who is lost "comes to himself" and returns, the rich blessings of the atonement are abundantly bestowed on him.

## THE GOOD SAMARITAN

The parable of the good Samaritan is a remarkable story of love for a neighbor in need. But in a significant way it also tells us about the love of Christ and his power to bless us through his atonement.

Jesus began the parable with these familiar words: "A certain man went down from Jerusalem to Jericho, and fell among thieves, which stripped him of his raiment, and wounded him, and departed, leaving him half dead."

Jerusalem was one of the highest points in ancient Israel, and Jericho was the lowest. We also have come down from heaven to earth, and we've fallen among enemies and trials here on earth. They have stripped us of our glory and wounded our spirits.

We know that in the parable a priest and a Levite saw the man's plight but passed him by. But then "a certain Samaritan, as he journeyed, came where [the wounded man] was: and when he saw him, he had compassion on him."

Christ has come on the same journey as we have, and he comes to where we are. When he sees our wounds, his heart is filled with love and compassion.

"And [the Samaritan] went to him, and bound up his wounds, pouring in oil and wine, and set him on his own beast, and brought him to an inn, and took care of him."

So also does Christ come to us and bind up our wounds, applying the astringent qualities of wine, representing repentance (and the blood of Christ), and the soothing qualities of oil, representing the atonement, which took place in a garden that produced olive oil. He carries us and takes us to a place of safety and cares for us.

"And on the morrow when he departed, he took out two pence, and gave them to the host, and said unto him, Take care of him; and whatsoever thou spendest more, when I come again, I will repay thee" (Luke 10:30–35).

Christ pays the price of our healing—whatever is required, he will pay.

## THE UNMERCIFUL SERVANT

This parable teaches that we must forgive one another if we hope to be forgiven by the Lord. But also, significantly, it emphasizes what it costs the Lord to forgive us.

In this parable, a king called in a servant to give an accounting of his stewardship. The servant owed ten thousand talents and could not pay. The king had the man bound and was prepared to sell him and his family as slaves to punish him for not paying his debt. The man pleaded for mercy and said he would pay. In a surprising turn of events, the king forgave the entire debt and set the man free.

Shortly thereafter, the servant met another man who owed him the relatively small amount of one hundred pence. The servant took the other man by the throat and demanded payment. His debtor pleaded for mercy, but the servant had the man cast into prison until he could pay the debt.

When the king learned what the servant had done, he was furious. "He delivered him to the tormentors, till he should pay all that was due unto him" (Matt. 18:34).

The message about forgiving one another is clear. But what does this teach us about the atonement?

In one interpretation of the story, we can consider the king as God and the servants as God's children. God requires all of us to give an accounting of our stewardships.

The servant in the parable owed ten thousand talents. This was an astronomical figure. One denarius was a day's wage for a common laborer, and it took ten thousand denarii to equal one talent. Thus, if a common laborer worked all year, taking only the Sabbath and a few holidays off, and if he saved all his money, it would take him thirty-three years to purchase *one* talent. It would take more than three hundred thousand years to purchase ten thousand talents.

For context, a year's combined taxes paid to Herod the Great by all of Judea, Idumea, Samaria, Galilee, and Perea in the year of his death (4 B.C.) came to only eight hundred talents.

How could the servant have accumulated so much debt? The answer is that it would not be possible—if we are talking about earthly debt. But the Lord intended us to see beyond the earthly example to the heavenly truth. Our debt to God is beyond measure and really beyond all reckoning.

In the parable, the king did the unexpected: he had compassion on the servant. (In the Greek, the word used means *godly compassion*.) In boundless and incomprehensible mercy, the king forgave the entire debt.

In his infinite love, our Heavenly Father is like the king in the parable. When we plead unto him, asking for mercy, he is "moved with compassion." He looses us from the bonds that hold us down and forgives us our great debt.

This parable teaches in a powerful way the goodness of God. We owe him everything we are, everything we have. King Benjamin put this beautifully: "In the first place, he hath created you, and granted unto you your lives, for which ye are indebted unto him. And secondly, he doth require that ye should do as he hath commanded you; for which if ye do, he doth immediately bless you; and therefore he hath paid you. And ye are still indebted unto him, and are, and will be, forever and ever" (Mosiah 2:23–24).

But beyond our temporal existence, we owe him our spiritual lives. Our Savior made the ultimate sacrifice to enable us to repent and be cleansed of our sins. When he forgives us of our wrongdoing, it is not a light thing for him. He paid a terrible price to atone for us. Yet he still forgives us freely when we repent with honest hearts. His forgiveness comes again and again. As imperfect as we are, he still reaches out to us—seven times, seventy times, seventy times seven times, an infinity of goodness.

If we come unto Christ with all our hearts; if we repent, receive the ordinances, and keep our covenants; and if we forgive others of their offenses against us, we place ourselves into the hands of Jesus Christ. We thereby come unto the "throne of grace" (Heb. 4:16) and receive the gifts and blessings of the atonement. Christ then pays "all that [is] due" on our account. But if we reject Christ and his commandments, and if we refuse to grant mercy to others around us, we are denied those blessings that could have been ours. As the Lord said through Joseph Smith: "Every man must repent or suffer. . . . Wherefore, I revoke not the judgments which I shall pass, but woes shall go forth, weeping, wailing, and gnashing of teeth. . . . If they would not repent they must suffer even as I" (D&C 19:4–5, 17).

CHAPTER 10

# ANGELS' FOOD, SCARLET, AND ALMONDS: THINGS THAT BEAR WITNESS OF CHRIST

IN THE WORDS OF PRESIDENT JOHN TAYLOR, "[There] were so many types, shadows and forms of which [Jesus] was the great prototype— the substance, the reality prefigured and foreshadowed by the other sacrifices which had been offered up from the beginning."[1] The scriptures present hundreds and perhaps thousands of types and shadows that prophesy of Jesus Christ, and certainly he is the chief focus of all scripture. As cited earlier, Moses 6:63 reveals that "all things bear record" of Jesus Christ, and Nephi testified that "all things which have been given of God from the beginning of the world, unto man, are the typifying of him [Christ]" (2 Ne. 11:4; see also Alma 34:14).

In presenting truths about Jesus, the prophets used a great number of symbols to provide insight into his life, mission, character, and atonement. They drew on the natural world, things in the heavens, the ancient Israelite temple and its components, places, cities, the cosmos, clothing, colors, liquids, numbers, rites of passage, foods, sacred vestments, plants, the animal kingdom, civil and religious positions, building and architectural components, various people, prophets, priests, and kings, historical events, animals, and many other things. All parts of the law of Moses—every particle—testified of Jesus and his sacrifice. As Amulek taught, "And behold, this is the whole meaning of the law [of Moses], every whit pointing to that great and last sacrifice; and that great and last sacrifice will be the Son of God" (Alma 34:14).

To provide a comprehensive treatment of all of the scriptural types and shadows that pertain to Jesus Christ would fill volumes. This chapter will deal with only a few—food (manna), the temple and its components, the seven cities of refuge, the colors white, red, scarlet, crimson, and the high priest's ephod. After dealing with these types, we will present a table that lists other types that pertain to one degree or another to the atonement.

## MANNA—ANGELS' FOOD, A SYMBOL OF JESUS, WHO IS THE BREAD OF LIFE

During the biblical period, a number of foods and liquids served as symbols that teach us about Jesus and his atonement, especially manna, which was the food that God provided for his people while they wandered in the wilderness. The children of Israel first received manna after they complained that they missed the fleshpots and bread of Egypt, at which point the Lord told Moses that he would "rain bread from heaven" (Ex. 16:4). This blessing from God was fulfilled when God "commanded the clouds from above, and opened the doors of heaven, and had rained down manna upon them to eat" (Ps. 78:23–24). "Manna" was also called "the corn of heaven," "angels' food" (Ps. 78:24–25), and "bread" (Ex. 16:15), and Exodus 16:31 describes manna as being "like coriander seed, white; and the taste of it was like wafers made with honey." God fed Israel this special bread for forty years (Ex. 16:35; Deut. 8:2–3); forty is a length of time that symbolizes a period of probation, testing, and tribulation (Gen. 7:4; Ex. 16:35; 24:18; Num. 14:33–34; 1 Kgs. 19:8; Ezek. 4:6; Matt. 4:2; Luke 4:2).[2] The manna ceased the day after the Israelites partook of grain in the promised land (Josh. 5:12), but to commemorate manna's significance to God's people, a jar of manna was kept in the ark of the covenant (Ex. 16:32–34; Heb. 9:4).

Manna is a powerful symbol of Jesus Christ, who is "the living bread" (John 6:51).[3] In the New Testament, when Jesus fed bread and fish to five thousand people near the Sea of Galilee, he referred to both manna *and* bread, saying: "I am the bread of life: he that cometh to me shall never hunger. . . . I am that bread of life. Your fathers did eat manna in the wilderness, and are dead. This is the bread which cometh down from heaven, that a man may eat thereof, and not die. I am the living bread which came down from heaven: if any man eat of this bread, he shall live for ever: and the bread that I will give is my flesh, which I will give for the life of the world" (John 6:35–51).

The chart below demonstrates various ways in which manna served as a type and shadow of Jesus Christ and his atoning sacrifice.

| **Manna** | **Jesus Christ** |
| --- | --- |
| God called the manna "bread" (Ex. 16:12, cf. v. 15). | Jesus called himself the "true bread," the "bread of life," and the "living bread" (John 6:32, 48, 51). |
| Manna provided the Israelites with temporal life (Ex. 16:11–35). | Jesus, the living bread, provides persons with eternal life: "I am the living bread . . . if any man eat of this bread, he shall live for ever" (John 6:51). |
| Manna was the bread that rained from heaven (Ex. 16:4). | Jesus came down from heaven" (John 6:38), and he is "the bread of God . . . which cometh down from heaven" (John 6:50; see also v. 33). |
| Manna was a gift from the Lord. "This is the bread which the Lord hath given you to eat" (Ex. 16:15). | "The gift of God is eternal life through Jesus Christ our Lord" (Rom. 6:23; D&C 14:7). |
| There was enough manna to fill every person: "They gathered every man according to his eating" (Ex. 16:16–18). | The atonement of Jesus Christ is infinite, sufficient to cover all of God's children, and fills those who are spiritually hungry: "I am the bread of life; he that cometh to me shall never hunger" (John 6:35). |

| Manna | Jesus Christ |
|---|---|
| Manna was undeserved. The Lord said, "I have heard the murmurings of the children of Israel: . . . at even ye shall eat flesh, and in the morning ye shall be filled with bread" (Ex. 16:12). | Jesus died for undeserving sinners: "For when we were yet without strength, in due time Christ died for the ungodly. . . . while we were yet sinners, Christ died for us" (Rom. 5:6, 8). |
| God commanded every man to gather manna. "This is the thing which the Lord hath commanded, Gather of it every man according to his eating" (Ex. 16:16). | Jesus commands his followers to partake of his flesh and blood through sacramental symbols (Matt. 26:26–27). |
| Those who overcome the world will be given "to eat of the hidden manna" (Rev. 2:17). | Jesus, the "living bread," is "hidden," or unknown, to the wicked but revealed to the righteous. |

## THE TEMPLE AND ITS COMPONENTS

Various components of the tabernacle foreshadow aspects of Jesus Christ's divine ministry and atoning sacrifice. These components include the tabernacle furniture (laver of brass, altars, lampstand, mercy seat), sacrifices, foods (shewbread), sacred objects (jar of manna, two tablets of stone, rod of Aaron), and various parts of the tabernacle (veil, horns of the altar). The rituals and performances (anointings, washings, sprinkling of blood, laying on of hands) also typified Jesus Christ and his mission, and even the tabernacle itself represented Christ's body, which is the "true tabernacle" (Heb. 8:2), the "sanctuary" (Ezek. 11:16), the "temple" (John 2:19–21), and the "dwelling place" (Ps. 90:1).

The components of the tabernacle and ancient Israelite temples that signified an aspect of Jesus Christ's atonement include the following:[4]

*Altar of incense.* Located directly in front of the temple's veil, the altar of incense specified that prayer (represented by incense) and Christ (represented by the veil) be the mediators by which one can approach God in the holy of holies (Ex. 30:1–10). The high priest burned incense on this altar twice daily, and once a year he was commanded to "make an atonement upon the horns . . . with the blood of the sin offering" (Ex. 30:7–10).

*Altar, sacrificial.* The sacrificial altar was an important place of atonement and was associated with blood sacrifices of various kinds, which pointed forward to Jesus Christ, the ultimate and infinite sacrifice. The high priest placed the blood of the bullock and goat upon the altar's horns to "make an atonement for the holy place" because of Israel's uncleanness (Lev. 16:16; see also vv. 27, 33). This act of atonement was so potent that it rendered the altar "most holy," to the point that the altar itself could convey holiness to whatever or whoever touched it: "Whatsoever toucheth the altar shall be holy" (Ex. 29:36–37).

*Horns of altar.* The horns represent power and strength (1 Sam. 2:10; Jer. 48:25; Ps. 75:10) or God's power to bring forth salvation. Also, in 2 Samuel, David calls the Lord "the horn of . . . salvation" (2 Sam. 22:3), a possible reference to the horns of the altar, whereon was placed the blood of the sin offering (Ex. 29:12).

*Lampstand.* The lampstand was located in the temple's holy place. Various parts of the lamp revealed Jesus: olive oil pointed to Christ, who is the Anointed One; light symbolized Jesus, who is the light of the world (John 1:9; 8:12); the seven branches of the lampstand formed a tree, representing Jesus as the tree of life; and "seven" signified perfection, pointing to Jesus' perfection. The lampstand was designed to represent an almond tree and had all the stages of an almond tree at once—buds, blossoms, flowers, and fruit (Ex. 25:31–39). This symbolized Jesus' miraculous power to give immortality and eternal life through the atonement.

*Laver of brass.* The laver was used for ablutions, or ritual washings (Ex. 30:18; Heb. 9:10; D&C 124:37). These washings symbolized the cleansing of the soul from sin and iniquity through the power of the atonement (cf. Eph. 5:26; Isa. 4:4).

*Manna, jar of.* The jar of manna was kept in the ark of the covenant. Manna, which saved the children of Israel temporally, represented Jesus Christ, the "living bread," who saves his people with mortality and eternal life (John 6:48–51).

*Mercy seat.* The mercy seat (part of the ark of the covenant), or the Lord's throne of atonement (Hebrew *capporet*), was a focal point of atonement and kingship. The throne resided in the holy of holies of the tabernacle and later Solomon's temple; it was constructed according to the Lord's command and instructions (Ex. 25:1–22); it housed the tablets of the law, a jar of manna, and Aaron's rod (Heb. 9:4); and it served as a meeting place between God and his prophet (Ex. 25:22; Num. 7:89). It was most holy, and the Lord punished those who trespassed against it (1 Sam. 6:19; 2 Sam. 6:6–7). The high priest sprinkled blood on the mercy seat on the Day of Atonement (Lev. 16:14–15). All of these factors regarding the mercy seat inform us regarding Jesus and his atonement.

*Rod of Aaron.* Aaron's rod was powerful and miraculous; at one point it became a serpent, which swallowed the Egyptian magicians' serpents; and later Aaron stretched out the rod and caused the waters to become blood (Ex. 4:2–4; 7:9–20). These miracles symbolize the power of Jesus Christ. On one occasion the rod "brought forth buds, and bloomed blossoms, and yielded almonds" (Num. 17:2–10). The Hebrew word for almond and almond tree is *shaked,* which denotes to wake up early, and the almond tree is "so called from its early waking out of winter's sleep."[5] In Israel, the almond tree buds and blossoms early in the season. As an almond tree, Aaron's rod symbolizes that Jesus Christ was the first to awaken at the resurrection; just as Aaron's rod budded and blossomed, and as the almond tree "wakes up early" in the spring, even so Jesus, as the firstfruits, woke up early in the resurrection. The rod was stored in the ark of the covenant with the tablets and jar of manna.

*Shewbread.* Shewbread (from the Hebrew) literally means "bread of the face" or "bread of the presence," referring to God's face or presence. The bread, eaten by the priests (Lev. 24:9), anticipated the emblems of the Lord's sacrament.

*Tabernacle.* Many scriptures testify that the tabernacle itself, and later the temple building of Jerusalem, also served as types of Jesus

Christ and his body. In Ezekiel the Lord told the Jews, who were scattered among the nations, that he would be "as a little sanctuary" to them (11:16). The Psalmist records Moses' prayer: "Lord, thou hast been our dwelling place in all generations" (Ps. 90:1). In his epistle to the Hebrews, Paul called Jesus "a greater and more perfect tabernacle" (Heb. 9:11). And the Lord compared himself to the temple when he said, "Destroy this temple, and in three days I will raise it up." The Jews, who thought that he referred to the temple of Herod, responded, "Forty and six years was this temple in building, and wilt thou rear it up in three days? But he spake of the temple of his body" (John 2:19–22). Jesus' resurrected body became a new and perfect tabernacle.

*Veil.* The temple veil that separated the holy place from the holy of holies symbolizes Jesus Christ's flesh (Heb. 9:3; 10:19–20). In other words, the veil, meaning the Lord, stands between humans and their entrance into the temple's holiest place (representing the celestial kingdom).

## THE SEVEN CITIES OF REFUGE

Another symbolic part of the law of Moses was the seven cities of refuge, which had to do with the law pertaining to a person who accidentally killed someone else (Num. 35:9–34). The law stated that if a person accidentally killed another, then he (the killer) was required to flee to one of the cities of refuge before the "revenger of blood" (Hebrew: "redeemer of blood")—or the next of kin for the one who was killed—caught him. After the accidental killer fled to a city of refuge, he had to remain there until the death of the high priest (the anointed high priest who served in the temple). If the accidental killer exited the city of refuge before the death of the high priest "and the revenger of blood find him without the borders of the city of his refuge, and the revenger of blood kill the slayer; he shall not be guilty of blood" (Num. 35:27). There were seven cities of refuge. Six—Kedesh, Shechem, Kirjath-arba, Bezer, Ramoth, and Golan—were strategically positioned in ancient Palestine, with three on the east and three on the west. Jerusalem was the seventh city because it housed the great temple, which signified the quintessential place of refuge. If someone accidentally slew another, he could flee to one of the six cities or to the temple's altar of sacrifice and grasp one of its altars, thus seeking asylum from the redeemer of blood (1 Kgs. 1:49–53; 2:28–34).

Three aspects of the laws of the cities of refuge have symbolisms that point to Jesus Christ and his atonement.

1. *The redeemer of blood.* It was the responsibility of the redeemer of blood to pursue and slay the person who accidentally killed the redeemer of blood's next of kin, therein cleansing the land of the blood that was shed. The Lord states that "blood it defileth the land: and the land cannot be cleansed of the blood that is shed therein, but by the blood of him that shed it. Defile not therefore the land which ye shall inhabit, wherein I dwell: for I the Lord dwell among the children of Israel" (Num. 35:33–34). The redeemer of blood foreshadowed Jesus Christ, who is the Great Redeemer. Both the redeemer of blood mentioned in Numbers 35 and the Great Redeemer administer justice; God administers perfect justice as the Redeemer of blood when he cleanses the land of its pollutions and defilements.

2. *Refuge.* The city of refuge symbolizes the Lord, who is our refuge from sin and from death. The scriptures identify the Lord as our refuge: "O Lord: I said, Thou art my refuge and my portion in the land of the living" (Ps. 142:5); "The eternal God is thy refuge" (Deut. 33:27); "The God of my rock; in him will I trust: he is my shield . . . my refuge, my Savior" (2 Sam. 22:3); "My refuge is in God" (Ps. 62:7); "God is our refuge" (Ps. 46:1).

Just as a person who accidentally killed another could flee for his life to one of the appointed cities of refuge—"that fleeing unto one of these cities he might live" (Deut. 4:42)—all of us may flee to the Lord Jesus from two of our greatest adversaries: sin and death. Through the power of Jesus' atonement, we can overcome sin and obtain forgiveness; we will also overcome death when we receive resurrected bodies. The apostle Paul summed up, saying we "have fled for refuge to lay hold upon the hope set before us" (Heb. 6:18); that hope is Jesus Christ (Heb. 6:19–20). In other words, we have fled to Jesus, who is our refuge, and laid hold upon the altar, that very sacred place of atonement in the temple.

3. *The high priest.* In the law of Moses, the person who accidentally slew another would remain in a city of refuge until the death of the reigning high priest, who was anointed with holy oil. That high priest typified Jesus, who is "the Apostle and High Priest of our profession" (Heb. 3:1). Similar to the high priest, Jesus was anointed with holy oil (*Messiah* [Hebrew] and *Christ* [Greek] mean "anointed one"). Just as the death of the ancient high priest freed the accidental killer from the confines of a city of refuge, allowing him to return to his homeland, so the death of Jesus Christ frees all humanity from the bondage of sin and death, allowing us to return to our heavenly homeland.

## WHITE, RED, SCARLET, AND CRIMSON

Four colors associated with the atonement are white, red, scarlet, and crimson. Although the last three colors are similar in appearance, especially when contrasted with white, there are subtle differences between the colors. Scarlet is a "brilliant red color," and crimson is a "rich, deep red color" that tends slightly to purple. The scriptures refer to all four colors with implicit or explicit references to Jesus Christ and the atonement. Red, scarlet, and crimson often signify Jesus Christ's blood, a reminder of the atonement.

The tabernacle of Moses, the focal point of sacrifice and atonement, had a number of red (or scarlet or crimson) components. This was not simply by coincidence or chance but by divine design. Worshippers who entered the tabernacle may have experienced visual magnificence as they viewed the colors of the various appurtenances. The courtyard gate's hanging, the door of the tent, the curtains of the tabernacle, and the veil that separated the holy of holies from the holy place were all made of finely twisted linen and embroidery in colors of blue, purple, and scarlet (Ex. 26:1, 31, 36; 36:8, 35, 37). Expert spinners, artisans, embroiderers, and weavers, or those "filled with wisdom of heart," made all of these appurtenances (Ex. 35:35). Further, the Lord commanded Moses, "Thou shalt make a covering for the tent of rams' skins dyed red" (Ex. 26:14).

The high priest's ephod was an elaborate and beautiful sacred vestment that also featured scarlet and other colors. To make the ephod, craftsmen first beat "gold into thin plates," then cut the gold into wires, and finally worked the gold wires in with blue, purple, and scarlet thread or yarn and fine linen (Ex. 39:3). Similarly, the ephod's girdle, the breastplate, and the hems of the robe each featured gold, blue, purple, and scarlet yarn together with fine linen (Ex. 39:5, 8, 24).

The colors red and scarlet figure prominently in the ceremony of the sacrifice of the red heifer. The law required the heifer to be red, the sacrifice of the heifer produced red blood, and the slaughtered beast was burned, together with hyssop, cedar wood, and scarlet wool (Num. 19:6, 18).

One of the most symbolic ceremonies in the law of Moses was the cleansing of lepers; this ceremony pertained to Jesus Christ and his atonement, as summarized in the following statement: "The priest shall make an atonement for him, and he shall be clean" (Lev. 14:20; see also 18–19, 29, 31). Scarlet was used in the ceremony, as well as two birds, cedar wood, hyssop, and blood (Lev. 14:4–6, 49–52).

Scarlet was also used in three unique Old Testament events. First, after teaching the Israelites the precepts of the law, Moses employed scarlet wool, together with calves' and goats' blood, water, and hyssop. In a sacred ceremony he sprinkled blood on the people, on the book of the law, and on the tabernacle and its vessels. Both the red blood and the scarlet wool had a part in this ceremony. After describing this event, Paul added these words: "And almost all things are by the law purged with blood; and without shedding of blood is no remission" (Heb. 9:18–22; see also Ex. 24:4–8).

The second unique event occurred when Tamar bore Zarah and Pharez; her midwife identified the firstborn son (Zarah) by placing a "scarlet thread upon his hand" (Gen. 38:28, 30). Pharez became a direct line ancestor of Jesus Christ (Matt. 1:3). Although we cannot be sure whether the scarlet thread had anything to do with Pharez's posterity, the event details an interesting use of this symbolic color.

The third unique event occurred when two Israelite spies instructed Rahab from Jericho to tie a scarlet thread in her window to signal to the Israelites to spare the lives of Rahab and her family (Josh. 2:18–20;

cf. Josh. 6:17–23). Once again, we cannot be sure of the role of the color scarlet in this story, but the scarlet thread may have somehow signaled deliverance to this family.

Another symbolic use of the color red can be seen in the robes of the Savior. Twice Jesus Christ is associated with wearing a red (or scarlet) robe. First, those who mocked him dressed him in a scarlet robe. Second, Jesus will wear a red robe at his second coming. Isaiah emphasized Jesus' red garments with these expressions: The Messiah "cometh from Edom" (*Edom* in Hebrew means *red*), has "dyed garments," will be "red in [his] apparel," and his "garments like him that treadeth in the winefat" (Isa. 63:1–2; D&C 133:46–48). Further, Jesus will announce that "I have trodden the winepress alone," "I will tread them in mine anger, and trample them in my fury" (thus making his garments red), and "their blood [referring to the wicked] shall be sprinkled upon my garments, and I will stain all my raiment" (Isa 63:3; D&C 133:50–51). John the Revelator referred to the Second Coming of Jesus when he wrote, "He was clothed with a vesture dipped in blood" (Rev. 19:13), and Elder Neal A. Maxwell noted that Jesus will be "attired in red apparel, reminding us whose blood redeemed us."[6]

The red clothing symbolizes at least three things: the blood Christ shed in performing the atonement (Luke 22:44; D&C 19:18); the blood (or sins) of the wicked that he took upon himself (blood and sins are equated in Jacob 1:19; see also 1 Pet. 3:18; Alma 33:22; 3 Ne. 11:11); and the blood of the unrepentant wicked he has slain in his wrath (Isa. 63:3; Lam. 1:15; D&C 133:48, 50–51).

The color white is also prominently associated with the atonement. The redeemed of the Lord will be dressed in white robes, which are made white through the Lamb's blood. In the book of Revelation, John states: "After this I beheld, and, lo, a great multitude, which no man could number, of all nations, and kindreds, and people, and tongues, stood before the throne, and before the Lamb, clothed with white robes, and palms in their hands; . . . And one of the elders answered, saying unto me, What are these which are arrayed in white robes? and whence came they? And I said unto him, Sir, thou knowest. And he said to me, These are they which came out of great tribulation, and have washed their robes, and made them white in the blood of the Lamb" (Rev. 7:9–14). The truth expressed in John's statement, "washed their robes, and made them white in the blood of the Lamb," is also found in the Book of Mormon (1 Ne. 12:10–11; Alma 5:21; Morm. 9:6). It is clear that the color white symbolizes purity and that a person's robes become pure and white only through that person's faith, faithfulness, and belief in Christ and his atoning sacrifice.

The symbolism of all four colors—white, red, scarlet, and crimson—is summarized in a single verse of Isaiah: "Though your sins be as scarlet, they shall be white as snow; though they be red like crimson, they shall be as wool" (Isa. 1:18). In this passage scarlet and crimson are both used to symbolize human blood, which in turn can signify iniquity. The Lord, through Isaiah, contrasts the bloodlike colors scarlet and crimson with two tangible materials, snow and wool, both of which are white and are therefore used to symbolize purity, innocence, and light.

## THE EPHOD, A HIGH PRIEST'S SACRED VESTMENT

In the setting of the ancient temple, priests put on sacred vestments to perform their rituals, sacrifices, and offerings. All eight pieces of the high priest's vestments—the headpiece, or "turban, bound cap" (footnote to Ex. 28:4), the sash, the tunic, and "undergarments of plain linen,"[7] the robe of the ephod, the breastplate, a golden plate of the headpiece (Ex. 28:6–30), and the ephod, or "special apron" (footnote to Ex. 39:2)—symbolize various aspects of the atonement. The ephod had attached to it the linen breastplate (Ex. 28:15–30), which bore twelve precious stones and the Urim and Thummim; also, two onyx stones were fastened to the shoulders of the vestment. Written upon the twelve precious stones and upon the two onyx stones were the names of the twelve tribes of Israel so that the high priest would "bear their names before the Lord upon his two shoulders" (Ex. 28:12).

"In two principal ways the ephod was a symbol of Christ. First, the Urim and Thummim (Hebrew for 'lights and perfections') represented the perfect Jesus, who, as the 'light of the world,' reveals his truths to the prophets. Second, the high priest (also a symbol of Christ) donned the ephod and entered the Holy of Holies to make atonement for the children of Israel [Christ also did this; Heb. 4:14; 9:24]. By having the names of the children of Israel twice attached to the ephod, the high priest (representing Christ) symbolically carried the twelve tribes into the holy of holies and there made atonement for them."[8]

## OTHER THINGS THAT BEAR WITNESS OF JESUS CHRIST

The following table lists various types and shadows, arranged alphabetically, that pertain to Jesus Christ and the atonement. Some of the listed items are directly associated with the atonement and others are marginally related. The list is representative and not comprehensive (for a discussion of things in the natural world that are types of Christ, see chapter 12).

| Symbol | Representation | Reference(s) |
|--------|---------------|--------------|
| Almond/almond tree | Almond and almond tree (Hebrew *shaked*) denotes "to wake up early" and symbolizes Jesus Christ (and his resurrection) as the first to awaken at the resurrection | Ex. 25:33–34; Num. 17:8; Jer. 1:11–12; 1 Cor. 15:20–23 |
| Baptism | Christ's death, burial, and resurrection | JST Gen. 17:5; Rom. 6:1–6 |
| Birth | Spiritual birth—blood, spirit, and water | Moses 6:59; Mosiah 5:7–8 |
| Blood | Sacrificial animal's blood anticipates Christ's; it is "blood that maketh an atonement for the soul" (Lev. 17:11) | John 6:54; Rom. 3:25; Heb. 9:14, 22; 13:12 |
| Blood upon the door at Passover | Lamb's blood provides temporal deliverance; Christ's blood provides spiritual deliverance | Ex. 12 |

| Symbol | Representation | Reference(s) |
|---|---|---|
| Blood, shedding of | The shedding of blood in animal sacrifices pointed to Christ's "atoning blood" (Mosiah 4:2) | Lev. 1–6 |
| Blood, washing when spilled on priest's garments | When sacrificial blood spilled on priest's garments, he was commanded to wash them in the temple; this symbolically anticipates the washing of our own garments "white through the blood of the Lamb" (Alma 13:11) | Lev. 6:27; 4:6, 17; Alma 5:21; 13:11; 3 Ne. 27:19 |
| Branch | A name of the Messiah, perhaps signifying a branch from the tree of life | Jer. 23:5–6; 33:15–17; Isa. 11:1–5 |
| Brazen serpent | A special object lesson that pertained to the lifting up of Jesus Christ on the cross | Num. 21:6–9; Hel. 8:14–15 |
| Cities of refuge | Christ signifies the "refuge," the "high priest," and the "avenger of blood" (Heb. "redeemer of blood") | Num. 35:6–34; Deut. 4:42; 33:17; Ps. 46:1; 62:7; Heb. 6:18 |
| Cornerstone | The Messiah is the "head stone of the corner," perhaps referring to the temple's cornerstone | Ps. 118:22; Matt. 21:42 |
| Cross | Christ was "lifted up on the cross and slain for the sins" (1 Ne. 11:33) | 1 Cor. 1:17; Philip. 3:18; Col. 1:20; Gal. 6:14; Heb. 12:2; 3 Ne. 27:14; D&C 138:35; Moses 7:55 |
| Cup, bitter | Jesus drank from the bitter cup during the work of the atonement | Matt. 26:39; 3 Ne. 11:11; D&C 19:18 |

| Symbol | Representation | Reference(s) |
|---|---|---|
| Day of Atonement | Sacrifices and symbols of this holy day held special significance to Christ's atoning sacrifice | Lev. 16; Heb. 7–9 |
| Door/gate | Jesus said, "I am the door: by me if any man enter in, he shall be saved" (John 10:9); Jesus is the "keeper of the gate" (2 Ne. 9:41) | John 10:7, 9; 2 Ne. 9:41 |
| Fire | The Lord is described as a "wall of fire," "consuming fire," and "refiner's fire." With fire he takes vengeance on the wicked; with fire he refines people. | Deut. 4:24; Zech. 2:5; Isa. 33:14; Mal. 3:2–3; Heb. 12:29; Isa. 66:15; 2 Thes. 1:7–8 |
| Fountain of water | The Lord is the "fountain of living waters" who gives life to people | Jer. 2:13; 17:13; see also Ezek. 36:24–25; Zech. 13:1 |
| Guide | God "will be our guide even unto death" | Ps. 48:14 |
| High priest | The high priest of ancient Israel served as a figure of the "High Priest of our profession, Christ Jesus" (Heb. 3:1; 4:14) | Lev. 21 |
| Horns of the altar | Representative of God's power to bring forth salvation | Ex. 29:12; 1 Sam. 2:10; 2 Sam. 22:3; Jer. 48:25; Ps. 75:10 |
| Incense | Aaron put fire from the altar on incense and made atonement for the people, thus halting a plague that killed 14,700 people | Num. 16:44–50 |

| Symbol | Representation | Reference(s) |
|---|---|---|
| Lamb | Signified Jesus, the lamb of God | Ex. 12:5; John 1:29; Moses 5:7 |
| Law of Moses | Various aspects of the law anticipated Christ's atonement | Gal. 3:24; Jacob 4:5; Mosiah 13:29–31; Alma 34:14 |
| Light | The Lord is the light of the world | Isa. 60:19; 3 Ne. 15:9 |
| Manna from heaven | Christ is the "true" and "living" bread from heaven | Ex. 16:11–35; John 6:32–57 |
| Mediator | Moses was the mediator of the first covenant, Christ of the second | JST Gal. 3:19–20; 1 Tim. 2:5 |
| Nail | Symbolized crucifixion and the nails that fixed Jesus to the cross | Isa. 22:20–25; Col. 2:14; Ezra 9:8 |
| Number One | One signifies unity; "that they may be one, even as we are one" (John 17:11, 21–22) | Gen. 2:24; Deut. 6:4; John. 10:16; Acts 4:32; 2 Cor. 13:11; D&C 38:27 |
| Number Seven | Seven denotes completeness, totality; connected to covenant making (Heb. root for *seven* [*sheva*] is same as Hebrew verb that means "to take an oath") | Ex. 12:15; 20:10; see also Lev. 13:21; 15:28; 25:4–5; Num. 23:1, 29; Deut. 16:13; Josh. 6:4–15; Matt. 18:21–22; Rev. 1:4, 12, 20; 5:5; 8:6; 15:1; 17:1; D&C 107:93. |
| Passover | Aspects of the Passover anticipated the sacrifice of Jesus Christ, who is "our Passover" | Ex. 12; 1 Cor. 5:7 |
| Plagues | The Messiah will destroy death at his resurrection; "O death, I will be thy plagues" | Hos. 13:14 |

| Symbol | Representation | Reference(s) |
|---|---|---|
| Priest | The office of a Levitical priest and the requirements placed on him anticipated Christ's atonement | Lev. 8:5–10; 9; 16; 17; 21:1, 16–23; Heb. 7:11–12, 21 |
| Purifier | As a goldsmith purifies gold, the Lord purifies souls | Mal. 3:3; 1 Pet. 1:22; Heb. 9:13–14 |
| Root | The Messiah has the qualities of a root, which gives life to the plant | Isa. 53:2; Rev. 22:16 |
| Sacrifices | Ancient sacrifices prefigured Christ's roles as offering, offerer, and priest | Lev. 1–7; Alma 34:13 |
| Sacrificial meal | The meal was eaten by the offerer and the priests in the temple; anticipated Christ's sacrifice, while the modern sacramental meal recalls it | Lev. 7:11–36 |
| Soap | The Lord is like fuller's soap | Mal. 3:2 |
| Temple | Jesus is our temple and "dwelling place" | Ps. 90:1; Isa. 8:14; Ezek. 11:16 |
| Veil of the temple | Represents Christ's flesh | Heb. 10:19–20 |
| Vestments, sacred | Various parts of the ancient priestly sacred vestments symbolize aspects of the atonement | Ex. 28:6–30 |
| Water | Jesus is the living water that saves Israel | Num. 20:7–11; John 4:10–14; Eph. 5:25–26 |
| Way | Jesus is the "way" to salvation | John 14:6 |
| Wine | Sacramental emblem that signifies Jesus' sacrifice | Moro. 5:2; D&C 20:79 |

## CHAPTER 11

# THE LION AND THE LAMB: THE ATONEMENT SYMBOLISM OF ANIMALS

A NUMBER OF ANIMALS—red heifers, rams and ewe lambs, he-goats and nanny goats, turtledoves, bulls, pigeons, and a bronze serpent—serve as symbols of Jesus Christ's atonement or sacrifice. The blood of the group of animals sacrificed in sacred ceremonies was shed in anticipation of Jesus' blood, which would flow in Gethsemane and on the cross. Female animals that were sacrificed had specific life-giving qualities that pointed to Jesus as the giver of immortality and eternal life; male animals had other qualities that served as types of Jesus. The animals' economic worth made them a sacrifice of value to Israelite households that offered them in sacred temples. None of these animals deserved to be slaughtered—meaning none of them had committed sins or transgressions that required their death. Rather, their innocence is symbolic of Jesus Christ's innocence, and their lack of blemishes pointed toward his perfection.

The bronze serpent belongs in a category of its own because it was not sacrificed like the lambs, bulls, goats, birds, and heifers. Its symbolism was unique in that it was lifted up on a pole as a prophecy that Jesus would be lifted up on the cross. This chapter will deal with all of these and other aspects of animals that are types and shadows of Jesus Christ's atonement (see also chapter 16, which, in part, deals with the atonement and the law of sacrifice).

## Sacrificial Animals Symbolize Jesus Christ's Atonement

Sacrificial animals died violent deaths in anticipation of Jesus' violent death on the cross. These animals were killed and gave up their lifeblood; the sacrifice of these animals anticipated Jesus' death and spilled blood. Whereas the animals' blood supported their physical life, Jesus' blood provides spiritual life for us. The violence associated with the animals' slaughter stood as a reminder that Jesus' death would be cruel and brutal.

Each of the sacrificial animals had characteristics that pointed to Christ.

*Lambs.* A lamb has qualities that typify Jesus and his great sacrifice. For example, a lamb signifies meekness, innocence, and submissiveness, qualities exhibited by Jesus during his trial only hours before his crucifixion. Once when Jesus approached John the Baptist, John pronounced these words: "Behold the lamb of God, which taketh away the sin of the world" (John 1:29). According to Isaiah's prophecy, Jesus was "brought as a lamb to the slaughter" (Isa. 53:7; Acts 8:32), meaning Jesus went to his death without resistance or protest.

The Passover lamb too anticipated Jesus' death. This lamb, like Jesus, was unblemished (Ex. 12:5; 1 Pet. 1:18–19), male (Ex. 12:5), did not experience broken bones at his death (Ex. 12:46; John 19:33), and made atonement for the people (Num. 28:22). The Passover lamb's blood saved ancient Israelites from physical death, and Christ's atoning blood saves souls from spiritual death (Ex. 12:13; Hel. 5:9). The lamb's meat was edible and clean according to Mosaic law, and the Israelites partook of it in anticipation of Jesus' broken flesh. In comparable ways, we now partake of sacramental bread in remembrance of his broken flesh.

*Bulls.* A fully grown bull, weighing about two thousand pounds, presents the image of great strength. One scriptural passage refers to the "strength of the ox" (Prov. 14:4), and others compare God's strength to that of a wild ox (NIV Num. 23:22; 24:8). To offer up one of these great bulls to the Lord was a sacrifice of great economic value because its hide, meat, and ability to produce offspring were surrendered at the time of its offering. Somewhat comparable to the bull with its unparalleled strength, Jesus Christ was omnipotent, or all-powerful, in his ability to work the atonement and provide eternal life to all who would follow him and keep his commandments.

*Turtledoves.* Ancient Israelites who lacked the economic means to offer a lamb as a sacrifice were permitted to offer a dove, a creature of lesser value. A dove, which belongs to the pigeon family, is known to be an affectionate bird, both to its mates and its offspring. In many cultures, in antiquity as well as in modern times, a dove is a symbol of peace. The correspondences between a dove and Jesus Christ are noteworthy—both spilled their blood when being offered up as sacrifices, and qualities of affection and peace are attributed to both. Jesus, of course, is called the Prince of Peace.

Beyond the lambs, bulls, and turtledoves, other sacrificial animals also possess qualities or attributes that pertain to Jesus Christ. Perhaps most important, these animals were all clean animals according to the law of Moses, and their blood looked forward to Jesus' atoning blood.

## SACRIFICED FEMALE ANIMALS WERE ALSO SYMBOLS OF CHRIST

*Ewe lambs.* Female lambs without blemish were sacrificed as symbols of Jesus Christ (Lev. 4:32; 14:10; Num. 6:14). Furthermore, in a prophecy about Jesus, Isaiah used the image of a female sheep, or ewe lamb (Hebrew *rachel*): "He was oppressed, and he was afflicted, yet he opened not his mouth: . . . and as a sheep before *her* shearers is dumb, so he openeth not his mouth" (Isa. 53:7; emphasis added). Isaiah's prophecy was precisely fulfilled during Jesus' trial when he appeared, first before Herod and later before Pilate. When Jesus stood before Herod, Luke records that Herod "questioned with him in many words; but [Jesus] answered him nothing" (Luke 23:9). And when Jesus appeared before Pilate, "the chief priests accused him of many things: but he answered nothing. And Pilate asked him again, saying, Answerest thou nothing? behold how many things they witness against thee. But Jesus yet answered nothing" (Mark 15:3–5). By answering nothing, Jesus fulfilled Isaiah's prophecy that "he openeth not his mouth."

Why were female lambs sacrificed to represent Jesus, who is a male? The answer pertains to the fact that ewes are the bearers of new life. They possess the capacity to give birth to one, two, or even more lambs at a time. Just as a ewe gives physical life, so Jesus gives spiritual life to his daughters and sons. "And now, because of the covenant which ye have made ye shall be called the children of Christ, his sons, and his daughters; for behold, this day he hath spiritually begotten you . . . ye are born of him and have become his sons and his daughters" (Mosiah 5:7).

*Female goats.* A goat is a ruminant mammal that has straight hair, usually has a beard, and often has hollow horns that curve backward. Goats are related to sheep but are frequently more aggressive, stronger, hardy, and lively. Goats eat vegetation, plants, leaves, flowers, fruits, and other foods. For a number of reasons, a female goat was highly prized by an Israelite family. By giving birth to two or three kids per year, she helped the family's economy by multiplying the herd's size. Further, she was of great value by providing milk (which was used to make various dairy products), wool, meat, leather, and fertilizer.

On certain occasions, God's law required the ritual sacrifice of female goats; Leviticus 4:28 refers to the offering of "a kid of the goats, a female without blemish." More important, however, this sacrifice was a type and shadow of Jesus Christ's divine sacrifice. Why a female goat? Perhaps to typify the Savior as a giver of life (see above).

*Red heifer.* The Lord revealed that the way to remove corpse defilement was through the sacrifice of a red heifer. A heifer is young female that has not given birth. Heifers can mate after they are about fifteen months old. The red heifer ceremony featured set prescriptions. The heifer had to be "without spot, wherein is no blemish, and upon which never came yoke" (Num. 19:2). The heifer was slaughtered and then burned, together with hyssop, cedar wood, and scarlet wool

(Num. 19:6, 18). Afterward, its ashes were placed in a vessel, and then fresh water (the Hebrew text reads literally "living water") was poured into the vessel over the ashes. This mixture of ashes and water constituted the water of cleansing that was sprinkled on obedient Israelites who had been defiled by the dead. God considered the purification rituals to be so vital to the Israelites that if the defiled person failed to adhere to the appropriate rituals that served to cleanse him, he would be cut off from the community because he defiled the sanctuary (Num. 19:13, 20).

There is much symbolism attached to the sacrifice of the red heifer. The ritual slaughter of a heifer is a genuine sacrifice of economic value because the heifer's owner gives up all the future benefits that this animal would yield—milk, calves, leather (for clothing and scrolls), and meat. More significant, the sacrifice of the heifer is symbolic of Jesus Christ's divine sacrifice; its blood points to Jesus' blood, and the fact that the heifer was a female and potential life-giver anticipates the life-giving force of Jesus' atonement. Two colors figure prominently in the ceremony: the *red* heifer and the *scarlet* wool. Both red and scarlet denote the color of blood, pointing to Jesus' blood. The symbolism of the water of cleansing pertains to the symbolic purification of the defiled person; just as water cleanses a person who has soiled hands, even so the water of cleansing ritually purifies the defiled soul.

In regard to the corpse itself, death pertains to lifelessness and the corruption of the physical body, both of which are opposite to God's eternal vitality and immortal life. Death, as the ultimate state of physical corruption, separates us from God. Further, humans are entirely helpless when it comes to sustaining their mortal lives beyond the natural processes of mortality. We must rely upon God for all things that sustain life, including oxygen, water, and food. To teach the principle that death stands opposite to God's immortality and eternal life, God revealed that a corpse communicates ritual defilement to the living (Num. 19). That is to say, according to God's law as revealed to Moses, when a person (male or female) touched a dead body, a human bone, or a grave, or whenever a person was in the presence of a dead body in a tent or a room, that person would be rendered ceremonially unclean (Num. 19).

This defilement often came about accidentally when one inadvertently walked on a grave or entered a room where someone had recently died; or the defilement sometimes came knowingly when family members prepared a loved one for burial, buried their dead, and so forth. Defilement also came during war. When the Israelites killed others or touched the slain, they were required to adhere to the red heifer rituals. For instance, Moses required Israelite combatants who battled the Midianites to follow the purification procedures before returning to camp (Num. 31:19–24).

There is yet another lesson attached to the laws associated with the red heifer and the dead. As we learned above, when a living person comes into contact with the dead through touching a corpse, bone, or grave, that living person is ritually defiled. The touching and subsequent defilement of the living recalls other scriptural passages about touching unclean things. For example, Paul warned the Corinthians to "touch not the unclean thing," a reference to idols (2 Cor. 6:17). Alma, the high priest, taught, "Come ye out from the wicked, and be ye separate, and touch not their unclean things" (Alma 5:57). Isaiah warned the righteous to "touch no unclean thing" (Isa. 52:11) and to "go ye out from Babylon" or "go ye out from among the nations, even from Babylon, from the midst of wickedness, which is spiritual Babylon" (D&C 133:5, 14; see also D&C 133:7; 38:42). The Lord through Moses commanded the Israelites not to touch the things of three wicked men—Korah, Dathan, and Abiram: Moses "spake unto the congregation, saying, Depart, I pray you, from the tents of these wicked men, and touch nothing of theirs, lest ye be consumed in all their sins" (Num. 16:26). In his revelation, John too heard a plea from heaven for God's people to come out of the wickedness of Babylon when he "heard another voice from heaven, saying, Come out of her, my people, that ye be not partakers of her sins, and that ye receive not of her plagues" (Rev. 18:4).

Just as the living are defiled by the dead, even so the living are defiled by the spiritually dead and by spiritually lifeless situations. Spiritual death surrounds us during mortality in this world, and it affects our innocence and virtue to the extent that we need Christ and his atonement to remove such defilements from our hearts and minds. Paul sums up: "The ashes of an heifer sprinkling the unclean, sanctifieth to the purifying of the flesh: How much more shall the blood of Christ, who through the eternal Spirit offered himself without spot to God, purge your conscience from dead works to serve the living God?" (Heb. 9:13–14).

## THE INNOCENCE OF SACRIFICIAL ANIMALS ANTICIPATES CHRIST'S BLAMELESSNESS

Although some animals are instinctively predatory, territorial, and ferocious, the scriptures do not reveal if or how they will be held accountable for their actions. Some, or perhaps all, animals, apparently, are innocent of crimes against God; it seems that they cannot sin or commit transgressions. President John Taylor taught regarding sacrificial animals and their blameless natures: "From the commencement of the offering of sacrifices the inferior creature had to suffer for the superior. *Although it had taken no part in the act of disobedience,* yet was its blood shed and its life sacrificed, thus prefiguring the atonement of the Son of God."[1] Further, President Heber C. Kimball taught that horses "are as good as we are in their sphere of action; they honour their calling, and we do not, when we abuse them. . . .

"I do not think that many ever suppose that animals are going to be resurrected."[2]

With these teachings regarding animals in mind, we can better comprehend why God commanded his people to sacrifice animals in similitude of the Savior. Jesus Christ died for us even though he was innocent of even the least sins; and in the same manner sacrificial animals did nothing to deserve death at the altar because of their own actions. Their death, of course, pointed to the sacrifice of the Son of God.

Not only are animals innocent of committing sins, but many animals are found in heaven. Joseph Smith taught much regarding beasts in heaven. "John saw the actual beast in heaven, showing to John that beasts did actually exist there."[3] In addition to Joseph Smith's teachings regarding animals, the book of Revelation provides much information concerning the status of animals in heaven (Rev. 4:6–9; 5:6–14; 6:1–7; 7:11; 14:3; 15:7; 19:4).

## ANIMALS' ECONOMIC WORTH MAKE THEM A SACRIFICE OF VALUE

In the context of animal sacrifice, the term *sacrifice* has a dual meaning. First, sacrifice refers to the ritual or ceremonial slaughter of an animal for the purposes of making an offering to God, which slaughter was conducted in similitude of the Savior's sacrifice. Second, sacrifice signifies the surrender to God of something of great value. This second meaning of sacrifice has relevance to the ancient Israelite family that gave up one of its finest animals to God. Consider the following points regarding the economic value to a family of a sacrificial animal, using a sheep as an example. The sheep without blemish, either male or female, might have served to perpetuate a fine species; a large sacrificial ram of two hundred to three hundred pounds would have yielded much meat for the family table; the female too would have yielded meat for the family; the sheep's wool would have produced warm clothing; and its hide might have been used for sandals, clothing, scrolls, bags, belts, or other items of value. And by sacrificing a ewe, the family surrendered the future value of that ewe in birthing lambs for years to come. Another example: a female goat in its prime might have provided the daily dairy needs (milk, cheese, butter) of an Israelite family. If the family sacrificed a female goat, they would have thus relinquished important food products for their dietary needs. In sum, all categories of sacrificial animals—heifers, bullocks, goats, even doves—dedicated to the Lord represented an economic sacrifice to a greater or lesser degree.

## CLEAN AND UNCLEAN ANIMALS IN LIGHT OF ANIMAL SACRIFICES

The Lord revealed to Moses a strict and specific diet code regarding unclean and clean animals. This code had both spiritual and temporal purposes. Temporally, the code protected the Israelites from disease and from unwise economic practices. "The vast majority of foods prohibited [in the law of Moses] are those that (1) are more likely to carry disease in the arid climate of the Sinai desert and/or the land of Canaan; or (2) are foolishly uneconomical to raise as food in the particular agrarian context of the Sinai desert and/or the land of Canaan."[4]

Spiritually, the dietary code prohibited the Israelites from partaking of animals that non-Israelite religious groups sacrificed to their idols and deities.[5] The Israelites were to remain a peculiar people and were not to eat, live, or worship like the nations around them. Moreover, the law of Moses instructed that the dietary code spiritually prepare the people to become holy, even as God is holy. "For I am the Lord your God: ye shall therefore sanctify yourselves, and ye shall be holy; for I am holy. . . . This is the law of the beasts, and of the fowl, and of every living creature that moveth in the waters, and of every creature that creepeth upon the earth: To make a difference between the unclean and the clean, and between the beast that may be eaten and the beast that may not be eaten" (Lev. 11:44, 46–47).

Rules regarding clean and unclean animals teach us regarding the law of sacrifice: only clean animals could be sacrificed, and only they could be eaten. Not a single unclean animal could be sacrificed or eaten. Birds of prey and scavengers, fish lacking fins and scales, insects other than the grasshopper family, reptiles, and certain mammals were unclean animals that could neither be eaten nor sacrificed. The accompanying chart specifies the clean and unclean animals. The Mosaic law was strict regarding which animals the Israelites were permitted to sacrifice because that sacrifice pointed to Jesus Christ, who was clean and pure.

Unclean animals signify the opposite of the clean animals. The scriptures set forth symbolic meanings of some of the animals that were pronounced unclean according to Mosaic law. For example, a woman lacking discretion is likened to a pig's snout (Prov. 11:22), a fool is compared to a dog that returns to his vomit (Prov. 26:11; cf. 2 Pet. 2:22), the wicked are compared to dogs and swine (Matt. 7:6), Satan is compared to a dragon (Rev. 12:9), and frogs are symbols of unclean spirits (Rev. 16:13).

# The Dietary Code: Unclean and Clean Animals

| Type | Unclean | Clean | References |
|---|---|---|---|
| Birds of prey and scavengers ("fowls") | Eagle, ossifrage, osprey, vulture, kite, raven, owl, night hawk, cuckow, hawk, little owl, cormorant, great owl, swan, pelican, gier eagle, stork, heron, lapwing, bat, and "all fowls that creep, going upon all four" | Birds not identified as unclean are considered to be clean and may be eaten | Lev. 11:13–20; Deut. 14:11–20 |
| Fish ("all that are in the waters") | Fish lacking fins and scales may not be eaten | Fish with fins and scales may be eaten | Lev. 11:9–12; Deut. 14:9–10 |
| Insects ("flying creeping things") | Those not of the grasshopper family; quadrupeds with wings | "These may ye eat of every flying creeping thing that goeth upon all four, which have legs above their feet, to leap withal upon the earth" (Lev. 11:21): locust, bald locust, beetle, and grasshopper | Lev. 11:21–25, 42 |
| Mammals ("beasts") | Animals that either do not have a parted hoof or do not chew the cud may not be eaten, including the camel, coney, hare, and swine | Mammals that have a parted hoof or cloven foot and that chew the cud may be eaten | Lev. 11:2–8, 26–31; Deut. 14:6–8 |
| "creeping things" | All are unclean: weasel, mouse, tortoise, ferret, chameleon, lizard, snail, mole | None | Lev. 11:29–31, 41–43 |

## THE LION AND THE LAMB

The scriptures refer to Jesus Christ as both the Lamb and the Lion (Isa. 31:4; Hosea 5:14; Rev. 5:5). That is to say, Jesus Christ has qualities that remind us of these two animals. With regard to the atonement, Christ is the embodiment of both the Lamb and the Lion. As the "Lamb of God, which taketh away the sin of the world" (John 1:29) he submissively, meekly, and with innocence faced his accusers and went to the slaughter, ultimately suffering death on the cross.

As the Lion, he with might and power overcame death and stands exalted in heaven, reigning forevermore with perfect majesty over his kingdom of Saints. Isaiah compared the Lord to a lion: "For thus hath the Lord spoken unto me, Like as a lion and the young lion roaring on his prey, when a multitude of shepherds is called forth against him, he will not be afraid of their voice, nor abase himself for the noise of them" (Isa. 31:4).

Revelation 5:5–6 places the lion and the lamb in the same setting. In Revelation 5:6 Christ is called "Lamb," but in 5:5 he is called "Lion," a creature hostile and adverse to the Lamb. Christ as the Lamb portrays one who is submissive, as a sacrificial victim who is "brought as a lamb to the slaughter" (Isa. 53:7), or one who condescended to descend below all things. Christ as the Lion depicts one who has power over all creatures and is a majestic, fearless king (as a lion is "king of the beasts") who possesses great strength. In this context the title is especially appropriate, because just as a lion prevails over other creatures, so Christ "prevailed to open the book" with seven seals (Rev. 5:5) (or, according to the RSV, Christ "has conquered, so that he can open the scroll and its seven seals").

"Jesus is a member 'of the tribe of Judah,' whose emblem is the lion (Gen. 49:9)."[6]

## THE BRONZE SNAKE—A SYMBOL OF CHRIST ON THE CROSS

As the Israelites traveled through the wilderness near the kingdom of Edom, they complained to God and Moses concerning what they considered to be a lack of adequate food and water. God responded to their complaints by sending poisonous snakes among them, killing many. The people recognized their error and pled with Moses to ask the Lord to remove the snakes. As a result of his prayer, "the Lord said unto Moses, Make thee a fiery serpent, and set it upon a pole: and it shall come to pass, that every one that is bitten, when he looketh upon it, shall live. And Moses made a serpent of brass, and put it upon a pole, and it came to pass, that if a serpent had bitten any man, when he beheld the serpent of brass, he lived" (Num. 21:8–9).

This historical incident affected the Israelites to such a great degree that for centuries they revered the bronze snake.[7] In fact, during the reign of King Hezekiah, the Israelites burned incense to it, which was an act of apostasy because they worshipped the symbol (the bronze snake) instead of that which was symbolized (Jehovah, or Jesus Christ). As a result of the Israelite apostasy, Hezekiah, a righteous ruler and great reformer, "removed the high places, and brake the images, and cut down the groves, and brake in pieces the brasen serpent that Moses had made: for unto those days the children of Israel did burn incense to it" (2 Kgs. 18:4).

The bronze serpent typifies Jesus Christ on the cross in several ways:

1. The serpent was attached to a pole; Jesus was nailed to the cross.

2. Both the serpent and Jesus were "lifted up." Nephi, Helaman's son, explained, "And as [Moses] *lifted up* the brazen serpent in the wilderness, even so shall he [Jesus] be *lifted up* who should come" (Hel. 8:14; emphasis added). Jesus also taught this doctrine: "As Moses lifted up the serpent in the wilderness, even so must the Son of man be lifted up: That whosoever believeth in him should not perish, but have eternal life" (John 3:14–15).

3. Whoever of the Israelites looked up at the serpent did not die from the venomous serpents but lived; and whoever looks to Jesus on the cross (by accepting Jesus and his atoning death) lives spiritually. Again, Nephi taught, "And as many as should *look upon that serpent* should live, even so as many as should *look upon the Son of God* with faith, having a contrite spirit, might live, even unto that life which is eternal" (Hel. 8:15; emphasis added).

4. Many Israelites who were bitten by the poisonous serpents died because it seemed too simple to look up at the bronze serpent in order to be healed. Nephi, Lehi's son, taught that the Lord "sent fiery flying serpents among them; and after they were bitten he prepared a way that they might be healed; and the labor which they had to perform was to look; and because of the simpleness of the way, or the easiness of it, there were many who perished" (1 Ne. 17:41). Similarly, people of all ages scoff at the idea of the cross because they deem it to be foolishness: "For the preaching of the cross is to them that perish foolishness, but unto us which are saved it is the power of God" (1 Cor. 1:18).

5. God "gave unto Moses power that he should heal the nations after they had been bitten by the poisonous serpents" (2 Ne. 25:20). Moses was a type and shadow of Jesus Christ, who heals the nations from spiritual disease and sin, and through the power of the resurrection the nations are healed from the sting of death.

## CHAPTER 12

# FROM STONES TO STARS: THE TESTIMONY OF EARTH AND SKY

THE SCIENTIST HENRY EYRING WROTE:

> There is probably no better way to deepen faith in the Gospel than to try to think out how this magnificently complicated world came about. Only a profound scholar of the physical sciences is able to calculate the utter improbability of any universe arising by chance. There is a deep meaning running through all that touches our lives. *The Gospel is to be found not only in the scriptures but in every detail of the world, if we can but read it.*[1]

This statement is consistent with what the Lord said to Adam—"all things are created and made to bear record of me," including "things which are in the heavens above, and things which are on the earth" (Moses 6:63). Even the natural world—the heavens and the earth—bears witness of Jesus Christ and his atonement. Here are a few examples.

## THINGS WHICH ARE ON THE EARTH

*Rock.* The fundamental, foundational (literally) substance of the earth is *rock*. It is the firm base of all else on the planet. The scriptures teach repeatedly that Jesus is the solid rock of the gospel (Deut. 32:4; Ps. 28:1; 62:2; 1 Cor. 10:1–4). As such, Christ and his atonement are the solid foundation upon which we can build. Like a rock, the atonement is steadfast and immovable.

Rock is ground up by other elements into sand and dirt. It is rock on which the earth's soil rests and from which plants and trees grow. Even sea plants and sea creatures require the nutrients that come from the underwater rock as it is gradually pulverized by the forces of nature. Thus the rock, when broken down, contributes to the life of all plants and animals on the entire earth. Likewise, through Christ's atonement we can receive the essential spiritual nourishment we all need.

Christ is also referred to as a stone. He is the chief cornerstone in the foundation of our eternal lives (Ps. 118:22–23; Isa. 28:16; Rom. 9:32–33; 1 Pet. 2:4–10). The cornerstone stands between two walls and gives strength and unity to the whole structure. Christ and his atonement serve as a foundation for our lives, give us strength, and increase the unity in our relationships with both God and man.

In Zechariah, the Lord refers to a stone that he has placed before the high priest, whose name was Joshua (a compound word that includes a form of *Jesus*). In relation to that stone—and also in relation to a servant called the Branch (see *Trees* below)—the Lord says, "I will remove the iniquity of that land in one day" (Zech. 3:9). The "one day" in which the Lord removed *our* iniquity was the literal day of atonement, which took place "once for all" (NIV Heb. 9:26) in the Garden of Gethsemane. That atonement was performed by Jesus, who was both the Branch and the Stone.

Anciently, stones were used to build altars on which the Lord's people offered sacrifice and at which they prayed. In other words, the altar was a mediating structure for those who wished to draw closer to God—just as Christ mediates to help us in that quest. Those altars were to be put together without the use of tools, and the rocks used were not to be cut by human hands (Ex. 20:25). The atonement does not come through human labor but through the loving act of God—it is given as a divine gift.

Isaiah taught that Christ is the foundation of our salvation. "Therefore thus saith the Lord God, Behold, I lay in Zion for a foundation a stone, a tried stone, a precious corner stone, a sure foundation" (Isa. 28:16).

Latter-day Saint author Lenet Hadley Read has written with insight:

> Under Mosaic law, stones symbolized judgment and justice, stoning being the means by which those who committed the most serious crimes were put to death.
>
> Interestingly, stones were also of ceremonial importance as symbols of judgment in the tabernacle and temple. It was commanded that the priest (a type of Christ, the true High Priest), when he "goeth in before the Lord," should wear a breastplate set with twelve precious stones. The breastplate was called the "breastplate of judgment," and the priest was to wear it that he might "bear the judgment of the children of Israel upon his heart" (Ex. 28:30).
>
> The use of *precious* stones to symbolize an atoning for the judgment of sins assumes greater implications when we consider Christ's mortal mission. As our Savior, Jesus would remove the judgment against all who would acknowledge his atoning act and accept his command to "go, and sin no more." In other words, Christ, the precious "living stone" (1 Pet. 2:4), the "head stone of the corner" of Israel (Ps. 118:22; Matt. 21:42), would "bear the judgment of Israel upon his heart."[2]

*Water.* Water is one of the most essential elements on earth for the growth and continuing life of plants and animals and humans. Without water, all fish and sea creatures die within minutes. Most animals and all humans die within days without water. Water can take a lifeless, arid desert and turn it into a fertile, teeming land. Water is necessary for cleansing that which has become dirty or befouled. The movement of water is a major source of electrical power on earth.

Water is an impressive symbol of the atonement. The atonement is essential for our growth and continuing life. It can take a spiritually lifeless, arid soul and help it become fertile and vital. It is necessary to cleanse souls that have become dirty or befouled. It is a major source of the spiritual power on earth.

When the people of Israel had no water and were facing death, Moses struck a rock and water flowed out (Num. 20:1–11). This was a literal event that also has symbolic meaning. The rock represented Christ, the source of both physical and spiritual life, and the water represented the life and Spirit that flow from him, made available to us through the atonement.

No wonder Jesus Christ is given in both the Old and New Testaments as the source, or fountain, of living water (Jer. 2:13; 17:13; John 4:10–14). He said to the woman at Jacob's Well in Samaria, "Whosoever drinketh of the water that I shall give him shall never thirst; but the water that I shall give him shall be in him a well of water springing up into everlasting life" (John 4:14). After feeding the five thousand by the Sea of Galilee, Jesus said, "He that cometh to me shall never hunger; and he that believeth on me shall never thirst" (John 6:35). Later, standing in the temple, Jesus cried out, "If any man thirst, let him come unto me, and drink. He that believeth on me, as the scripture hath said, out of his belly shall flow rivers of living water" (John 7:37–38). After recording this last statement, John added a parenthetical explanation: "This spake he of the Spirit" (John 7:39).

When we come unto Christ through ordinance and obedience, we receive the Holy Ghost, who will help to quench all our spiritual thirst. The Spirit can act as an agent of our spiritual cleansing. He can change us from dry, arid souls, those who are spiritually dead, to those who are teeming with spiritual life. We thus have a source of power within us that never ends. All these things are made possible through the atonement of Christ, an offering in which he poured out water in sacrifice for us (John 19:34) so that we could partake of the living water forever. The "fountain of living waters . . . are a representation of the love of God" (1 Ne. 11:25). "God so loved the world, that he gave his only begotten Son" (John 3:16). Christ so loved the world that he gave himself a ransom for the children of men (Ether 12:33; D&C 34:3).[3]

*Trees.* Trees are symbols of stability and strength. Many trees live far longer than humans. They provide shade for those who are hot and weary. Through the process of photosynthesis, they give necessary oxygen to both man and animals on the earth. Many trees are a source of delicious food, providing us with a great variety of nuts and fruits. The bark and leaves of certain trees have been found to have valuable medicinal qualities.

Symbolically, Jesus Christ is represented by a tree. He is the root, which gives life to the plant (Isa. 53:2; Rev. 22:16); the Branch (Jer. 23:5–6; 33:15–17; Isa. 11:1–5); and a stem (Isa. 11:1–4; D&C 113:1–2). His love is symbolized by the tree of life, as Nephi learned (1 Ne. 11:21–22, 25). Christ, with his love and the power of his atonement, also yields the fruit of the tree of life, which fruit ultimately is eternal life (1 Ne. 15:36; D&C 14:7). This fruit, Lehi said, "was desirable to make one happy. . . . It was most sweet, above all that I ever before tasted. . . . It filled my soul with exceedingly great joy. . . . It was desirable above all other fruit" (1 Ne. 8:10–12). When we pluck this precious fruit from the tree, we are promised, "Ye shall feast upon [it] even until ye are filled, that ye hunger not, neither shall ye thirst" (Alma 32:42).

The fruit also directly represents the atonement, through the emblems of the sacrament. Alma, quoting the Savior, said, "Come unto me and ye shall partake of the fruit of the tree of life; yea, ye shall eat and drink of the bread and the waters of life freely" (Alma 5:34).[4]

As a tree, Christ has all the symbols mentioned above. He stands firm when other plants wither. He is a place of refuge. He provides life to all—in fact, he is *the* Life, our eternal life (John 11:25; 14:6). The fruit of his tree is nourishing above all other fruit. That fruit brings the greatest joy on earth and in eternity. He heals us through the "balm in Gilead" (Jer. 8:22), a salve that was prepared from a tree.

All this points to the atonement of our Savior performed through his infinite love. It also is firm, a source of refuge, and an essential blessing unto eternal life. The gift of the atonement provides unparalleled strength and nourishment and great joy. It is the source of spiritual, emotional, and physical healing. John the Beloved learned that those who partake of the tree of life receive eternal life (Rev. 22:14); in the same way, those who partake of the atonement of Jesus Christ will receive that blessed life in the presence of God.

The apostle Peter used a tree as a direct symbol of the atonement when he wrote that Christ "his own self bare our sins in his own body on the tree, that we, being dead to sins, should live unto righteousness: by whose stripes ye were healed" (1 Pet. 2:24; see also Acts 5:30; 10:39; 13:29).

Related to the tree is the vine. Jesus said: "I am the true vine, and my Father is the husbandman. . . . Abide in me, and I in you. As the branch cannot bear fruit of itself, except it abide in the vine; no more can ye, except ye abide in me. I am the vine, ye are the branches: he that abideth in me, and I in him, the same bringeth forth much fruit: for without me ye can do nothing" (John 15:1, 4–5; see also 1 Ne. 15:15).

The vine is the source of strength, nourishment, and life for the branches, just as the Savior and his atonement provide us with strength, nourishment, and life. If the vine is unhealthy, the branches will fail to bear fruit and will ultimately die. But Jesus Christ is our true vine. We are absolutely dependent on him. Without him we will die; without him we have no hope of eternal life. But if we are united with Christ and receive the blessings of his atonement, we will bring forth much fruit.

*The Holy Land.* Latter-day Saint scholar Truman G. Madsen has written:

> "All things bear record of me." (Moses 6:63.) So we have been taught. But when our feet first touched the ground of Israel more than a decade ago, we still cherished the fallacy that the Master's words were the only vehicle for his gospel message. Environment and circumstance mattered little if at all, we thought. We soon learned otherwise! During his ministry, the Teacher of teachers invoked his surroundings to verify his revelatory acts and sayings. The cosmos was his visual aid, and the setting sprang to life through his words and actions. In the very rocks, in the very fountains and mountains, in the very trees of Israel his meaning is lodged—meanings that can reach the center of the soul.[5]

Many aspects of the Holy Land carry symbolic meaning, as is evident to anyone who has studied the parables of Jesus Christ.[6] But some elements of the geography stand specifically as types of Christ and his atonement.

The riches of the land symbolize the riches of the atonement of Christ: "For the Lord thy God bringeth thee into a good land," he said to Moses, "a land of brooks of water, of fountains and depths that spring out of valleys and hills; a land of wheat, and barley, and vines, and fig trees, and pomegranates; a land of oil olive, and honey; a land wherein thou shalt eat bread without scarceness, thou shalt not lack any thing in it; a land whose stones are iron, and out of whose hills thou mayest dig brass. When thou hast eaten and art full, then thou shalt bless the Lord thy God for the good land which he hath given thee" (Deut. 8:7–10). Just as the land provided for every physical need, so does Christ's atonement provide for our every spiritual need.

Abraham was commanded to go to a specific place to offer his only son in sacrifice: Mount Moriah (Gen. 22:2–3, 9). Later, David purchased that very location at great expense, saying, "This is the house of the Lord God, and this is the altar of the burnt offering for Israel" (1 Chr. 22:1). When Solomon later built the temple there, it became the center point of all sacrificial offerings for the children of Israel (2 Chr. 3:1). During the time of Christ, an impoverished widow cast into the temple treasury "all that she had, even all her living" (Mark 12:44). Each of these offerings of sacrifice prefigured the infinite sacrifice of Jesus Christ, which (after Gethsemane) was offered on Mount Moriah, at a place called Golgotha.

One crucial aspect of Jesus' experience in Gethsemane was foreshadowed in a small way by King David. David and his followers crossed over the brook Kidron, as did Jesus and his disciples (2 Sam. 15:23; John 18:1). In Gethsemane, which was on the Mount of Olives, Jesus had a dreadful contest with the adversary in which He was assailed in unimaginable ways. In that dark battle, the Savior literally shed blood through his pores. In a type of that experience, though admittedly only a weak shadow, David was attacked on the Mount of Olives by Shimei, who "came forth, and cursed still as he came. And he cast stones at David, and at all the servants of king David. . . . And thus said Shimei when he cursed, Come out, come out, thou bloody man, and thou man of Belial. . . . Behold, thou art taken in thy mischief, because thou art a bloody man. . . . And as David and his men went by the way, Shimei went along on the hill's side over against him, and cursed as he went, and threw stones at him, and cast dust" (2 Sam. 16:5–8, 13).

The principal waters of the Holy Land seem to point to important truths relating to the Savior and his atonement. The Jordan River flows down from Mount Hermon, the highest point of the entire land. The name *Jordan* comes from a Hebrew word meaning *descender.* The river has the lowest elevation of any in the world. It flows first into the Sea of Galilee, the lowest fresh-water lake in the world. It then meanders down the length of the land of Palestine until it reaches the Dead Sea, the lowest salt-water lake in the world. Thus do we move into mortality by going down from the high point of heaven unto the earth. Quite literally, we fall from a height to a depth. Once we are here, our passage down the river of life inevitably takes us to death. Yet, as symbolized by his baptism in the very waters of Jordan, Jesus Christ was submerged in mortality but came forth again in perfect resurrected form. Even though we cannot escape death, we will be renewed by Christ. This renewal is symbolized by the experience of Naaman the leper, who followed Elisha's instructions to dip seven times in the Jordan River, and "his flesh came again like unto the flesh of a little child, and he was clean" (2 Kgs. 5:14). Ezekiel also gives the wonderful symbolism of the living waters flowing from the temple to heal the waters of the Dead Sea (Ezek. 47:8–9). In the same way, the atonement of Christ can flow into our lives, heal us from spiritual death, and raise us from literal death.

*The wilderness.* Many of the events in the scriptures take place in the wilderness: when Adam and Eve were cast out of the Garden of Eden, they went into the wilderness; Abraham traveled in the wilderness before he reached the promised land; Moses and the children of Israel wandered there for forty years; Lehi and his family fled the city of Jerusalem to go into the wilderness; later, Nephi left his murderous brethren and went into the wilderness to find a place of safety.

The wilderness symbolizes our struggle with the trials of mortality. In the wilderness are found thirst, hunger, heat, thorns, the sweat of the brow, and, as the experience of Jesus in the wilderness teaches us, the temptations and afflictions of the adversary.

But the Lord seeks to bless us in our wilderness. The powers and blessings of his atonement are sufficient to help us through all our mortal trials, and he sends those blessings freely. As the Lord said to the children of Israel through Moses:

> Remember all the way which the Lord thy God led thee these forty years in the wilderness, to humble thee, and to prove thee, to know what was in thine heart, whether thou wouldest keep his commandments, or no.
>
> And he . . . fed thee with manna, which thou knewest not, neither did thy fathers know; that he might make thee know that man doth not live by bread only, but by every word that proceedeth out of the mouth of the Lord doth man live.
>
> Thy raiment waxed not old upon thee, neither did thy foot swell, these forty years. (Deut. 8:2–5)

These blessings were literal, but they also show how the Lord will care for us spiritually through his atonement. Later the Lord reminded the people of symbolic blessings he would give us:

> For the Lord's portion is his people; Jacob is the lot of his inheritance.
>
> He found him in a desert land, and in the waste howling wilderness; he led him about, he instructed him, he kept him as the apple of his eye.
>
> As an eagle stirreth up her nest, fluttereth over her young, spreadeth abroad her wings, taketh them, beareth them on her wings: so the Lord alone did lead him. . . .
>
> He made him ride on the high places of the earth, that he might eat the increase of the fields; and he made him to suck honey out of the rock, and oil out of the flinty rock; butter of kine, and milk of sheep, with fat of lambs, and rams of the breed of Bashan, and goats, with the fat of kidneys of wheat; and thou didst drink the pure blood of the grape. (Deut. 32:9–14)

160

That last statement is a pointed reminder that even though our trials may seem too great to bear, the grace (or enabling power) of Christ will always be there for us, and through him we will be able to "drink the pure blood of the grape."

Those faithful Saints wandering in the wilderness of mortality are like Abraham, who, though he "sojourned in the land of promise," was "as in a strange country, . . . for he looked for a city which hath foundations, whose builder and maker is God." He and the other righteous ones of old "confessed that they were strangers and pilgrims on the earth." As such, they "desire a better country, that is, an heavenly" (Heb. 11:9–10, 13, 16). And through Christ, they will come to that heavenly country and leave behind the mortal wilderness forever.

## THINGS WHICH ARE IN THE HEAVENS ABOVE

*Light.* Light is one of the most important elements of life on earth. It enables photosynthesis, which allows plants to develop the nutrients we all need—and which also produces oxygen for us to breathe. Natural light helps the human body produce vitamin D, without which humans would die. Light is energy and a source of power. It reaches across the universe faster than anything else we know. And light is necessary to enable us to see—it reveals those things that are around us. It makes it possible for people to perform their daily labors.

Jesus Christ is literally the light of the world (John 8:12; 12:46; Mosiah 16:9; 3 Ne. 18:2; D&C 10:57–58). As such, he possesses all the qualities of light listed above, both physically and spiritually. As inhabitants of the earth, we receive the blessings of physical light as a pure gift.

All humankind also receives the blessings of spiritual light, or the Light of Christ. The light that comes from Christ "enlighteneth your eyes," and that "same light . . . quickeneth your understandings." That light "is in all things, . . . giveth life to all things, . . . [and] is the law by which all things are governed" (D&C 88:11, 13).

As our Light, then, Jesus Christ is the very source of our life. He energizes and empowers us to "live and move and have our being" (Acts 17:28). By his light we can see and know truth. Without it we are in darkness. As we draw closer to the Savior through covenants and obedience, we receive marvelous blessings through the atonement. As the Lord has revealed, "He that receiveth light, and continueth in God, receiveth more light; and that light groweth brighter and brighter until the perfect day" (D&C 50:24). Surely it is no coincidence that when God created the earth, on the very first day he said, "Let there be light" (Gen. 1:3). Christ is the beginning and the end; in both a literal and a symbolic sense, he, as the light, was present at the beginning even of the earth.

Paul wrote that the Father helps us to be "partakers of the inheritance of the saints in light" (Col. 1:12). That inheritance of light includes all the blessings of the atonement of Christ. Those blessings, symbolized by light itself, include the gift of eternal life and eternal light, the energy and power we require to function spiritually, the enlightenment that fills our mind with truth, and much more. "Every good gift and every perfect gift is from above," wrote James, "and cometh down from the Father of lights" (James 1:17).

*Sun.* The sun is the primary source of light for everything on earth. Jesus Christ "is in the sun, and the light of the sun, and the power thereof by which it was made" (D&C 88:7). Other scriptures make the connection between the Lord and the sun. For example, Psalm 84:11 says plainly, "The Lord God is a sun." And Malachi 4:2 refers to Christ as the "Sun of righteousness [who shall] arise with healing in his wings." The brightness of the Lord's appearance is typically compared to the sun (Matt. 17:2; Acts 26:13; Rev. 1:16; D&C 110:2–3; JS–H 1:16–17). In the celestial world, we will not need the sun—the Lord will provide all our light (Isa. 60:19; Rev. 21:23; 22:5).

What do we learn about the atonement from knowing that Christ is as the sun? The sun gives us light (discussed above), warmth, and gravitation. Without the sun the earth would literally freeze—all would instantly die. Without gravitation the planets, including earth, would spin off into space. The sun is also a source of energy—it gives energy directly through its heat. It creates carbohydrate energy within plants through photosynthesis; it is a key part of the water cycle (causing evaporation and affecting air pressure zones), and water is an essential element in creating electrical energy; and the sun has an effect on earth's winds, which in turn affect the weather cycles and can be harnessed as wind energy. Finally, the sun is the dominating and governing force in the solar system.

All these characteristics of the sun are symbolic of characteristics of Christ and his atonement. He gives us light (both physical and spiritual) and spiritual warmth. He holds all things together. He provides the energy, or power, with which we are saved. The atonement of Christ is literally the dominating force in our lives. In fact, as Latter-day Saint scholar Hugh Nibley has written:

> In its sweep and scope, atonement takes on the aspect of one of the grand constants in nature—omnipresent, unalterable, such as gravity or the speed of light. Like them it is always there, easily ignored, hard to explain, and hard to believe in without an explanation. Also, we are constantly exposed to its effects whether we are aware of them or not. Alma found that it engages the mind like a physical force, focusing thought with the intensity of a laser beam (see Alma 36:17–19). Like gravity, though we are rarely aware of it, it is at work every moment of our lives, and to ignore it can be fatal. It is waiting at our disposal to draw us on.[7]

*Star.* Jesus said, "I am . . . the bright and morning star" (Rev. 22:16). And the book of Numbers records that he is the "Star out of Jacob" (Num. 24:17). There has been much scholarly discussion about the star that heralded the birth of Christ—the star that prompted the "wise men from the east" (Matt. 2:1) to search out the newly born king—but the exact identity of that star remains a mystery. The "bright and morning star" is clearly Venus, however. Venus is the brightest "star" in the sky; depending on its location relative to the earth, it is often the first star seen in the evening sky (and thus is also called the evening star) or is the last star to disappear in the morning.[8]

Like the "bright and morning star," the atonement of Christ is the brightest part of the gospel. Just as Venus is there at the beginning and ending of day and night, the glory of Christ's love and the power of his atonement shine in the darkness from beginning to end.

Further, stars shine in the darkness, just as the atonement shines in spiritual darkness. Stars are necessary to help us navigate our way through an otherwise black night; so likewise can the atonement provide direction to our lives, even when we feel we're struggling with little light.

President Gordon B. Hinckley also compared the Savior to the North Star: "Like the Polar Star in the heavens, regardless of what the future holds, there stands the Redeemer of the world, the Son of God, certain and sure as the anchor of our immortal lives. He is the rock of our salvation, our strength, our comfort, the very focus of our faith.

"In sunshine and in shadow we look to Him, and He is there to assure and smile upon us."[9] The same, of course, could be said of his atonement: it is always there, always in proper place, "certain and sure as the anchor of our immortal lives."

*Constellations.* The constellations in the sky (particularly the northern hemisphere) tell a story that corresponds to much of the mythology of the ancient Greeks and Romans. But where did they get the stories? As Nibley has written, virtually all mythologies of the ancient world descended from the true gospel stories told by the earliest prophets:

> A student confronted for the first time by classical and Oriental myths that read like reruns of well-known Bible stories—such as the garden of Eden episode and the Flood—often goes into a sort of shock, emerging from which he announces to family and friends that he has just discovered a fact of life: the Bible is just a lot of mythology.
>
> Such a conclusion may be the result of a faulty approach to the Bible as well as to the myths. The first thing to do in such a case is to apply cold packs and calm the student down. . . .
>
> Some of the earliest religious writers were edified by the Egyptian [myths], and the later Fathers of the traditional church diligently catalogued those heathen myths and doctrines that most closely resembled their own beliefs as proof that the gentiles had always pirated the true teachings of the prophets and patriarchs.
>
> The idea was that the Egyptians had picked up a lot of stuff from the Israelites during the latter's sojourn in Egypt, and of course the Egyptians got it all mixed up. Also, since Adam, Enoch,

Noah, and Abraham had all left writings behind long before Moses, it was only to be expected that in times of apostasy their teachings, in contaminated form, should fall into profane hands.

There is a good deal to be said for this theory, for the myths and rites of all the ancient world, if traced backward in time, do show a marked tendency to conform more and more to a few basic themes and to converge on a limited geographical area as their apparent place of origin. . . . There is a very real relationship between the biblical and the worldwide pagan traditions. . . .

. . . If we know . . . that the gospel has been on the earth from time to time ever since the days of Adam, then it is easily understandable that recognizable fragments of it should be seen floating around in sundry times and places.[10]

Elsewhere Nibley wrote: "Greek mythology is an endless procession of familiarly recurring themes. . . . Thus we may see that Greeks have all the original building blocks, but they have admittedly lost the blueprints and never tire of trying to put the parts back together again in the proper order. I. E. S. Edwards says much the same thing about the Egyptians."[11]

Thus, those with eyes to see can recognize the true works of God in the flawed works of Zeus or Jupiter. They can see truth about God the Father, the atonement of Christ, the resurrection, and the battle with Satan in the Egyptian story of Isis, Osiris, Horus, and Set. And, by extension, they can see something of the story of Christ and his atonement in the constellations that fill the earth's sky.

The existence of the constellations in a form much as we know them now can be dated to nearly as early as 400 B.C., when Eudoxus, a Greek scientist, received a sphere from Egypt detailing them.[12] Millennia earlier, the book of Job suggested that the Lord himself had formed at least some of the constellations: "By his spirit he hath garnished the heavens; his hand hath formed the crooked serpent" (Job 26:13)—"the crooked serpent" referring to one of the prominent constellations. Earlier in the same record, Job says that the Lord "spreadeth out the heavens, . . . [and] maketh Arcturus, Orion, and Pleiades, and the chambers of the south" (Job 9:8–9; see also Job 38:31–32).

The story told by the constellations is remarkable. Here are some of the primary signs of the zodiac, with some of their related constellations (called decans). Like Hebrew parallelism, the stories of the constellations are repeated again and again in different ways.

*Virgo,* or a virgin, holds a branch (which could symbolize Christ as the Branch) and an ear of corn (symbolizing the seed of life); one of the decans shows a woman with an infant child on her lap; another depicts a centaur, which was half man and half horse (which could symbolize Christ as half man, half God); and the third shows Bootes (meaning "the coming one"), with another branch and a sickle (used in the harvest).

*Libra,* representing the scales of judgment, is also sometimes called the Altar, on which the sacrifice is made; accompanying decans are the Cross; Lupus, the wolf (often called the Victim); and Corona, or the crown (all of which could symbolize the sacrifice of Jesus Christ and the crown of victory he won).

*Scorpio* depicts a great enemy with claws ready to entrap the sacrificial victim; related decans show the Serpent, seeking to wound the heel of the nearby man; Ophiuchus, the Serpent Holder, wrestling the serpent into submission; and Hercules, the Strong One, crushing the head of the Dragon with his foot—all seemingly apparent symbols of Christ's atonement.

*Capricorn,* the Goat-fish, another symbolic creature with two natures, is being slain by an arrow; decans include a wounded eagle falling to its death, and the Dolphin, rising up again—a seeming reference to Christ's death and resurrection.

*Aries* is the ram or the lamb, a familiar symbol of Christ; in the decans we see the Sea Monster holding the Fishes bound—but Perseus, another great hero, is killing the monster.

Other constellations include Aquarius, the Water Bearer, pouring a river of water from a huge vase, which may symbolize the living water the Savior gives us; Orion, the glorious man who is destroying the enemy with a two-edged sword; Auriga, the Shepherd; and Leo, the lion king, who is crushing the serpent with its foot.[13]

## CHAPTER 13

# THE MAN OF SORROWS: PROPHECIES OF CHRIST'S MORTAL MINISTRY AND ATONEMENT

PROPHECIES OF JESUS CHRIST'S FIRST coming served to prepare people for Jesus' condescension, mortal ministry, and atoning sacrifice. God's holy men and women prophesied under the power of the Holy Ghost, and the prophets' chief message to the world's inhabitants has always been about Jesus Christ—his birth, nature, character, mortal ministry, sufferings, atoning sacrifice, death, resurrection, second coming, and millennial reign.[1] Joseph Smith taught this important truth: "The fundamental principles of our religion are the testimony of the Apostles and Prophets, concerning Jesus Christ, that He died, was buried, and rose again the third day, and ascended into heaven; and all other things which pertain to our religion are only appendages to it."[2] All of the ancient prophets taught and prophesied of Jesus Christ, as the Book of Mormon prophet Jacob and others have so testified (Jacob 7:11; see also Luke 24:27; 3 Ne. 9:16; D&C 20:26).

The accompanying chart sets forth prophecies concerning Jesus Christ. Although the focus of this book is the atonement, other prophecies about Jesus have been included in order to set a broad context that pertains to his mortal life and ministry. The chart is representative, not comprehensive, and does not deal with Jesus' second coming or millennial reign.

Of course, some prophecies are general in their illumination while others are specific. For example, the prophecy that reveals that Jesus will come out of Egypt (Hos. 11:1; Matt. 2:15) is somewhat general, while the Psalmist's prophecy regarding Christ's words "Why hast thou forsaken me?" was uttered verbatim by Jesus on the cross (Ps. 22:1; Matt. 27:46) and is specific. Several other prophecies were fulfilled in a precise manner, such as the prophecy regarding Jesus' name—his "name shall be Jesus Christ, the Son of God" (2 Ne. 25:19; Mosiah 3:8).

| | |
|---|---|
| Jesus prepared from the beginning | • "He who was prepared from the foundation of the world" (Ether 3:14) |
| | • "Chosen from the beginning" (Moses 4:2) |
| | • "Whom shall I send? . . . Here am I, send me" (Abr. 3:27) |
| Jesus' forerunner | • John precedes Jesus as "the voice of one crying in the wilderness" (Matt. 3:3; Isa. 40:3) |
| | • John prepares "the way of the Lord" (1 Ne. 10:7–8; 11:27) |
| Jesus' birth | • Born of a virgin (Isa. 7:14; Matt. 1:23; 1 Ne. 11:18) |
| | • "His mother shall be called Mary" (Mosiah 3:8; Alma 7:10) |
| | • "Unto us a child is born" (Isa. 9:6) |
| | • "He shall grow up . . . as a tender plant" (Isa. 53:2) |
| | • Descendant of David (Isa. 9:7; 11:1; Jer. 23:5; 33:15; Matt. 1:1; John 7:42; D&C 113:1–2) |
| | • Specific year of his coming (1 Ne. 19:8; Hel. 14:2) |
| | • "He shall . . . be born of a woman" (Alma 19:13) |
| | • "I shall take upon me flesh and blood" (Ether 3:9) |
| | • "Lord Omnipotent . . . shall dwell in a tabernacle of clay" (Mosiah 3:5) |

|                    |                                                                                      |
| ------------------ | ------------------------------------------------------------------------------------ |
|                    | • Condescension(s) (1 Ne. 11:16–20; 2 Ne. 9:53; Jacob 4:7)                           |
|                    | • Would be born "at Jerusalem" (Alma 7:10)                                            |
|                    | • Comes forth from Bethlehem (Micah 5:2; Matt. 2:1, 6)                                |
|                    | • "In the body he shall show himself unto those at Jerusalem" (2 Ne. 9:5)             |
| Jesus' names       | • His "name shall be Jesus Christ, the Son of God" (2 Ne. 25:19; Mosiah 3:8)          |
|                    | • Jesus Christ (Moses 6:52; 8:23–24; Ether 3:14–16)                                   |
|                    | • He is named "Immanuel" (Isa. 7:14)                                                  |
|                    | • He is named "Wonderful, Counsellor, The mighty God, The everlasting Father, The Prince of Peace" (Isa. 9:6) |
|                    | • He is the Shepherd (Gen. 49:24; Ps. 23:1; John 10:14; 1 Ne. 13:41)                 |
|                    | • Savior (1 Ne. 21:26; Isa. 43:11)                                                   |
|                    | • Jehovah (Abr. 1:16; John 8:58)                                                     |
|                    | • Redeemer (Job 19:25; Isa. 47:4)                                                    |
|                    | • Messiah (Isa. 61:1; Dan. 9:26; Matt. 16:16; 1 Ne. 10:4; 2 Ne. 1:10)                |
|                    | • "Christ . . . should be his name" (2 Ne. 10:3)                                      |
| Jesus' childhood   | • He comes out of Egypt (Hos. 11:1; Matt. 2:15)                                       |
|                    | • He would "be called a Nazarene" (Matt. 2:23)                                        |
|                    | • Mary and Jesus in Nazareth (1 Ne. 11:13, 20)                                        |
| Jesus' baptism     | • John baptizes "the Messiah with water" (1 Ne. 10:9–10; 11:27)                       |
|                    | • Jesus is baptized to "fulfil all righteousness" (2 Ne. 31:5–6)                      |

| | |
|---|---|
| Jesus and the Holy Ghost | • After Jesus' baptism the Holy Ghost shall "abide upon him" (1 Ne. 11:27) |
| | • "The Holy Ghost descended upon him in the form of a dove" (2 Ne. 31:8) |
| Jesus' disposition | • "He had done no violence, neither was any deceit in his mouth" (Isa. 53:9) |
| | • He is righteous (Jer. 23:5–6) |
| | • He is "a man of sorrows" (Isa. 53:3) |
| | • He is "acquainted with grief" (Isa. 53:3) |
| | • He serves as a loving shepherd (Gen. 49:24; Isa. 40:10–11; Ezek. 34:11–31) |
| | • He delights to do God's will (Ps. 40:7–8) |
| | • He is full of understanding and power (Isa. 11:1–5) |
| | • A light out of darkness (Isa. 9:1–2) |
| | • A sure foundation and cornerstone (Isa. 28:16) |
| Jesus and temptation, hunger, and thirst | • "He shall suffer temptation, and pain of body, hunger, thirst, and fatigue, even more than man can suffer, except it be unto death" (Mosiah 3:7) |
| | • "Suffering pains and afflictions and temptations of every kind" (Alma 7:11) |
| | • Jesus "suffereth temptation" (Mosiah 15:5) |
| Jesus' ministry | • He will "preach good tidings unto the meek" (Isa. 61:1) |
| | • Teachings are rejected (Isa. 6:9–10) |
| | • Dwells "beyond Jordan, in Galilee of the nations" (Isa. 9:1) |
| | • "Christ . . . should come among the Jews" (2 Ne. 10:3) |
| | • Has a zeal for God's house (Ps. 69:9) |

- Prays for adversaries (Ps. 109:4)
- Comes in the Lord's name (Ps. 118:26)
- "He shall not fail nor be discouraged" (Isa. 42:4)
- Taught with parables (Ps. 78:2; Matt. 13:35)
- Jesus loves his disciples as a shepherd (Isa. 40:10–11; Ezek. 34:11–31)
- "He went forth ministering unto the people" (1 Ne. 11:28, 31)
- He "shall go forth amongst men, working mighty miracles" (Mosiah 3:5; 15:6; 2 Ne. 10:4)

| | |
|---|---|
| Jesus' healings and casting out of devils | • The Lamb heals the sick, lame, blind, deaf, diseased, raises the dead, and casts out devils and unclean spirits (1 Ne. 11:31; Mosiah 3:5–6) |
| Jesus' priesthood | • The Melchizedek Priesthood "after the order of the Son of God" (JST Gen. 14:28)<br>• "Thou art a priest for ever after the order of Melchizedek" (Ps. 110:4; Heb. 7:3; Alma 13:7–9)<br>• A priest upon his throne (Zech. 6:12–13) |
| Jesus and the brokenhearted | • "He hath sent me to bind up the brokenhearted" (Isa. 61:1)<br>• He comforts "all that mourn" (Isa. 61:2) |
| Jesus' rejection | • People "hid [their] faces from him" (Isa. 53:3)<br>• People "esteemed him not" (Isa. 53:3)<br>• People "like sheep have gone astray" (Isa. 53:6)<br>• He is a stumbling block and snare to Israel and Jerusalem's inhabitants (Isa. 8:13–15)<br>• Rejected like a building stone that is rejected by builders (Ps. 118:22)<br>• Hated for no reason (Ps. 35:19; 69:4) |

- Jesus was mocked, scourged, cast out, and "disowned by his people" (Mosiah 15:5)
- The "multitudes . . . cast [Jesus] out from among them" (1 Ne. 11:28)
- "Because of priestcrafts and iniquities, they . . . stiffen their necks against him" (2 Ne. 10:5)
- "They will reject him, because of their iniquities" (2 Ne. 25:12)
- They will "reject the stone upon which they might build" (Jacob 4:15)

| | |
|---|---|
| Jesus' triumphal entry | • He is a king who comes to Jerusalem, "lowly, and riding upon an ass" (Zech. 9:9; Matt. 21:5)<br>• People would say of Jesus, "Blessed be he that cometh in the name of the Lord" (Ps. 118:26; Mark 11:9; Luke 19:38; John 12:13) |
| Jesus' betrayal | • Betrayed for "thirty pieces of silver" (Zech. 11:12; Matt. 26:15)<br>• The thirty pieces of silver were cast to the potter (Zech. 11:13; Matt. 27:9–10)<br>• Betrayed by a familiar friend (Ps. 41:9; Acts 1:16–20)<br>• He will receive wounds in his hands in the "house of [his] friends" (Zech. 13:6) |
| Jesus' trial | • False witnesses rise up (Ps. 35:11)<br>• Silent before his accusers (Isa. 53:7)<br>• Hid not his "face from shame and spitting" (Isa. 50:6)<br>• "Assembly of the wicked have inclosed me" (Ps. 22:16)<br>• "God of Abraham . . . yieldeth himself . . . into the hands of wicked men" (1 Ne. 19:10) |

| | |
|---|---|
| | • "Brought as a lamb to the slaughter" (Isa. 53:7; Matt. 26:57; 27:2, 12) |
| | • "The Son of the everlasting God was judged of the world" (1 Ne. 11:32) |
| Jesus' sufferings | • "Surely he hath borne our griefs and carried our sorrows" (Isa. 53:4) |
| | • "He is despised and rejected" (Isa. 53:3) |
| | • "He was wounded" (Isa. 53:5) |
| | • He was "bruised" (Isa. 53:5) |
| | • He received "stripes" (Isa. 53:5; 1 Pet. 2:21–25) |
| | • "He was oppressed, and he was afflicted" (Isa. 53:7) |
| | • "He openeth not his mouth" (Isa. 53:7) |
| | • He was "stricken" (Isa. 53:8) |
| | • He gives his "back to the smiters" and his "cheeks to them that plucked off the hair" (Isa. 50:6; John 18:22; 19:3) |
| | • He hid not his "face from shame and spitting" (Isa. 50:6; Mark 14:65) |
| | • Jesus will be smitten (Zech. 13:7; Matt. 26:31) |
| | • His visage marred (Isa. 52:14) |
| | • "Son of God suffereth according to the flesh" (Alma 7:13; 16:19; Mosiah 18:2) |
| Jesus' atonement for our sins and iniquities | • "He was wounded for our transgressions, he was bruised for our iniquities" (Isa. 53:5) |
| | • "The Lord hath laid on him the iniquities of us all" (Isa. 53:6; 1 Pet. 2:21–25) |
| | • "For the transgression of my people was he stricken" (Isa. 53:8; Acts 8:32–35; Rev. 5:6, 12; 13:8) |

- "He shall bear their iniquities" (Isa. 53:11)
- "He bare the sin of many" (Isa. 53:12; Rom. 4:25; Heb. 9:28)
- Jesus will bruise Satan (Gen. 3:15; Rom. 16:20)
- "Redemption cometh through Christ" (Mosiah 16:15; 2 Ne. 1:10)
- Redemption would come through Jesus' "death and sufferings" (Alma 21:9)
- "Christ, who shall come . . . to redeem the world" (Hel. 5:9; Ether 3:14)
- He was "slain for the sins of the world" (1 Ne. 11:33)
- "He offereth himself a sacrifice for sin" (2 Ne. 2:7)
- "Blood of Christ atoneth for their sins" (Mosiah 3:16)
- "He shall atone for the sins of the world" (Alma 34:8; 42:15)
- "Son of God hath atoned for original guilt" (Moses 6:54)
- "Redemption . . . brought to pass through the . . . sufferings, and death of Christ" (Mosiah 18:2)
- "Sufferings and death of Christ atone" (Alma 22:14)
- "Make intercession for all" (2 Ne. 2:9)
- "Reconciled unto him through the atonement of Christ" (Jacob 4:11)
- "To finish the transgression, and to make an end of sins, and to make reconciliation for iniquity" (Dan. 9:24)
- "Blood cometh from every pore" (Mosiah 3:7)
- He will "take upon him the sins of his people" (Alma 7:13)

| | |
|---|---|
| Jesus' atonement for our pains, infirmities, sicknesses, griefs, and sorrows | • "He suffereth the pains of all men" (2 Ne. 9:21)<br>• "He will take upon him their infirmities" (Alma 7:12)<br>• He will "take upon him the pains and the sicknesses" (Alma 7:11)<br>• "He has borne our griefs, . . . and carried our sorrows" (Isa. 53:4)<br>• "Wherefore, it must needs be an infinite atonement" (2 Ne. 9:7) |
| Jesus' infinite atonement | • "The atonement . . . is infinite for all mankind" (2 Ne. 25:16)<br>• "It must be an infinite and eternal sacrifice" (Alma 34:10)<br>• "Nothing which is short of an infinite atonement . . . will suffice for the sins of the world" (Alma 34:12) |
| Jesus' atonement satisfies justice and mercy | • "For the atonement satisfieth the demands of his justice" (2 Ne. 9:26; Mosiah 15:8–9, 26–27)<br>• "The plan of mercy could not be brought about except an atonement should be made" (Alma 42:15)<br>• "God himself atoneth for the sins of the world, to bring about the plan of mercy, to appease the demands of justice" (Alma 42:15) |
| Jesus' atonement redeems humankind from physical death and the Fall | • "He will take upon him death, that he may loose the bands of death which bind his people" (Alma 7:12)<br>• The resurrection comes because of Jesus' "death and sufferings" and "the atonement of his blood" (Alma 21:9) |

- The "death of Christ shall loose the bands of this temporal death" (Alma 11:42)
- "He may bring to pass the resurrection of the dead" (2 Ne. 2:8)
- "Save it should be an infinite atonement this corruption could not put on incorruption" (2 Ne. 9:7)
- Jesus "suffereth the pains of all men . . . that the resurrection might pass upon all men" (2 Ne. 9:21–22; Mosiah 15:7–9, 20–27)
- "There was a plan of redemption laid, which shall bring to pass the resurrection of the dead" (Alma 12:25; 11:39–45)

| | |
|---|---|
| Jesus' crucifixion | - "He was numbered with the transgressors" (Isa. 53:12) |
| | - He asked his Father, "Why hast thou forsaken me?" (Ps. 22:1; Matt. 27:46) |
| | - People laughed at him and scorned him (Ps. 22:7–8; Matt. 27:30–31, 39; Mark 15:29) |
| | - While on the cross he was thirsty (Ps. 22:15; John 19:28) |
| | - They give him gall and vinegar to drink (Ps. 69:20–21; Matt. 27:48) |
| | - His hands and feet are pierced (Ps. 22:16; Matt. 27:35) |
| | - He would be crucified with a "nail in a sure place" (Isa. 22:23) |
| | - People will look on the pierced Jesus (Zech. 12:10; John 19:37) |
| | - The piercing causes wounds in his hands (Zech. 13:6) |

- Jesus is "poured out like water" (Ps. 22:14; John 19:34)
- Lots cast for his vesture (Ps. 22:18; Matt. 27:35)
- People say, "He trusted on the Lord that he would deliver him: let him deliver him" (Ps. 22:8; Matt. 27:43; Luke 23:35)
- Crucifixion is described (Ps. 22:14–15)
- He says, "Into thine hand I commit my spirit" (Ps. 31:5)
- No bones broken (Ps. 34:20; John 19:32–36)
- Jesus would be "lifted up upon the cross" (1 Ne. 11:33; Moses 7:55)
- He is "lifted up" and "crucified" (1 Ne. 19:10)
- "They crucify the God of Israel" (1 Ne. 19:13)
- "They should scourge him and crucify him" (2 Ne. 6:9)
- The people "stiffen their necks against him, that he be crucified" (2 Ne. 10:5)
- "They will crucify him" (2 Ne. 25:13; 10:3, 5)

| | |
|---|---|
| Jesus' death | • "He is brought . . . to the slaughter" (Isa. 53:7)<br>• He is "cut off out of the land of the living" (Isa. 53:8)<br>• He is "with the rich in his death" (Isa. 53:9)<br>• "He hath poured out his soul unto death" (Isa. 53:12)<br>• Jesus the Messiah would be slain (1 Ne. 10:11)<br>• He "layeth down his life" (2 Ne. 2:8)<br>• "Becoming subject even unto death" (Mosiah 15:7)<br>• "Sufferings, and death of Christ" (Mosiah 18:2; 3 Ne. 6:20) |

| | |
|---|---|
| | • "He will take upon him death" (Alma 7:12; 16:19) |
| | • "Shall Messiah be cut off, but not for himself" (Dan. 9:26) |
| | • "Suffereth himself to . . . die for all men" (2 Ne. 9:5) |
| | • The Messiah is slain (1 Ne. 10:11) |
| | • "He offereth himself a sacrifice for sin" (2 Ne. 2:7) |
| | • "He will swallow up death in victory" (Isa. 25:8) |
| Signs at Jesus' death | • "Three days of darkness . . . sign given of his death" (1 Ne. 19:10) |
| | • "Signs given unto my people of . . . his death" (2 Ne. 26:3; Hel. 14:14; 3 Ne. 11:2) |
| | • Cities destroyed, lightnings, earthquakes, thunderings (1 Ne. 12:4–6) |
| | • Sun, moon, and stars darkened, lightnings, thunderings, tempests, highways and cities become desolate, rocks broken, "mountains laid low" (Hel. 14:23; see also vv. 20–28) |
| Jesus' burial | • "He made his grave with the wicked" (Isa. 53:9) |
| | • Jonah is a type that Christ would remain three days and nights in the tomb (Jonah 1:17) |
| | • "He is laid in a sepulchre" (2 Ne. 25:13) |
| | • He is "buried in a sepulchre" (1 Ne. 19:10) |
| Jesus' visit to the spirit world | • He will "bring out the prisoners from the prison, and them that sit in darkness out of the prison house" (Isa. 42:7; see also 49:9) |
| | • "I have sent forth thy prisoners out of the pit" (Zech. 9:11) |
| | • He proclaims "liberty to the captives, and the opening of the prison to them that are bound" (Isa. 61:1) |

| | |
|---|---|
| Jesus' resurrection | • He will "stand at the latter day upon the earth" as a resurrected being (Job 19:25; see also 1 Sam. 2:6; Ezek. 37:12–13) |
| | • Jesus' soul would not be left in hell, and his body will not "see corruption" (Ps. 16:10; Acts 2:27; 13:35; see also Jonah 2:6) |
| | • "He will swallow up death in victory" (Isa. 25:8) |
| | • His "dead body" will arise (Isa. 26:19) |
| | • He will destroy graves at the resurrection (Hos. 13:14) |
| | • He will hold the keys of the resurrection (Isa. 22:22) |
| | • "He should rise from the dead" (1 Ne. 10:11; 2 Ne. 26:1) |
| | • Jesus would "rise from the dead, with healing in his wings" (2 Ne. 25:13) |
| | • "Messiah hath risen from the dead" (2 Ne. 25:14) |
| | • "He shall rise the third day from the dead" (Mosiah 3:10) |
| Jesus' exaltation and blessings | • Sits at God's right hand (Ps. 110:1) |
| | • Given dominion and glory (Ps. 72:1–19) |
| | • Ascended to heaven (Ps. 68:18) |
| | • Has an eternal throne and kingdom (Ps. 45:6) |
| | • "He shall be exalted and extolled, and be very high" (Isa. 52:13) |
| | • "He shall see his seed" (Isa. 53:10) |
| | • "He shall prolong his days" (Isa. 53:10) |

- "The pleasure of the Lord shall prosper in his hand" (Isa. 53:10)
- "He . . . shall be satisfied" (Isa. 53:11)
- He will have "a portion with the great" (Isa. 53:12)
- "He shall divide the spoil with the strong" (Isa. 53:12)

---

## CHAPTER 14

# WALKING ON WATER AND OTHER MIRACLES: WITNESSES OF ATONING POWER

SOME OF THE MOST IMPRESSIVE WORKS of God on earth are the miracles his prophets—and the Savior himself—performed. On one level, these miracles show forth the power of God to the blessing of man. On a deeper, perhaps more profound level, miracles bear witness of and teach truth about the atonement of Jesus Christ.

Jesus' power was prefigured in stories from the Old Testament, where incredible power is manifest in the lives of Enoch, Melchizedek, Moses, Joshua, Elijah, Elisha, and others. As just one example, Elijah sealed the heavens so it would not rain for three and a half years, was miraculously fed by ravens during a drought, blessed a widow's barrels of meal and oil so they would not go empty, raised a young boy from the dead, called down fire from heaven, opened the heavens so it would rain again, divided the waters of the Jordan River, and rode a chariot of fire into heaven. Of course, Elijah did all these things through the power of God.

The mortal Messiah did even greater works. His power was manifest in such miracles as changing water to wine, walking on water, stilling a storm, multiplying loaves and fishes, healing the sick (lame, blind, leprous, and others), raising the dead, casting out devils, and many more.

Each miracle Jesus did was literal—a marvelous manifestation of his power in heaven and on earth. But the physical miracles also show us Christ's power in the spiritual realm to bless us, to succor us, to lift us, to change us, and to bring us to life eternal. Each physical miracle is a type of what he will do for us spiritually through the power of the atonement. When he healed the physically blind, he attested to his power to heal the spiritually blind. When he stilled the storm, he made manifest that he can succor us in the violent spiritual storms of our lives. When he cast out devils, he showed that he has power over Satan—as well as over the weaknesses within us.

President Howard W. Hunter, then a member of the Quorum of the Twelve Apostles, taught of the spiritual meaning of the miracles of Christ in the October 1979 general conference:

> There was an incident in the life of the Savior that was mentioned by Matthew, Mark, and Luke. A significant part of the story is told by Mark in only two short verses and five words of the following verse. Let me read them to you.
>
> "And, behold, there cometh one of the rulers of the synagogue, Jairus by name; and when he saw him [that is, when he saw Jesus], he fell at his feet,
>
> "And besought him greatly, saying, My little daughter lieth at the point of death: I pray thee, come and lay thy hands on her, that she may be healed; and she shall live.
>
> "And Jesus went with him" (Mark 5:22–24).
>
> The reading time of that portion of the story is about thirty seconds. It is short and uncomplicated. The visual picture is clear and even a child could repeat it without difficulty. But as we spend time in thought and contemplation, a great depth of understanding and meaning comes to us. We conclude that this is more than a simple story about a little girl who was sick and Jesus went to lay his hands on her. Let me read these words to you again: . . .
>
> ". . . I pray thee, come and lay thy hands on her, that she may be healed; and she shall live." These are not only the words

of faith of a father torn with grief but are also a reminder to us that whatever Jesus lays his hands upon lives. If Jesus lays his hands upon a marriage, it lives. If he is allowed to lay his hands on the family, it lives. . . .

. . . When they got to the home of the ruler of the synagogue, Jesus took the little girl by the hand and raised her from the dead. In like manner, he will lift and raise every man to a new and better life who will permit the Savior to take him by the hand.[1]

The story of the raising of the daughter of Jairus from the dead literally happened. It bears witness of the Savior's power over death for all of us. It also bears testimony of the power and love of Christ, activated through his atonement, to lift us and bring us to "a new and better life."

Latter-day Saint author Bruce Satterfield presents an interesting insight into the miracles recorded in the Gospel of John. There, he notes, Jesus' miracles are juxtaposed with his teachings regarding his mission as the Savior. Each of the miracles recorded by John, then, bears witness of Christ's atoning power.

> John wrote his gospel to convince his readers that Jesus was the one anointed to save man from sin. He stated: "And many other signs truly did Jesus in the presence of his disciples, which are not written in this book: But these are written, that ye might believe that Jesus is the Christ, the Son of God; and that believing ye might have life through his name" (20:30–31).
>
> In this statement, John calls the Savior's miracles "signs" rather than miracles. He saw within each miracle a truth verifying that Jesus is the Christ. . . . He associated each sign with a discourse given by the Savior that reflects the miracle. It appears that the sign and miracle should be read in conjunction with each other with the miracle being a sign that verifies the truth taught in the discourse. . . . The following is a list of the miracles and discourses:
>
> 1. **Sign:** Water converted to wine (2:1–11)
>    **Discourse**: The natural man converted to the spiritual man (3:1–21)
> 2. **Sign:** Bringing life to the nobleman's son (4:46–54)

**Discourse:** The living waters that bring everlasting life (4:1–42)

3. **Sign:** The healing of the invalid on the Sabbath (5:1–18)
   **Discourse:** The Divine Son, the Lord of the Sabbath (5:19–47)

4. **Sign:** Miracle feeding of the multitude with bread (6:1–15)
   **Discourse:** Christ is the bread of life (6:22–66)

5. **Sign:** Jesus walks on water (6:12–21)
   **Discourse:** Christ, who will walk into the presence of the Father, offers living water to all (7:14–39)

6. **Sign:** Healing of the man born blind (9)
   **Discourse:** Christ is the Light of the World (8:12–59)

7. **Sign:** The raising of Lazarus from the dead (11)
   **Discourse**: Christ, the Good Shepherd, will lay down his life for his sheep, that he might bring about the resurrection (10:1–18).[2]

By way of example, let's look at two of Christ's miracles to see how they teach of his atonement. If we were to read with the Spirit and with understanding, we could gain similar insights into many of the other miracles he performed.

## THE MIRACLE OF THE LOAVES AND FISHES

The miracle of feeding the five thousand with only a few loaves and fishes is recorded in all four of the Gospels (Matt. 14:14–21; Mark 6:32–44; Luke 9:10–17; John 6:1–14), although there are some key differences among the four accounts. For example, only John records that the miracle was followed by the stunning "bread of life" sermon (John 6:22–66), and only Luke mentions that the miracle occurred in Bethsaida (Luke 9:10). Examining this miracle part by part will illustrate the way in which it casts light on the atonement of Jesus Christ.

> And [Jesus took the apostles], . . . and went aside privately into a desert place belonging to the city called Bethsaida. And the people, when they knew it, followed him: and he received them,

and spake unto them of the kingdom of God, and healed them that had need of healing. (Luke 9:10–11)

We also are in a desert place, a mortal world filled with trial and difficulty. When we choose to follow Jesus, he will teach us (through the Spirit and through mortal ministers) about his kingdom. He will heal us spiritually through his power. (Interestingly, the account in Mark doesn't simply say that they followed Jesus, but that they *ran* to do so.)

And Jesus, when he came out, saw much people, and was moved with compassion toward them, because they were as sheep not having a shepherd: and he began to teach them many things. (Mark 6:34)

When Jesus sees us, he is moved with compassion toward us—he is filled with pure love. Without him we are "as sheep not having a shepherd." But if we will turn our hearts to him and his duly called representatives, he will teach us "many things."

And when the day was now far spent, his disciples came unto him, and said, This is a desert place, and now the time is far passed: Send them away, that they may go into the country round about, and into the villages, and buy themselves bread: for they have nothing to eat. (Mark 6:35–36)

Again we see the emphasis that we are living in a spiritual desert, and that time is passing us by. True spiritual nourishment comes only when we stay with Jesus, rather than going elsewhere to find it. The account in John indicates that Jesus fully recognized both the need and the solution: "When Jesus then lifted up his eyes, and saw a great company come unto him, he saith unto Philip, Whence shall we buy bread, that these may eat? And this he said to prove him: for he himself knew what he would do" (John 6:5–6).

He answered and said unto them, Give ye them to eat. And they say unto him, Shall we go and buy two hundred pennyworth of bread, and give them to eat? He saith unto them, How many loaves have ye? go and see. And when they knew, they say, Five, and two fishes. (Mark 6:37–38)

The blessings of the atonement cannot be purchased. They come only from Christ, by miracle. He is desirous that we all be given what we need. As the Lord said through Isaiah, "Every one that thirsteth, come ye to the waters, and he that hath no money; come ye, buy, and eat; yea, come, buy wine and milk without money and without price" (Isa. 55:1).

> And he commanded them to make all sit down by companies upon the green grass. And they sat down in ranks, by hundreds, and by fifties. And when he had taken the five loaves and the two fishes, he looked up to heaven, and blessed, and brake the loaves, and gave them to his disciples to set before them; and the two fishes divided he among them all. (Mark 6:39–41)

The blessings of the atonement are often ministered unto us through the Lord's servants. Christ gives direction and authority to those who hold the priesthood; those called to serve, in turn, bless us in small groups. We receive as we follow Jesus in what he commands us to do. Even when the Lord's servants are part of the process, however, the blessings we receive come directly from the Lord himself, who is joined with the Father in giving the blessing. Further, everyone who comes unto Christ is able to receive: "divided he among them *all*."

Latter-day Saint scholar Thomas R. Valletta adds another insight into John's account: "John's words foreshadow the sacrament of the Lord's Supper, wherein Jesus 'took' the bread, gave 'thanks,' and 'gave' it to His Apostles to eat (see Matt. 26:26; Mark 14:22; Luke 22:19; 1 Cor. 11:24). The phraseology effectively alerts the reader to the possible sacramental symbolism of both the miraculous multiplication of the loaves and of the manna of the Exodus."[3]

> And they did all eat, and were filled: and they took up of the fragments that remained twelve baskets full. And they that had eaten were about five thousand men, beside women and children. (Matt. 14:20–21)

The Lord gives us enough grace and to spare. We are filled, and there is always more remaining for us and for others in need.

> Then those men, when they had seen the miracle that Jesus did, said, This is of a truth that prophet that should come into the world. (John 6:14)

When we partake of the blessings of the atonement, the miracle that lifts and fills us, we are constrained to testify, "This is of a truth" Jesus the Christ, whom the prophets testified would come into the world.

The next day, Jesus gave further meaning to the miracle, saying that in a crucial way he was the very bread that gives life:

> And Jesus said unto them, I am the bread of life; he that cometh to me shall never hunger; and he that believeth on me shall never thirst. . . . This is the bread which cometh down from heaven, that a man may eat thereof, and not die.
>
> Your fathers did eat manna in the wilderness [or desert], and are dead. But I am the living bread which came down from heaven; if any man eat of this bread, he shall live for ever; and the bread that I will give is my flesh, which I will give for the life of the world. . . . Whoso eateth my flesh, and drinketh my blood, hath eternal life; and I will raise him up in the resurrection of the just at the last day. (JST John 6:35, 49–51, 54)

The atonement of Christ can meet our deepest need, just as the miracle of the loaves and fishes met the needs of the people in that desert. The bread could not be multiplied by the apostles—they could not meet this need of the people. But Christ could.

Both miracles (multiplying food and offering the sacrifice of the atonement) are performed by the power of Christ because he loves us. When we read about the loaves and fishes, we can think of what the true bread is, and how it can bless us forever.

## WALKING ON WATER

What kind of man can walk on water? It's one thing to use the power of God to divide a sea or a river so that people can walk across on dry ground—as Moses and later Joshua did (Ex. 14:21–22; Josh. 3:14–17). It's quite another to actually walk across the top of water. And Jesus performed this singular miracle not on a glass-level sea but in the midst of a storm. In doing so he proceeded faster across the water than the apostles' ship was able to go (Mark 6:48), and he then helped one of his mortal followers to walk on the water as well (Matt. 14:28–29).

Jesus' walk on water demonstrated in a remarkable way his power over the elements and suggests his power over all things—including sin and death. This miracle is recorded in three of the Gospels (Matt. 14:22–36; Mark 6:45–56; John 6:15–21). It occurred immediately following the miracle of the loaves and fishes.

> When Jesus therefore perceived that they [those who had witnessed the miracle of the loaves and the fishes] would come and take him by force, to make him a king, he departed again into a mountain himself alone. And when even was now come, his disciples went down unto the sea, and entered into a ship, and went over the sea toward Capernaum. And it was now dark, and Jesus was not come to them. (John 6:15–17)

Even when we experience Christ's power in our lives, there will be times when we feel that the Spirit is not as close as it was. It may feel as though we are crossing over a sea in the darkness of night—and even though we may hope and expect that the Savior's influence will return, it may not come as soon as we desire.

> But the ship was now in the midst of the sea, tossed with waves: for the wind was contrary. And in the fourth watch of the night Jesus went unto them, walking on the sea. (Matt. 14:24–25)

The storm of our life sometimes gets worse, with heavy waves and a contrary wind. The account in Mark says that Jesus "saw them toiling in rowing" (Mark 6:48). We may see that we're making no headway and may even feel that we are threatened with destruction. John called the wind "a great wind" (John 6:18). Even though it may feel that the Lord is far from us, he actually is near and is fully aware of our need. To help us grow, he may not come immediately—the fourth watch of the night would have fallen in the dark hours just before the dawn. Yet the Savior *will* come to us in our need, sometimes in a manner that will seem truly miraculous.

Of this part of the story Latter-day Saint author Robert England Lee asked:

> What would it be like to row all night, being tossed by the waves and the wind, making no progress? Can we feel the pain in our hands, stomach, thighs, shoulders, and back? Can we feel the beating of the waves against our bodies? Can we see the blackness of the night? If we sense these things, we may have a deeper appreciation for what Alma called the "endless night of darkness" (Alma 41:7). In those words Alma described the condition of souls who had not repented, which would be the condition of all souls if there had been no atonement, and repentance were not possible. The ship on the sea may be seen as a type of the endless condition of all mankind if there were no Redeemer. . . .
>
> Alma explained that all will not be consigned to an endless night of darkness, for "mercy claimeth the penitent, and mercy cometh because of the atonement; and the atonement bringeth to pass the resurrection of the dead; and the resurrection of the dead bringeth back men into the presence of God" (Alma 42:23).[4]

The scriptural account of this miracle continues:

> But when they saw him walking upon the sea, they supposed it had been a spirit, and cried out: for they all saw him, and were troubled. And immediately he talked with them, and saith unto them, Be of good cheer: it is I; be not afraid. (Mark 6:49–50)

When we see the presence of the Lord in our lives, he will immediately reassure us that he has come to bring the blessing we have sought: "Be of good cheer; it is I; be not afraid."

> And Peter answered him and said, Lord, if it be thou, bid me come unto thee on the water. And he said, Come. And when Peter was come down out of the ship, he walked on the water, to go to Jesus. But when he saw the wind boisterous, he was afraid; and

beginning to sink, he cried, saying, Lord, save me. And immediately Jesus stretched forth his hand, and caught him, and said unto him, O thou of little faith, wherefore didst thou doubt? (Matt. 14:28–31)

Not only will the Lord come to us, but he will also help us to come to him, even if it seems that the gap between us is impassible, even if it seems impossible for us so to come. Like Peter, some are anxious at all costs to come unto Christ. When our faith and desire are sufficient, through his grace we will be enabled to "go to Jesus." But if we then focus on the temptations of the adversary or the turbulent circumstances of our life and give way to fear, we will again begin to slip away from him, perhaps in ways that could take our very lives, speaking spiritually. Even then, if we will cry out to Jesus, "Lord, save me," he will stretch "forth his hand" and catch us.

Robert England Lee wrote:

> What would it have been like to be Peter at that moment? What would it be like to know that we were powerless to deliver ourselves from the sea? Can we feel our hearts breaking and the contrition of our spirits as our arm stretches up in hope and our voice cries out, "Save me, Lord"? Can we feel the power in the outstretched hand of the Son of God as he grasps our own feeble arm and pulls us from the deep? If we can feel these things, we can begin to appreciate the meaning of the atonement of Christ in our lives, for without him we too are powerless to be delivered from the night of endless darkness. The difference between being without Christ in the world and having him as our companion is illustrated by Mark when he said, "And he went up unto them into the ship; and the wind ceased" (Mark 6:51).[5]

We next read in the Gospel account:

> And when they were come into the ship, the wind ceased. Then they that were in the ship came and worshipped him, saying, Of a truth thou art the Son of God. (Matt. 14:32–33)

When Jesus comes more fully into our troubled lives, he will help the storms to cease. John wrote that they "willingly" received Jesus into the ship (John 6:21). Then we will be constrained to acknowledge his divinity, with which he will bless us with the great blessings of his atonement, and we will exclaim, "Of a truth thou art the Son of God."

> Then . . . immediately the ship was at the land whither they went. (John 6:21)

When we receive Jesus Christ and his power into our lives, acknowledging him for who he is, he will quickly take us to the spiritual land we seek.

> And when they were come out of the ship, straightway they knew him, and ran through that whole region round about, and began to carry about in beds those that were sick, where they heard he was. And whithersoever he entered, into villages, or cities, or country, they laid the sick in the streets, and besought him that they might touch if it were but the border of his garment: and as many as touched him were made whole. (Mark 6:54–56)

When we participate in the miracle of the blessing that Jesus Christ brings, we want to show others what he can do in their lives. Their faith will also be strengthened, and many will choose to come unto Christ to partake of the healing power of his atonement.

The very works of Christ bore testimony of the truth and power of the atonement. His miracles, marvelous in their own right, stand as witnesses through the generations of the Savior's power over all things.

## CHAPTER 15

# SON OF GOD, SON OF MAN:
# A LIFE OF CONTRADICTIONS

JOSEPH SMITH TAUGHT THAT JESUS "descended in suffering below that which man can suffer; or, in other words, suffered greater sufferings, and was exposed to more powerful contradictions than any man can be. But, notwithstanding all this, he kept the law of God, and remained without sin."[1]

The apostle Paul also referred to contradictions. We must look unto "Jesus the author and finisher of our faith," he said, "who for the joy that was set before him endured the cross, despising the shame, and is set down at the right hand of the throne of God. For consider him that endured such contradiction of sinners against himself, lest ye be wearied and faint in your minds" (Heb. 12:2–3).

Here Paul captures the essence of the contradictions Jesus experienced: He suffered beyond all our suffering because of "the joy that was set before him," which joy includes the blessing of our eternal salvation. The "contradiction of sinners" is alternatively translated as "rebellion of sinners" or "opposition of sinners."[2] This is an astounding contradiction: those who most need the Savior (although we all desperately need him) rebel against him, oppose him, and put him to death.

The contradictions the Savior suffered began with his condescension: the God of all creation descended to earth as an infant to suffer all that mankind suffers and more (1 Ne. 19:9–10). He left behind his exalted station and his glory to be clothed in human flesh. During his life and his atonement, he "descended below them all" (D&C 122:8). But in the end he ascends above them all and, as Paul testified, Jesus "is set down at the right hand of the throne of God" (Heb. 12:2). Through that final triumphant ascent, he is able to lift all men to him.

A poetic summary of the contradictions Jesus experienced was poignantly captured by Parley P. Pratt in a beloved hymn. Each couplet identifies a true paradox of his mortal existence.

> *Jesus, once of humble birth,*
> *Now in glory comes to earth.*
> *Once he suffered grief and pain;*
> *Now he comes on earth to reign.*
>
> *Once a meek and lowly Lamb,*
> *Now the Lord, the great I Am.*
> *Once upon the cross he bowed;*
> *Now his chariot is the cloud.*
>
> *Once he groaned in blood and tears;*
> *Now in glory he appears.*
> *Once rejected by his own,*
> *Now their King he shall be known.*
>
> *Once forsaken, left alone,*
> *Now exalted to a throne.*
> *Once all things he meekly bore,*
> *But he now will bear no more.*[3]

The accompanying table details some of the paradoxes or contradictions the Savior suffered during his mortal life.

# Paradoxes in the Life of the Messiah

| Jesus as a Mortal | Jesus from the Eternal Perspective |
|---|---|
| Was born in a dark and lowly stable | At his birth, angels proclaimed him, and a bright new star shone in the heavens |
| "There was no room for them in the inn" (Luke 2:7) | "The earth is the Lord's and the fulness thereof" (Ps. 24:1) |
| As an infant babe, was forced with his parents to flee from earthly powers by going into Egypt | As Jehovah, led the children of Israel from Egypt by heavenly power |
| Came not in glory but quietly, virtually in secret | Was truly a God |
| Came not to command but to obey the will of his Father | Was the true and lawful King |
| Lived a relatively obscure and inconspicuous mortal life | At his Second Coming, "every eye shall see him" (Rev. 1:7) |
| Mingled with the sick, lame, deaf, blind, leprous, the possessed of devils, the publicans and sinners, the despised Samaritans | Had ruled and reigned in the heavens—not only over one world but also over countless numbers of them |
| Was "despised and rejected of men" (Isa. 53:3) | Is Lord of all the hosts of heaven |
| Was called "a gluttonous man, and a winebibber, a friend of publicans and sinners" (Luke 7:34) | Never did anything but that which was perfectly true and right |
| Was accused of having a devil | Was the greatest enemy of Satan and had power over all devils |
| "The Son of man hath not where to lay his head" (Luke 9:58) | Had created "worlds without number" (Moses 1:33) |
| Was subject to cold, sickness, and pain | Now has a resurrected, perfect body |

| Jesus as a Mortal | Jesus from the Eternal Perspective |
|---|---|
| Healed multitudes | Received wounds for us |
| Was not recognized as the King of the Jews | Will return as King of all kings and Lord of all lords |
| Rode on a borrowed donkey as he entered Jerusalem for the final time | Will return riding "clouds of heaven" and a heavenly white horse (Matt. 26:64; Rev. 14:14; 19:11) |
| Suffered more greatly for sin (ours) than anyone in history | Was sinless |
| Was betrayed for thirty pieces of silver, the price of a common slave | Prophetically called "Wonderful, Counsellor, The mighty God, The everlasting Father, The Prince of Peace" (Isa. 9:6) |
| Was betrayed by a kiss | A kiss typically is a symbol of intimate affection |
| Meekly and submissively yielded to arrest | Could have called tens of thousands of angels to come to his aid |
| Permitted the wicked to smite him | At his Second Coming, will smite the wicked |
| Was slapped, spat upon, and mocked | Performed the atonement so that his oppressors could be forgiven |
| Was treated with hatred and disdain in his last hours | In his last hours, gave his disciples "a new commandment . . . , That ye love one another; as I have loved you" (John 13:34) |
| Was falsely judged by the people to be evil | Will be the great Judge of all |
| "The world, because of their iniquity, shall judge him to be a thing of naught" (1 Ne. 19:9) | Is Jehovah, Lord of heaven and earth |

| Jesus as a Mortal | Jesus from the Eternal Perspective |
| --- | --- |
| Unrighteous priests asked, "By what authority doest thou these things? and who gave thee this authority?" (Matt. 21:23) | Was and is the source of all true authority |
| Was accused of blasphemy, of giving offense to God | Was God himself |
| Was commanded by the high priest: "I adjure thee by [in the name of] the living God . . ." (Matt. 26:63) | Was and is "the living God" |
| Was declared "guilty of death" (Matt. 26:66) | Was guilty of nothing, while his accusers were "guilty of death" |
| Mockingly told, "prophesy unto us" (Matt. 26:68) | Was and is the source of all true prophecy |
| The murderer Barabbas (meaning "son of the father") was released in exchange for the execution of Jesus | Was innocent of any wrong and was the true Son of the Father |
| Mocked by Roman soldiers, who placed a false royal robe of scarlet and crown of thorns on him and said, "Hail, King of the Jews" (Matt. 27:29) | Truly was the king of the Jews |
| Was condemned by false witnesses | Bears the titles of "faithful witness" (Rev. 1:5; 3:14) and "truth" (John 14:6) |
| Was crucified between two thieves | Had given the command, "Thou shalt not steal" (Ex. 20:15) |
| Suffered excruciating pain on the cross | Pleaded from the cross that the Father would forgive his tormentors |
| Cried out on the cross, "I thirst" (John 19:28) | Created the rivers, streams, brooks, fountains, lakes, and oceans |
| Died as a purported criminal and breaker of the law | Was the source of the law, which he kept perfectly |
| Was placed in a borrowed tomb | Rose up as Master of the universe |

Brigham Young University professor Gary L. Bunker summarizes Christ's life of contradictions with these words: "He drank the bitter cup that we might drink the sweet. He was taken captive that we might be delivered. He was mocked that we might be more merciful. He was spat upon that we might be more sensitive. He was scourged that we might be sanctified. He was judged of the world that we might be justified. He was bruised that we might be blessed. He was wounded that we might be made whole. He died, that we might live."[4]

And Elder Neal A. Maxwell, of the Quorum of the Twelve, bore this testimony of the contradictions Christ suffered:

> For Jesus, in fact, irony began at His birth. Truly, He suffered the will of the Father "in all things from the beginning." (3 Ne. 11:11.) This whole earth became Jesus' footstool (see Acts 7:49), but at Bethlehem there was "no room . . . in the inn" (Luke 2:7) and "no crib for his bed." (*Hymns,* 1985, no. 206.)
>
> At the end, meek and lowly Jesus partook of the most bitter cup without becoming the least bitter. (See 3 Ne. 11:11; D&C 19:18–19.) The Most Innocent suffered the most. Yet the King of Kings did not break, even when some of His subjects did unto Him "as they listed." (D&C 49:6.) Christ's capacity to endure such irony was truly remarkable. . . .
>
> In heaven, Christ's lofty name was determined to be the only name on earth offering salvation to all mankind. (See Acts 4:12; 2 Ne. 25:20; see also Abr. 3:27.) Yet the Mortal Messiah willingly lived so modestly, even, wrote Paul, as a person "of no reputation." (Philip. 2:7.) . . .
>
> As the Creator, Christ constructed the universe, yet in little Galilee He was known merely as "the carpenter's son." (Matt. 13:55.) . . .
>
> As Jehovah, Jesus issued the original commandment to keep the Sabbath day holy, but during His mortal Messiahship, He was accused of violating the Sabbath, because on that day He gave healing rest to the afflicted. (See John 5:8–16.) . . .

Yet, even with all the ironies, sad ironies, there is the grand and glad irony of Christ's great mission. He Himself noted that precisely because He was "lifted up upon" the cross, He was able to "draw all men unto [him]," and being "lifted up by men," even so should "men be lifted up by the Father." (3 Ne. 27:14.)[5]

## CHAPTER 16

# DRINKING THE BITTER CUP: GETHSEMANE

WE SING IN "O LITTLE TOWN of Bethlehem": "The hopes and fears of all the years/Are met in thee tonight."[1] The hopes of the long millennia before Christ came was that God would provide a Savior to lift us from the world of sin and death. The fears were that the Savior might not come, or that somehow he might fail in his mission. Of course, God keeps all his promises, and in the baby Jesus the long-promised Messiah finally arrived on the earth. It wasn't until Gethsemane, however, that the Savior came to his ultimate purpose on the earth—to take upon him, in his innocence and purity, both sin and death—giving him power over both, not only for himself but for us as well. The fulfillment of that purpose continued on the cross and reached its culmination when he emerged from the tomb a resurrected, glorified being and ascended into the presence of the Father.

The Savior's perfect character, complete oneness with the Father, infinite love, and divine power all came together in the olive vineyard called Gethsemane. The scriptural accounts of the events in that garden, as well as the immediately preceding events, are filled with symbolisms and other insights that deepen our understanding of what actually occurred there. Here are a few examples.

## The Preparations

*The Passover.* As the last Passover of Jesus' life approached, "when the passover must be killed" (Luke 22:7), "Jesus knew that his hour was come that he should depart out of this world unto the Father, having loved his own which were in the world, [and] he loved them unto the end" (John 13:1). On Thursday evening of Jesus' last week, he sat down with the Twelve Apostles for the Passover meal. They apparently partook of the traditional symbolic menu, all of which points to Jesus Christ and his atonement and celebrates his power of deliverance (see chapter 2). "And he said unto them, With desire I have desired to eat this passover with you before I suffer" (Luke 22:15).

But Jesus then adapted part of the ceremony to point directly to his impending offering: "And as they were eating, Jesus took bread, and brake it, and blessed it, and gave to his disciples, and said, Take, eat; this is in remembrance of my body which I give a ransom for you. And he took the cup, and gave thanks, and gave it to them, saying, Drink ye all of it. For this is in remembrance of my blood of the new testament, which is shed for as many as shall believe on my name, for the remission of their sins. And I give unto you a commandment, that ye shall observe to do the things which ye have seen me do, and bear record of me even unto the end" (JST Matt. 26:22–25).

Throughout Jesus' entire life, his every act was purposeful—and here he took advantage of a powerful teaching opportunity. With his suffering and death only hours away, Jesus sought to point the minds and hearts of his disciples to the significance of that which would take place in Gethsemane and on Golgotha. The apostles may not have fully understood what he was telling them. But at the Last Supper, for them as well as for us, the Savior taught that he would give his body "a ransom" for us, and that his blood would be "shed . . . for the remission of [our] sins."

*The washing of the disciples' feet.* After administering the sacrament to the apostles, Jesus "riseth from supper, and laid aside his garments; and took a towel, and girded himself." He poured water into a basin "and began to wash the disciples' feet, and to wipe them with the towel wherewith he was girded." When Peter protested, Jesus explained, "If I wash thee not, thou hast no part with me." Then he added, "He that is washed needeth not save to wash his feet, but is clean every whit: and ye are clean." After he had finished, he sat back down again and said, "If I then, your Lord and Master, have washed your feet; ye also ought to wash one another's feet. For I have given you an example, that ye should do as I have done to you" (John 13:4, 5, 8, 10, 14–15).

The lessons of the washing of feet apply directly to the atonement that would soon take place: Jesus gives himself to our need. He serves. He has power to make us clean. And when we follow his example of selfless service, we more fully become one, united through the *at-oning* power of Christ.

Jesus freely gave this gift to the apostles (as he freely gives all gifts), "knowing that the Father had given all things into his hands, and that he was come from God, and went to God" (John 13:3). Sadly, Judas received this ordinance as well, to his own condemnation. Then he left the group to proceed with his betrayal, for "Satan entered into him" (John 13:27).

*The teachings.* After administering the washing of feet, the Savior gave some precious teachings pertaining to his divine commission from the Father and to the atonement—including such themes as his oneness with the Father, his power to take us to the Father, the oneness that comes through love, and the peace and comfort that can come through union with the Spirit. Only the apostle John recorded these truths (and thus all references are to the Gospel of John).

For example, *the Savior emphasized the blessing of oneness and unity with both the Father and the Son,* both in the present and in future glory, which comes through the atonement:

"He that receiveth me receiveth him that sent me" (13:20).

"In my Father's house are many mansions. . . . I go to prepare a place for you, . . . that where I am, there ye may be also" (14:2–3).

"I am the way, the truth, and the life: no man cometh unto the Father, but by me" (14:6).

"Because I live, ye shall live also. At that day ye shall know that I am in my Father, and ye in me, and I in you" (14:19–20).

*He taught that we would receive Comforters and peace,* even in his absence; these blessings too flow from the atonement:

"I will pray the Father, and he shall give you another Comforter, that he may abide with you for ever; . . . he dwelleth with you, and shall be in you. I will not leave you comfortless: I will come to you" (14:16–18).

"He that loveth me shall be loved of my Father, and I will love him, and will manifest myself to him. . . . And my Father will love him, and we will come unto him" (14:21, 23).

"Peace I leave with you, my peace I give unto you: not as the world giveth, give I unto you. Let not your heart be troubled, neither let it be afraid" (14:27; see also 16:33).

*He emphasized our need to receive his love and to strengthen our relationship with him and with one another,* which are also blessings of the atonement:

"A new commandment I give unto you, That ye love one another; as I have loved you. . . . By this shall all men know that ye are my disciples" (13:34–35).

"I am the vine, ye are the branches: He that abideth in me, and I in him, the same bringeth forth much fruit: for without me ye can do nothing" (15:5).

"As the Father hath loved me, so have I loved you: continue ye in my love. . . . I have kept my Father's commandments, and abide in his love" (15:9–10).

"Greater love hath no man than this, that a man lay down his life for his friends. Ye are my friends, if ye do whatsoever I command you. . . . I have called you friends" (15:13–15).

Finally, *he testified of his relationship with the Father,* which was an essential contributing factor to his ability to perform the atonement:

"I came forth from the Father, and am come into the world: again, I leave the world, and go to the Father. . . . I am not alone, because the Father is with me" (16:28, 32).

*The hymn.* Before going into the Garden of Gethsemane, Jesus and his disciples sang a hymn (Matt. 26:30; Mark 14:26). This was a traditional part of the Passover experience. Earlier in the ceremony the participants would sing the first part of the Hallel, Psalms 113 and 114. (The Hallel included many repetitions of the expression "Hallelu Yah!" meaning "Praise the Lord," "Praise Yah," or "Praise Jehovah!") Later in the Passover service, the participants would sing Psalms 115 through 118; it seems likely that these were the words that Jesus and the disciples sang at the end of the Last Supper.

The Hallel is Christ-centered poetry. For example, it is from Psalm 118 that we have this important prophecy of the rejection of Christ: "The stone which the builders refused is become the head stone of the corner. This is the Lord's doing; it is marvellous in our eyes. . . . Blessed be he that cometh in the name of the Lord" (vv. 22–23, 26). It's important to note that every detail of the Passover service symbolizes the bondage of Israel and God's deliverance of his people. The Hallel focuses on the goodness of God and his delivering power from sin and trouble, a deliverance that comes from his infinite atonement. Thus, a very short time before Christ began his suffering in the Garden of Gethsemane, he and his disciples likely sang such testimonies of the atonement as the following example:

> *Blessed be the name of the Lord from this time forth and for evermore. . . .*
> *Who is like unto the Lord our God, who dwelleth on high,*
> *Who humbleth himself to behold the things that are in heaven, and in the earth!* (Ps. 113:2, 5–6)
>
> *Ye that fear the Lord, trust in the Lord: he is their help and their shield.*
> *The Lord hath been mindful of us: he will bless us.* (Ps. 115:11–12)
>
> *The sorrows of death compassed me, and the pains of hell gat hold upon me: I found trouble and sorrow.*
> *Then called I upon the name of the Lord; O Lord, I beseech thee, deliver my soul.*

> *Gracious is the Lord, and righteous; yea, our*
> *God is merciful. . . .*
> *For thou hast delivered my soul from death,*
> *mine eyes from tears, and my feet from falling. . . .*
> *What shall I render unto the Lord for all his*
> *benefits toward me?*
> *I will take the cup of salvation, and call upon*
> *the name of the Lord. . . .*
> *O Lord, truly I am thy servant; . . . thou hast*
> *loosed my bonds.* (Ps. 116:3–5, 8, 12–13, 16)

> *O give thanks unto the Lord; for he is good: be-*
> *cause his mercy endureth for ever. . . .*
> *The Lord is on my side; I will not fear: what*
> *can man do unto me? . . .*
> *The Lord is my strength and song, and is be-*
> *come my salvation. . . .*
> *Open to me the gates of righteousness: I will go*
> *into them, and I will praise the Lord: . . .*
> *I will praise thee: for thou hast heard me, and*
> *art become my salvation. . . .*
> *Thou art my God, and I will praise thee: thou*
> *art my God, I will exalt thee.*
> *O give thanks unto the Lord; for he is good: for*
> *his mercy endureth for ever.* (Ps. 118:1, 6, 14, 19,
> 21, 28–29)

*The great Intercessory Prayer.* After uttering the teachings noted above, and perhaps after the hymn, Jesus offered what has been called the great Intercessory Prayer, a prayer of a perfect, sinless son pleading for his fallen brothers and sisters on the earth (John 17). The Gospels record many instances of Jesus seeking time alone with his Father for prayer; but this is the only prayer to which the words have been preserved in this detail. The burden of the prayer consisted of Christ as the great high priest interceding in behalf of his fellows, asking with deep yearnings that we might be united with one another as Christ and the

Father are united, and that we might be united with the Father and the Son. This unity or oneness is the work of the atonement.

Almost immediately before going to the Garden of Gethsemane, then, Christ reached up to heaven in a prayer outlining some of the key purposes of the atonement. By carefully studying this prayer (and a similar one offered among the Nephites, recorded in 3 Nephi 19:19–29), we can more fully understand why Christ's atoning sacrifice was offered. (A more detailed discussion of the Intercessory Prayer is found in chapter 8.)

*The brook Kidron.* After Jesus offered the Intercessory Prayer, "he went forth with his disciples over the brook Cedron [or Kidron], where was a garden, into the which he entered, and his disciples" (John 18:1). Kidron means "dark" or "black." The Kidron is also known as the Valley of Jehoshaphat (Joel 3:2), which means "Jehovah judges"; it is indeed a symbolic place of judgment. It was also a traditional place of burial, a place of mourning. South of the Kidron is the Hinnom Valley. Jeremiah called this valley the "valley of slaughter" (Jer. 7:32). There, apostate Jews sacrificed their children to the false god Molech. During New Testament times the Hinnom Valley was called Gehenna; it became the city's garbage dump. Always burning with fires and filled with stench, it was known as a symbol of hell.

In walking to the Garden of Gethsemane, therefore, Jesus descended from the area of the Temple Mount and entered a valley of darkness, mourning, and judgment. Connecting to this valley not far away is a valley of slaughter and unholy sacrifice—a symbol of hell. It is meaningful to contemplate that the very physical geography through which Jesus passed is symbolic of the spiritual passage he would make in the Garden of Gethsemane, at the trial before the Jewish and Roman authorities, and during the suffering on the cross.

As an additional connection, the brook Kidron was used to carry away from the city the blood of animals sacrificed in the temple.[2] Since Jesus performed the atonement at the time of Passover, the blood of many lambs likely would have been carried in the waters of the Kidron at the very time the true Sacrificial Lamb crossed it to make his way to the garden.[3]

*The garden.* Some of the most eternally significant events in human history occurred in a garden or grove. Adam and Eve were brought together as the parents of the human race in a garden. They subsequently fell from spiritual life to spiritual death in that same garden. The atonement for that fall—and for all the sins of mankind—was performed in an olive vineyard called a garden. Christ was buried in a tomb surrounded by a garden and soon was resurrected to endless life there. At the beginning of the last dispensation, Joseph Smith knelt in a "garden" of trees, or a grove near his home, and received one of the grandest and most glorious manifestations ever given to a human soul. Further, in the end of this earth's telestial existence, it will be "renewed and receive its paradisiacal glory" (A of F 1:10). Thus, our history began in a garden, was changed in a garden in the meridian of time, and, in a grove, was set again on the proper course in the last days; and in the Millennium, the entire globe will be a garden.

The Garden of Gethsemane was also a "temple." The temple that had been authorized by the Lord and dedicated by Solomon was destroyed by Nebuchadnezzar. It was later replaced by the Temple of Zerubbabel, which was partially destroyed but then rebuilt by Herod. It was the Temple of Herod that was in use in Jesus' day, but it was under the direction of apostate priests. Temples are the preeminent places of sacrifice, and it seems vital that the greatest sacrifice ever offered on the face of the earth—the atonement—be made in a temple. One study has noted eleven characteristics that the ancient temple and the Garden of Eden had in common.[4] Interestingly, the Garden of Gethsemane, on the day Jesus entered there to perform the atonement, fit many of those shared characteristics. Hence, like the temple and the Garden of Eden,

- The Garden of Gethsemane contained the tree of life, who was Jesus Christ himself.

- It was associated with the living waters, the source of which is Jesus Christ. (Living waters will flow from the temple, figuratively and literally, in the last days.)

- It was associated with a mountain, being located on the Mount of Olives. (In the scriptures, mountains often stand as substitutes for temples; and temples are often constructed on mountains.)

- It was guarded by divinely appointed beings. The Garden of Eden was guarded by cherubim, which were also found in the ancient temple. The Garden of Gethsemane was guarded by divinely appointed apostles, as well as, perhaps, the angel who ministered to Christ.

- It was a place of sacrifice. In fact, a significant part of the greatest sacrifice of all time, the sacrifice to which all other sacrifices pointed, took place in the Garden of Gethsemane.

- It included revelation as an essential element. A key part of Christ's sacrifice involved the revelation of the Father's will, which Christ then fully yielded himself to.

- It was a focal point for the presence of God. (Of course, unlike us, the Savior was never separated from his Father—until that separation was required by the offering of the atonement). In the Garden of Gethsemane, Christ approached the Father in most sacred and holy prayer.

- It involved sacred vestments. Ancient temples featured clothing that is sacred and unique, as do modern temples. In the Garden of Gethsemane, Christ's clothing was made sacred above all, touched by the very blood of the infinite atonement (Luke 22:44).

- It brought God's children to the ultimate abundance; the grace of Christ is the source of many of the greatest blessings we enjoy in this life.

## THE OFFERING

*The olive press.* The word *Gethsemane* comes from the Hebrew and means "oil press." The Garden of Gethsemane was an olive vineyard that apparently included one or more olive presses, used to produce olive oil. Truman G. Madsen has explained how the olive press worked:

To produce olive oil, the refined olives had to be crushed in a press. The mellowed and seasoned olives were placed in strong bags and flattened on a furrowed stone. Then a huge crushing circular rock was rolled around on top, paced by a mule or an ox and a stinging whip. Another method used heavy wooden levers or screws twisting beams downward like a winch upon the stone with the same effect: *pressure, pressure, pressure—until the oil flowed. . .*

. . . The root word for *Messiah* in the book of Daniel means "anointed one," with connotations of coronation and ordination. This was the night when in the hardest of hard ways, he would become the *anointing* one. . . . In eventual triumph the Messiah was to say, "I have trodden the . . . press" (in this case the winepress, not the olive press, but the two merge in allegory as in life) "and none were with me." . . . It is one thing to take off one's sandals and trample the grapes in the stone vat. It is another to be trodden upon, trampled, crushed until the very tissues of the heart cry out for relief and release and until "mercy hath compassion on mercy and claimeth her own" (D&C 88:40), "that he may know, according to the flesh, how to succor his people." (Alma 7:12.)[5]

Isaiah alluded to the incessant pressure of the oil press in Gethsemane. The King James Version tells us "he was bruised for our iniquities" (Isa. 53:5); but a better translation from the Hebrew indicates that "he was *crushed* for our iniquities." There is a significant difference between "bruised" and "crushed"—our Savior experienced the far greater suffering.

*The winepress.* Elsewhere, the Lord compared the harrowing experience in the Garden of Gethsemane to a winepress. "I have trodden the wine-press alone," he has declared, "and have brought judgment upon all people; and none were with me" (D&C 133:50; see also Isa. 63:3, 5; Rev. 14:20; D&C 76:107; 88:106).

Anciently, winepresses and olive presses were sometimes used interchangeably. Several people would get into the press, a rock-lined pit with a mosaic or plaster floor, and, holding onto one another, smash the grapes or olives with their feet until the fruit turned into a thick pulp. Unless one held onto others in the press, it was almost impossible to lift one's feet in the thick sludge to tromp the grapes into juice. It also became very slippery, and without others in the press to hang onto for support, it was very easy to fall. . . . Ironically, in a place named for an activity that required several participants, one Man suffered for all men—the greatest contradiction in the history of created things.[6]

The blood of the winepress will stain his garments, and the returning Lord will therefore wear red garments in his second coming (Isa. 63:1–3; Rev. 19:13; D&C 133:46–51). That bloodstain "symbolizes at least three things: the blood Christ shed in performing the Atonement (Luke 22:44; D&C 19:18); the blood (or sins) of the wicked that he took upon himself (blood and sins are equated in Jacob 1:19; see also 1 Pet. 3:18; Alma 33:22; 3 Ne. 11:11); and the blood of the unrepentant wicked he has slain in his wrath ([Isa.] 63:3; Lam. 1:15; D&C 133:48, 50–51)."[7]

*The blood.* The blood of the Savior was a key element of his sacrifice. As the Lord said through Moses, "It is the blood that maketh an atonement for the soul" (Lev. 17:11). The Book of Mormon echoes this truth. King Benjamin taught, "Salvation was, and is, and is to come, in and through the atoning blood of Christ, the Lord Omnipotent" (Mosiah 3:18). And Aaron declared that "there could be no redemption for mankind save it were through the death and sufferings of Christ, and the atonement of his blood" (Alma 21:9; see also Hel. 5:9). And we read in latter-day scripture: "Jesus the mediator of the new covenant . . . wrought out this perfect atonement through the shedding of his own blood" (D&C 76:69).

In his offering in the Garden of Gethsemane, Christ gave all that was required—every whit. He bled through "every pore" (Mosiah 3:7; D&C 19:18; see also JST Luke 22:44)—or through every portion of his skin. Later, in his trials with the authorities and on the cross, he offered even more, yielding his blood through the crown of thorns, the severe scourging, the nails through his hands and feet, and the spear into his side.

Why did the Savior bleed from every pore? Brigham Young

suggested an answer when he said: "At the very moment, at the hour when the crisis came for him . . . , the Father withdrew Himself, withdrew His spirit, and cast a veil over Him. . . . If he had had the power of God upon Him, He would not have sweat blood; but all was withdrawn from him, and a veil was cast over him."[8]

Truly the atonement of Christ came through "the shedding of his own blood." And we with faith can cry out, as did the people of King Benjamin, "O have mercy, and apply the atoning blood of Christ that we may receive forgiveness of our sins, and our hearts may be purified; for we believe in Jesus Christ, the Son of God" (Mosiah 4:2). Because of the sacrifice of his blood and because of the blood on his garments, our own garments can be made white, and we can be made pure (Alma 5:21–22, 27; 13:11; 34:36; 3 Ne. 27:19).

*The sacrifice.* The atonement of Jesus Christ was typified by sacrifice from the very beginning. When Adam and Eve were cast out of the Garden of Eden, they were commanded to "offer the firstlings of their flocks, for an offering unto the Lord." They obeyed, even though they didn't understand the purpose of those sacrifices. Later an angel appeared to Adam and explained, "This thing is a similitude of the sacrifice of the Only Begotten of the Father, which is full of grace and truth" (Moses 5:5, 7).

Why was the atonement typified by the sacrifice of animals? The obvious reason is that the animals gave their life—and their blood—in the process. Jesus, the Lamb of God, would do the same. But every person, every animal ever born will die—billions upon billions of individuals and creatures for many thousands of years. Many of those deaths would be premature; many would die by violence. Surely the sacrifice of Christ means more than his life and his blood, precious though those are.

What was unique about the sacrifice of our Savior?

- That sacrifice was the essence of his mission on the earth—that is why he came!

- His very birth on earth was a great sacrifice; he condescended to

210

leave his celestial home, where he reigned in power and glory, and to subject himself to the pains and indignities of human life.

- By descending to mortality, he (even God!) faced the real possibility of falling himself. In his condescension he took upon himself not only mortal flesh but also the mortal test. If he were somehow protected from a personal fall, his sacrifice would be less than genuine.

- He was the only completely pure person to walk the earth. Yet in a terrible sacrifice he received unto himself the sins of all the world.

- He was the only person who had such power that he could choose not to die. But he yielded himself unto death to open the door to resurrection for all mankind.

All these were essential elements of the sacrifice of Jesus Christ, offered in Gethsemane and on the cross of Calvary.

*The suffering.* The atoning sacrifice of Christ involved the deepest, most excruciating suffering ever experienced by any creature on the face of the earth—or of any earth in the entire universe. The physical suffering on the cross, terrible as it was, was intensified and magnified manyfold by his emotional and spiritual suffering. That greater suffering began in the Garden of Gethsemane and culminated on Golgotha. And what was the source of that suffering? King Benjamin gives the answer: "Behold, blood cometh from every pore, so great shall be his anguish for the wickedness and the abominations of his people" (Mosiah 3:7).

In brief phrases the Gospels describe his experience in Gethsemane (remember: this is Jehovah, suffering as only a God could suffer!):

Mark wrote that "he . . . began to be sore amazed, and to be very heavy" (Mark 14:33). Another translation of "sore amazed" is "terrified surprise."[9] What could be the cause of that "terrified surprise"? As Jehovah, as the great Creator, Jesus knew all things in heaven and on earth—except one. Because he was perfect, he did not know what sin felt like. "Now, in an instant, he began to feel all the sensations and effects of sin, all the guilt, anguish, darkness, turmoil, depression, anger, and physical sickness that sin brings. All of this the Savior felt and much, much more."[10]

Matthew recorded that the Savior said, "My soul is exceeding sorrowful, even unto death" (Matt. 26:38), and then "he . . . fell on his face, and prayed" (Matt. 26:39). His pain and agony and "terrified surprise" were so great that he must have felt overwhelmed, and he fell on his face as he prayed!

Luke adds a most important detail, touched on above: "And being in an agony he prayed more earnestly: and his sweat was as it were great drops of blood falling down to the ground" (Luke 22:44). Jesus did all things perfectly. All his prayers were perfect, truly with an earnest heart and real intent. But here he prayed more earnestly, and in the intensity of his suffering, his blood literally oozed through his pores and fell to the ground. Latter-day revelation gives this sobering insight about the circumstances of that bleeding: "[This] suffering caused myself, even God, the greatest of all, to tremble because of pain, and to bleed at every pore, and to suffer both body and spirit" (D&C 19:18).

The Lord gives us a glimpse of the suffering we would experience if we refuse to repent: "[Those] sufferings [will] be sore—how sore you know not, how exquisite you know not, yea, how hard to bear you know not" (D&C 19:15). This passage is describing the torture of one solitary soul who is suffering as a result of his or her own sins. But in the Savior the torture would be magnified to an infinite, incomprehensible level, since, as he said, "I, God, have suffered these things for all, that they might not suffer if they would repent" (D&C 19:16).

Some of our latter-day apostles and prophets have sought to put the magnitude of Christ's horrific suffering into words.

President John Taylor taught: "There came upon Him the weight and agony of ages and generations, [an] indescribable agony. . . . Hence His profound grief, His indescribable anguish, His overpowering torture. . . .

"Groaning beneath this concentrated load, this intense, incomprehensible pressure, this terrible exaction of Divine justice, . . . placed below all things, His mind surcharged with agony and pain, lonely . . . and forsaken, in his agony the blood oozed from His pores."[11]

In his masterpiece, *Jesus the Christ,* Elder James E. Talmage wrote that "He struggled and groaned under a burden such as no other being who has lived on earth might even conceive as possible. . . . [He suffered] a spiritual agony of soul such as only God was capable of experiencing."[12]

President Marion G. Romney wrote of suffering so great that "no man, nor set of men, *nor all men put together,* ever suffered what the Redeemer suffered in the Garden."[13]

Elder Neal A. Maxwell taught: "The cumulative weight of all mortal sins—past, present, and future—pressed upon that perfect, sinless, and sensitive Soul! All our infirmities and sicknesses were somehow, too, a part of the awful arithmetic of the Atonement. . . . His suffering [was] as it were, *enormity* multiplied by *infinity.*"[14]

As Elder Maxwell emphasized, the suffering in the garden was brought about by more than sin—every human burden, pain, difficulty, trial, sorrow, sickness, weakness—everything that separates us from God or that makes us unlike God was "part of the awful arithmetic of the Atonement."

Elder Jeffrey R. Holland testified of this truth when he wrote:

> The total cost of such combined spiritual and physical suffering is incalculable. Yet the iniquities, including the sorrows and sadness, of every mortal being who ever has lived or will live in this world were laid across one lonely set of shoulders. . . .
>
> . . . Christ. . . [took] upon himself our mortal sicknesses and infirmities, our earthly trials and tribulations, our personal heartaches and loneliness and sorrows—all done in addition to taking upon himself the burden of our sins. . . .
>
> . . . He knows the deepest and most personal burdens we carry. He knows the most public and poignant pains we bear. He descended below all such grief in order that he might lift us above it. There is no anguish or sorrow or sadness in life that he has not suffered in our behalf and borne away upon his own valiant and compassionate shoulders.[15]

And in his classic work, *Believing Christ,* Stephen A. Robinson explained: "Human nature makes us want to quantify, to measure the atonement of Christ, but his ordeal is off any scale; it is beyond our comprehension. . . .

*All* the negative aspects of human existence brought about by the Fall, Jesus Christ absorbed into himself. He experienced vicariously in Gethsemane all the private griefs and heartaches, all the physical pains and handicaps, all the emotional burdens and depressions of the human family. . . .

. . . In that infinite Gethsemane experience, the meridian of time, the center of eternity, he lived a billion billion lifetimes of sin, pain, disease, and sorrow.

God uses no magic wand to simply wave bad things into nonexistence. The sins that he remits, he remits by making them his own and suffering them. The pain and heartaches that he relieves, he relieves by suffering them himself. . . . All that the Fall put wrong, the Savior in his atonement puts right. It is all part of his infinite sacrifice—of his infinite gift.[16]

No wonder Elder Orson F. Whitney described Christ's offering as suffering "the piled up agony of the human race."[17]

*The bitter cup.* "And he went a little further, and fell on his face, and prayed, saying, O my Father, if it be possible, let this cup pass from me: nevertheless not as I will, but as thou wilt" (Matt. 26:39). Even though in his extremity the Savior asked repeatedly if there might be another way, he did not hesitate once he understood the answer. "The will of the Son [was] swallowed up in the will of the Father" (Mosiah 15:7). He had sought the Father's will from the beginning, and this most difficult of moments brought no exception.

The cup that Jesus then drank has elsewhere been called "the bitter cup" (3 Ne. 11:11; D&C 19:18). A cup is a frequently used symbol in the scriptures. Typically, it refers to God's wrath or indignation—those who drink of the cup receive the terrible judgments of God (Isa. 51:17; Jer. 25:15; 2 Ne. 8:17; Mosiah 3:25–26; 5:5; D&C 29:17; 43:26). In the Garden of Gethsemane, the Father gave Christ to drink of such a cup (John 18:11; 3 Ne. 11:11). In other words, part of the atoning process required that the Savior partake of the "cup of his fury—thou hast drunken the dregs of the cup of trembling wrung out" (2 Ne. 8:17), the "cup of the wine of the fierceness of his wrath" (Rev. 16:19; see also Alma 40:26; D&C 76:107).

Jesus was "in all points tempted like as we are, yet [he was] without sin" (Heb. 4:15), but God "hath made him to be sin for us" so that "we might be made the righteousness of God in him" (2 Cor. 5:21). That process, wherein Christ became "sin for us" so we could be "made the righteousness of God in him," brings to us the gift of grace. But Christ's gift of grace, though freely offered, was not freely obtained by the giver. It came at the price of drinking the awful and bitter cup. Sinless and guiltless, he did not deserve God's punishment for any thought, feeling, or act, great or small. But in taking upon himself our sins, he became "guilty of all" (James 2:10). In his guilt, he was required to drink of the cup of God's wrath.

Elder Boyd K. Packer has said: "Upon Him was the burden of all human transgression, all human guilt. . . .

". . . By choice, [Christ] accepted the penalty . . . for brutality, immorality, perversion, and corruption, for addiction, for the killings and torture and terror—for all of it that ever had been or all that ever would be enacted upon this earth."[18]

By receiving that guilt and accepting the penalty, Jesus Christ made an astounding sacrifice of love: he drank the cup till it was emptied, and humankind could become fully free of the effects of the Fall, as well as of our personal sins and weaknesses.

Because Christ drank of the bitter cup, we can partake of the cup representing the blood he shed for us, the cup of remembrance (3 Ne. 18:8; Moro. 5:1). And, through his grace, we can say with the Psalmist: "My cup runneth over. Surely goodness and mercy shall follow me all the days of my life" (Ps. 23:5–6).

*The battle.* The atonement in the Garden of Gethsemane involved a "supreme contest with the powers of evil."[19] The Savior was "attacked by the powers of darkness."[20] "He faced the awesome power of the evil one."[21] "In that hour of anguish Christ met and overcame all the horrors that Satan, 'the prince of this world' [John 14:30] could inflict."[22]

We have scriptural record of others who have wrestled with this great adversary. After Moses had a marvelous interchange with the Lord, "The presence of God withdrew from Moses, that his glory was not upon Moses; and Moses was left unto himself." Then, "behold, Satan came tempting him, saying: Moses, son of man, worship me." Moses recognized the deception and sought to cast Satan out: "Get thee hence, Satan; deceive me not." But Satan did not leave. Again Moses commanded, "Depart hence, Satan."

> And now, when Moses had said these words, Satan cried with a loud voice, and ranted upon the earth, and commanded, saying: I am the Only Begotten, worship me.
>
> And it came to pass that Moses began to fear exceedingly; and as he began to fear, he saw the bitterness of hell. Nevertheless, calling upon God, he received strength, and he commanded, saying: Depart from me, Satan, for this one God only will I worship, which is the God of glory.
>
> And now Satan began to tremble, and the earth shook; and Moses received strength, and called upon God, saying: In the name of the Only Begotten, depart hence, Satan.
>
> And it came to pass that Satan cried with a loud voice, with weeping, and wailing, and gnashing of teeth; and he departed hence, even from the presence of Moses, that he beheld him not. (Moses 1:9, 12, 16, 18–22)

When Joseph Smith sought the Lord in the Sacred Grove, he was physically attacked by Satan. Joseph wrote:

> I kneeled down and began to offer up the desires of my heart to God. I had scarcely done so, when immediately I was seized upon by some power which entirely overcame me, and had such an astonishing influence over me as to bind my tongue so that I could not speak. Thick darkness gathered around me, and it seemed to me for a time as if I were doomed to sudden destruction.
>
> But, exerting all my powers to call upon God to deliver me out of the power of this enemy which had seized upon me, and at the very moment when I was ready to sink into despair

and abandon myself to destruction—not to an imaginary ruin, but to the power of some actual being from the unseen world, who had such marvelous power as I had never before felt in any being—just at this moment of great alarm, I saw a pillar of light exactly over my head, above the brightness of the sun, which descended gradually until it fell upon me.

It no sooner appeared than I found myself delivered from the enemy which held me bound. (JS–H 1:15–17)

Alma the Younger described the wrestle he had with the horrors of sin in the process of his repentance. He told of "wading through much tribulation" and suffering "an everlasting burning." His soul was in "the gall of bitterness and bonds of iniquity. I was in the darkest abyss. . . . My soul was racked with eternal torment" (Mosiah 27:28–29).

In another account of the same experience, Alma said: "I was racked with eternal torment, for my soul was harrowed up to the greatest degree and racked with all my sins. . . . I was tormented with the pains of hell. . . . So great had been my iniquities, that the very thought of coming into the presence of my God did rack my soul with inexpressible horror. . . . I [was] racked, even with the pains of a damned soul. . . . I was thus racked with torment. . . . [I was] in the gall of bitterness, and . . . encircled about by the everlasting chains of death. . . . There could be nothing so exquisite and so bitter as were my pains" (Alma 36:12–18, 21).

We don't have a specific record of Jesus' experience with such things in the Garden of Gethsemane. But we do know that his anguish was so great that he "sweat . . . great drops of blood" (Luke 22:44). We know that he pleaded that, if it were possible, the bitter cup might pass from him. We know that he "descended below [us] all" (D&C 122:8). And we know that at that hinge point of eternity, Satan surely would unleash all his arsenal, bring forth his most powerful associates, send out all his fiery darts—that he would do all in his dark and awesome power to prevent the atoning sacrifice of the meek and humble Lamb that knelt alone on a dark hillside in the meridian of time.

Jesus met all that terrible onslaught, and more, with the power of

217

his righteousness and the power of his love. "In that hour of anguish Christ met and overcame all the horrors that Satan . . . could inflict. . . .

"From the terrible conflict in Gethsemane, Christ emerged a victor."[23]

As Elder David B. Haight testified using simple and heartfelt language: "The Savior took upon Himself the burden of the sins of mankind. . . . He suffered an agony and a burden the like of which no human person would be able to bear. In that hour of anguish our Savior overcame all the power of Satan."[24]

*The solitary offering.* Again and again the Lord saved his people through the actions of one person: Noah, Joseph of Egypt, Moses, Samson, and others. Each of these is a type of Christ, who was required to offer the atonement by himself, without help from God or man. His apostles were nearby, but they slept through most of the experience. Further, in Gethsemane the disciples "began . . . to complain in their hearts, wondering if this be the Messiah" (JST Mark 14:36). An angel was sent for a time to strengthen and comfort him, but the angel could not remove the trial, nor could he perform the atonement in Jesus' behalf. As God, Christ himself had to atone for the sins of his people, and he had to do it alone.

Jesus possessed a fulness of the Holy Spirit (JST John 3:34). But even that sweet and ever-constant companion had to leave him. That in itself was a supreme sacrifice for the one Sinless Man, a sacrifice of overwhelming love.

The Psalmist foresaw Jesus' solitary offering and wrote, "Reproach hath broken my heart; and I am full of heaviness: and I looked for some to take pity, but there was none; and for comforters, but I found none" (Ps. 69:20).[25]

*The deaths.* Because God was the literal Father of Jesus Christ in the flesh and because Jesus never committed sin, neither physical nor spiritual death had any power over him. Yet by taking upon himself our sins, he "suffered . . . spiritual death in the Garden of Gethsemane, and shed his blood, which dropped like sweat, in our behalf. Later he suffered physical death on the cross in our behalf. By suffering these two deaths, he paid the debt legally and completely. He atoned for Adam's transgressions unconditionally for all men; and he atoned for our sins on conditions of our repentance."[26]

In performing the atonement, Jesus willingly took upon himself these deaths.

Imagine meeting someone who is in the filthiest, darkest, most spiritually benighted state possible. Would you ever, under any circumstances, voluntarily change places with him? How would it feel to leave your spiritually, emotionally, and physically comfortable condition and take his place? Now imagine the Savior in his purity, the one Being who had never sinned, changing places with such an individual. That shocking reversal is precisely what happened. Jesus took the soul that was physically and spiritually dead and entered into death for him, offering him life eternal.

No wonder Jacob exclaimed: "O the greatness of the mercy of our God, the Holy One of Israel! For he delivereth his saints from that awful monster the devil, and death, and hell, and that lake of fire and brimstone, which is endless torment" (2 Ne. 9:19).

*The weeping God.* We do not have a God who is distant, who cannot understand our pain and our struggle. "We have not an high priest which cannot be touched with the feeling of our infirmities" (Heb. 4:15). He knows the difficulties, the anguish, the endless trial of mortal life. He "was in all points tempted like as we are, yet without sin" (Heb. 4:15). He offered the infinite atonement "with strong crying and tears" (Heb. 5:7) unto the Father, and his prayers were heard because of his reverent submissiveness (NIV Heb. 5:7).[27]

Jesus Christ "knows our need, to our weakness is no stranger."[28] Though he has "ascended into heaven," yet he still has "the bowels of mercy; being filled with compassion towards the children of men" (Mosiah 15:9). Even though "all we like sheep have gone astray" (Isa. 53:6), even though he could say of us, as he did of some of the Saints in Joseph Smith's day, "They were slow to hearken unto the voice of the Lord their God; . . . in the day of their peace they esteemed lightly my counsel; but, in the day of their trouble, of necessity they feel after me." Even after all that, he adds, "Verily I say unto you, notwithstanding their sins, my bowels are filled with compassion towards them. I will not utterly cast them off; and in the day of wrath I will remember mercy" (D&C 101:7–9).

That compassion was manifested in a poignant way in Jesus' visit to the Nephites. After teaching them, he said, "Behold, my bowels are filled with compassion towards you. . . . I have compassion upon you; my bowels are filled with mercy." Then, after uttering a prayer so marvelous and sacred that it could not be recorded, "he wept, and the multitude bare record of it." He blessed "their little children, one by one, . . . and when he had done this he wept again" (3 Ne. 17:6–7, 21–22).

Where the Nephites saw Jesus weeping for joy, Enoch saw "the God of heaven" weeping for sorrow. "And Enoch bore record of it, saying: . . . How is it that thou canst weep, seeing thou art holy, and from all eternity to all eternity?" The Lord answered that from the beginning he had given man knowledge of his plan, and agency, and also a "commandment, that they should love one another, and that they should choose me, their Father"—but they had ignored the commandment and had followed Satan. "Wherefore," the Lord asked, "should not the heavens weep, seeing these shall suffer?"

Then Enoch himself wept and refused to be comforted. But the Lord, who knows the end from the beginning, said: "Lift up your heart, and be glad; and look. . . . And behold, Enoch saw the day of the coming of the Son of Man, even in the flesh; and his soul rejoiced, saying: The Righteous is lifted up, and the Lamb is slain from the foundation of the world; and through faith I am in the bosom of the Father, and behold, Zion is with me."

Then the Lord bore testimony to Enoch, saying, "I am Messiah, the King of Zion, the Rock of Heaven, which is broad as eternity; whoso cometh in at the gate and climbeth up by me shall never fall; wherefore, blessed are they of whom I have spoken, for they shall come forth with songs of everlasting joy" (Moses 7:28, 33, 37, 44, 47, 53).

Our Savior, who wept in pain and anguish in the Garden of Gethsemane, weeps for sorrow at our sins and in compassion for our mortal hurts and weakness and trouble. We do not have a God who "cannot be touched with the feeling of our infirmities" (Heb. 4:15), for he experienced them all, descending below us all, and, conquering all, he ascended up on high with power to help us all.

Knowing that he knows, then, knowing that he understands, knowing that he has experienced all we have experienced, and more, knowing that he loves us with a pure and everlasting love, "let us therefore come boldly unto the throne of grace, that we may obtain mercy, and find grace to help in time of need" (Heb. 4:16).

## CHAPTER 17

# THE CRUEL CROSS: THE CRUCIFIXION

IN A POWERFUL SERMON TITLED "The Sacramental Covenant," Elder Melvin J. Ballard spoke movingly of Abraham's sacrifice of his son, Isaac, and compared that event to the Father's offering of his Son. He talked of the heartbreaking commandment Abraham received to sacrifice his precious son, the son he had waited long decades for. Abraham and Isaac traveled three days to the appointed mount, when Isaac asked, "Where is the lamb for a burnt offering?" (Gen. 22:7). As Elder Ballard related the story, "It must have pierced the heart of Father Abraham to hear the trusting and confiding son say: 'You have forgotten the sacrifice.'" Abraham responded by promising that the Lord would provide.

They climbed the mountain and built an altar. ". . . Then Isaac was bound, hand and foot, kneeling upon the altar. I presume Abraham, like a true father, must have given his son his farewell kiss, his blessing, [and] his love, and his soul must have been drawn out in that hour of agony toward his son who was to die by the hand of his own father. Every step proceeded until the cold steel was drawn, and the hand raised that was to strike the blow to let out the life's blood when the angel of the Lord said: 'It is enough.'"

> Our Father in heaven went through all that and more, for in his case the hand was not stayed. He loved his Son, Jesus Christ, better than Abraham ever loved Isaac, . . . and yet he allowed this

well-beloved Son to descend from his place of glory and honor . . . down to the earth, a condescension that is not within the power of man to conceive. He came to receive the insult, the abuse, and the crown of thorns. God heard the cry of his Son in that moment of great grief and agony, in the garden when, it is said, the pores of his body opened and drops of blood stood upon him, and he cried out: "Father, if thou be willing, remove this cup from me."

Even fathers and mothers on earth are unable to "stand by and listen to the cry of their children in distress . . . and not render aid and assistance." They will put themselves at great risk to save one of their children. The Father "loved his Son, and he could have saved him. . . . He saw that Son condemned; he saw him drag the cross through the streets of Jerusalem and faint under its load. He saw that Son finally upon Calvary; he saw his body stretched out upon the wooden cross; he saw the cruel nails driven through hands and feet, and the blows that broke the skin, tore the flesh, and let out the life's blood of his Son. He looked upon that."

In the case of our Father, the knife was not stayed, but it fell, and the life's blood of his Beloved Son went out. His Father looked on with great grief and agony over his Beloved Son, until there seems to have come a moment when even our Savior cried out in despair: "My God, my God, why hast thou forsaken me?"

In that hour I think I can see our dear Father behind the veil looking upon these dying struggles until even he could not endure it any longer; and, like the mother who bids farewell to her dying child, has to be taken out of the room, so as not to look upon the last struggles, so he bowed his head, and hid in some part of his universe, his great heart almost breaking for the love that he had for his Son. Oh, in that moment when he might have saved his Son, I thank him and praise him that he did not fail us, for he had not only the love of his Son in mind, but he also had love for us. I rejoice that he did not interfere, and that his love for us made it possible for him to endure to look upon the sufferings of his Son and give him finally to us, our Savior and our Redeemer.[1]

Indeed we do rejoice that "God so loved the world, that he gave his only begotten Son, that whosoever believeth in him should not perish, but have everlasting life" (John 3:16). But at what cost did the Father give his Son? At what cost did the Son give himself? We have considered the terrible suffering in Gethsemane; it brought enough pain and anguish that it would literally have killed someone with lesser strength (Mosiah 3:7). Had that been the entirety of the atonement, we would have cause to praise God forevermore. But more was required. After a long night of horror, agony, and suffering beyond mortal comprehension, after an extended battle with Satan, after the exhaustion of a spiritual exertion that resulted in the Savior's bleeding through *every* pore, a continuing trial awaited—torture and torment at the hands of wicked men, the excruciating pains of the cross, the profound sense of loneliness and loss when the Father's presence departed, the final demands of the atonement on the cross, and, finally, the death of the One who least deserved death.

## Before the Crucifixion

*The betrayals and the arrest.* After the labors in the Garden, Jesus emerged with his disciples, only to be confronted by a contingent of chief priests and elders led by Judas Iscariot. Jesus did not wait for them to approach him, but he first went to them: "Whom seek ye?" They responded, "Jesus of Nazareth." As the King James Version of this account records, Jesus then said, "I am he," which phrase is repeated twice in the passage. But the story in the original Greek has one small difference in wording, which makes a great difference in meaning. Rather than saying, "I am he," Jesus said, "I am" (John 18:4–8).

Centuries earlier, Moses asked the Lord to identify himself by name, and Jehovah gave the same answer: "I Am" (Ex. 3:14). The chief priests and elders surely recognized the meaning behind Jesus' words—"As soon then as he had said unto them, I am . . . , they went backward, and fell to the ground" (John 18:6; the italic *he* was supplied by the KJV translators).

At some point in the confrontation, after Peter had struck off the ear of Malchus, the high priest's servant, and Jesus had healed it, "all the disciples forsook him, and fled" (Matt. 26:56). This must have been wrenching for Jesus, although he knew in advance it would happen. Earlier in the evening Jesus had said, "All ye shall be offended because of me this night: for it is written, I will smite the shepherd, and the sheep shall be scattered" (Mark 14:27). But there were two disciples who followed Jesus and the arresting party, perhaps from a distance: Simon Peter and another who remains unnamed, presumably John the Beloved (John 18:15).

The involvement of "the chief priests, and captains of the temple, and the elders" (Luke 22:52) marked a significant betrayal of Jesus, the Son of God. Their assignment was to serve in the temple of the Lord. Their priesthood had been given to their fathers (many generations earlier) by the Lord. And yet, chillingly, "those responsible for the care of the Temple were also responsible for the Savior's premeditated murder."[2] They had sold their souls to preserve their position as the religious leaders of the people, and this they did because they were under "the power of darkness" (Luke 22:53).

The arrest involved another betrayal of someone who should have been one of Jesus' greatest defenders—one of the select group of Jesus' closest disciples, the apostle Judas Iscariot. Judas also was under "the power of darkness." As John records, "Satan entered into him" (John 13:27). The One whose entire life was perfectly devoted to doing the Father's will was betrayed by one who turned his life to doing the will of "the father of all lies," whose object and desire was and is "to deceive and to blind men, and to lead them captive at his will, even as many as would not hearken unto [the Lord's] voice" (Moses 4:4).

Among the Jews of Jesus' day, a kiss was a mark of respect; it was common for disciples to greet their leaders or teachers with such a kiss. When Jesus visited the home of Simon the Pharisee, Jesus rebuked him for failing to offer a kiss (Luke 7:45). Later, Paul counseled the Saints to "greet all the brethren with an holy kiss" (1 Thess. 5:26). Thus, it was particularly offensive for Judas to identify his Master with a kiss of betrayal. In Proverbs 27:6, we read, "Faithful are the wounds of a friend; but the kisses of an enemy are deceitful." And so it was with Judas.

Even though Jesus had willingly identified himself, and even though he had healed the ear of Malchus after Peter had struck it off, he was immediately forced to submit to an indignity. As Elder Bruce R. McConkie has written, Jesus was then "led away with a rope around his neck, as a common criminal."[3] The use of such a rope fulfilled the type established by the scapegoat in the law of Moses. On the Day of Atonement, the sins of the people were transferred to its head, and it was led with a noose around its neck into the wilderness, there to perish (Lev. 16:21–22).

The story of the sacrifice of Isaac prefigures the arrest of Jesus, as well as his actual offering on the cross. After identifying their intended victim just outside the Garden of Gethsemane, "the band and the captain and the officers of the Jews took Jesus, and bound him" (John 18:12). Isaac also was bound in preparation for his sacrifice: "And they came to the place which God had told him of; and Abraham built an altar there, and laid the wood in order, and bound Isaac his son, and laid him on the altar upon the wood" (Gen. 22:9). (Note that after Jesus was bound, he also eventually was "laid . . . upon the wood," on an altar called the cross.) Further, the binding and offering of Isaac occurred on Mount Moriah, which later became known as the temple mount, the same general location where Jesus was bound and offered.

*The trials.* After Jesus was bound, he was taken to a series of trials. He appeared before Annas, the former high priest; Caiaphas, the then-current high priest, and "the chief priests, and elders, and all the council" (Matt. 26:59)[4]; Pontius Pilate, the Roman governor of Judea; Herod Antipas, the tetrarch of Galilee and Perea, who was staying in Jerusalem during the Passover celebration; and back again to Pilate. It is remarkable that three representative groups—the three leading authorities of the day—had a hand in the trial and death of Jesus Christ. These were the church (in the form of the chief priests and the council), the Jewish governor, and the Roman governor. Jews and Gentiles alike were responsible for the wicked dealings of that dark morning. Perhaps the Father wanted to underscore that no earthly group is fully innocent; all are culpable of sin; in one degree or another, the choices of all human beings have contributed to the need for the atonement, and, though all have at least some guilt, all can partake of the blessings of grace offered by a Savior who freely accepted a torturous death that we might live.

The trials of Jesus were marked by false accusations: that Jesus planned to destroy Herod's temple (Mark 14:57–58), that Jesus was "perverting the nation" (Luke 23:1–2), that Jesus was guilty of blasphemy (Matt. 26:65–66), that he "stirreth up the people" (Luke 23:5). Jesus' typical response to the accusations was silence, fulfilling the marvelous prophecy uttered by Isaiah: "He was oppressed, and he was afflicted, yet he opened not his mouth: he is brought as a lamb to the slaughter, and as a sheep before her shearers is dumb, so he openeth not his mouth" (Isa. 53:7).

Jesus was not entirely silent during these trials, however. The one exception was his appearance before Herod, at which Herod "questioned with him in many words; but he answered him nothing"—even though "the chief priests and scribes stood and vehemently accused him" (Luke 23:9–10). He took opportunity to bear testimony of himself, perhaps to increase the accountability of those who plotted his death and perhaps also to let future generations know that he knew, even in his extremity, precisely who he was.

When Caiaphas asked with directness, "Art thou the Christ, the Son of the Blessed?" Jesus answered, "I am: and ye shall see the Son of man sitting on the right hand of power, and coming in the clouds of heaven" (Mark 14:61–62). Not only did Jesus answer the direct question with an equally direct response, but once again he also identified himself in terms the high priest would recognize as referring to Jehovah, whose name was "I Am." As Elder James E. Talmage wrote, "It was an unqualified avowal of divine parentage, and inherent Godship."[5]

Before Pilate, Jesus testified, "My kingdom is not of this world: if my kingdom were of this world, then would my servants fight, that I should not be delivered to the Jews: but now is my kingdom not from hence." Pilate responded by asking, "Art thou a king then?" Jesus answered with yet another testimony: "Thou sayest that I am a king. To this end was I born, and for this cause came I into the world, that I should bear witness unto the truth. Every one that is of the truth heareth my voice" (John 18:36–37).

*Torture and humiliation.* Every stage of these trials of Jesus was marked by torture and humiliation. He experienced scourging, smiting, spitting, a crown of thorns, nakedness, mocking, and blasphemy. He was bound by those who arrested him. He was struck by an officer when he appeared before Annas. When he stood before Caiaphas, they "spit in his face, and buffeted him; and others smote him with the palms of their hands" (Matt. 26:67). "And the men that held Jesus mocked him, and smote him. And when they had blindfolded him, they struck him on the face, and asked him, saying, Prophesy, who is it that smote thee?" (Luke 22:63–64). In Jesus' meeting with Herod, the ruler and "his men of war set him at nought, and mocked him, and arrayed him in a gorgeous robe" (Luke 23:11).

After Jesus' second meeting with Pilate, the Roman governor "scourged Jesus" and "delivered him to be crucified." The scourging, which involved a vicious beating with a whip designed to tear the flesh, was painful enough to kill some of its victims. But Jesus survived to receive additional torments. Then the Roman soldiers "took Jesus" and "stripped him, and put on him a scarlet robe. And when they had platted a crown of thorns, they put it upon his head, and a reed in his right hand: and they bowed the knee before him, and mocked him, saying, Hail, King of the Jews! And they spit upon him, and took the reed, and smote him on the head" (Matt. 27:26–30).

Such abuse of the literal Son of God was prophesied by seers with remarkable vision. Nephi wrote that "the world, because of their iniquity, shall judge him to be a thing of naught; wherefore they scourge him, and he suffereth it; and they smite him, and he suffereth it. Yea, they spit upon him, and he suffereth it." Then Nephi added a powerful witness of why the Savior would submit himself to such mistreatment: "because of his loving kindness and his long-suffering towards the children of men" (1 Ne. 19:9). And King Benjamin taught, "He cometh unto his own, that salvation might come unto the children of men even through faith on his name; and even after all this they shall consider him a man, and say that he hath a devil, and shall scourge him, and shall crucify him" (Mosiah 3:9).

President Spencer W. Kimball has written eloquently of the godly

228

character and self-control Jesus manifested during his long hours of trial and torture:

> In quiet, restrained, divine dignity he stood when they cast their spittle in his face. He remained composed. Not an angry word escaped his lips. They slapped his face and beat his body. Yet he stood resolute, unintimidated. . . .
>
> He who created the world and all that is in it, he who made the silver from which the pieces were stamped which bought him, he who could command defenders on both sides of the veil—stood and suffered.
>
> What dignity! What mastery! What control! . . .
>
> Yet still further tests came. Though pronounced innocent, he was scourged. Unworthy men lashed him, the pure and the Holy One, the Son of God. One word from his lips and all his enemies would have fallen to the earth, helpless. All would have perished, all could have been as dust and ashes. Yet, in calmness, he suffered.
>
> Even when delivered to the soldiers to be crucified, he prayed for them who despitefully used him. How he must have suffered when they violated his privacy by stripping off his clothes and then putting on him the scarlet robe! . . .
>
> With a reed in his hand, a scarlet robe over his shoulders, and a crown of thorns on his head, he was made to suffer indignity: they laughed and mocked and jeered and challenged him. Taking the reed from his hand, they would strike him on the head. Yet he stood there, the model of long-suffering.[6]

No one has ever suffered as the Son of God suffered. But the suffering of his servants can help us to more fully comprehend what he experienced. When Joseph Smith cried out in anguish in Liberty Jail (D&C 121:1–3), the Lord answered with a marvelous revelation of comfort and truth. Included in the answer were some vital hints and clues about the pains of Christ's earthly experience, including the atonement. Even though the Lord was describing experiences of Joseph Smith, He was also, as we learn in the last verse of this extract, describing His own:

The ends of the earth shall inquire after thy name, and fools shall have thee in derision, and hell shall rage against thee. . . .

If thou art called to pass through tribulation; if thou art in perils among false brethren; . . . if thou art accused with all manner of false accusations; if thine enemies fall upon thee; if they tear thee from the society of thy father and mother and brethren and sisters . . . with a drawn sword . . . , and thou be dragged to prison, and thine enemies prowl around thee like wolves for the blood of the lamb; and if thou shouldst be cast into . . . the hands of murderers, and the sentence of death passed upon thee; . . . if fierce winds become thine enemy; if the heavens gather blackness, and all the elements combine to hedge up the way; and above all, if the very jaws of hell shall gape open the mouth wide after thee, know thou, my son, that all these things shall give thee experience, and shall be for thy good.

The Son of Man hath descended below them all. Art thou greater than he? (D&C 122:1–8)

*Barabbas.* Even though he found no basis for the things of which Jesus was accused (Luke 23:14), Pilate sought to appease the crowd, which was clamoring for Jesus' death. Accordingly, the governor offered them a choice—should he put Jesus to death, or Barabbas, who had been incarcerated for sedition and murder? Seemingly to Pilate's surprise, the mob cried out for the death of Jesus, and Barabbas was set free (Matt. 27:15–26).

According to some codices, Barabbas's first name was Jesus, and his last name literally means "son of the father." Thus, Jesus of Nazareth, the Son of the Father, was killed, while Jesus Barabbas, "the son of the father," was allowed to go free. Jesus of Nazareth was innocent of all sin, while Jesus Barabbas was guilty of heinous sins. In a stunning development, the innocent died for the guilty.

This story can be seen as a shocking type of the atonement. Jesus of Nazareth was the preeminent Son, the Only Begotten Son in the flesh—but all of us are also sons. We may not have committed heinous sins, but we also are guilty; but in his love, the Innocent One died for us, that we might have life.

There is yet one additional symbolic connection in this brief story. In the law of Moses the priests were instructed to take two goats on the Day of Atonement. One was the scapegoat, which was set free. The other was the sacrificial goat, which was killed on the altar, thus symbolically removing the sins of the people (Lev. 16:7–22). On the final and actual day of atonement, the last day of Christ's life, the temple priests and the people cried for Barabbas to be set free, while Christ was killed for the sins of the people.

## Jesus Christ Crucified

*Types of Christ's death.* The scriptures prefigured the death of Christ in a number of types and shadows. For example:

- After the fall of Adam and Eve, they were naked and needed to be clothed. In recounting that event to Moses, the Lord said, "Unto Adam, and also unto his wife, did I, the Lord God, make coats of skins, and clothed them" (Moses 4:27). Where did the coats of skins come from? Presumably, the Lord sacrificed animals to bless and benefit the man and the woman and to provide a covering for them. In the same way, God the Father offered the life of his Son to bless and benefit the people of the earth, and to "cover" their sins through the atonement (the sense of covering here is not to hide, but to protect one from the consequences of choices, or the required punishment).

- When the children of Israel were thirsty in the wilderness, Moses struck the rock to bring forth the water of life (Ex. 17:5–7; Num. 20:7–13). The striking symbolized the slaying of Christ (the Rock), and the water symbolizes the living waters Christ provides. (For a more detailed discussion of this story, see chapter 7.)

- In another incident in the wilderness, the people came to a place where the waters were bitter; at Marah, "therefore the name of it was called Marah" (which means "bitterness"). When the people "murmured against Moses," the Lord instructed him to cast a specific tree into the water, and "the waters were made sweet" (Ex. 15:23–25).

The people were then able to drink the water and live. In the same way, Christ (the tree of life) is cast into the bitter waters of life; by his sacrifice, the bitterness of life can be made sweet, and through him, we can partake of godly power and blessing unto eternal life.

• Many of the provisions of the law of Moses pertaining to sacrifice and the tabernacle point to Christ and the manner of his death, as well as the atoning power that flows from that sacrifice. (For a discussion of blood sacrifices and the temple, see chapters 2 and 4.)

• At one point in the wanderings of the children of Israel, "the soul of the people was much discouraged because of the way." They complained "against God, and against Moses," accusing them of bringing them "out of Egypt to die in the wilderness." The Lord then punished them by sending "fiery serpents among the people, and they bit the people; and much people of Israel died." When the people recognized their sin and sought to repent, the Lord provided a means of deliverance. Speaking to Moses, he said, "Make thee a fiery serpent, and set it upon a pole: and it shall come to pass, that every one that is bitten, when he looketh upon it, shall live." Then "Moses made a serpent of brass, and put it upon a pole, and it came to pass, that if a serpent had bitten any man, when he beheld the serpent of brass, he lived" (Num. 21:4–9). (For a fuller discussion of the brass serpent, see chapter 11.)

When Nephi (son of Helaman) taught his people about the event, he tied it directly to the atonement of Christ, specifically noting the means by which Christ should die: "Did he [Moses] not bear record that the Son of God should come? And as he lifted up the brazen serpent in the wilderness, even so shall he be lifted up who should come. And as many as should look upon that serpent should live, even so as many as should look upon the Son of God with faith, having a contrite spirit, might live, even unto that life which is eternal" (Hel. 8:14–15).

• Only days before his crucifixion, the Savior told a parable that foretold his death. In the parable of the wicked husbandmen, a man planted a vineyard and then left the country, leaving his vineyard in the care of husbandmen. After a time he sent a servant to receive payment for the use of his land, but "the husbandmen beat him, and sent him away empty." The owner sent others, who also were beaten, treated shamefully, wounded, and cast out. Finally the owner said, "I will send my beloved son: it may be they will reverence him when they see him." But the wicked husbandmen said, "This is the heir: come, let us kill him, that the inheritance may be ours." Accordingly, "they cast him out of the vineyard, and killed him" (Luke 20:9–15).

In the same way, the Father left the gifts of the earth in the care of his children here—in particular, he left the covenant in the care of the temple priests and elders in Jerusalem. But when he sent prophets to them, they beat them, stoned them, and cast them out (Matt. 23:31; see also Hel. 13:33; 3 Ne. 8:25). Finally, when the Father sent his own "beloved son," the wicked people of his day killed him outside the city, fulfilling the prophecy uttered only three days before.

*"The place of a skull."* Matthew, Mark, and John all record (with slightly differing language) that Jesus was taken "unto the place Golgotha, which is, being interpreted, The place of a skull" (Mark 15:22; Matt. 27:33; John 19:17). In the Joseph Smith Translation, the Prophet changed the word "skull" to more properly read "burial." Apparently, the place of execution and the place of burial were essentially the same (John 19:41).

Public executions held a definite appeal to the Romans. Their desire seemed to be twofold: to publicly humiliate, or shame, the victim; and to hold him up as a public example. It is a sad irony that Christ, the Great Exemplar of righteousness, should be used as an example of the fate of a criminal or an enemy of the state.

Jerusalem at the time of Passover would have been teeming with people. The population of the city (which was already the largest in the land) would have swelled manyfold. John's record says that many people saw Jesus and the two thieves dying on their crosses, and many saw the testimony inscribed above Jesus' head: "Jesus of Nazareth the King of the Jews," written in Hebrew, Latin, and Greek, so people of many nationalities could read it (John 19:19–20).

In writing to the Hebrews, Paul made reference to Christ being crucified outside the city. He spoke of a form of burnt offering that was to be performed outside the camp of the children of Israel and compared it to the death of Jesus Christ: "We have an altar, whereof they have no right to eat which serve the tabernacle. For the bodies of those beasts, whose blood is brought into the sanctuary by the high priest for sin, are burned without the camp. Wherefore Jesus also, that he might sanctify the people with his own blood, suffered without the gate. Let us go forth therefore unto him without the camp, bearing his reproach" (Heb. 13:10–13).

*The cross.* Jesus was placed on the cross at the third hour of the day, which would have been at 9:00 A.M., Friday morning. Why did the Romans use a cross for their executions? It is likely that it was the most horrible form of suffering they were able to devise. In the classic *Life of Christ,* Frederic Farrar wrote,

> A death by crucifixion seems to include all that pain and death can have of the horrible and ghastly—dizziness, cramp, thirst, starvation, sleeplessness, traumatic fever, tetanus, publicity of shame, long continuance of torment, horror of anticipation, mortification of untended wounds, all intensified just up to the point at which they can be endured at all, but all stopping just short of the point which would give to the sufferer the relief of unconsciousness. The unnatural position made every movement painful; the lacerated veins and crushed tendons throbbed with incessant anguish; the wounds, inflamed by exposure, gradually gangrened; the arteries, especially of the head and stomach, became swollen and oppressed with surcharged blood; and, while each variety of misery went on gradually increasing, there was added to them the intolerable pang of a burning and raging thirst. Such was the death to which Christ was doomed.[7]

"No word can be found adequate to describe so monstrous a proceeding,"[8] the Roman statesman Cicero wrote, as a man who likely had opportunity to see that monstrous proceeding firsthand (Cicero died in 43 B.C.). It is noteworthy that the words *excruciating* and *crucifixion* derive from the same Latin root (*crucis*).

If the Romans used crucifixion because it was so dreadful a way to die, why did the Father require the Son to die in that manner? Here are some possibilities:

First, it was required that the Son descend below all things. The descent brought together a combination of the intense suffering in the Garden of Gethsemane, the sleepless night, the deep pain of betrayal, the sadistic treatment of the Romans and Jews, the brutality of the cross, the spiritual death of a sinless being, and more—all combined in an emotionally heightened state that has sometimes, with meaning, been called "the passion."

Second, death by crucifixion represented a curse on the victim. Paul wrote, "Christ hath redeemed us from the curse of the law, being made a curse for us: for it is written, Cursed is every one that hangeth on a tree" (Gal. 3:13). Thus, in submitting himself to crucifixion, Jesus Christ was "made a curse for us," in keeping with the pronouncement in the law of Moses: "And if a man have committed a sin worthy of death, and he be to be put to death, and thou hang him on a tree: His body shall not remain all night upon the tree, but thou shalt in any wise bury him that day; (for he that is hanged is accursed of God . . . )" (Deut. 21:22–23).

Third, the symbolism of crucifixion is instructive. The arms are reached out as in surrender. The crucified individual was forced into that position and held there by the cruelest of means—but Christ willingly drank of this portion of the bitter cup, that the will of the Father might be done in every detail.

The arms stretched out suggest another symbolism: that of wings. On more than one occasion the Lord referred to the blessings of his "wings."

I bare you on eagles' wings, and brought you unto myself. (Ex. 19:4)

As an eagle stirreth up her nest, fluttereth over her young, spreadeth abroad her wings, taketh them, beareth them on her wings: so the Lord alone did lead him. . . . He made him ride on the high places of the earth. (Deut. 32:11–13)

How excellent is thy lovingkindness, O God! therefore the children of men put their trust under the shadow of thy wings. (Ps. 36:7)

Be merciful unto me, O God, be merciful unto me: for my soul trusteth in thee: yea, in the shadow of thy wings will I make my refuge. (Ps. 57:1)

Unto you that fear my name shall the Sun of righteousness arise with healing in his wings. (Mal. 4:2)

Behold, I will gather them as a hen gathereth her chickens under her wings, if they will not harden their hearts. (D&C 10:65)

The ark of the covenant was protected and covered with the wings of the cherubim (Ex. 25:20), again suggesting the outstretched arms of the atoning Lord. Those outstretched arms are mentioned often in the Old Testament: "The Lord brought us forth out of Egypt with a mighty hand, and with an outstretched arm, and with great terribleness, and with signs, and with wonders" (Deut. 26:8). "And I myself will fight against you with an outstretched hand and with a strong arm, even in anger, and in fury, and in great wrath" (Jer. 21:5). (For other examples of the Lord's outstretched arm, see Ex. 6:6; Deut. 4:34; 5:15; 7:19; 1 Kgs. 8:42; Ps. 136:12; Jer. 32:17, 21; Ezek. 20:33–34.)

*The prophecy of Psalm 22.* Psalm 22 is a remarkable prophecy of the crucifixion of Jesus Christ. It includes details about the way in which he was treated, actual words he said on the cross, and the division of his garments by the Roman soldiers. The psalm also contains a vivid description of what happened to Jesus' physical body while on the cross. The accompanying chart compares passages from Psalm 22 with statements by Matthew, Mark, Luke, and John.

# PSALM 22 AND ITS FULFILLMENT IN CHRIST

| Psalm 22 | Fulfillment in Christ |
|---|---|
| My God, my God, why hast thou forsaken me? why art thou so far from helping me, and from the words of my roaring? (v. 1) | And about the ninth hour Jesus cried with a loud voice, saying, . . . My God, my God, why hast thou forsaken me? (Matt. 27:46) |
| Our fathers trusted in thee: they trusted, and thou didst deliver them. They cried unto thee, and were delivered. (vv. 4–5) | He trusted in God; let him deliver him now, if he will have him. (Matt. 27:43) |
| But I am a worm, and no man; a reproach of men, and despised of the people. (v. 6) | They spit upon him . . . smote him on the head . . . they had mocked him. (Matt. 27:30–31) |
| All they that see me laugh me to scorn: they shoot out the lip, they shake the head, saying, (v. 7) | They that passed by reviled him, wagging their heads. (Matt. 27:39; Mark 15:29) |
| He trusted on the Lord that he would deliver him: let him deliver him, seeing he delighted in him. (v. 8) | And the people stood beholding. And the rulers also with them deride him, saying, He saved others; let him save himself, if he be Christ. (Luke 23:35) |
| I am poured out like water, and all my bones are out of joint: my heart is like wax; it is melted in the midst of my bowels. (v. 14) | One of the soldiers with a spear pierced his side, and forthwith came there out blood and water. (John 19:34) |
| My strength is dried upon like a potsherd; and my tongue cleaveth to my jaws; and thou hast brought me into the dust of death. (v. 15) | Jesus, knowing that all things were now accomplished, that the scripture might be fulfilled, saith, I thirst. (John 19:28) |
| For dogs have compassed me: the assembly of the wicked have inclosed me: (v. 16) | Chief priests, elders, multitude, soldiers, scribes, thieves. (Matt. 27:20–44) |

| Psalm 22 | Fulfillment in Christ |
|---|---|
| They pierced my hands and my feet. (v. 16) | And they crucified him. (Matt. 27:35) And again another scripture saith, They shall look on him whom they pierced. (John 19:37, citing Zech. 12:10) |
| I may tell all my bones: they look and stare upon me. (v. 17) | But when they came to Jesus, and saw that he was dead already, they brake not his legs. (John 19:33) |
| They part my garments among them, and cast lots upon my vesture. (v. 18) | And they crucified him, and parted his garments, casting lots: that it might be fulfilled which was spoken by the prophet, They parted my garments among them, and upon my vesture did they cast lots. (Matt. 27:35) |

Truly the Lord revealed details of the crucifixion a thousand years before it took place. Because the chart shows only portions of this powerful poetic prophecy, following is a longer extract. What feelings we experience as we read this psalm of our suffering Savior!

*My God, my God, why hast thou forsaken me?*
*Why art thou so far from helping me, and from the words of my roaring? . . .*
*I am . . . a reproach of men, and despised of the people.*
*All they that see me laugh me to scorn:*
*They shoot out the lip [sneer at me];*
*They shake the head, saying,*
*He trusted on the Lord that he would deliver him:*
*Let him deliver him. . . .*
*Be not far from me;*
*For trouble is near; for there is none to help. . . .*
*They gaped upon me with their mouths, as a ravening and a roaring lion.*
*I am poured out like water,*

*And all my bones are out of joint:*
*My heart is like wax;*
*It is melted in the midst of my bowels.*
*My strength is dried up like a potsherd [broken pottery];*
*And my tongue cleaveth to my jaws;*
*And thou hast brought me into the dust of death.*
*For dogs have compassed me:*
*The assembly of the wicked have enclosed me:*
*They pierced my hands and my feet. . . .*
*They part my garments among them,*
*And cast lots upon my vesture.*
*But be not thou far from me, O Lord: O my strength,*
*Haste thee to help me.*
*Deliver my soul.* (Ps. 22:1, 6–8, 11, 13–16, 18–20)

*The words on the cross.* The words Jesus uttered on the cross reveal much about the character and experience of the mortal Messiah. Included in those words are seven short, impressive sermons:

1. "Father, forgive them; for they know not what they do" (Luke 23:34).

This statement is clarified in the Joseph Smith Translation: "Father, forgive them; for they know not what they do (Meaning the soldiers who crucified him)" (JST Luke 23:35). The Roman soldiers came from another society and culture; they were not of the covenant; they had not received the lifelong training in the law and scriptures and tradition that the Jews had. Even more damning for the Jews of that day, those who most clamored for Jesus' death were the religious leaders—those who stood as caretakers of the law and temple of Jehovah. When Jehovah came to dwell with them in the flesh, they rejected him and plotted his murder. The soldiers, however, were innocent in the sense that they did not understand who they were crucifying; in fact, since Jesus was dying the death of a criminal, they surely assumed he was a criminal.

In Jesus' concern for all people, as he suffered in the very act of becoming our advocate and mediator, he acted as advocate and mediator for the very men who had participated in his torture.

239

2. "Verily I say unto thee, To day shalt thou be with me in paradise" (Luke 23:43).

This statement was uttered to one of the thieves, who expressed a feeling that Christ was innocent of a crime (Luke 23:41). The Prophet Joseph Smith taught that "paradise" more correctly meant "the world of spirits."[9] The thief may not have understood what Jesus meant—what was his understanding of God's plan?—but Christ's words clearly were intended to be a comfort to the thief. Again, in his suffering, the Savior was thinking of the needs of those around him.

3. "Woman, behold thy son! . . . Behold thy mother!" (John 19:26–27).

Standing by the cross were Jesus' mother, a few other female disciples, and the apostle John. What mother can bear to stand by and watch her beloved son suffer and die? Even though Mary knew from the beginning that this son was to be "the Son of the Highest," who would "reign over the house of Jacob for ever" (Luke 1:32–33), her heart was surely broken to see the agonizing torture and torment he suffered on the cross. With his own heart filled with compassion for his mother, even in the midst of his own pains, Jesus spoke to both Mary and John and indicated that Jesus was passing the care for his mother to his faithful friend. "And from that hour that disciple took her unto his own home" (John 19:27). (The word from which "woman" is translated was in Jesus' time a term of endearment.)

4. "My God, my God, why hast thou forsaken me?" (Matt. 27:46).

This deep soul cry fulfilled a prophecy recorded in Psalm 22, where these exact words are found. Hours earlier, in the dark hours of the night, Jesus had suffered spiritual death in the Garden of Gethsemane, where the Father's Spirit had left him alone (see chapter 16). That Spirit apparently returned to assist him through the hours of his trial and afflictions. But at or before the ninth hour of the day (about 3:00 P.M.), Jesus again suffered the loss of the Father's presence, and in his anguish cried out in a loud voice: "Eloi, Eloi, lama sabachthani? which is, being interpreted, My God, my God, why hast thou forsaken me?" (Mark 15:34). By this point the earth had been shrouded in darkness for three hours.

The loss of the Spirit again signified spiritual death. As part of the infinite atonement, it was necessary that Jesus experience the consequences of sin to the very depths. Everyone else who has ever lived has tasted the fruits of sin; all have suffered loss of the Spirit. But Christ was without sin, "a lamb without blemish and without spot" (1 Pet. 1:19). Before the Garden of Gethsemane, he had never known the feeling of being abandoned by his Father, nor did he deserve to know. And now that terrible, wrenching, empty feeling had returned. It was the ultimate loneliness, a source of agony and spiritual pain that only the truly repentant can begin to understand. It brought him into "the very atmosphere of hell itself, the deepest pit of despair, the darkest depression."[10] It "placed Jesus in His own Outer Darkness, in which He paid the price for sin by Himself—without a deliverer to take Him down from the cross or to lessen His agony."[11] "Even for the Savior, greater pain or anguish was not possible. One simply cannot go lower than below *all* things."[12]

5. "I thirst" (John 19:28).

What an irony that the source of living waters should be surrounded by people and yet have no way to quench his thirst! After Jesus had been hanging on the cross for six hours, "knowing that all things were now accomplished, that the scripture might be fulfilled, [he] saith, I thirst" (John 19:28). He had suffered and given all that was required. He had attended to the needs of others, even in his own extreme distress. Surely he had been thirsty the entire time. But now, not strictly to satisfy his thirst but also in part to fulfill prophecy, he said, "I thirst." A "vessel full of vinegar" was nearby, set there to be given to those crucified, and someone "filled a spunge with vinegar, and put it upon hyssop, and put it to his mouth" (John 19:29).[13]

Hyssop (a woody plant) was used in expressing a type of Christ's atonement at the first Passover. Moses commanded the children of Israel to kill the Passover lamb and, using "a bunch of hyssop" to apply the blood to the lintel and the doorposts (Ex. 12:21–22). Now it was used again in the last moments of the atonement.

Thus prophecy was fulfilled: "They gave me also gall for my meat; and in my thirst they gave me vinegar to drink" (Ps. 69:21).

6. "It is finished" (John 19:30).

Immediately after taking the vinegar, Jesus said, "It is finished." The Greek word from which this is translated (*tetelestai*) suggests completeness or fulfillment. Jesus had completed and fulfilled all the requirements of the atonement.

The Joseph Smith Translation gives a more complete account of these words: "Jesus . . . cried again with a loud voice, saying, Father, it is finished, thy will is done" (JST Matt. 27:54). Jesus had done the Father's will from the beginning. Even in premortality he had said, "Father, thy will be done, and the glory be thine forever" (Moses 4:2). Now he came to the end of his sufferings with the same spirit. He had never wavered from seeking that will. Even in the Garden of Gethsemane, when he wondered if the cup might pass, he consistently and earnestly added, "Nevertheless not as I will, but as thou wilt" (Matt. 26:39). It was with that same heart that he completed his atoning task.

7. "Father, into thy hands I commend my spirit" (Luke 23:46).

This cry also was uttered "with a loud voice," suggesting that Jesus had strength remaining within him. But as soon as he said these words, "he gave up the ghost" (Luke 23:46). The atonement was complete; his life was complete; he had done all he had been sent to do. The task was finished. Now, even though Jesus had suffered the pains of hell when the Father's Spirit departed, he knew he would be entering into the presence of God in his resurrection and would sit down at his right hand, there to rule in majesty and glory forever.

This statement was another fulfillment of Old Testament prophecy: "Into thine hand I commit my spirit: thou hast redeemed me, O Lord God of truth" (Ps. 31:5).

Through his atonement on the cross, Jesus also fulfilled a choice messianic prophecy of Isaiah, wherein the Father made promises regarding his most beloved Son: "I will clothe him with thy robe, and strengthen him with thy girdle, and I will commit thy government into his hand: and he shall be a father to the inhabitants of Jerusalem, and to the house of Judah. And the key of the house of David will I lay upon his shoulder; so he shall open, and none shall shut; and he shall shut, and none shall open. And I will fasten him as a nail in a sure place; and he shall be for a glorious throne to his father's house. And they shall hang upon him all the glory of his father's house" (Isa. 22:21–24).

*Atonement on the cross.* Some misunderstand and believe that the entirety of the atonement for our sins occurred in Gethsemane, while the crucifixion was essential so that Christ could offer his life for us. While it is true that the Savior had to die in order to overcome death (see, for example, Heb. 2:9), it is also true that his suffering for our sins, which began in Gethsemane, recurred on the cross. This understanding is well supported in latter-day scripture. In two successive revelations given in June 1831 in Kirtland, Ohio, the Lord said that he "was crucified for the sins of the world" (D&C 53:2; 54:1).

Thus we know that Christ suffered for our sins in Gethsemane, and he suffered for our sins on the cross. The magnitude of Christ's offering reaches far past our ability to imagine or comprehend. "If we interpret the holy word aright," Elder Bruce R. McConkie wrote, "all of the anguish, all of the sorrow, and all of the suffering of Gethsemane recurred during the final three hours on the cross, the hours when darkness covered the land. Truly there was no sorrow like unto his sorrow, and no anguish and pain like unto that which bore in with such intensity upon him."[14]

*The physical death.* Death had no power over Christ; to the contrary, Christ had power over death. Jesus said, "For as the Father hath life in himself; so hath he given to the Son to have life in himself" (John 5:26). Later he taught, "Therefore doth my Father love me, because I lay down my life, that I might take it again. No man taketh it from me, but I lay it down of myself. I have power to lay it down, and I have power to take it again. This commandment have I received of my Father" (John 10:17–18).

God has all power over life and death. He has established laws whereby spirits enter physical bodies to begin their mortal lives, and he has established laws whereby the spirit leaves the body in death. He can shorten life or prolong life according to his will and purposes. He can change a person's body through a process called translation so that the person lives indefinitely, impervious to physical pain, sickness, injury, or (presumably) aging. God personally lives forever; his body cannot degrade, decay, or atrophy in any way. He has "life in himself." And just as the Father has such life, he gave his Son power to have "life in himself." Jesus Christ was the literal biological son of the Father. As such, he could not die unless he chose to die.

The pain and torture on the cross were terribly real. The Savior suffered intense exhaustion and loss of blood. But these things did not bring the death of Christ. He died through an act of will, a choice, and he would not make that choice until all was complete, or, as he said, "finished" (John 19:30).

He died in the ninth hour of the day, or about 3:00 P.M. On that day, at that very moment, the Jews were killing lambs for their Passover feast. The Lamb slain from the foundation of the world, the sacrifice symbolized by slain lambs for two thousand years—this Lamb voluntarily gave up his life, in sacrifice, on the very day God's chosen people were preparing to celebrate their divine deliverance from their enemies, a deliverance that came with an outstretched arm and with mighty power.

It was required that "bodies should not remain upon the cross on the sabbath day" (John 19:31), which would begin in only hours, at dusk. Therefore, to assure that those crucified were really dead, it was the custom for the Romans to break their legs. Acting on a request from the Jews, Pilate so instructed that the legs of Jesus and the two thieves be broken; then the bodies would be removed from the cross and buried. The soldiers accordingly broke the legs of the two thieves, "but when they came to Jesus, and saw that he was dead already, they brake not his legs: But one of the soldiers with a spear pierced his side, and forthwith came there out blood and water. For these things were done, that the scripture should be fulfilled, A bone of him shall not be broken. And again another scripture saith, They shall look on him whom they pierced" (John 19:33–34, 36–37).

The piercing of Jesus' side was prophesied by Simeon when the infant Jesus was taken to the temple for the required offering. Simeon, who had been moved by the Spirit to go to the temple that day, saw Mary and Joseph and Jesus. "And Simeon blessed them, and said unto Mary his mother, Behold, this child is set for the fall and rising again of many in Israel; and for a sign which shall be spoken against; (Yea, a sword shall pierce through thy own soul also,) that the thoughts of many hearts may be revealed" (Luke 2:34–35). The Joseph Smith Translation clarifies the latter part of this prophecy, pointing it directly to the crucifixion: "Yea, a spear shall pierce through him to the wounding of thine own soul also" (JST Luke 2:35).

This repeats a prophecy uttered by Isaiah. The King James Version of Isaiah 53:5 says, "He was *wounded* for our transgressions," but the original Hebrew reads differently: "He shall be *pierced* for our transgressions" (emphasis added). And so he was.

*The testimony of all nature.* Beginning at about the sixth hour of the day (or noon), "there was darkness over all the land" (Matt. 27:45), and the "sun was darkened" (Luke 23:45). Such darkness was understandable. Jesus Christ is the light of the world (3 Ne. 1:15). He is "in the sun, and the light of the sun, and the power thereof by which it was made. . . . Which light proceedeth forth from the presence of God to fill the immensity of space" (D&C 88:7, 12). With the light of the world suffering and dying, the light that flowed from him surely would dim and darken.

That darkness continued for three hours, until Christ's offering was complete. Then, at his death, "the earth did quake, and the rocks rent" (Matt. 27:51). This fulfilled a prophecy spoken by Nephi; he said that "the rocks of the earth must rend," and some on the earth, not knowing of the events in Jerusalem, would be led to exclaim, "The God of nature suffers" (1 Ne. 19:12). Enoch the seer beheld the same events: "The Lord said unto Enoch: Look, and he looked and beheld the Son of Man lifted up on the cross, after the manner of men; and he heard a loud voice; and the heavens were veiled; and all the creations of God mourned; and the earth groaned; and the rocks were rent" (Moses 7:55–56; see also Hel. 14:21–24).

President John Taylor recorded the effects of the crucifixion on the earth—and the worlds beyond—when he wrote:

> Not only did His agony affect the mind and body of Jesus, causing Him to sweat great drops of blood, but by reason of some

principle, to us unfathomable, His suffering affected universal nature. . . .

When he gave up the ghost, the solid rocks were riven, the foundations of the earth trembled, earthquakes shook the continents and rent the isles of the sea, a deep darkness overspread the sky, the mighty waters overflowed their accustomed bounds, huge mountains sank and valleys rose, the handiwork of feeble men was overthrown, their cities were engulphed or consumed by the vivid shafts of lightning, and all material things were convulsed with the throes of seeming dissolution. . . .

Thus, such was the torturing pressure of this intense, this indescribable agony, that it burst forth abroad beyond the confines of His body, convulsed all nature, and spread throughout all space.[15]

The combination of these events was so impressive that the Gentile soldiers who were present at the crucifixion "feared greatly" and cried out, "Truly this was the Son of God" (Matt. 27:54).

*The veil of the temple.* Another highly symbolic and significant event occurred at the moment of Jesus' death: "Behold, the veil of the temple was rent in twain from the top to the bottom" (Matt. 27:51). The veil protected the holy of holies from profane eyes. It protected the dwelling place of God on the earth. Only the high priest could go through that veil, and then only on the Day of Atonement. When the holy of holies, or most holy place, was "unveiled," it became desecrated, unclean, *unholy.* The Jews would have been horrified at the violation of their most holy place.

What they may not have understood was that the veil was ripped open by the hand of God. It also represented a powerful symbol of the atonement: the rending of Christ's body with the nails and the rending of the temple veil both ultimately signified the same thing: that God was making a new covenant with his people, a covenant whereby they could enter his presence without the mediation of an Aaronic high priest (Heb. 9:24; 10:19–20). Christ himself, through the atonement, would be "mediator of the new covenant, who wrought out this perfect atonement through the shedding of his own blood" (D&C 76:69), which atonement would be the "great and last sacrifice" (Alma 34:10).

*The burial.* Joseph of Arimathaea was "a rich man" and "an honourable counsellor." He also was "a disciple of Jesus" who "waited for the kingdom of God" (Matt. 27:57; Mark 15:43; John 19:38). At real risk to himself (John 19:38), Joseph "went in boldly unto Pilate, and craved the body of Jesus" (Mark 15:43). That request was granted. According to Luke's testimony, Joseph took the body down from the cross (Luke 23:53); but in Matthew's account "Pilate commanded the body to be delivered" (Matt. 27:58). In either event, Joseph was joined by Nicodemus, another wealthy disciple of Christ who belonged to the Sanhedrin. Joseph "bought fine linen" (Mark 15:46), and Nicodemus "brought a mixture of myrrh and aloes, about an hundred pound weight" (John 19:39). Then these two faithful men "took . . . the body of Jesus, and wound it in linen clothes with the spices, as the manner of the Jews is to bury. Now in the place where he was crucified there was a garden; and in the garden a new sepulchre, wherein was never man yet laid. There laid they Jesus therefore because of the Jews' preparation day; for the sepulchre was nigh at hand" (John 19:40–42).

"And the women also, which came with him from Galilee, followed after, and beheld the sepulchre, and how his body was laid. And they returned, and prepared spices and ointments; and rested the sabbath day according to the commandment" (Luke 23:55–56).

## "THIS IS THE GOSPEL"

The gospel of Jesus Christ, which is the gospel of the Father, is many things. It includes the truths found in the Articles of Faith. We believe in a Godhead of three separate persons; we believe that Adam is responsible for his sins and that we are responsible for our own; we believe that the atonement of Jesus Christ will save all who come unto Christ in obedience; we believe in such essentials as faith in Jesus Christ, repentance, baptism, and the gift of the Holy Ghost; we believe that the gospel is sheltered in a Church with a divinely inspired organization; we believe in many gifts of the Spirit; and so forth.

The gospel is also found in the temple, where marvelous truths are taught to the faithful. The gospel is found throughout the scriptures, which present a collection of multifaceted gems of truth that collectively are the good news from on high.

Though all that is true, there are four places in the scriptures where the Lord says plainly, "This is the gospel" or "This is my gospel."

In two instances where the Lord makes that declaration, he defines "my gospel" as "repentance and baptism by water, and then cometh the baptism of fire and the Holy Ghost, even the Comforter, which showeth all things, and teacheth the peaceable things of the kingdom" (D&C 39:6; see also D&C 33:11–12). These are gifts and blessings available to the obedient; they come through the atonement of Jesus Christ.

In one instance, the Lord focuses on his condescension and his atonement, including the crucifixion: "And *this is the gospel,* the glad tidings, which the voice out of the heavens bore record unto us—that he came into the world, even Jesus, to be crucified for the world, and to bear the sins of the world, and to sanctify the world, and to cleanse it from all unrighteousness; that through him all might be saved whom the Father had put into his power and made by him" (D&C 76:40–42; emphasis added).

In a final instance, the Lord combines the two concepts—the gospel comprises his atoning mission on the earth and the gifts of repentance, baptism, and reception of the Holy Ghost that are made possible through that mission:

> Behold I have given unto you my gospel, and *this is the gospel* which I have given unto you—that I came into the world to do the will of my Father, because my Father sent me.
>
> And my Father sent me that I might be lifted up upon the cross; and after that I had been lifted up upon the cross, that I might draw all men unto me, that as I have been lifted up by men even so should men be lifted up by the Father, to stand before me, to be judged of their works, whether they be good or whether they be evil—
>
> And for this cause have I been lifted up; therefore, according

to the power of the Father I will draw all men unto me, that they may be judged according to their works.

And it shall come to pass, that whoso repenteth and is baptized in my name shall be filled; and if he endureth to the end, behold, him will I hold guiltless before my Father at that day when I shall stand to judge the world. . . .

Now this is the commandment: Repent, all ye ends of the earth, and come unto me and be baptized in my name, that ye may be sanctified by the reception of the Holy Ghost, that ye may stand spotless before me at the last day.

Verily, verily, I say unto you, *this is my gospel;* and ye know the things that ye must do in my church; for the works which ye have seen me do that shall ye also do; for that which ye have seen me do even that shall ye do. (3 Ne. 27:13–16, 20–21; emphasis added)

Clearly these are essential truths. Out of all the gospel teachings the Lord has given us, here is the core: know that Christ came into the world to do the Father's will, which brought him to the singular act of the atonement, including the crucifixion; and if we have faith in that atonement, we must repent of our sins, be baptized, endure to the end, and become sanctified through the cleansing blood of Jesus Christ.

## SIGNS OF THE OFFERING

Jesus, our Savior, has retained within his body the marks or signs of his atoning sacrifice. When he returns in his Second Coming, "Then shall the Jews look upon me and say: What are these wounds in thine hands and in thy feet?" And Jesus will respond: "These wounds are the wounds with which I was wounded in the house of my friends. I am he who was lifted up. I am Jesus that was crucified. I am the Son of God." And then, he says, the Jews "shall . . . weep because of their iniquities; then shall they lament because they persecuted their king" (D&C 45:51–53; see also Zech. 13:6).

But these signs are not only for the Jews. To all those who may feel forsaken or forgotten by the Lord, he asks: "Can a woman forget her sucking child, that she should not have compassion on the son of her womb? yea, they may forget, yet will I not forget thee." And then he adds this heartbreaking truth about a terrible cost of the atonement: "Behold, I have graven thee upon the palms of my hands" (Isa. 49:15–16).

Elder Jeffrey R. Holland has given this humbling reassurance:

> When we stagger or stumble, He is there to steady and strengthen us. In the end He is there to save us, and for all this He gave His life. However dim our days may seem, they have been a lot darker for the Savior of the world. As a reminder of those days, Jesus has chosen, even in a resurrected, otherwise perfected body, to retain for the benefit of His disciples the wounds in His hands and in His feet and in His side—signs, if you will, that painful things happen even to the pure and the perfect; signs, if you will, that pain in this world is *not* evidence that God doesn't love you; signs, if you will, that problems pass and happiness can be ours. . . . It is the wounded Christ who is the Captain of our souls, He who yet bears the scars of our forgiveness, the lesions of His love and humility, the torn flesh of obedience and sacrifice.
>
> These wounds are the principal way we are to recognize Him when He comes. He may invite us forward, as He has invited others, to see and to feel those marks. If not before, then surely at that time, we will remember with Isaiah that it was for us that a God was "despised and rejected . . . ; a man of sorrows, and acquainted with grief," that "he was wounded for our transgressions, he was bruised for our iniquities: the chastisement of our peace was upon him; and with his stripes we are healed" (Isa. 53:3, 5).[16]

## REMEMBERING HIS SACRIFICE

The gift of the atonement, including the suffering through the crucifixion, is like any other gift: it needs to be received to have true meaning in our lives. And to be received with the greatest impact, the significance of the offering must be *felt* as well as cognitively recognized. Elder Holland referenced this truth when he spoke of contemplating the details of the atonement: "So much of the mystery of [Jesus'] power and ministry tear at my *mind:* the circumstances of his birth, the breadth and variety of his ministry and miracles, the self-summoned power of his resurrection—before all of these I stand amazed and say, 'How did he do it?' But here with disciples who abandoned him in his hour of greatest need, here fainting under the weight of his cross and the sins of all mankind which were attached to it, here rent by piercing spikes in his palms and in his wrists and in his feet—here now the amazement tears not at my *mind* but at my *heart.*"[17]

How can we better remember the sacrifice of our Savior, with *feeling?*

Mormon suggested one way in an impressive invitation to his son, Moroni, to continually ponder the sacrifice of the Savior: "My son, be faithful in Christ; and may . . . Christ lift thee up, and may his *sufferings* and *death,* and the *showing his body* unto our fathers, and his *mercy and long-suffering,* and the hope of his glory and of eternal life, rest in your mind forever" (Moro. 9:25; emphasis added).

This is an invitation we can receive for ourselves. In fact, in a touching statement in this dispensation, the Lord invites us to contemplate his offering in a specific and deeply personal way: "Look unto me in *every thought;* doubt not, fear not. Behold the *wounds* which pierced my side, and also the *prints of the nails* in my hands and my feet. Be faithful, keep my commandments, and ye shall inherit the kingdom of heaven" (D&C 6:36–37; emphasis added).

Of course, we promise to always remember him each week as we partake of the sacrament. We "eat in remembrance of the *body*" of Christ and "in remembrance of the *blood* . . . which was shed for [us]" (D&C 20:77, 79; emphasis added). (Some Saints silently substitute *I* and *me* for the words *we, they,* and *them* as they listen to the sacrament prayers, which can give the experience a powerful new dimension.)

As we continue in faithfulness, being taught by the Spirit and strengthened and cleansed by the atonement, we may someday reach the point where we can speak of Christ's sacrifice as Elder McConkie so powerfully did in his stirring last testimony: "I testify that [Jesus Christ] is the son of the Living God and was crucified for the sins of the world. . . .

"I am one of his witnesses, and in a coming day I shall feel the nail marks in his hands and in his feet and shall wet his feet with my tears.

"But I shall not know any better then than I know now that he is God's Almighty Son, that he is our Savior and Redeemer, and that salvation comes in and through his atoning blood and in no other way."[18]

And so we must ever remember, with true feeling for the gift that has been offered and for the incomprehensible price of that offering. As President Gordon B. Hinckley, then a member of the Quorum of the Twelve, admonished:

> No member of this Church must ever forget the terrible price paid by our Redeemer who gave his life that all men might live— the agony of Gethsemane, the bitter mockery of his trial, the vicious crown of thorns tearing at his flesh, the blood cry of the mob before Pilate, the lonely burden of his heavy walk along the way to Calvary, the terrifying pain as great nails pierced his hands and feet, the fevered torture of his body as he hung that tragic day, the Son of God crying out, "Father, forgive them; for they know not what they do." (Luke 23:34.)
>
> This was the cross, the instrument of his torture, the terrible device designed to destroy the Man of Peace, the evil recompense for his miraculous work of healing the sick, of causing the blind to see, of raising the dead. This was the cross on which he hung and died on Golgotha's lonely summit.
>
> We cannot forget that. We must never forget it, for here our Savior, our Redeemer, the Son of God, gave himself a vicarious sacrifice for each of us.[19]

CHAPTER 18

# "HANDLE ME AND SEE": THE RESURRECTION

OUR LIVES CAN CHANGE IN A DAY, an hour, a moment. One day the disciples of Jesus Christ were feeling lost, bereft, filled with grief and confusion: the man whom they called Messiah had been slain and laid in a tomb. The hopes of some were shattered; some surely were filled with doubt; others, who retained their faith in Jesus as the Christ, may have wondered how the prophecies could possibly be fulfilled. "As yet they knew not the scripture, that he must rise again from the dead" (John 20:9; see also Mark 16:11–14).

The next day, "when it was yet dark" (John 20:1), Mary Magdalene and other women (Mark 16:1; Luke 24:10) went to the tomb of Christ. It was empty. But two angels met them and, in an instant, enlightened their understandings. "Fear not ye," the angels said, "for we know that ye seek Jesus, who was crucified. He is not here; for he is risen, as he said" (JST Matt. 28:4–5).

The angels sent the women to "tell his disciples that he is risen from the dead" (Matt. 28:7).

Hearing word of the women's experience, Peter and John ran to the tomb. Christ's body was gone, but his grave clothes remained, neatly folded (John 20:2–8).

Later, Mary Magdalene returned to the sepulcher, weeping. Overcome with concern and grief, she saw a man she mistook for the gardener—and had a thrilling interchange with her risen Savior (John 20:11–18).

That afternoon, two disciples were walking to Emmaus. They were deep in conversation about the events of the day, wondering what it all meant, when they met a man who taught them from the Old Testament prophets about Christ. Then, after teaching them, he revealed himself as the resurrected Jesus. "And their eyes were opened, and they knew him" (Luke 24:31; see also vv. 13–35).

While these disciples were giving a report to the apostles and others, "Jesus himself stood in the midst of them, and saith unto them, Peace be unto you." Then, because they feared they were seeing a ghost, or a spirit, Jesus said, "Behold my hands and my feet, that it is I myself: handle me, and see; for a spirit hath not flesh and bones, as ye see me have" (Luke 24:36, 39).

Years later, Paul gave this testimony:

> I delivered unto you first of all that which I also received, how that Christ died for our sins according to the scriptures; and that he was buried, and that he rose again the third day according to the scriptures: and that he was seen of Cephas, then of the twelve:
>
> After that, he was seen of above five hundred brethren at once; of whom the greater part remain unto this present, but some are fallen asleep.
>
> After that, he was seen of James; then of all the apostles. (1 Cor. 15:3–7)

At another time, another place, Jesus appeared to the faithful among the Nephites. There, in a marvelous and very physical way, he manifested the reality of his resurrected body. At his invitation, "the multitude went forth, and thrust their hands into his side, and did feel the prints of the nails in his hands and in his feet; and this they did do, going forth one by one until they had all gone forth, and did see with their eyes and did feel with their hands, and did know of a surety and did bear record, that it was he, of whom it was written by the prophets, that should come" (3 Ne. 11:15).

## A MIRACLE OF MIRACLES

Over the millennia of the earth's history, God has shown forth many mighty miracles. He parted the Red Sea so the Israelites could cross in safety as they fled from the murderous Egyptians. He blessed Gideon and his three hundred to defeat an army of fifteen thousand. He enabled Elijah to call down fire from heaven. On more than one occasion Christ healed large multitudes. The mortal Messiah raised Lazarus and others from the dead. Later, Christ descended from heaven in a marvelous way to manifest himself unto the Nephites.

But every other miracle, great as each one was, pales when compared to the greatest public manifestation of God's power[1]: Christ's resurrection from the dead. Never before had someone risen from the grave in immortal form. When Christ arose he did so in a glorified, perfected body (although he retained the marks of his crucifixion as a witness of his offering), never to die again.

Just as remarkable, through that process he conquered death for all living things. The ultimate enemy, before which all were powerless for thousands of years, was overcome once and for all (and at one singular point, for all people of all time).

The scope of the resurrection truly is infinite. It affects every member of the human family in every age of the world. It blesses every person from every world created by Christ. It reaches back to the beginning of time and forward to the end of the world. It blesses animals, plants, and the earth itself. No dead body will ever be forgotten—all will be resurrected. No dead body will be lost in the utmost parts of the earth or the waters of the sea or the ashes of destruction—the Lord knows all, and all will rise from the dead. There will be no exceptions.

Not only does resurrection bless us with immortality, but it also blesses us as a necessary element of our experiencing at-one-ment with God. Through the resurrection we can be lifted up to eternal life, where we can have life *like* God and life *with* God.

The atonement for sin and the atonement for death work in tandem with each other. Both are essential for us to come to true godliness. If we were redeemed from death but not cleansed from sin, we would rise from the grave as corrupted souls. If we were sanctified from sin but never resurrected, we would not be corporeal as God is, and we would never attain to a fulness of joy (D&C 93:33–34).

The resurrection was the culminating act of the marvelous atonement of Christ. It is "the visible, outward manifestation of the more invisible and inward spiritual triumph of the Atonement." As such, "it remains the grand, central fact at the heart of the Christian message. It is the sublime reality that sets Christianity apart from all other religions."[2] Thus the resurrection, supremely important in its own right, also stands as a symbol of the many other blessings of the atonement. If the resurrection is real and true, then Christ's other powers to bless and lift us unto the Father are likewise real.

Speaking of the resurrection as the culmination of the atonement, President Gordon B. Hinckley said: "Of all the victories in human history, none is so great, none so universal in its effect, none so everlasting in its consequences as the victory of the crucified Lord who came forth in the Resurrection that first Easter morning.

"We laud the captains and the kings, we praise the nations that are victorious against oppressors. We appropriately build monuments to remember their sacrifices and their triumphs over the forces of oppression. But great and important as are these achievements, none can compare with the victory of the lonely, pain-racked figure on Calvary's cross who triumphed over death and brought the gift of eternal life to all mankind."[3]

As with other elements of the atonement, both the scriptures and the natural world contain many witnesses and symbols of the resurrection of Jesus Christ—and of our resurrection. This chapter includes some examples.

## THE NATURAL WORLD

*Birth*. Birth into mortality involves the spirit entering the body and the body leaving the mother's womb. Similarly, resurrection involves the spirit entering the body and the body leaving the grave. Hence, birth into mortality is a type of resurrection into immortality. President

Brigham Young once stated, "The resurrection from the dead may also, with propriety, be called a birth."[4] President Charles W. Penrose also likened resurrection to birth: "I want to impress . . . the fact that the resurrection will prove to be just as natural as birth."[5]

*Sleep.* Nightly sleep is a type and a shadow for death, and awakening in the morning symbolizes the resurrection. Daniel used the word *sleep* to refer to death and *awake* to refer to the resurrection: "And many of them that sleep in the dust of the earth shall awake, some to everlasting life, and some to shame and everlasting contempt" (Dan. 12:2).

*Morning.* The prophets have frequently referred to the "morning of the first resurrection," which is the resurrection that will take place at Christ's second coming. President Harold B. Lee, for example, declared: "I know that God lives. I know that he has opened the doors to the glorious resurrection. He is biding the time when He shall come again, when the trump shall sound and those who are ready to come forth in the morning of the resurrection shall come forth to be caught up in the clouds of heaven to meet Him. God grant that we may live to be worthy to be among those who will be with Him."[6]

It may be that the *morning* of the day is a type that looks forward to the resurrection. The first obvious parallel is that Christ was resurrected in the morning (Mark 16:1–6), Sunday morning, now known as Easter morning.

There are other parallels. Morning comes at daybreak, or sunrise, which corresponds with the increased light that people will gain at the resurrection. During the night, we sleep, a similitude to those who are sleeping in their graves. Then in the morning, we rise out of bed, in likeness of our rising out of the grave. During sleep, we have no consciousness, but upon awakening we have full consciousness. Similarly, during the sleep of death our bodies have no consciousness, but at the resurrection our bodies, united with our spirits, will have full consciousness. Morning brings physical refreshment to those who have slept, just as the resurrection will give eternal vigor to our souls. "As we rise in the morning from our night's rest, so it will be with us in the resurrection," said President Penrose.[7]

*Seasons.* The cycles of the seasons are a beautiful and clear type of the resurrection. The springtime, when all is fresh and new, can symbolize birth into mortality. We grow and mature through the long days of summer, when the sun shines brightly. We bear much fruit in our maturity. Then, in autumn, we decline as the days become shorter and cooler. In the winter the earth settles down for a cold spell. Many of the plants die or go into a dormant state. Then, again in spring, the plants send forth their shoots, the leaves begin to develop and bud, and life returns. Just as this pattern suggests the normal cycle of mortality, so also can the death in winter and the new life in spring symbolize the universal and blessed power of the resurrection.

*Hibernation.* Hibernation coincides with the seasons. Some species of animals go into a semidormant state for many weeks or months, often hidden in the earth. Then, as the sun warms the earth again, they come forth, ready for a new year and a new life. So it is with us in the resurrection.

*The chrysalis.* The life cycle of the butterfly (as well as some other insects) is symbolic of the resurrection. It begins as a larva, or caterpillar, which can crawl but is rather limited in movement. Then it builds a cocoon, a type of grave where it is encased and unable to move. After a time of dormancy, it seems to return to life and emerges from the chrysalis stage as a beautiful new creature.

*Sown seeds.* Paul compared the sowing of seeds in the earth to death and burial, and the maturing and ripening of grain to the resurrection (1 Cor. 15:35–38). In his analogy, the sown seed will "die" when it is buried in the ground. It is then "quickened" (v. 36) when it breaks forth from the ground and produces grain or fruit. The quickening of the seed is comparable to the resurrection of the human soul, according to Paul's analogy. Additionally, Paul called the seed a "body" (v. 38), comparing it to a person. He credited God for the harvested grain (verses 37–38), an important point in his analogy because God is also the power by which people are resurrected.

## SCRIPTURE STORIES

*Jonah and the great fish.* Jonah's experience with the great fish typified Jesus' death and resurrection. Both were buried in their respective tombs, Jonah in the belly of the fish and Jesus in the belly of the earth. Both spent approximately three days and three nights there; and both were brought forth on the third day. As Elder Bruce R. McConkie wrote, "Jonah's burial in and coming forth from the 'great fish' (Jonah 1:15–17; 2) symbolizes the death, burial, and resurrection of Christ."[8]

*The baptism of Jesus Christ.* The baptism of Christ was symbolic of his death and resurrection. His immersion prefigured his death and burial, and coming forth from the water anticipated his resurrection, or coming forth from the grave. In Romans 6:3–11, a discourse on baptism, Paul used many terms that pertain to death—*dead, buried, death,* and *died.* He also used terms that speak of the resurrection—*raised up, newness of life, resurrection, live, raised from the dead, liveth,* and *alive.* Of course, these symbolisms apply to us as well. On the one hand, our own baptism into The Church of Jesus Christ of Latter-day Saints represents the "death" of our disobedient, sinful selves and our spiritual "resurrection" into a newness of life. On the other hand, our baptism symbolizes our physical death and resurrection.

*The raising of Lazarus.* The raising of Lazarus from the dead typifies the resurrection from the dead. Language used in the Lazarus account pertains to both death and the resurrection—*died, rise again,* and *life* (John 11:21–26). Just as Lazarus died and was brought back to life through the power of Jesus Christ, so too will all the dead be brought back to life in the resurrection through the power of Jesus' atonement.

Jesus used the setting of Lazarus's death to teach concerning the resurrection. Previous to Lazarus's renewal to life, Jesus testified to Martha, Lazarus's sister, "I am the resurrection, and the life: he that believeth in me, though he were dead, yet shall he live" (John 11:25).

*The budding of Aaron's rod.* In Numbers 16, a large group of Israelites rebelled against Moses and Aaron, demanding the priestly office for themselves. The Lord responded by slaying the rebels. Then, in Numbers 17, the Lord gave additional instruction to show Israel whom he had chosen for the priesthood. He told the people to prepare twelve rods, one for each tribe of Israel, and to write on each rod the name of the prince who led that tribe. Aaron's name was to be inscribed on the rod of Levi. "And thou shalt lay them up in the tabernacle of the congregation before the testimony, where I will meet with you. And it shall come to pass, that the man's rod, whom I shall choose, shall blossom: and I will make to cease from me the murmurings of the children of Israel, whereby they murmur against you" (vv. 4–5).

The next day, eleven of the rods still lay dead on the ground, but "behold, the rod of Aaron for the house of Levi was budded, and brought forth buds, and bloomed blossoms, and yielded almonds" (v. 8). Moses took the rods and showed them "unto all the children of Israel," and they saw which rod lived and which remained dead (v. 9).

This story demonstrates God's power over life and death in the plant kingdom—but it also serves as a beautiful type of the resurrection of Christ. Where all others who have died have remained lifeless and dead, only Christ has borne fruit unto life after his death—and many have seen and borne witness.

*Other stories.* The scriptures have a number of other stories that are types of the resurrection:

In the Garden of Eden, Adam lay down and fell into a deep sleep. When he arose, he received a new bride and a new life, and he was blessed to walk and talk with God. Likewise, Christ was laid down at the Garden Tomb in the sleep of death. He arose unto a new life, where he is able to walk and talk with God—and in time he will receive his bride, the faithful Saints.

Noah entered the ark (representing the tomb) and spent many days riding over the waters of death. But he and his family were preserved and remembered by God, even while they were in the tomb. When they were brought forth by God's power, they emerged into a new world.

Isaac was laid as a sacrifice on the altar of death. Paul writes: "By faith Abraham, when he was tried, offered up Isaac: and he that had received the promises offered up his only begotten son, of whom it was said, That in Isaac shall thy seed be called: accounting that God was able to raise him up, even from the dead; from whence also he received him in a figure [or type]" (Heb. 11:17–19). The sacrifice was fully accounted unto both Abraham and Isaac "for righteousness" (D&C 132:36), and Isaac then rose up from the altar by the power of God (manifest through the visitation of an angel) unto life.

Joseph of old was cast into a pit, symbolizing the grave. Then he was brought out and sold into bondage in a strange country, where he was separated from his family. Eventually, though, he was reunited with his family and became the salvation of his people.

The Jaredites left a world that was about to be changed forever. Through the power of Christ they were preserved as they crossed the dark waters of death, "buried" in enclosed barges. Finally they arrived to a new life in a new land, the "promised land" (Ether 6:7, 12), which signifies heaven (Alma 37:45–46).

## God's Power over Death

The scriptures give abundant evidence of God's power over death. His power over death from a variety of causes underscores and witnesses to his power over death in the ultimate sense, the resurrection.

*Protected from death.* Again and again the Lord has shown his ability to protect his people from death. Consider the stories of Enoch and his enemies; Noah, his family, and the ark; Abraham on the altar; Lot and his family when the cities of the plain were destroyed; Isaac on the altar; Joseph when his brothers conspired to kill him; Moses in the bulrushes; Moses and Joshua on countless occasions against the Egyptians, the Canaanites, and other enemies; the children of Israel when they looked on the brass serpent; Elijah during the drought and later when the king's soldiers came against him; David when Saul sought to kill him; Shadrach, Meshach, and Abed-nego in the fiery furnace; Daniel in the den of lions; Jonah and the great fish; Jesus stilling the deadly seas on which the disciples rode in a ship; Peter, James, John, and Paul when the Jewish leaders sought their death; Nephi[1] when he faced Laban and then the elders of the city; Nephi[1] when his brothers conspired to kill him; Abinadi, who was preserved until he could deliver all his testimony; the sons of Mosiah when they went to preach to the murderous Lamanites; Ammon when he protected the king's flocks from robbers and when he faced the angry father of King Lamoni; the valiant stripling warriors; Samuel the Lamanite when the people cast stones and shot arrows at him; Nephi[2] and his brother Lehi,[4] who were protected by encircling fire in the prison; Nephi[2] when he was accused of killing the chief judge; the righteous Nephites who were to be put to death for expecting the sign of Christ's birth; Moroni[2], who was charged with preserving the record of the people of Lehi; and many, many more.[9]

*Raising people from the dead.* We have mentioned the raising of Lazarus from the dead. But every person who has ever been raised from the dead by the power of the priesthood can appropriately be viewed as a type and a shadow of the resurrection. This includes the widow's son raised by Elisha (1 Kgs. 17:17–24); several people raised by Jesus (Jairus's daughter, the young man of Nain, and Lazarus [Mark 5:22–43; Luke 7:11–17; John 11]); Tabitha, or Dorcas, who was raised by Peter (Acts 9:36–43); Eutychus, who was raised by Paul (Acts 20:7–12); Timothy, raised by his brother Nephi[3] (3 Ne. 7:19; 19:4); and others.[10]

*Translated beings.* Those who have been translated by the power of God enter a type of intermediate state in which they cannot die until God decrees that they should be changed. Like those who are resurrected, translated beings have remarkable bodies that are not akin to mortal bodies. Like translated beings, resurrected souls will never taste of death or experience physical pain, and Satan has no power over them. Both resurrected personages and translated beings have the power to hide their true identity from mortals, and both have power over the elements of the earth (3 Ne. 28:7–9, 15–32, 36–40).

## THE RESURRECTION AND THE LIFE

Jesus is "the resurrection and the life" (John 11:25). Through him, and only through him, do we receive the priceless gifts of resurrection and eternal life. Only through his atonement is the Father able to accomplish his "work and [his] glory—to bring to pass the immortality and eternal life of man" (Moses 1:39).

In addition to the symbols noted above, the New Testament gives us three important symbols of the resurrection: the temple of Jesus' body, the house not made with hands, and the firstfruits.

*The temple of Jesus' body.* In the second chapter of his Gospel, the apostle John told of Jesus' cleansing the temple of Herod (John

2:13–22). The Jews who witnessed this astonishing event demanded that Jesus justify his actions: "What sign shewest thou unto us, seeing that thou doest these things?" (v. 18).

Jesus answered with a brief response: "Destroy this temple, and in three days I will raise it up" (v. 19). He referred, of course, to his own resurrection—the power by which he would be resurrected also gave him authority to cleanse the temple of Herod. The Jews did not understand his meaning, thinking he referred to the destruction of Herod's temple, which towered over them as they spoke. It had taken forty-six years to build the temple—how could this man Jesus rebuild it in three days? But John added a clarifying phrase to erase all confusion: "He spake of the temple of his body" (John 2:21).

After Jesus was killed and then resurrected, "his disciples remembered that he had said this unto them; and they believed the scripture, and the word which Jesus had said" (John 2:22). Thus, Jesus' metaphor of the temple of his body was a powerful and effective testimony of the reality of his resurrection.

*The house not made with hands.* The apostle Paul used a similar metaphor when he bore witness of the resurrection:

> For we know that if our earthly house of this tabernacle were dissolved, we have a building of God, an house not made with hands, eternal in the heavens.
>
> For in this we groan, earnestly desiring to be clothed upon with our house which is from heaven: if so be that being clothed we shall not be found naked. For we that are in this tabernacle do groan, being burdened: not for that we would be unclothed, but clothed upon, that mortality might be swallowed up of life.
>
> Now he that hath wrought us for the selfsame thing is God, who also hath given unto us the earnest of the Spirit. (2 Cor. 5:1–5)

The apostle Paul contrasted mortal bodies with immortal, resurrected bodies, using the architectural terms *house, tabernacle,* and *building* as metaphors. The mortal body, Paul wrote, is an "earthly house," a "tabernacle" that will eventually be "dissolved." By contrast, a resurrected body is a "building of God," a "house not made with hands" that is "eternal in the heavens," a "house which is from heaven."

Paul also used imagery pertaining to clothing and nakedness; he contrasted *clothed* personages with those who are *naked* and *unclothed*. In Paul's imagery, we are clothed with a body during mortality, "unclothed" of that body at death, and then clothed upon with a glorious body at the resurrection. Nephi also used the words *clothed* and *robe* in the context of the resurrection of the righteous. At that great event, he taught, "the righteous shall . . . [be] clothed with purity, yea, even with the robe of righteousness" (2 Ne. 9:13–14).

Elder Jeffrey R. Holland extended this imagery when he wrote: "As a universal gift flowing from the atonement of Christ, the Resurrection will clothe with a permanent, perfected, restored body every spirit ever born into mortality. Furthermore, for every person who accepts the principles and ordinances of the gospel, that person's body will be something of a robe of righteousness. Therein is the redemption of the soul, and therein is a fulness of joy throughout all eternity."[11]

*The firstfruits of the resurrection.* Countless billions of people had died before the time of Christ, and all remained in the grave. No one at any time, whether prophet, king, or healer, had power to permanently raise a dead body from the grave. Christ was the first. As such, Paul called him the *firstfruits:* "But now is Christ risen from the dead, and become the firstfruits of them that slept. . . . But every man in his own order: Christ the firstfruits; afterward they that are Christ's at his coming" (1 Cor. 15:20, 23).

The Mosaic law required individual Israelites to bring "the first of the firstfruits of [their] land" (Ex. 23:19) as an offering to the Lord. The firstfruits, including grains and fruits, had to be the first ripened as well as the choicest foods (Num. 18:12–13). Firstfruits also included selected processed foods, such as olive oil, wine, flour, or dough.

In this image, the planting of a seed in the earth may be likened unto Christ's body being "planted" in the sepulcher at his death (see 1 Cor. 15:35–38). But, having been buried in the earth, the plant did not remain there. It blossomed and bore fruit, and the seeds of that fruit would then produce plants that would bear additional fruit. Thus, the "firstfruits" yield much additional fruit. The firstfruits also had to be the choicest of the crop. In a very real sense Jesus was and is the choicest of all God's children.

Jesus used a similar image during the last week of his life, after his triumphal entry into Jerusalem. He said: "The hour is come, that the Son of man should be glorified. Verily, verily, I say unto you, Except a corn of wheat fall into the ground and die, it abideth alone: but if it die, it bringeth forth much fruit" (John 12:23–24).

## CHAPTER 19

# THE LIMITLESS ATONEMENT: ITS MAGNITUDE, POWER, AND SCOPE

THREE BOOK OF MORMON PASSAGES use *infinite* when describing the atonement:

First, "The atonement . . . is infinite for all mankind" (2 Ne. 25:16).

Second, "Wherefore, it must needs be an infinite atonement—save it should be an infinite atonement this corruption could not put on incorruption. Wherefore, the first judgment that came upon man must needs have remained to an endless duration. And if so, this flesh must have laid down to rot and to crumble to its mother earth, to rise no more" (2 Ne. 9:7).

Third, "For it is expedient that there should be a great and last sacrifice; yea, not a sacrifice of man, neither of beast, neither of any manner of fowl; for it shall not be a human sacrifice; but it must be an infinite and eternal sacrifice. . . . There can be nothing which is short of an infinite atonement which will suffice for the sins of the world. . . . And behold, this is the whole meaning of the law, every whit pointing to that great and last sacrifice; and that great and last sacrifice will be the Son of God, yea, infinite and eternal" (Alma 34:10–14).

*Infinite* literally means "not finite" or "not finished," and synonyms of *infinite* include endless, limitless, boundless, and eternal. Thus, passages that describe the atonement as infinite imply that the atonement is not bound to a single sphere or space, such as our earth, solar system, or universe, but rather that it is infinite in its scope. The atonement is not limited to a specific number of God's children; it reaches through time retrospectively (backward in time) and prospectively (forward in time) and blesses all of God's children regardless of when they experienced or will experience mortality. The atonement is not limited to God's children—all of his creations benefit from the atonement, including creatures (fish, fowl, animals), earths, and more. The atonement is eternal, wrought by the Eternal God, covering much more than our sins; it affects our pains, sicknesses, rebellions, crimes, infirmities, addictions, and mental, physical, and emotional weaknesses; it affects our griefs, infirmities, little children, and more. To sum up, the atonement is a "perfect atonement" (D&C 76:69) in all aspects.

## THREE IMAGES—CARDINAL DIRECTIONS, CLOUDS, AND GUILT OFFERINGS

Various scriptural images provide nuances that are instructive with regard to the meaning of infinite, including the following three: cardinal directions, clouds, and guilt offerings. First, Psalm 103:12 used cardinal directions to suggest God's power to infinitely remove our transgressions: "As far as the east is from the west, so far hath he removed our transgressions from us." The distance between east and west, of course, is endless and immeasurable; so too, God's ability to remove our transgressions is infinite.

Second, through Isaiah the Lord compares thick clouds to his blotting out of our sins and transgressions. The Lord revealed, "I have blotted out, as a thick cloud, thy transgressions, and, as a cloud, thy sins: return unto me; for I have redeemed thee" (Isa. 44:22). The image of clouds evokes endlessness—just as thick clouds continually form, reshape, disappear, and reappear in the sky, God forevermore forgives those who return (Hebrew *shub,* "to repent") to him.

Third, the guilt offering of the Mosaic law includes an element that suggests infinity. According to Leviticus (5:14–19; 7:1–10), the guilt offering (Hebrew *asham*) deals with offenses against God or humans that could be estimated and for which a restitution of six-fifths was required. It is this restitution payment that suggests infinity because it represents more than wholeness, beyond wholeness, or infinity. In his great prophecy of the suffering servant in Isaiah 53, Isaiah foretold that Jesus Christ would become a guilt offering ("Thou shalt make his soul an offering for sin" [v. 10]). This means that Jesus paid 120 percent for our collective offenses (our sins and wrongdoings). If Jesus paid the exact amount of our offenses—100 percent—then his sacrifice would have been finite, but he paid the full amount plus more.

## THE ATONEMENT COVERS MANY WORLDS AND THEIR INHABITANTS

In Doctrine and Covenants 76, Joseph Smith and Sidney Rigdon gave a powerful testimony of Jesus Christ, witnessing that "by him, and through him, and of him, the worlds are and were created, and the inhabitants thereof are begotten sons and daughters unto God" (v. 24). This testimony reveals a significant doctrine regarding the atonement—that Christ is the Creator and Savior of many worlds, and that the redeemed inhabitants of those worlds are his begotten sons and daughters. Later, Joseph wrote a poetic rendition of Doctrine and Covenants 76, confirming the doctrine that inhabitants of other worlds are begotten sons and daughters of God and giving an inspired explanation of Jesus Christ's infinite atonement:

> And I heard a great voice bearing record from heav'n,
> He's the Saviour and Only Begotten of God;
> By him, of him, and through him, the worlds were all made,
> Even all that career in the heavens so broad.
> Whose inhabitants, too, from the first to the last,
> Are sav'd by the very same Saviour of ours;
> And, of course, are begotten God's daughters and sons
> By the very same truths and the very same powers.[1]

These lines reemphasize that the inhabitants of other earths are also saved by our Savior, Jesus Christ. They do not have a different Savior;

his atonement is not bound to this earth only, but rather it is infinite in its reach throughout the broad expanse of universes and galaxies. Those who dwell on other earths too are spiritually begotten of him and become his daughters and sons. As Elder Bruce R. McConkie observed, through Christ's "infinite atonement the inhabitants of those worlds are adopted into the divine family as heirs with himself."[2]

The poem also reveals that those inhabitants are saved by the "same truths and the very same powers" by which we are saved. What truths? The truths regarding Jesus Christ, his divine Sonship, role in the creation, atoning sacrifice, redeeming love, everlasting mercy, and much more. Further, the inhabitants of other worlds likely have prophets, scriptures, and ordinances, as do we, all of which focus on Jesus Christ. And what powers? The same powers that are upon our earth—that is, the powers of the priesthood that are "centered" in Jesus Christ[3]: the power to heal the sick and brokenhearted, the power to raise the dead to mortality and to resurrect souls to immortality, the power to cast out devils and to overcome Satan and his temptations forevermore, and the power to return souls to Heavenly Father's presence.

In sum, Jesus Christ's atonement is limitless in its power to redeem myriad souls from worlds without number. Jesus Christ indeed is the Lord and Redeemer of the universe. "The mercy of the Atonement," wrote Elder Russell M. Nelson, "extends not only to an infinite number of people, but also to an infinite number of worlds created by Him."[4]

## THE ATONEMENT WILL REDEEM OUR PHYSICAL EARTH

Various truths regarding the planet earth were revealed to Joseph Smith on December 27, 1832, at Kirtland, Ohio. Composing what is now Doctrine and Covenants 88, these truths demonstrate the earth's significance to God and to those who dwell upon it and include several points: that Christ is the power by which the earth was made (v. 10), that the earth will fill "the measure of its creation" (vv. 19, 25), that the earth will "be crowned with glory," which is "the presence of God the Father" (v. 19), that the earth is governed by and moves in its times and seasons through God's law (vv. 42–43), that symbolically, the earth possesses wings—the power to move (v. 45; see also D&C 77:4), that we are instructed to learn of things "in the earth, and under the earth" (v. 79), that one of the signs of the times is that the earth will "tremble and reel to and fro as a drunken man" (v. 87), that the "end of the earth" will be found at the end of the Millennium (v. 101), that the earth was "made and created" so that celestial souls might "possess [the earth] forever and ever" (v. 20), that "the poor and the meek of the earth shall inherit it" (v. 17), and finally, that "the righteous shall inherit" it (v. 26).

In addition, Doctrine and Covenants 88 also provides information regarding the earth and the atonement: the earth is obedient—it "abideth the law of a celestial kingdom," and it "transgresseth not the law" (v. 25); the earth will "be sanctified" (v. 26); the earth will "die" (v. 26); "notwithstanding [the earth] shall die, it shall be quickened again, and shall abide the power by which it is quickened" (v. 26). One definition of the verb "to quicken" is "to make alive," and the expression that the earth "shall be quickened again" suggests that the earth will be resurrected.

Our prophets and apostles have also taught regarding the earth's resurrection and redemption, confirming and expounding upon the doctrines revealed in Doctrine and Covenants 88. President Joseph Fielding Smith wrote, "This earth itself, upon which we stand . . . shall receive the resurrection and come forth to be crowned as a celestial body, and to be the abode of celestial beings eternally."[5] More specifically, he also wrote, "The earth, as a living body, will have to die and be resurrected, for it, too, has been redeemed by the blood of Jesus Christ."[6] Parley P. Pratt expressed his testimony of this doctrine when he uttered these words: "Christ offered himself a sacrifice for this earth. . . . Christ died for the earth and for the elements."[7] Finally, President Brigham Young summarized, "Jesus Christ . . . came in the meridian of time to redeem the earth and the children of men from the original sin that was committed by our first parents."[8]

From the scriptures and the added testimony of modern-day prophets, we see that Christ's atonement is not limited to the creatures that walk upon the earth, but that the atonement actually covers the earth itself. Eventually, through the infinite atonement, Christ will extend the blessings of resurrection and exaltation to the physical earth, just as he will extend them to all of the inhabitants of the earth.

## THE ATONEMENT COVERS ANIMALS, FISH, AND CREEPING THINGS

The Lord revealed to Joseph Smith a number of doctrines pertaining to the eternal nature of animals and the animal kingdom. Joseph recorded that "the heaven and the earth shall be consumed and pass away, and there shall be a new heaven and a new earth," that "all things shall become new, even the heaven and the earth, and all the fulness thereof, both men and beasts, the fowls of the air, and the fishes of the sea; and not one hair, neither mote, shall be lost, for it is the workmanship of mine hand" (D&C 29:22–25).

The Prophet taught that animals do exist in heaven, and commenting on John's book of Revelation, he said:

> John saw the actual beast in heaven, showing to John that beasts did actually exist there. . . .
> John saw curious looking beasts in heaven; he saw every creature that was in heaven—all the beasts, fowls and fish in heaven—actually there, giving glory to God. . . .
> I suppose John saw beings there of a thousand forms, that had been saved from ten thousand times ten thousand earths like this—strange beasts of which we have no conception: all might be seen in heaven. . .
> . . . John heard the words of the beasts giving glory to God, and understood them. God who made the beasts could understand every language spoken by them.[9]

In addition to showing John the presence of beasts in heaven, the Lord also revealed to him that creatures have abilities that demonstrate intelligence and understanding. In Revelation 5, John witnessed "the sacred adulation of more than one hundred million angels" (Rev. 5:9–12). This is followed by John hearing "all creatures of the earth and sea praise the Lamb. They repeat four of the seven terms of praise voiced by the angels: *blessing, honor, glory,* and *power.*"[10] According to Revelation 5:13, "Every creature which is in heaven, and on the earth, and under the earth, and such as are in the sea, and all that are in them, heard I saying, Blessing, and honour, and glory, and power, be unto him that sitteth upon the throne, and unto the Lamb for ever and ever." Commenting on this verse, Joseph Smith said: "Revelation 5:13 proves that John saw beasts in heaven and heard them speak praise to God. [I] do not know what language they speak."[11]

The presence of beasts, fowls, and fish in heaven is yet another testimony of the infinite power of Jesus Christ's atonement. The atonement is not limited to the human family; it extends to all other living creatures. Regarding the redemption of beasts, fowls, fish, creeping things, and even insects, President Young taught, "The earth itself, and mankind upon it, the brute beasts, the fish of the sea, and the fowls of heaven, the insects, and every creeping thing with all things pertaining to this earthly ball—all are in the hands of the Savior, and he has redeemed them all."[12]

Others have borne witness of the salvation of animals through the atonement. For example, President Young's words are unambiguous: "Christ offered himself a sacrifice for this earth, for men, for the animals, for fishes, and the creeping things. . . . Christ died, his blood was spilt."[13] President Young summarized the teaching regarding the redemption of animals with the message that Jesus Christ is ". . . the Savior of the whole world of mankind, and of all creatures pertaining to the earth. . . . All will be redeemed by the blood of the Son of God."[14]

## THE ATONEMENT COVERS LITTLE CHILDREN

One of the great blessings of the restoration of the gospel is that the scriptures of the restoration, which include the Book of Mormon and Doctrine and Covenants, reveal truths regarding the atonement and little children—for example, that little children (those under the age of eight) are not to be baptized. In Mormon 8, Mormon vehemently speaks out against baptizing children, saying, "He that supposeth that little children need baptism is in the gall of bitterness and in the bonds of iniquity; for he hath neither faith, hope, nor charity; wherefore, should he be cut off while in the thought, he must go down to hell" (v. 14). Why did Mormon use such strong language against those who baptize little children? Because the atonement, which is at the very heart of the matter, saves all little children. Anyone who says "that little children need baptism," wrote Mormon, "setteth at naught the atonement of him and the power of his redemption" (v. 20).

In the same chapter, Mormon detailed the following doctrines regarding little children: "little children are whole" (v. 8); "little children . . . are not capable of committing sin" (v. 8); "the curse of Adam is taken from them in me, that it hath no power over them" (v. 8); "little children need no repentance" (v. 11); "little children need no . . . baptism" (v. 11); "little children are alive in Christ, even from the foundation of the world" (v. 12); "all children are alike" (v. 17); "they are all . . . partakers of salvation" (v. 17); "little children cannot repent" (v. 19); "they are all alive in him because of his mercy" (v. 19); "all little children are alive in Christ" (v. 22). These statements provide a summary of how the atonement affects little children, showing that the atonement is infinite in its capacity to cover infants and little children, who are alive in Christ. Similar passages of scripture reinforce truths about little children and the atonement (Mosiah 3:16; D&C 29:1, 46; 74:7).

## THE ATONEMENT COVERS THE RESURRECTION OF ALL HUMANKIND

In addition to providing salvation for the righteous children of God, the atonement universally provides resurrection for both the wicked and the righteous. Jesus himself taught, "For the hour is coming, in the which all that are in the graves shall hear his voice, and shall come forth; they that have done good, unto the resurrection of life; and they that have done evil, unto the resurrection of damnation" (John 5:28–29; see also 1 Cor. 15:21–22). In addition, many prophets have shared their testimonies of this doctrine. In the Book of Mormon, Amulek taught, "For behold, the day cometh that all shall rise from the dead and stand before God, and be judged according to their works" (Alma 11:41; see also Alma 40:4–5). And Moroni directly linked the resurrection to Jesus' death, saying: "The death of Christ bringeth to pass the resurrection, which bringeth to pass a redemption from an endless sleep, from which sleep all men shall be awakened by the power of God when the trump shall sound; and they shall come forth, both small and great, and all shall stand before his bar, being redeemed and loosed from this eternal band of death, which death is a temporal death" (Morm. 9:13).

Each of the three passages cited in the previous paragraph use the word *all* when referring to the resurrection—"*all* that are in the graves"; "*all* shall rise from the dead"; and "from which sleep *all* men shall be awakened." The use of *all* underscores the universality of the resurrection. As Paul wrote, Jesus tasted "death for every man" (Heb. 2:9). Christ's atonement is so complete and so universal that every soul will be resurrected, including those bodies that have been lost over the millennia from human knowledge—seafarers lost at sea, wandering travelers, explorers, pioneers whose bodies were buried and then lost on the plains, warriors killed in battle in earth's remotest areas, or whole villages that have been destroyed or swallowed up by earthquake, fire, tsunami, or other forces of destruction.

## The Atonement Is Retrospective

Although Jesus' divine sacrifice took place at a specific point in time, his atonement is effective both retrospectively and prospectively. In other words, the atonement saves all those who lived before the time of Christ as well as all who have lived or who will live since Christ's sacred experience in Gethsemane and Calvary during the meridian of time.

Long before Gethsemane and Calvary, the atonement was effectual, and its effects have always reached all the way back to the premortal life. The expression "the Lamb of God slain from the foundation of the world" (Rev. 13:8) refers to the retrospective nature of the atonement— indeed, "the atonement which was prepared from the foundation of the world" (Mosiah 4:7; see also 1 Ne. 10:18; Mosiah 15:19; Alma 12:30; Ether 3:14). Elder Russell M. Nelson provided this important witness regarding Jesus' premortal knowledge that he would eventually become our Savior: "Even before the Creation was completed, the premortal Jehovah understood the need for an atonement. Even before breath was put into the man Adam, the Christ knew that He would be required to serve as a Savior. He understood His responsible role. He was to be born into mortality to suffer, to bleed, and to die."[15]

That Christ was foreordained to bring about the atonement is also evident from Peter's statement that we are redeemed "with the precious blood of Christ, as of a lamb without blemish and without spot: Who verily was foreordained before the foundation of the world" (1 Pet. 1:19–20). Christ's foreordination apparently took place in the first grand council in heaven, where "we were all present, and saw the Savior chosen and appointed and the plan of salvation made, and we sanctioned it."[16]

Another evidence that Christ's atoning sacrifice was retrospective comes from a passage in Revelation that states that the atonement effected victory in the war in heaven. Revelation 12 provides significant elements regarding the war in heaven: "And there was war in heaven: Michael and his angels fought against the dragon; and the dragon fought and his angels, and prevailed not; neither was their place found any more in heaven. And the great dragon was cast out, that old serpent, called the Devil, and Satan, which deceiveth the whole world: he was cast out into the earth, and his angels were cast out with him. . . . And they overcame him by the blood of the Lamb, and by the word of their testimony" (Rev. 12:7–9, 11). This passage tells us that the righteous were eventually victorious because "they overcame [Satan] by the blood of the Lamb, and by the word of their testimony" (Rev. 12:11). Ultimately, they conquered Satan by the blessings of the atonement of Christ, which atonement was wrought by the shedding of his blood (Rev. 7:14; 1 Pet. 1:18–19; 1 Ne. 12:10–11; 2 Ne. 9:6–26; Alma 34:36). Thus, the power of the atonement was retroactive eons before Jesus lived his mortal life and became the sacrificed Lamb in Jerusalem.

In addition to the explicit testimony of the retroactive power of the atonement, the scriptures contain many examples of people who received the blessings of the atonement before the atonement actually occurred. Enos, for instance, lived centuries before Christ and yet heard a voice declare, "Enos, thy sins are forgiven thee, and thou shalt be blessed." Enos knew then that his "guilt was swept away" (Enos 1:5–6). Alma, the son of Alma, also received the benefits of the atonement decades before Jesus came to the earth as the mortal Messiah. He had been a man who was "racked, even with the pains of a damned soul . . . racked with torment, . . . harrowed up by the memory of [his] many sins, . . . in the gall of bitterness, and . . . encircled about by the everlasting chains of death" (Alma 36:16–18). But after repenting of his gross sins, he recorded: "I could remember my pains no more; yea, I was harrowed up by the memory of my sins no more. And oh, what joy, and what marvelous light I did behold; yea, my soul was filled with joy as exceeding as was my pain! . . . There can be nothing so exquisite and sweet as was my joy" (Alma 36:19–21). Because of the atonement's retrospective nature, all of these blessings came to Enos and Alma before Christ's sufferings and death.

The key to the retrospective nature of the atonement is recorded in Mosiah 3:13, which details that all humankind can receive a remission of their sins, saying that "whosoever should believe that Christ should come, the same might receive remission of their sins, and rejoice with exceedingly great joy, even as though he had already come among them" (Mosiah 3:13; see also Jarom 1:11). This scripture shows the incredible and infinite power of the atonement to reach forward and backward through time, saving those who had already lived and giving some the faith to believe in Christ "as though he had already come."

## THE ATONEMENT COVERS ALL OUR SINS

For our benefit, understanding, and accountability, the prophets have defined sin, saying "sin is the transgression of the law" (1 John 3:4); "all unrighteousness is sin" (1 John 5:17); the person who "knoweth to do good, and doeth it not, to him it is sin" (James 4:17); and whoever "cometh not unto me [Jesus] is under the bondage of sin" (D&C 84:51). If one were to list and categorize all the sins of the human race, it would take pages and pages; also, the list would always remain incomplete because people continually discover or create new ways to sin. Inasmuch as our iniquities are so great, we require an infinite atonement. As Alma 34:12 states, "Therefore there can be nothing which is short of an infinite atonement which will suffice for the sins of the world." The atonement is wonderfully comprehensive because it covers all of our sins, and neither the devils nor wicked humans can devise a sin that will not be covered by Christ's sufferings in Gethsemane and Calvary.[17] As President Boyd K. Packer stated: "There is no habit, no addiction, no rebellion, no transgression, no apostasy, no crime exempted from the promise of complete forgiveness. That is the promise of the atonement of Christ."[18]

The prophets have testified that the "blood of Jesus . . . cleanseth us from all sin" (1 John 1:7), "Christ died for our sins" (1 Cor. 15:3), "he was manifested to take away our sins" (1 John 3:5), he "washed us from our sins in his own blood" (Rev. 1:5). Elder Neal A. Maxwell explained it this way: "The cumulative weight of all mortal sins—past, present, and future—pressed upon that perfect, sinless, and sensitive Soul!"[19] Likewise, President James E. Faust, then a member of the Quorum of the Twelve, asserted, "All of the terrible individual and collective sins of mankind were taken upon the Lord's shoulders."[20] Through the infinite atonement of Jesus Christ, all of our many sins are covered, and salvation from sin is always provided.

## The Atonement Covers Our Pains, Sicknesses, Infirmities, and More

The atonement is comprehensive and limitless in its coverage of our mortal sufferings. It goes well beyond our personal and collective sins, for Jesus Christ also took upon himself our pains, sicknesses, infirmities, griefs, and sorrows. In the Book of Mormon, the prophet Alma testified: "And he shall go forth, suffering pains and afflictions and temptations of every kind; and this that the word might be fulfilled which saith he will take upon him the pains and the sicknesses of his people. And . . . he will take upon him their infirmities" (Alma

7:11–12; see also D&C 18:11). Note the complete inclusiveness of the terms *pains, sicknesses,* and *infirmities.* The word *pains* likely refers to the broad span of afflictions experienced by mortals, whether they are physical or emotional pains; *sicknesses* probably refers to all categories of sicknesses—physical, emotional, and mental; and *infirmities* covers our lack of physical vitality and strength, and our feeble, decrepit, or debilitated conditions. In explaining this marvelous aspect of the atonement, Alma proceeded to say that Christ experienced these things that "he may be filled with mercy, according to the flesh, that he may know according to the flesh how to succor his people" (Alma 7:12).

During mortality, each of us experiences deep and intense sadness. We may lose a family member in death, we may feel profound remorse over our sins, we may witness a loved one commit a grievous sin, we may personally be innocent victims of another's sin, and we will undoubtedly endure similar highly emotional circumstances. At certain points in our lives, our profound sorrow can cause our hearts to break with grief. But just as the Messiah took upon himself our sicknesses and infirmities, he also "hath borne our griefs, and carried our sorrows" (Isa. 53:4). Because of this aspect of the atonement, we are able to turn our broken hearts over to the Lord to be healed. And Jesus Christ, just as he heals all of us from sin, will heal our broken hearts.

## THE PERFECT ATONEMENT

Because of its limitless coverage of all sins and all pains for all creatures on all earths in all times, the infinite atonement is beyond our understanding. President Gordon B. Hinckley's words capture the magnificence of Christ's sacrifice on our behalf: "I sense in a measure the meaning of His atonement. I cannot comprehend it all. It is so vast in its reach and yet so intimate in its effect that it defies comprehension. When all is said and done, when all of history is examined, when the deepest depths of the human mind have been explored, there is nothing so wonderful, so majestic, so tremendous as this act of grace when the Son of the Almighty, the prince of His Father's royal household, . . . gave His life in ignominy and pain."[21]

## CHAPTER 20

# ALL THIS FOR ME? PARTAKING OF CHRIST'S MARVELOUS GRACE

AS MORTALS IN A FALLEN WORLD, we are in a terrible plight: By ourselves, we don't have the ability to adequately deal with the negative aspects of life. We also are unable to adequately develop the godly attributes we need to enter into God's presence. And yet we often act as if we do have to do these things on our own.

Certainly we need to do our very best. But without Christ, we will fail to adequately deal with the negative aspects of our lives. And we will fail to adequately develop the positive qualities we need to return to God. Gratefully, the grace of Jesus Christ can help us with this plight.

We know we need grace to be *saved*—Christ, through his atonement, has conquered death for us, and if we will do our part, he also helps us conquer sin. But we also need grace to help us with our everyday plight. We read in *True to the Faith,* an official Church publication:

> In addition to needing grace for your ultimate salvation, you need this enabling power *every day of your life.* As you draw near to your Heavenly Father in diligence, humility, and meekness, *He will uplift and strengthen you through His grace.* . . . Reliance upon His grace enables you to *progress and grow* in righteousness. . . .

Grace enables you to help build God's kingdom, a service you cannot give through your strength or means alone. . . .

If you ever become discouraged or feel too weak to continue living the gospel, remember the strength you can receive through the enabling power of grace.[1]

Grace delivers the powers of God to us through the atonement. This understanding gives new meaning to the words of the hymn "Come, Thou Fount of Every Blessing":

> *Oh to grace how great a debtor*
> *Daily I'm constrained to be!*
> *Let thy goodness, like a fetter,*
> *Bind my wandering heart to thee.*[2]

## WHEN CAN WE RECEIVE THIS GRACE?

Nephi wrote in a familiar passage, "For we labor diligently to write, to persuade our children, and also our brethren, to believe in Christ, and to be reconciled to God; for we know that it is by grace that we are saved, after all we can do" (2 Ne. 25:23). Some feel that we cannot ask for grace along the way—that we have to do all *we* can do *first*. But many of us feel we can never do enough. We never feel we do all we can, though we wear ourselves out trying. Surely we could have taken one more step, done one more thing, said one more prayer, participated in one more act of service. Accordingly, we never feel we can ask for grace, the divine power that will make the difference. We sometimes become discouraged and troubled.

But remember what the Brethren have told us in *True to the Faith*, in the passage just cited: "You need this enabling power every day of your life. . . . He will uplift and strengthen you through His grace."[3]

We also have this truth expressed in the LDS Bible Dictionary: "It is . . . through the grace of the Lord that individuals, through faith in the atonement of Jesus Christ and repentance of their sins, receive strength and assistance to do good works that they otherwise would not be able to maintain if left to their own means."[4]

The Brethren are not contradicting Nephi. He said, "It is by grace that we are *saved,* after all we can do." As we talk about ultimate salvation this is certainly true. Our final salvation occurs through Christ, after all we can do.

But we also need much grace as we proceed to our final goal. We need God's strength and assistance every step along the way—through help with temptation, gifts of the Spirit, repentance and forgiveness, and so forth. Thus, we can see why Nephi wrote in 2 Nephi 25, "And we talk of Christ, we rejoice in Christ, we preach of Christ, [and] we prophesy of Christ, . . . that our children may know to what source they may look for a remission of their sins" (v. 26)—and to that we could add: that our children may know to what source they can look for their daily emotional and spiritual sustenance.

## DEPENDENT ON THE LORD

To fully receive of the blessings of grace, we must recognize our dependence on Christ, relying on his merits and his power. Again we read from Nephi: "And now, . . . after ye have gotten into this strait and narrow path, I would ask if all is done? Behold, I say unto you, Nay; for ye have not come thus far save it were by the word of Christ with unshaken faith in him, *relying wholly upon the merits of him who is mighty to save*" (2 Ne. 31:19; emphasis added).

We can rely on his merits and mercy because, as Alma testified in Alma 5, "I know that Jesus Christ shall come, yea, the Son, the Only Begotten of the Father, full of grace, and mercy, and truth" (v. 48).

In John 15:1–5, Jesus taught of our utter dependence on him in the allegory of the vine and the branches:

> I am the true vine, and my Father is the husbandman. . . .
>
> Abide in me, and I in you. As the branch cannot bear fruit of itself, except it abide in the vine; no more can ye, except ye abide in me.
>
> I am the vine, ye are the branches: He that abideth in me, and I in him, the same bringeth forth much fruit: for without me ye can do nothing.

But if we choose to be independent of Christ or inappropriately self-sufficient, we won't seek to be strengthened and nourished by him. We won't abide in him—and we certainly won't be allowing him to abide in us.

## Grace Can Help Us with the Challenges of Our Lives

Grace can help us with such challenging aspects of our lives as sin, weakness, trials, griefs, and mistakes. In other words, Christ's grace is an enabling power that will assist and strengthen us in all these things. Some of these truths have been discussed in chapter 19, but let's briefly look at the challenging areas of life the atonement can help us with.

*First, the Savior's atonement can cleanse us from sin,* if we come unto him and follow his commandments. Isaiah lamented, "All we like sheep have gone astray" (Isa. 53:6). But, he testified, Christ provided the answer: "He was wounded for our transgressions, he was bruised for our iniquities: . . . and with his stripes we are healed" (vv. 5–6). "Come now, and let us reason together, saith the Lord," Isaiah recorded earlier, "though your sins be as scarlet, they shall be as white as snow; though they be red like crimson, they shall be as wool" (Isa. 1:18).

How is it done? Through partaking of the cleansing power of the atonement of Jesus Christ, which comes to us as we exercise faith, repent, enter into covenant, and continue in obedience. But in giving that answer, we must acknowledge that even though we must sacrifice all we can in the process, the greater sacrifice was made by our Savior.

*Second, the blessings of grace can help us with our weaknesses.* "If men come unto me," the Lord said, speaking to Moroni, "I will show unto them their weakness. I give unto men weakness that they may be humble; and my grace is sufficient for all men that humble themselves before me; for if they humble themselves before me, and have faith in me, then will I make weak things become strong unto them" (Ether 12:27). We already have weaknesses. Those weaknesses, if we will, can help us to be humble. If we then come unto Christ in humility and faith, he will help us to see those weaknesses more clearly, and he will then help us turn those weaknesses into strengths.

President James E. Faust, while a member of the Quorum of the Twelve Apostles, taught that the atonement covers "our foolishness."[5] That is another category of human weakness the Savior suffered for.

*Third, grace can help us with our pains, our trials and troubles, our burdens, and our afflictions.* Elder Neal A. Maxwell wrote, "Since not all human sorrow and pain is connected to sin, the full intensiveness of the Atonement involved bearing our pains, infirmities, and sicknesses, as well as our sins"[6] (see Alma 7:11). Certainly this includes emotional as well as physical pain, spiritual as well as physical infirmity. That doesn't mean he will necessarily remove those problems. But he will help us in them. We all have experienced the promise we sing of in "How Firm a Foundation":

> *When through fiery trials thy pathway shall lie,*
> *My grace, all sufficient, shall be thy supply.*[7]

*Fourth, grace can help us with our griefs and sorrows.* "Surely he hath borne our griefs, and carried our sorrows," Isaiah said (Isa. 53:4). Mortal life brings grief and sorrow to all of us. Our Savior has already borne those griefs and sorrows for us. When we turn to him, we are able to receive help and support with such difficulties of life.

*Fifth, the grace of Christ can help us with our innocent mistakes.* Elder Bruce C. Hafen taught this reassuring truth: "The Savior's victory can compensate not only for our sins but also for our inadequacies; not only for our deliberate mistakes but also for our sins committed in ignorance, our errors of judgment, and our unavoidable imperfections."[8] Elsewhere he said, writing with his wife, Marie: "The same power that compensates for and heals us from the effects of our conscious sins also compensates for and heals us from the same kinds of effects—the pain, the bitterness, the sorrow—caused by our unintentional mistakes and the natural adversities we suffer."[9]

## Grace Is Also the Source of Essential Blessings

Our Heavenly Father is the source of the gifts that enable us to become like him. Paul wrote to the Ephesians: "Unto every one of us is *given* grace according to the measure of the *gift* of Christ. . . . When he ascended up on high, he led captivity captive, and *gave gifts* unto men" (Eph. 4:7–8; emphasis added).

Our desire in this life is not only to be forgiven of our sins but also to be able to become one with God. We desire to grow in the attributes of Christ. There is much we can do on our own to develop those attributes. But in their ultimate form, they come as gifts from God through his grace.

Robert L. Millet eloquently wrote of the power of Christ to bring growth and change when he said:

> What mortal can snatch pride and selfishness, lust and lewdness from a natural man and create a clean heart in its place? Indeed, no man but the Man of Holiness and the Son of Man can do such things; these are works and wonders beyond the power of even the most spiritually mature Saints to do. . . . The miracle of change, the miracle associated with the renovation and regeneration of fallen man, is the work of a God. . . .
>
> . . . The transformations from a fallen nature to a spiritual nature, from worldliness to holiness, from corruption to incorruption, and from imperfection to perfection are accomplished because divine powers bring them to pass. They are acts of grace.[10]

Some of the enriching blessings we can receive through grace include power against temptation, greater ability to be obedient, spiritual gifts, magnified abilities, compensating blessings, having things set right, and improved relationships. Each of these is vitally important to our happiness and progress on the earth.

*First, power against temptation.* We understand this blessing of grace when we sing in the hymn "Abide with Me":

*I need thy presence, ev'ry passing hour.*
*What but thy grace can foil the tempter's power?*[11]

In the scriptures, the Lord has clearly promised us power against temptation. For example, we read in Alma 13: "Humble yourselves before the Lord, and call on his holy name, and watch and pray continually, that ye may not be tempted above that which ye can bear, and thus be led by the Holy Spirit" (v. 28). And in Doctrine and Covenants section 3: "You should have been faithful; and he would have extended his arm and supported you against all the fiery darts of the adversary; and he would have been with you in every time of trouble" (v. 8).

If we try to overcome the adversary without the help of the Lord, we will fail. But when we receive his help, and when we do our part, we will succeed.

*Second, greater ability to be obedient.* Even though the gospel plan requires us to exercise our agency to be obedient to the Lord's commands, the Lord is willing to help us in our efforts. Paul taught an important truth when he admonished us to "work out [our] own salvation with fear and trembling" (Philip. 2:12). Throughout our lives we should "work out [our] own salvation" with an awareness that a failure to do so will bring grave and eternal consequences. Hence, Paul's encouragement to attend to the issues of our salvation "with fear and trembling."

But, as Paul taught clearly elsewhere, all our efforts to work out our salvation won't save us—no matter how hard we work and no matter how much we fear and tremble—unless we receive the blessings of the atonement of Christ. In that same letter to the Philippians, in the next phrase, Paul then emphasized that we are partners with God in the process of salvation, and that he assists us in our obedience: "For it is God which worketh in you both to will and to do of his good pleasure" (Philip. 2:13). God helps us "to will and to do"; in other words, if we allow him to do so, he first helps us with our desire to choose to follow him, and then he helps us as we move forward.

This same truth—that the Lord will help us in our efforts to obey him—is plainly taught in the Book of Mormon. "I will go and do the things which the Lord hath commanded," Nephi said to his father, "for I know that the Lord giveth no commandments unto the children of men, save he shall prepare a way for them that they may accomplish the thing which he commandeth them" (1 Ne. 3:7). Later, Nephi testified in his writing, "If it so be that the children of men keep the commandments of God he doth nourish them, and strengthen them, and provide means whereby they can accomplish the thing which he has commanded them" (1 Ne. 17:3).

These blessings of assistance in our obedience are helps through the grace of Jesus Christ.

*Third, spiritual gifts.* Spiritual gifts sent from on high are a significant manifestation of God's grace. Notice the repetition of the word *gifts* in Doctrine and Covenants 46: "Seek ye earnestly the best *gifts.* . . . For . . . they are given for the benefit of those who love me and keep all my commandments, and him that seeketh so to do. . . . And all these *gifts* come from God" (D&C 46:8–9, 26; emphasis added).

Note that we don't have to be perfectly keeping all the commandments to receive God's gifts. His gifts, he said, "are given for the benefit of those who love me and keep all my commandments, *and* him that seeketh so to do" (D&C 46:9; emphasis added).

One of God's marvelous gifts, available through grace, is peace of heart and mind. As Jesus said: "Peace I leave with you, my peace I *give* unto you: not as the world giveth, *give* I unto you. Let not your heart be troubled, neither let it be afraid" (John 14:27; emphasis added).

Another spiritual gift through grace is the light of revelation, which will give us heavenly guidance and direction. We are all in great need of direction from on high, and through the Lord's grace, we can receive the guidance we need. James wrote in a well-known passage, "If any of you lack wisdom, let him ask of God, that *giveth* to all men liberally, and upbraideth not; and it shall be *given* him" (James 1:5; emphasis added).

A third gift of the Spirit, through grace, is charity, or the pure love of Christ. We all know charity as the greatest of the gifts of God. But notice who the Lord desires to give this gift to. As Mormon taught: "Pray unto the Father with all the energy of heart, that ye may be filled with this love, which he hath *bestowed* upon all who are true followers of his Son, Jesus Christ" (Moro. 7:48; emphasis added).

In Ether 12, Moroni recorded that charity flows at least in part from grace: "And it came to pass that I prayed unto the Lord that he would *give unto the Gentiles grace,* that they might have *charity*" (Ether 12:36; emphasis added).

Joy is another gift of the Spirit we receive through grace. "I will *impart* unto you of my Spirit, which shall enlighten your mind, which shall fill your soul with joy," the Lord has said (D&C 11:13; emphasis added). The word *impart* here indicates that the Spirit that brings joy comes as a gift. When we observe the conditions of receiving this gift, then the gift becomes ours.

Alma and his fellow missionaries went on a very long and difficult mission to the Lamanites, filled with trials and privations. But as we read in Alma 31: "The Lord . . . gave them strength, that they should suffer no manner of afflictions, save it were swallowed up in the joy of Christ" (Alma 31:38). Through the gift of grace, they were able to experience joy despite their difficulties.

*Fourth, magnified abilities.* Latter-day prophets have repeatedly taught that the Lord will magnify our abilities through grace. President Ezra Taft Benson said: "In the service of the Lord [we] have even greater powers than in ordinary responsibilities. . . . He will not permit us to fail if we do our part. *He will* magnify *us* even beyond our own talents and abilities when necessary. This I know." And then he added, "[This] is one of the sweetest experiences that can come to a human being."[12]

In the October 1984 general conference, President Gordon B. Hinckley taught this same truth: "You have come out of the world as partakers of the restored gospel of Jesus Christ . . . , and if you are living worthy of it, the Lord will honor you in it and *magnify you.*"[13]

Elder Henry B. Eyring, speaking to all those who receive callings in the Church, said:

> Just as God called you and will guide you, He will magnify you. You will need that magnification. . . .
>
> There will be times when you will feel overwhelmed. One of

the ways you will be attacked is with the feeling that you are inadequate. Well, you are inadequate to answer a call to represent God with only your own powers. But you have access to more than your natural capacities, and you do not work alone. . . .

. . . God magnifies those He calls, even in what may seem to you a small or inconspicuous service. You will have the gift of seeing your service magnified. . . .

There is yet another way the Lord will magnify you in your call to His service. You will feel at some time, perhaps at many times, that you cannot do all you feel you must. The heavy weight of your responsibilities will seem too great. You will worry that you can't spend more time with your family. You will wonder how you can find the time and the energy to meet your responsibilities beyond your family and your calling. You may feel discouragement and even guilt after you have done all you could to meet all your obligations. I have had such days and such nights. Let me tell you what I have learned. . .

. . . [When I have done my best] I know then that I have done enough for the promise made by Joseph Smith to be fulfilled once again: "Let us cheerfully do all things that lie in our power; and then may we stand still, with the utmost assurance, to see the salvation of God, and for his arm to be revealed."[14]

Whether we are serving in the Church, serving as parents in the home, or honorably engaged in temporal affairs, when we seek and do the Lord's will in our lives, he will magnify us where we fall short. That is one of the blessings of grace. In fact, some have held that this blessing is commonly granted. Joseph Fielding McConkie wrote: "Among the faithful Latter-day Saints, experiences in which they have been able to function beyond their natural abilities are common. Such experiences constitute one of the most prevalent forms of revelation."[15]

*Fifth, compensating blessings.* Because of the grace of Christ, we can receive compensation for losses we suffer through no fault of our own. Elder Vaughn J. Featherstone wrote: "Justice demands that there be compensating blessings for every particle of suffering we go through innocently. . . . A loving Savior can remove every heartache. . . . He can fill the soul with joy, marvelous light, and exquisite sweetness. If He did that only for the sinful, He would not be just. But He is a merciful God, and He has done it for the innocent and the repentant alike."[16] And Elder Hafen wrote, "The Savior grants not only a continuing remission of our sins, but he will also help compensate for our inadequacies, heal the bruises caused by our unintentional errors, and strengthen us far beyond our natural capacity in times of acute need."[17]

The compensating blessings through grace include help for our losses through trials; for blessings we're not able to receive, despite our best efforts; and for our failures and inabilities, after we've done all we can do.

*Sixth, having things set right.* There is much pain and suffering in this world that we experience through no fault of our own. There is much injustice and inequity. And there is pain that we may bring upon others that we don't have power to heal. The atonement of Christ can help to set things right for us and those we have harmed, as we (and they) seek this sweet blessing from a God who loves us.

President Boyd K. Packer taught this very truth: "Restoring what you cannot restore, healing the wound you cannot heal, fixing that which you broke and you cannot fix is the very purpose of the atonement of Christ."[18]

Nearly two years later Elder Richard G. Scott added this testimony: "The Atonement will not only help us overcome our transgressions and mistakes, but in His time, it will resolve all inequities of life—those things that are unfair which are the consequences of circumstance or others' acts and not our own decisions."[19]

*Seventh, improved relationships.* The atonement can help us become at-one with God and with our fellow man, perfecting and improving all our relationships. When Jesus offered the Great Intercessory Prayer shortly before entering the Garden of Gethsemane, he pleaded with the Father, "Holy Father, keep through thine own name those whom thou hast given me, that they may be one, as we are" (John 17:11). Later in the prayer he said:

> Neither pray I for these alone, but for them also which shall believe on me through their word; that they all may be one; as

thou, Father, art in me, and I in thee, that they also may be one in us: that the world may believe that thou hast sent me.

And the glory which thou gavest me I have given them; that they may be one, even as we are one: I in them, and thou in me, that they may be made perfect in one; and that the world may know that thou hast sent me, and hast loved them, as thou hast loved me. (John 17:20–23)

In this poignant prayer, our Savior calls on the Father in our behalf, asking that we might become one with each other in a godly union, and that we likewise will become one with God. This is one of the great purposes of the atonement, or the at-one-ment: to receive heavenly help, or grace, and to strengthen and perfect our relationships with God and with one another.

M. Catherine Thomas, a Latter-day Saint scholar, reflected on this aspect of the atonement when she wrote:

> The Lord Jesus Christ's atonement for you and me made possible an at-one-ment society. . . . The powers in the atonement apply to our lives and are accessible to you and me right now. These powers have implications for every relationship we have. . . . These powers may hold the secret to making right relationships endure and may help us to know what is wrong with potentially good relationships that are going wrong. . . .
>
> . . . Atonement, literally at-one-ment, is a word . . . which means reconciliation or to come back into a relationship after a period of estrangement. This word points to what has happened to man—he has fallen from a relationship, even many relationships, and from a knowledge of the oneness of the premortal children. . . . Christ wrought the atonement to restore us to the heavenly society. So we might say that the word rendered atonement by the early biblical translators could have been more accurately rendered re-at-one-ment or reunion. Christ wrought the great Reunion. . . .
>
> The work of Christ is the work of reintegration. Scriptural uses of atonement or at-one-ment suggest that Christ intends to bring us to oneness in heaven and to that social harmony that we experienced before the world was.[20]

## The Atonement Provides a Lifting Power

During Jesus' last week on earth, he told his listeners that he was going to die. "Except a corn of wheat fall into the ground and die, it abideth alone: but if it die, it bringeth forth much fruit" (John 12:24), he said to them. "And I, if I be lifted up from the earth, will draw all men unto me" (John 12:32).

Because he, the Son of God, willingly allowed himself to be lifted up on the cross, he had power to lift us up to celestial glory. Later, among the Nephites, he reiterated this truth:

> My Father sent me that I might be lifted up upon the cross; and after that I had been lifted up upon the cross, that I might draw all men unto me, that as I have been lifted up by men even so should men be lifted up by the Father, to stand before me, to be judged of their works, whether they be good or whether they be evil—and for this cause have I been lifted up; therefore, according to the power of the Father I will draw all men unto me, that they may be judged according to their works. (3 Ne. 27:14–15)

The atonement has lifting power. This power functions not only to lift us up to judgment in the resurrection, but it can also lift us here and now. Through the power of his atonement, Christ can lift us—

from sin to sanctification,
from sorrow and burden to joy and gladness,
from natural human abilities to heavenly/spiritual endowments,
from a mortal/temporal environment to a spiritual one,
from a fallen soul to a saint,
from a saint to a perfected, exalted being,
from a fallen world to the presence of God.

We have become estranged from God through sin. Yet we need his assistance to be able to walk a godly walk, with heavenly strength, through each day. Every gift we receive from our Father—every blessing of enabling grace—is made possible through Christ and his atonement. All that he offers to us is possible because of his atonement.

Elder David A. Bednar gave an excellent summary of how we need the grace of Christ both to overcome the fallen world and to be lifted up:

> Prophets throughout the ages have emphasized the dual requirements of (1) avoiding and overcoming bad and (2) doing good and becoming better. Consider the penetrating questions posed by the Psalmist:
>
> "Who shall ascend into the hill of the Lord? or who shall stand in his holy place?
>
> "He that hath clean hands, and a pure heart; who hath not lifted up his soul unto vanity, nor sworn deceitfully" (Psalm 24:3–4).
>
> Brothers and sisters, it is possible for us to have clean hands but not have a pure heart. Please notice that both clean hands and a pure heart are required to ascend into the hill of the Lord and to stand in His holy place.
>
> Let me suggest that hands are made clean through the process of putting off the natural man and by overcoming sin and the evil influences in our lives through the Savior's Atonement. Hearts are purified as we receive His strengthening power to do good and become better. All of our worthy desires and good works, as necessary as they are, can never produce clean hands and a pure heart. It is the Atonement of Jesus Christ that provides both a *cleansing and redeeming power* that helps us to overcome sin and a *sanctifying and strengthening power* that helps us to become better than we ever could by relying only upon our own strength. The infinite Atonement is for both the sinner and for the saint in each of us.[21]

Without Jesus Christ and his grace we are lost. We will neither have the power to overcome sin and weakness nor the ability to sufficiently change and develop the attributes of Christ in our lives.

But through the power of his atonement, Christ gives us all we need. He can help us overcome the negative pull of this fallen world, he can help us overcome the troubles and burdens of this life, he can help us to become as God is.

We can be bold in seeking the grace of God—meaning all the

blessings of the atonement—to bless us in our lives. As the apostle Paul wrote to the Hebrews, "Let us therefore come boldly unto the throne of grace, that we may obtain mercy, and find grace to help in time of need" (Heb. 4:16). And that grace, when we receive it, is sufficient.

CHAPTER 21

# THE UNIQUENESS OF CHRIST: ATTRIBUTES AND CHARACTERISTICS OF THE REDEEMER

OF ALL OUR FATHER'S CHILDREN, ONLY one was uniquely qualified to become the Redeemer. Jehovah, his premortal name,[1] was different from his fellows in that he was the firstborn in the spirit. Only he (with the possible exception of the Holy Ghost, whose identity and premortal relationships have not been revealed) was actually a God, a member of the divine godhead, before he came to earth. He was selected and ordained from the beginning to be the Savior of mankind, the "Lamb slain from the foundation of the world" (Rev. 13:8). He was filled with perfect love for his Father and for all his brothers and sisters.

Jehovah became known as Jesus Christ in mortality. Again in his mortal condition he was uniquely qualified to be the Redeemer. God was the father of his mortal being, giving Jesus power over death. Even though Jesus was tempted repeatedly, he remained spotless, utterly without sin throughout his entire mortal life. He was perfectly submissive to his Father's will—to a degree that was simply unparalleled among all his fellows, in any age. He was willing to set at risk his godhood to come to a fallen earth, where he would be subject to pain, suffering, hunger, emotional and physical stress, and great temptation. He was willing to offer himself in the ultimate sacrifice to bless and lift others.

294

This chapter focuses on the unique attributes and qualifications of the appointed Savior, primarily from the point of view of scriptural symbolism. As we will discover again and again, the scriptures are filled with images of Christ, each of which points to his life and sacrifice. Each bears a testimony of the reality of his divine mission. Of course, it would be a mistake to seek a correlation between every little detail of a type, shadow, or symbol and the life of Christ. An obvious example is the sheep used in Israel's sacrifices. They were to be without blemish, but they were mortal in a way that Christ was not. The fact that they were free of blemish is symbolic. Their ultimate mortality was not.

Still, there is much we can learn about the attributes and characteristics of the Atoner from the details of scriptural symbols. These are clues given by a loving Father to help us see patterns and truths about Christ throughout the scriptures.

*Firstborn in spirit.* According to the law of the Hebrews, the firstborn male in a family had both special responsibilities and unique privileges. He was given a double portion of the inheritance—a privilege. But with that extra portion he was to care for his widowed mother, unwed sisters, minor siblings, and others with special needs. This law was a wise way to care for the needs of a family. It was also representative of God's law in the heavens.

Since Jesus was the firstborn of all the Father's children, he had special privileges. His worthiness, his willingness, and his supreme intelligence combined with his right as the Firstborn to bring about his call into the godhead. There he served during the creation of the earth and throughout all the years of the Old Testament period. But he also had the great responsibility of being the son chosen to perform the act of atonement for his fallen brothers and sisters. This would require a sacrifice unlike any other on earth, exceeding all other sacrifices by an order of many magnitudes.

The sacrifice of Isaac, the firstborn and chosen son of Abraham, prefigured the sacrifice of the Firstborn and Chosen Son of the Father. When animals were sacrificed under the law of Moses, they were to be the firstborn. (These symbols were discussed at greater length in chapters 4 and 6.)

*God in premortality.* The Book of Mormon testifies that only the sacrifice of a god would be sufficient to effect an infinite atonement (Alma 34:8–16; 42:15). Jesus Christ was that God. Nephi testified, "The God of our fathers, who were led out of Egypt, out of bondage, and also were preserved in the wilderness by him, yea, the God of Abraham, and of Isaac, and the God of Jacob, yieldeth himself . . . as a man, into the hands of wicked men, to be lifted up, . . . and to be crucified, . . . and to be buried in a sepulchre" (1 Ne. 19:10). The apostle John bore witness that Christ was a God in premortality when he expressed in beautiful poetic language: "In the beginning was the Word, and the Word was with God, and the Word was God. The same was in the beginning with God" (John 1:1–2). And when Jesus appeared to the Nephites, he referred to "the holiness which is in Christ, who was before the world began" (3 Ne. 26:5).

*Savior from the beginning.* In order to bless all of mankind, from beginning to end, the Atoner needed to have power that stretched back to Adam and Eve and went onward to the last human being. Thus the scriptures teach that Jesus Christ was, as noted above, the "Lamb slain from the foundation of the world" (Rev. 13:8). It is significant that he is our Alpha and Omega, the first and the last, the beginning and the end (Rev. 1:8, 11; 22:13; 3 Ne. 9:18). He is "from everlasting to everlasting" (D&C 61:1), "whose course is one eternal round, the same today as yesterday, and forever" (D&C 35:1). For that reason, he identified himself to Moses as "I Am" (Ex. 3:14).

*The Creator.* Jesus Christ is the creator of the world, acting under the direction of the Father. As John taught, "All things were made by him; and without him was not any thing made that was made" (John 1:3). He created the earth and sky, the rocks and water, the trees and grass, and the birds and animals. He commanded the stars to move in a designated order and the planets to orbit around the stars. As Creator, he has power over the physical world, a power that was manifest repeatedly in the miracles of the mortal Messiah. That same power is an essential element of the atonement—the atoning acts performed in Gethsemane and on Golgotha stand with the creation as the greatest manifestations of power in all time. Jesus' descriptions of himself as the true vine, the bread of life, the source of living water, and "the life" (John 14:6) all point to him as a source of strength and life. (For further discussion on the scriptural symbolisms pointing to Christ's power, see chapters 14 and 22.)

*The Only Begotten Son of God.* Every person on earth was born first as a *spirit* child to God the Father. But Jesus Christ was the only person ever to have God the Father as the father of his *body.* This divine parentage gave Christ power over death; with that power he could choose when and even whether to die. He taught, "As the Father hath life in himself; so hath he given to the Son to have life in himself" (John 5:26). Thus, because he had a mortal mother, he *could* die. But because he had an exalted, immortal father, he did not *have* to die.

It is clear in the scriptures that Jehovah had power over death. Each time the scriptures record an instance where one of his servants prevailed over this ultimate enemy, the triumph came through the power of Christ, providing thereby a type and shadow of that which was to come through our Redeemer. Elijah was able to raise a boy from the dead (1 Kgs. 17:17–23), a miracle that Jesus repeated on several occasions. Righteous Shadrach, Meshach, and Abed-nego were thrown into a furnace so hot that it killed their would-be executioners—and yet through God's power they survived, accompanied by one "like the Son of God" (Dan. 3:25; see also vv. 12–30). Daniel was thrown into a den of vicious lions, but through God's power he survived unscathed (Dan. 6:16–27). Alma and Amulek were cast into prison and much tormented until God destroyed the prison and all who were within its walls— except Alma and Amulek, who were preserved by God's power (Alma 14:17–29). Enemies of God and his truth repeatedly sought to kill the three Nephite disciples who were translated. "And they did cast them into furnaces of fire, and they came forth receiving no harm. And they also cast them into dens of wild beasts, and they did play with the wild beasts even as a child with a lamb; and they did come forth from among them, receiving no harm" (4 Ne. 1:32–33).

Just as Christ, the Only Begotten Son of the Father, was able to empower his servants to prevail over death, so did he himself have that power both in heaven and on earth. Yet each of those who were so preserved, eventually died (or will die). Only Christ had within himself the power to overcome death forever.[2]

*Born of a virgin.* Even though Christ had God as his father, as noted, he had a mortal woman as his mother. It was required that she be a woman of absolute purity; further, she must be a virgin so that there could be no question about the fatherhood of her child.

The scriptures give several remarkable examples of God's power over the womb. Sarah, wife of Abraham, bore a child when she was well past menopause; in fact, Paul called her "past age" and Abraham "as good as dead" (Heb. 11:11, 12)! Rachel, the wife of Jacob, was able to conceive only after much pleading with the Lord (Gen. 30:22–24). Hannah (the mother of Samuel) and Elisabeth (the mother of John the Baptist) both conceived their sons through the grace and blessing of God (1 Sam. 1:9–11, 17–20; Luke 1:5–7, 13, 24–25). These stories not only show God's hand in the lives of those who were so blessed, but they also stand as marvelous types of the birth of Christ.

*Perfect and sinless in all his choices.* The scriptures give examples of two men who were called perfect: Noah was a "just man and perfect in his generations, and Noah walked with God" (Gen. 6:9); Job was "perfect and upright" (Job 1:1; 2:3). The Lord commanded Abraham to "walk before me, and be thou perfect" (Gen. 17:1); and the children of Israel were likewise commanded to be perfect (Deut. 18:13; 1 Kgs. 8:61). Some men were said to have a "perfect heart": David before his sin with Bathsheba (see 1 Kgs. 11:4), Hezekiah (2 Kgs. 20:3; Isa. 38:3), and Asa (see 2 Chr. 15:17). The sacrifices that Israel offered to the Lord were to be "perfect to be accepted; there shall be no blemish therein" (Lev. 22:21). All these were in similitude of the Savior of the world, who was perfect, flawless, without spot.

Jesus Christ was tempted, yet without sin. Elder Neal A. Maxwell wrote: "Jesus' character necessarily underwrote His remarkable atonement. Without Jesus' sublime character there could have been no sublime atonement! His character is such that He 'suffered all manner of temptation,' yet He gave temptations 'no heed.' (Alma 7:11; D&C 20:22.)"[3]

*Perfectly submissive to the Father's will.* Abinadi taught how the

Savior would be submissive to the Father even in great difficulty. He said: "Because he dwelleth in flesh he shall be called the Son of God, and having subjected the flesh to the will of the Father. . . . And thus the flesh becoming subject to the Spirit, or the Son to the Father, being one God, suffereth temptation, and yieldeth not to the temptation, but suffereth himself to be mocked, and scourged, and cast out, and disowned by his people" (Mosiah 15:2, 5). This submissiveness was foreshadowed by the sacrifice of sheep in the law of Moses. Sheep are generally docile, quiet, and patient. After they are trained to be led, they follow readily. When they are caught, they struggle at first but then quickly become submissive. Sheep are thus a deeply meaningful symbol of the submissive Savior.

Another type of Christ is worthy Job, who experienced suffering greater than most men ever imagine: in one day he lost all his oxen, asses, sheep, and camels (a total of 11,500 animals), along with all of his many servants except for four; in the same day he lost all his children—seven sons and three daughters. His response was a picture of submissiveness: "Then Job arose, and rent his mantle, and shaved his head, and fell down upon the ground, and worshipped, and said, Naked came I out of my mother's womb, and naked shall I return thither: the Lord gave, and the Lord hath taken away; blessed be the name of the Lord. In all this Job sinned not, nor charged God foolishly" (Job 1:20–22). All this could likewise be said of Jesus Christ in his extremity.

*Descended below all things.* It was necessary that the Savior partake of the full mortal experience. If he had been exempted from any part of what we go through in mortality, it could be said that he doesn't know, doesn't understand what we feel or how we suffer. Instead, he descended below all things. The story of Job gives an Old Testament type of that descent. Job lost all his wealth, his children, and his health. His friends turned on him, falsely accusing him of having committed sin. Even his wife said to him, "Dost thou still retain thine integrity? curse God, and die" (Job 2:9). When the Lord spoke to Joseph Smith about his "adversity" and "afflictions," he contrasted him to Job: "Thou art not yet as Job; thy friends do not contend against thee, neither charge thee with transgression, as they did Job" (D&C 121:10).

But Jesus descended below even this.

In the process he increased in his *experiential* understanding of our mortal plight. As Jehovah, his understanding of all things was perfect and complete. After all, he was God, one with the Father. But experiencing something deepens and perfects our understanding of it. The descent of Christ, and the experiences that accompanied it, are what Alma was referring to when he said:

> And he shall go forth, suffering pains and afflictions and temptations of every kind; and this that the word might be fulfilled which saith he will take upon him the pains and the sicknesses of his people.
>
> And he will take upon him death, that he may loose the bands of death which bind his people; and he will take upon him their infirmities, that his bowels may be filled with mercy, according to the flesh, that he may know according to the flesh how to *succor* his people according to their infirmities.
>
> Now the Spirit knoweth all things; nevertheless the Son of God suffereth according to the flesh that he might take upon him the sins of his people, that he might blot out their transgressions according to the power of his deliverance; and now behold, this is the testimony which is in me. (Alma 7:11–13; emphasis added)

It's important to note that the word *succor* used here is found in a similar context in the book of Hebrews: "In that he himself hath suffered being tempted, he is able to succour them that are tempted" (Heb. 2:18). Elder Jeffrey R. Holland said of that word: "To *succor* means 'to run to.' I testify that Christ will run to us, and is running even now, if we will but receive the extended arm of His mercy."[4]

*Motivated by love and filled with power.* The trials of the atonement—and the difficulties of a lifetime of perfection—would be so great that the Savior would require two additional characteristics: he would have to be motivated by pure love and he would have to be filled with godly power. Jesus had these qualifications to a much greater degree than any other person who has ever come to earth.

## CHAPTER 22

# LOVE, POWER, AND SACRIFICE: KEYS TO THE ATONEMENT

LOVE AND POWER WERE NECESSARY elements of the atonement; and sacrifice was the necessary mode. Christ embodied all three of these elements in perfection. He brought to the earth perfect love, he exercised complete power, and he offered the ultimate sacrifice.

His sacrifice was made possible because of his love and his power. If he had had the love but not the power, he would not have been able offer a sacrifice of infinite proportions. If he had had the power but not the love, he might not have been willing. Gratefully, in Jesus Christ—and only in him—we are blessed with a perfect combination of love and power, which were brought together in the sacrifice of all sacrifices.

These elements of the Savior's mission are taught clearly in the Book of Mormon: Another Testament of Jesus Christ and emphasized in the speeches of Nephi, King Benjamin, Abinadi, and Alma, as well as the Savior himself in Third Nephi. For example, Nephi saw a marvelous vision of the mission of the mortal Messiah, wherein he began to understand "the condescension of God"—or the descent of God from his celestial realms to the fallen earth. His growing understanding was characterized by this testimony: "I know that he *loveth* his children; nevertheless, I do not know the meaning of all things."

Later in the same vision, Nephi recorded: "I beheld that he went forth ministering unto the people, in *power* and great glory. . . . And I beheld multitudes of people who were sick. . . . And they were healed by the *power* of the Lamb of God."

Finally, concerning sacrifice, he wrote: "And I . . . beheld the Lamb of God, that he was taken by the people; yea, the Son of the everlasting God was judged of the world. . . . And I, Nephi, saw that he was *lifted up upon the cross and slain* for the sins of the world" (1 Ne. 11:16–17, 28, 31–33; emphasis added).

Abinadi saw the same combination of sacrifice, power, and love. The Son of God, he said, "suffereth temptation, and yieldeth not to the temptation, but *suffereth himself to be mocked, and scourged, and cast out, and disowned* by his people. . . . [And] he shall be *led, crucified, and slain.*" This same being would exercise power, Abinadi said, in working "*many mighty miracles* among the children of men" and would gain "the *victory over death;* giving the Son *power to make intercession* for the children of men." Having done that, he would ascend on high in love, "having the *bowels of mercy;* being *filled with compassion* towards the children of men" (Mosiah 15:5–9; emphasis added).

President Ezra Taft Benson said regarding these essential elements of Christ's character:

> No mortal being had the power or capability to redeem all other mortals from their lost and fallen condition, nor could any other voluntarily forfeit his life and thereby bring to pass a universal resurrection for all other mortals.
>
> Only Jesus Christ was able and willing to accomplish such a redeeming act of love.
>
> We may never understand nor comprehend in mortality *how* He accomplished what He did, but we must not fail to understand *why* He did what He did.
>
> Everything He did was prompted by His unselfish, infinite love for us.[1]

President Benson also said: "He was *able* to accomplish His mission because He was the Son of God and He possessed the power of God. He was *willing* to accomplish His mission because He loves us."[2]

Love, power, sacrifice—this chapter will consider each of these essential elements of Christ's mission separately.

## THE LOVE OF CHRIST

Jesus was filled with perfect love for both God and man, and that love was an essential component of his mission of redemption. When Nephi saw the vision that included the tree of life, he learned that it represented "the love of God" (1 Ne. 11:22, 25). That tree (or God's love) was presented in the context of the mission and sacrifice of Christ. "And I, Nephi, saw that he was lifted up upon the cross and slain for the sins of the world" (1 Ne. 11:33). Later, Nephi taught that Jesus would suffer trials and indignities—and death—at the hands of others "because of his loving kindness and his long-suffering towards the children of men" (1 Ne. 19:9).

The scriptures give a number of examples of self-sacrifice because of love. When the people of Israel made the golden calf and offered sacrifices to it, Moses said to them, "Ye have sinned a great sin: and now I will go up unto the Lord; peradventure I shall make an atonement for your sin." In his compassion, Moses pleaded before the Lord, saying, "If thou wilt forgive their sin—; and if not, blot me, I pray thee, out of thy book which thou hast written" (Ex. 32:30–32). Moses was willing to forfeit his place in eternity in his heartfelt desire to help save his people's spiritual lives.

Another helpful example can be seen in the story of the stripling warriors in the book of Alma. As part of their repentance for past heinous sins, the parents of these young men had sworn an oath that they would never again take up arms against an enemy. Yet the Lamanites were threatening, and death seemed to be the certain result. The stripling warriors, who had not taken the oath, went to war to protect their people even though it was a reasonable expectation that some, or many, would be killed (Alma 53:10–18).

The Book of Mormon gives another powerful example of this principle. The sons of Mosiah, in their own repentance and as an act of pure love, decided they must preach the gospel to the Lamanites. Others warned them of the extreme danger of their enterprise (Alma 26:23–24) because they were going to preach to "a wild and a hardened and a ferocious people; a people who delighted in murdering the Nephites" (Alma 17:14). The sons of Mosiah went to preach anyway, doing so in similitude of their Savior in a desire to save the souls of those they came to love, even at risk to their own lives.

The Savior's love was prefigured by prophetic symbolisms of the shepherd and the sheep, the protective wings of the mother hen, the father and his child, and the husband and wife. For example, Isaiah recorded, "He shall feed his flock like a shepherd: he shall gather the lambs with his arm, and carry them in his bosom, and shall gently lead those that are with young" (Isa. 40:11). The imagery here is significant. Christ won't just go seeking the lost sheep, as we know a good shepherd would. He will feed them. He will carry them in his arms, holding them close. He will lead them gently with his love.

Jesus consistently manifested love in his interactions with others—in teaching, healing, and ministering. When the word *compassion* is used in the New Testament, it is translated from a Greek word pointing us to *godly* compassion, or the pure love of Christ. Christ's compassion, then, does not flow from ordinary love, or even from extraordinary human love. It flows from godly love. In the Gospels, we see Christ have compassion on the two blind men by the wayside (Matt. 20:34), the leper in Galilee (Mark 1:41), the widow of Nain (Luke 7:13), a great multitude who had sick among them (Matt. 14:14), a multitude who had been with him for three days and had no food (Mark 8:2), and many others.

One story that particularly demonstrates Christ's pure love is the account of the raising of Lazarus from the dead:

"Now a certain man was sick, named Lazarus, of Bethany." And his sisters, Mary and Martha, sent word to Jesus, saying, "Lord, behold, *he whom thou lovest* is sick." And the account adds, "Now *Jesus loved* Martha, and her sister, [Mary], and Lazarus."

We know Jesus delayed going to Bethany, that the power of God might be manifest. When he finally arrived and saw the grief of this family that he loved, "he groaned in the spirit, and was troubled, and

304

said, Where have ye laid him? They said unto him, Lord, come and see. Jesus wept. Then said the Jews, *Behold how he loved him!* . . . Jesus therefore again *groaning in himself* cometh to the grave" (John 11:1–5, 33–38; emphasis added).

He commanded that the stone blocking the cave be removed and then commanded Lazarus to come forth. The emotions expressed in this touching account make it clear that Jesus truly did love those he served.

## THE POWER OF CHRIST

The story of Lazarus is an example not only of great love but also of great power. The prophets foretold that Jesus would come with *power*. For example, as noted above, King Benjamin prophesied, "Behold, the time cometh, . . . that *with power, the Lord Omnipotent* [omnipotent means "all powerful"] . . . shall come down from heaven among the children of men, . . . and shall go forth amongst men, *working mighty miracles*" (Mosiah 3:5; emphasis added).

The Gospels record the fulfillment of those prophecies. Mark records, "The Son of man hath *power on earth to forgive sins*" (Mark 2:10; emphasis added). Luke wrote: "And Jesus returned in the *power* of the Spirit into Galilee. . . . And they were astonished at his doctrine: for his *word was with power*" (Luke 4:14, 32; emphasis added). Luke further recorded, "Then he called his twelve disciples together, and gave them *power* and authority over all devils, and to cure diseases" (Luke 9:1; emphasis added). Not only did Jesus have great power, but he was also able to share it with others.

John recorded what Jesus said in prayer to the Father, referring to himself: "Thou hast given him *power over all flesh*" (John 17:2; emphasis added).

Christ's power was repeatedly manifest in the many miracles he performed. And it became particularly focused when he performed the infinite atonement in the Garden of Gethsemane.

It was necessary that the Atoner have power over Satan. This power was prophesied almost from the very beginning of this earth's existence.

After Satan, in the form of a serpent, tempted Adam and Eve, and after our first parents fell, the Lord pronounced a curse and a blessing. Even before the Lord gave consequences to Adam and Eve, He spoke to the serpent (or Satan): "Because thou hast done this thou shalt be cursed above all cattle, and above every beast of the field; upon thy belly shalt thou go, and dust shalt thou eat all the days of thy life; . . . and I will put enmity between thy seed and her seed; and *he shall bruise thy head,* and thou shalt bruise his heel" (Moses 4:20–21; emphasis added).

Examples in scripture repeatedly manifest the unparalleled power of Christ. We see his power in the works of his servants Moses, Joshua, Elijah, Elisha, Nephi, Ammon, and many others, all of whom obtained their power from on high. We see it in Christ's power during his earthly ministry to still the waters, to feed the multitude, and to heal the withered hand. With such power, Christ can conquer even the greatest enemies of all: death and sin.

"I am Alpha and Omega, Christ the Lord," Jesus has said in our day, "yea, even I am he, the beginning and the end, the Redeemer of the world. I, having accomplished and finished the will of him whose I am, even the Father, concerning me—having done this that I might subdue all things unto myself—retaining all power, even to the destroying of Satan and his works at the end of the world" (D&C 19:1–3).

## THE SACRIFICE OF JESUS CHRIST

Jesus Christ's love and power came together in his sacrifice. That sacrifice had three parts: (1) the condescension of Jehovah, (2) a lifetime of trial, (3) the infinite, atoning sacrifice of a god.

The condescension of Jehovah is the beginning of the story of all stories. The Creator of the universe, even the God of the Old Testament, comes down to earth to dwell as a man, beginning his life as a helpless infant and ending his life in an incredible, incomprehensible sacrifice offered for all mankind.

Suppose you heard that the literal son of God, the God of the entire universe, was going to be born. What would you expect? You'd probably expect that God would choose to send his Son to a world of righteousness, one that would honor him.

It might make sense that God would send his Son with such heavenly and earthly manifestations that all the world would know without question that the Son of God had been born.

You'd likely imagine that God would send his Son to a prominent city in a prominent nation and to a family of wealth and prestige. Perhaps he'd send his Son to be the mortal son of the greatest emperor on earth.

You might think that God would send his Son to live in a time of comfort and a time when arts and sciences would be at their peak.

You might suppose God would send his Son to the finest hospital in the history of earth, with the best equipment, clean surroundings, and superbly trained doctors and nurses.

You might think that God would send his Son to a time and place where he could obtain the best training and education that had ever been available.

Of course, in God's wisdom and love for his children, none of this was appropriate for the mission of the Only Begotten Son of the Father. An outline of the condescension of the great Jehovah underscores the sacrifice he offered just in coming to the earth to dwell as a mortal man:

He arrived on earth as a helpless baby, completely dependent on the care of others.

He was born in a cave, in utter poverty and obscurity.

He was born with a presumed stain on the legitimacy of his parentage.

He was born in an insignificant country, one of the minor subject nations of the great world power.

He became a refugee in a foreign land as an infant.

He was reared as the son of poor parents, learning a trade with his hands.

He grew up in a small village far from the seat of power of his country, which was far from the seat of power of the ruling empire.

He continued in obscurity for his first thirty years.

He became an itinerant with no home, dependent on the goodness of others for food and lodging.

He was persecuted throughout his ministry, threatened with death, spat upon, cursed, accused of having a devil.

He was betrayed by one of his closest associates.

He was denied by one of his closest friends.

He was abandoned by his disciples.

He was put to death on trumped-up charges, having been sentenced to die as a criminal.

He suffered a most painful and humiliating death.

He was buried in a borrowed tomb.

Such was the condescension of Christ!

Jesus suffered a lifetime of trial. We know that his suffering in the Garden of Gethsemane was beyond our comprehension. But that was the culmination of many years of trials that preceded it. Alma wrote that he would suffer "pains and afflictions and temptations of every kind" and that he would "take upon him" the pains, sicknesses, and infirmities of mortality (Alma 7:11).

And Isaiah's testimony never fails to touch our hearts:

He is despised and rejected of men; a man of sorrows, and acquainted with grief: . . . he was despised, and we esteemed him not.

Surely he hath borne our griefs, and carried our sorrows: yet we did esteem him stricken, smitten of God, and afflicted.

But he was wounded for our transgressions, he was bruised for our iniquities. . . .

He was oppressed, and he was afflicted. (Isa. 53:3–7)

## Love, Power, and Sacrifice: Jesus' Final Hours

The Savior's love, power, and sacrifice all came together in a remarkable way during his final hours. (Christ's last two days, including a detailed discussion of Gethsemane and Calvary, are addressed in detail in chapters 16 and 17.) During those hours, Christ's pure love was plainly manifest. For example, he manifest selfless and thoughtful love to his disciples at the Last Supper—knowing he was soon going to be performing the awful atonement. After they had eaten, he rose up from the supper, set aside his garments, and wrapped a towel around his waist. Then he poured water into a basin, washed the disciples' well-traveled feet, and wiped them with the towel. Then, the apostle John wrote: "After he had washed their feet, and had taken his garments, and was set down again, he said unto them, Know ye what I have done to you? . . . If I, . . . your Lord and Master, have washed your feet; ye also ought to wash one another's feet. . . . For the servant is not greater than his lord; neither he that is sent greater than he that sent him" (John 13:12–16; see also vv. 4–5).

Here Christ had the burden of the world on his shoulders. He knew that in a few hours he would be offering a sacrifice more painful and more difficult (by an exponential factor) than any offered at any other time or place. But he took time to serve in a private and personal way, to bless and to strengthen his disciples. He took the time to tenderly show his love.

Jesus' great Intercessory Prayer, offered shortly after the washing of feet, was a pure expression of love. As the Savior pleads for the blessings of eternity for those who believe and follow him, he mentions the word *love* or the idea of godly *unity* nearly twenty times (see John 17).

There were other manifestations of great love from the cross. John recorded: "When Jesus therefore saw his mother, and the disciple standing by, whom he loved, he saith unto his mother, Woman, behold thy son! Then saith he to the disciple, Behold thy mother! And from that hour that disciple took her unto his own home" (John 19:26–27).

In the preceding hours, Jesus had undergone incomprehensible suffering in the Garden of Gethsemane. He had been mocked, beaten, scourged, and spat upon. He was nailed to a cruel cross as he spoke, but his heart reached out with love and concern to his mother, seeking to do the only thing he could to bless her.

In his love, he likewise was concerned about his tormentors: "Then said Jesus, Father, forgive them; for they know not what they do" (Luke 23:34).

In Nephi's great testimony, he observed that love was the motivating force that would enable Jesus to withstand with perfect forbearance the abuse he would suffer in his final hours: "And the world, because of their iniquity, shall judge him to be a thing of naught; wherefore they scourge him, and he suffereth it; and they smite him, and he suffereth it. Yea, they spit upon him, and he suffereth it, *because of his loving kindness* and his long-suffering towards the children of men" (1 Ne. 19:9–10; emphasis added).

In addition to *love,* the atoning sacrifice of Christ represents the most incredible demonstration of *power* this world has ever seen.

*The atonement required the power to resist all evil.* In his message to the Hebrews, Paul wrote: "[Look] unto Jesus the author and finisher of our faith; who for the joy that was set before him endured the cross, despising the shame, and is set down at the right hand of the throne of God. . . . Ye have not yet resisted unto blood, striving against sin" (Heb. 12:2, 4). (As the New International Version puts it, "In your struggle against sin, you have not yet resisted to the point of shedding your blood.") This seems to be an allusion to Jesus' mighty struggle in the Garden of Gethsemane. We don't resist sin to the point of bleeding through our pores—but Jesus did. Even though the adversary unleashed on him the greatest assault ever sent against man, Jesus "resisted unto blood, striving against sin"—for us. Because of his power, he not only authored our faith, but he also finished it, accomplishing every necessary thing until he truly could say at the end, "It is finished" (John 19:30).

*The atonement required the power for Jesus to receive all mortal pain and suffering into himself—willingly—and to survive.* There is nothing that mortals can suffer that Jesus didn't overcome. As President Benson wrote: "It was in Gethsemane that Jesus took on Himself the sins of the world, in Gethsemane that His pain was equivalent to the cumulative burden of all men, in Gethsemane that He descended below all things so that all could repent and come to Him.

"The mortal mind fails to fathom, the tongue cannot express, the pen of man cannot describe the breadth, the depth, the height of the suffering of our Lord—nor His infinite love for us."[3] President Howard W. Hunter added that "the sinless Son of God" took upon him "not only the sins and temptations of every human soul who will repent, but all of our sickness and grief and pain of every kind. He suffered these afflictions as we suffer them, according to the flesh. He suffered them all. He did this to perfect his mercy and his ability to lift us above every earthly trial [Alma 7:11–12]."[4]

*The atonement required the power to stand against the power of the adversary.* The scriptures give suggestions of that dark power. In Ephesians 6, Paul warned of the power of the devil and said, "We wrestle not against flesh and blood, but against principalities, against powers, against the rulers of the darkness of this world, against spiritual wickedness in high places" (Eph. 6:12). Elsewhere Satan is described as a "great red dragon" and "that old serpent, called the Devil," who was filled with "great wrath" (Rev. 12:3, 9, 12). And Peter described him as "a roaring lion, [who] walketh about, seeking whom he may devour" (1 Pet. 5:8). Jesus was able to face that great adversary—and conquer him with power.

*The atonement required that Christ have the power to lay down his life and take it up again*—something that had never happened before in the history of the world. Because of the power Christ exercised in his atonement, he gained victory over "that monster, death and hell" (2 Ne. 9:10). And because of that victory, through Christ, we will be resurrected as he was, and, if we will, we also can overcome sin.

## CHAPTER 23

# FOREVER LOST: CALAMITOUS CONSEQUENCES WITHOUT THE ATONEMENT

JUST AS THE ATONEMENT PROVIDES US with the opportunity to be eternally exalted, without Jesus Christ and his atoning sacrifice we would be eternally fallen and lost; Satan would have complete power over us, and we would eventually become like him—filthy, miserable, and lacking any degree of merit. We would be wholly forlorn, pitiful, and lonely souls, deficient of any sort of value and forever remaining without hope of ever becoming clean and pure before God. Repentance and forgiveness would be no more than imaginary concepts, and our faith would be in vain.

"If it weren't for the atonement," Elder Bruce R. McConkie wrote, "we could write the Gospel off as a myth and the whole purpose of the creation would be frustrated."[1] Without the atonement, decay and corruption would reign supreme, for the resurrection, with all its joys, miracles, and glories, would not exist. Without the atonement of our Savior, Jesus Christ, all of us would perish forevermore. We would be cut off from God's presence, love, light, glory, and power throughout the eternities. Ultimately, in the words of Elder Neal A. Maxwell, the "atonement . . . saves us from meaninglessness."[2]

To illustrate the unthinkable calamity that would exist for

humankind had there been no atoning sacrifice, President Joseph
Fielding Smith wrote about a deep and dark pit.

> A man walking along the road happens to fall into a pit so
> deep and dark that he cannot climb to the surface and regain his
> freedom. How can he save himself from his predicament? Not by
> any exertions on his part, for there is no means of escape in the
> pit. He calls for help and some kindly disposed soul, hearing his
> cries for relief, hastens to his assistance and by lowering a ladder,
> gives to him the means by which he may climb again to the sur-
> face of the earth.
>
> This was precisely the condition that Adam placed himself
> and his posterity in, when he partook of the forbidden fruit. All
> being together in the pit, none could gain the surface and relieve
> the others. The pit was banishment from the presence of the Lord
> and temporal death, the dissolution of the body. And all being
> subject to death, none could provide the means of escape.
>
> Therefore, in his infinite mercy, the Father heard the cries of
> his children and sent his Only Begotten Son, who was not subject
> to death nor to sin, to provide the means of escape. This he did
> through his infinite atonement and the everlasting gospel.[3]

Of course, our situations would be much worse if we were without
the atonement than if we had merely fallen into a pit, and our escape
from the pit of sin and death is much more important than our escape
from any physical pit. Ultimately, without the atonement we would all
become devils, our bodies would stay in the earth, our spirits would remain in prison, our faith would be vain, we would not be able to merit
anything of ourselves, all of us would be forever lost, and in the end we
all would perish.

## WITHOUT THE ATONEMENT,
## WE WOULD BECOME DEVILS

The prophets have described the disastrous consequences we would
experience if there were no atonement or resurrection. For example,
the prophet Jacob, brother of Nephi, articulated seven appalling

circumstances, including that we would become devils. Jacob's words are: "For behold, if the flesh should rise no more our spirits must become subject to that angel who fell from before the presence of the Eternal God, and became the devil, to rise no more. And our spirits must have become like unto him, and we become devils, angels to a devil, to be shut out from the presence of our God, and to remain with the father of lies, in misery, like unto himself; yea, to that being who beguiled our first parents, who transformeth himself nigh unto an angel of light, and stirreth up the children of men unto secret combinations of murder and all manner of secret works of darkness" (2 Ne. 9:8–9).

In sum, without the resurrection, (1) we would become subject to Satan, (2) we would become like Satan, (3) we would become devils, (4) we would become "angels to a devil," (5) we would be eternally shut out from God's presence, (6) we would live forever with Satan, who is "the father of lies" and the instigator of murder and "secret works of darkness," and (7) we would live "in misery."

Later in Jacob's same speech, he used the expressions *awful monster, death, hell, devil, lake of fire and brimstone,* and *endless torment* to portray the terrible condition that would exist for all of us had there been no atonement: "For the atonement satisfieth the demands of his justice upon all those who have not the law given to them, that they are delivered from that awful monster, death and hell, and the devil, and the lake of fire and brimstone, which is endless torment; and they are restored to that God who gave them breath, which is the Holy One of Israel" (2 Ne. 9:26).

The testimony of President Joseph Fielding Smith also provides a summary of what life without Jesus' divine redemptive act would be like: "What a dreadful situation we would have been in without this infinite atonement! Our bodies returning to the dust there to remain forever; our spirits becoming subject to Satan, and we would have had no recourse. How grateful we should be for the mercies of our Eternal Father and his beloved Son that the way was opened for our escape."[4]

## WITHOUT THE ATONEMENT, OUR BODIES WOULD REMAIN IN THE EARTH

Death is defined as the separation of the body and the spirit. The resurrection is the opposite of death, because it is the reunion of the spirit and body, "to be united never again to be divided" (D&C 138:17). Without the resurrection, our physical bodies would never reunite with our spirits; rather, they would rot and decay in mother earth to the point of complete disintegration—forever. In his teachings on the infinite atonement, the prophet Jacob said that unless the atonement were infinite, "this corruption could not put on incorruption." The effects of the fall would have "remained to an endless duration," and our bodies would be "laid down to rot and to crumble" in the earth, "to rise no more" (2 Ne. 9:7). President Marion G. Romney wrote: "The atonement of the Master is the central point of world history. Without it, the whole purpose for the creation of the earth and our living upon it would fail. . . .

". . . Without it, no man or woman would ever be resurrected."[5]

## WITHOUT THE ATONEMENT, OUR SPIRITS WOULD REMAIN IN PRISON

Just as our bodies would be unable to be resurrected, our spirits too would be unable to progress and would remain in prison. In a record of a vision received October 3, 1918, President Joseph F. Smith used language that describes the state of the dead—both the righteous and the wicked, as captives in prison. President Smith declared that the dead are "spirits in prison" and "captives who were bound"; specifically, they were bound with "the bands of death," "the chains of death," and "the chains of hell." Also, "the dead had looked upon the long absence of their spirits from their bodies as a bondage" (D&C 138:16, 18, 23, 28, 31, 50). But mercifully, the resurrection frees the dead from their prison. President Smith referred to that freedom by using such words as "liberty," "fulness of joy," and "deliverance."

Jesus Christ, through his atonement, is the one who provides that freedom, for he is our "Redeemer and Deliverer" (D&C 138:17–18, 23, 31, 49). Verses 23 and 24 provides this insight: "And the saints rejoiced in their redemption, and bowed the knee and acknowledged the Son of God as their Redeemer and Deliverer from death and the chains of hell. Their countenances shone, and the radiance from the presence of the Lord rested upon them, and they sang praises unto his holy name."

## Without the Atonement, Our Faith Would Be in Vain

Faith is a first principle of the gospel, and by faith our lives are blessed in numerous ways (Heb. 11; Ether 12). First and foremost, by faith we accept Jesus Christ into our hearts, and accepting Christ brings truth to our minds, light to our countenances, and great joy to our souls. Further, when we have faith in Christ and his atonement, we have hope that we can be cleansed from sin and raised from the dead in the resurrection.

Other blessings and powers of faith are diverse and numerous. By faith earlier Saints "subdued kingdoms, wrought righteousness, obtained promises, stopped the mouths of lions, quenched the violence of fire, escaped the edge of the sword, out of weakness were made strong, waxed valiant in fight, turned to flight the armies of the aliens. Women received their dead raised to life again" (Heb. 11:33–35). By faith people have been able to withstand torture, mockings, scourgings, imprisonment, stonings, destitution, afflictions, torments, and wanderings (Heb. 11:35–38; cf. also JST Gen. 14:30–31).

These various examples are only a sampling of the powers and blessings of faith. However, our faith is only possible through the atonement; without the atonement, our faith would be empty and ineffective. People would not be able to do righteous works and obtain promises from the Lord, make weak things become strong, divide the seas, turn back armies, or stand in God's presence. As Paul stated: "If Christ be not risen, then is our preaching vain, and your faith is also vain. . . . If in this life only we have hope in Christ, we are of all men most miserable" (1 Cor. 15:14, 19).

President Brigham Young effectively summarized what would happen to faith and hope if the atonement were taken away from the plan of salvation: "The moment the atonement of the Savior is done away, that moment, at one sweep, the hopes of salvation entertained by the Christian world are destroyed, the foundation of their faith is taken away, and there is nothing left for them to stand upon. When it is gone all the revelations God ever gave to the Jewish nation, to the Gentiles, and to us are rendered valueless, and all hope is taken from us at one sweep."[6]

## WITHOUT THE ATONEMENT, WE "COULD NOT MERIT ANYTHING OF [OURSELVES]"

Without Christ's sufferings, death, and atonement for our sins, we would not be worthy of anything of ourselves, and we would remain undeserving souls. Neither our attempts at providing good works nor our desire for personal righteousness would help us. We cannot, by ourselves, become righteous, pure, or holy, and we cannot with our own power obtain forgiveness of our sins. Christ is the essential part of any formula that includes our becoming righteous, pure, holy, or obtaining forgiveness of our sins. In the Book of Mormon, Aaron taught this significant doctrine regarding merit: "And since man had fallen he could not merit anything of himself; but the sufferings and death of Christ atone for their sins, through faith and repentance, and so forth; and that he breaketh the bands of death, that the grave shall have no victory, and that the sting of death should be swallowed up in the hopes of glory" (Alma 22:14).

## WITHOUT THE ATONEMENT, ALL OF US WOULD BE FOREVER LOST

Through testimonies in the scriptures, we can understand with surety that without the atonement, all humankind would be lost. The prophets have consistently maintained that "all mankind were in a lost and in a fallen state, and ever would be save they should rely on this Redeemer" (1 Ne. 10:6), that "if there should be no atonement made all mankind must be lost" (Jacob 7:12), and that "mankind . . . would have been endlessly lost were it not that God redeemed his people from their lost and fallen state" (Mosiah 16:4).

*Lost,* according to a dictionary published in 1828 (a dictionary in use when Joseph Smith translated the Book of Mormon), is defined as "ruined; destroyed; wasted or squandered"; "not able to find the right way"; "bewildered; perplexed"; "not perceptible to the senses."[7] Each of these definitions describes our condition when we lack the atonement in our lives. Without the atonement, we would be *ruined, destroyed, wasted,* and *squandered,* not just throughout mortality but also throughout eternity; to recall Abinadi's words, we would be "endlessly lost" (Mosiah 16:4).

Without the atonement, we would *not be able to find the right way.* Jesus provides the way, which is the plan of salvation; in fact, he himself *is* the Way. If we lacked the atonement in our lives, we would remain *bewildered* and *perplexed* regarding who we are and what our divine purposes are. Similarly, inasmuch as the devil lacks the atonement, he is lost. In fact, one of Satan's names is *Abaddon,* meaning *lost* and *destruction.*[8] "And they had a king over them, which is the angel of the bottomless pit, whose name in the Hebrew tongue is Abaddon" (Rev. 9:11).

## Without the Atonement, "All Men Must Perish"

A number of Book of Mormon prophets declared that had it not been for Jesus' redeeming sacrifice, all of us would perish. These prophets utilized the expressions "must perish" and "must unavoidably perish" to describe such a woeful circumstance: "For were it not for the redemption which [Jesus] hath made for his people, which was prepared from the foundation of the world, I say unto you, were it not for this, all mankind must have perished" (Mosiah 15:19); "Were it not for the atonement, which God himself shall make for the sins and iniquities of his people, . . . they must unavoidably perish" (Mosiah 13:28); "And my soul delighteth in proving unto my people that save Christ should come all men must perish" (2 Ne. 11:6). And finally, "For it is expedient that an atonement should be made; for according to the great plan of the Eternal God there must be an atonement made, or else all mankind must unavoidably perish; yea, all are hardened; yea, all are fallen and are lost, and must perish except it be through the atonement which it is expedient should be made" (Alma 34:9).

## CHAPTER 24

# MAKING IT OURS:
## PERSONALIZING THE ATONEMENT

THE ATONEMENT IS THE GREATEST GIFT God offers his children. The Savior offered himself in the garden and on the cross so that we could be blessed in every needful way—cleansed of our sins, transformed in our very beings so we become more like our Father, strengthened in our weaknesses, assisted in our trials and our sorrows. These gifts are available for everyone in the world, everyone who has ever lived or ever will live. God excludes no one—although we can by our choices exclude ourselves from much of what he offers. Though they are freely offered, these gifts can be received only as we make the atonement personal in our lives.

How, then, can we come to the blessings of the atonement? The scriptures are filled with explanations and testimonies of how to come unto Christ and receive of his atonement. The process is deceptively simple. Moroni capsulized it with plainness when he said that we must "come unto Christ, and be perfected in him" (Moro. 10:32). But knowing that simple charge is not enough. How do we so come?

There are many ways that we can deepen our understanding of the process Moroni speaks of. One approach is to seek to deconstruct some of the stories in the scriptures to see the model they present. Doing so shows us an inspired pattern that points the way to more fully partake of all that the Savior offers us. That pattern includes the following steps:

- Have a vision of the blessings of the atonement that are offered to you.

- Recognize your need for those blessings, and be filled with a powerful desire to receive them.

- Recognize that Christ is the source of those blessings, and trust that he wants to give them to you.

- Have a broken and humble heart, a sense of helplessness without him.

- Ask for the blessings you desire.

- Learn what God requires for you to receive those blessings.

- Obey what you've learned.

- Be filled with gratitude for what you receive.

Let's see how this pattern unfolds in several scriptural examples. Though the sequence may shift in these accounts, all of the elements of the pattern occur in each example (although sometimes they are implied rather than explicit). As you read these accounts, seek to feel the depth of emotion in each one. It's not enough just to intellectually know about the atonement, even if we know a great deal. Instead, it needs to sink deep within our hearts.

## ALMA THE YOUNGER

Alma and the sons of Mosiah went about "seeking to destroy the church of God" (Alma 36:6). An angel appeared to them to stop them. Then, without planning in advance, Alma began to go through the steps of receiving the blessings of the atonement.

- *Recognize your need for those blessings, and be filled with a powerful desire to receive them.*

"And he said unto me: If thou wilt of thyself be destroyed, seek no more to destroy the church of God. . . . When I heard [those] words

. . . I was struck with . . . great fear and amazement [that] perhaps I should be destroyed" (Alma 36:9, 11).

• *Have a broken and humble heart, a sense of helplessness without him.*

"But I was racked with eternal torment, for my soul was harrowed up to the greatest degree and racked with all my sins. . . . Yea, . . . so great had been my iniquities, that the very thought of coming into the presence of my God did rack my soul with inexpressible horror" (Alma 36:12, 14).

• *Have a vision of the blessings of the atonement that are offered to you. Recognize that Christ is the source of those blessings, and trust that he wants to give them to you.*

"And it came to pass that as I was thus racked with torment, . . . behold, I remembered also to have heard my father prophesy unto the people concerning the coming of one Jesus Christ, a Son of God, to atone for the sins of the world" (Alma 36:17).

• *Ask for the blessings you desire. Learn what God requires for you to receive those blessings. And obey what you've learned.*

"Now, as my mind caught hold upon this thought, I cried within my heart: O Jesus, thou Son of God, have mercy on me, who am in the gall of bitterness, and am encircled about by the everlasting chains of death" (Alma 36:18).

• *Be filled with gratitude for what you receive.*

"And now, behold, when I thought this, I could remember my pains no more; yea, I was harrowed up by the memory of my sins no more. And oh, what joy, and what marvelous light I did behold; yea, my soul was filled with joy as exceeding as was my pain!" (Alma 36:19–20).

## ZEEZROM

Zeezrom was an enemy of the Church. When Alma and Amulek tried to teach the people, Zeezrom engaged them in a battle of words, seeking, successfully, to turn others from the truth. Partly as a result of his lying words, Alma and Amulek were thrown into prison and many of their followers were killed. Later Zeezrom came to himself and sought repentance and forgiveness. His experience also fits the pattern of how we can receive the blessings of the atonement.

- *Recognize your need for those blessings, and be filled with a powerful desire to receive them.*

"Zeezrom lay sick at Sidom, with a burning fever, which was caused by the great tribulations of his mind on account of his wickedness. . . . And . . . his many . . . sins . . . did harrow up his mind until it did become exceedingly sore, having no deliverance" (Alma 15:3).

- *Have a vision of the blessings of the atonement that are offered to you. Recognize that Christ is the source of those blessings, and trust that he wants to give them to you.*

"Now, when he heard that Alma and Amulek were in the land of Sidom, his heart began to take courage; and he sent a message immediately unto them, desiring them to come unto him" (Alma 15:4).

- *Have a broken and humble heart, a sense of helplessness without him. Ask for the blessings you desire.*

"And . . . they went immediately . . . unto Zeezrom; and they found him upon his bed, sick . . . ; and his mind also was exceedingly sore because of his iniquities; and when he saw them he stretched forth his hand, and besought them that they would heal him" (Alma 15:5).

- *Recognize that Christ is the source of those blessings, and trust that he wants to give them to you.*

"And it came to pass that Alma said unto him, taking him by the hand: Believest thou in the power of Christ unto salvation? And he answered and said: Yea, I believe all the words that thou hast taught" (Alma 15:6–7).

• *Learn what God requires for you to receive those blessings.*

"And Alma said: If thou believest in the redemption of Christ thou canst be healed" (Alma 15:8).

• *Obey what you've learned.*

"And he said: Yea, I believe according to thy words. And then Alma cried unto the Lord, saying: O Lord our God, have mercy on this man, and heal him according to his faith which is in Christ. And when Alma had said these words, Zeezrom leaped upon his feet, and began to walk" (Alma 15:9–11).

• *Obey what you've learned. Be filled with gratitude for what you receive.*

"And Alma baptized Zeezrom unto the Lord; and he began from that time forth to preach unto the people" (Alma 15:12).

## THE PRODIGAL SON

Earlier (chapter 9) we discussed the parable of the prodigal son, but let's review it here from the perspective of coming unto Christ and receiving the gifts of the atonement. One way to read this parable is to think of the father as Christ and the prodigal as us:

"A certain man had two sons: And the younger of them said to his father, Father, give me the portion of goods that falleth to me. And he divided unto them his living. And not many days after the younger son gathered all together, and took his journey into a far country, and there wasted his substance with riotous living" (Luke 15:11–13). But the time came when the prodigal son entered into the process of coming unto Christ.

• *Recognize your need for those blessings and be filled with a powerful desire to receive them.*

"And when he had spent all, there arose a mighty famine in that land; and he began to be in want. . . . And he would fain have filled his belly with the husks that the swine did eat: and no man gave unto him" (Luke 15:14, 16).

> • *Have a vision of the blessings of the atonement that are offered to you. Recognize that Christ is the source of those blessings, and trust that he wants to give them to you.*

"And when he came to himself, he said, How many hired servants of my father's have bread enough and to spare, and I perish with hunger!" (Luke 15:17).

> • *Have a broken and humble heart, a sense of helplessness without him. Ask for the blessings you desire.*

"I will arise and go to my father, and will say unto him, Father, I have sinned against heaven, and before thee, and am no more worthy to be called thy son: make me as one of thy hired servants" (Luke 15:18–19).

> • *Learn what God requires for you to receive those blessings. Obey what you've learned. Be filled with gratitude for what you receive.*

"And he arose, and came to his father. But when he was yet a great way off, his father saw him, and had compassion, and ran, and fell on his neck, and kissed him.

"And the son said unto him, Father, I have sinned against heaven, and in thy sight, and am no more worthy to be called thy son.

"But the father said to his servants, Bring forth the best robe, and put it on him; and put a ring on his hand, and shoes on his feet: and bring hither the fatted calf, and kill it; and let us eat, and be merry: for this my son was dead, and is alive again; he was lost, and is found" (Luke 15:11–24).

## Twenty-First Century Types

The pages of this book review many types of Christ, from Old Testament figures to the scriptural miracles to the modern ordinances. But as we personalize the atonement, making it come alive in our lives, we manifest a final and most important type: ourselves.

"I am the light of the world," Jesus said (John 9:5). But those who follow him, who partake fully of his atonement, become as he is. "Ye are the light of the world," he said to those who hearkened unto him (Matt. 5:14).

We receive our light from him—but as we do so, we become types of our Savior.

We even receive the title of *savior*. As the Lord said through Joseph Smith, the righteous are "set to be a light unto the world, and to be the saviors of men" (D&C 103:9).

We have no power within ourselves to save others (or even ourselves). But when we align ourselves with Christ and partake of the powers of his atonement, we can help in the process of salvation—and in doing so, we are types of Christ.

Latter-day Saint scholar Andrew C. Skinner has given us a valuable lesson on personalizing the types of the atonement:

> Our challenge is to take the lessons taught in the ancient written testimonies and use them to become more Christlike. . . . Perhaps the greatest lesson on types and similitudes is the one which some of us find the most difficult to accept, but by not accepting it, we rob ourselves of the true picture of our own relationship and similarity to God: We too are similitudes of the Messiah.
>
> All persons who take upon themselves the name of Christ are a similitude of Christ. Every person who is baptized as Christ was baptized is a similitude of Christ. Every man who holds the Melchizedek Priesthood "is or should be a type of Christ," said Elder Bruce R. McConkie. . . . In short, every person who is washed, anointed, and ordained in the name of Christ, every person who immerses himself or herself in living the gospel of Christ, every person who is a witness of Christ—all these are living, walking, breathing similitudes of the Lord Jesus Christ.[1]

## BRINGING IT INTO OUR HEARTS

The atonement of Jesus Christ can change our lives and everything about them. But first we have to let the significance of the Savior's offering sink into our hearts. Elder Orson F. Whitney, an apostle who served from 1906 to 1931, had an experience with the atonement that affected everything about his life thereafter. He had a dream or vision in which he saw himself "in the Garden of Gethsemane, a witness of the Savior's agony." After leaving the apostles in a group to pray, Jesus "passed over to the other side, where He also knelt and prayed . . . 'Oh my Father, if it be possible, let this cup pass from me; nevertheless not as I will, but as thou wilt.'

"As He prayed the tears streamed down his face, which was toward me. I was so moved at the sight that I also wept, out of pure sympathy. My whole heart went out to him; I loved him with all my soul, and I longed to be with him as I longed for nothing else."

Elder Whitney saw Jesus return to the apostles, who had fallen asleep, awaken them, and then return to his prayer. "Three times this occurred, until I was perfectly familiar with his appearance—face, form and movements. He was of noble stature and majestic mien. . . the very God that he was and is, as meek and humble as a little child."

Then the circumstances changed. "Instead of before, it was after the crucifixion." Elder Whitney could see that the Savior was about to ascend into heaven.

> I could endure it no longer. I ran from behind the tree, fell at his feet, clasped Him around the knees, and begged him to take me with him.
>
> I shall never forget the kind and gentle manner in which He stooped, raised me up, and embraced me. . . . and said in tenderest tones: "No, my son; these have finished their work; they can go with me; but you must stay and finish yours." Still I clung to Him. Gazing up into his face—for he was taller than I—I besought him fervently: "Well, promise me that I will come to you at the last." Smiling sweetly, He said: "That will depend entirely upon yourself." I awoke with a sob in my throat, and it was morning.[2]

## CHAPTER 25

# "I Cannot Say the Smallest Part": An Appreciation for the Atonement

THE LITERATURE OF FAITH IS FILLED WITH eloquent expressions of gratitude and awe for the atonement of our Savior, Jesus Christ. Joseph Smith was moved upon by the Spirit to pen one such expression, rejoicing in Jesus Christ, the blessings that flow from his atonement, and his work in the latter days:

> Now, what do we hear in the gospel which we have received? A voice of gladness! A voice of mercy from heaven; and a voice of truth out of the earth; . . . a voice of gladness for the living and the dead; glad tidings of great joy. . . .
>
> Let your hearts rejoice, and be exceedingly glad. Let the earth break forth into singing. Let the dead speak forth anthems of eternal praise to the King Immanuel. . . . .
>
> Let the mountains shout for joy, and all ye valleys cry aloud; and all ye seas and dry lands tell the wonders of your Eternal King! And ye rivers, and brooks, and rills, flow down with gladness. Let the woods and all the trees of the field praise the Lord; and ye solid rocks weep for joy! And let the sun, moon, and the morning stars sing together, and let all the sons of God shout for joy! And let the eternal creations declare his name forever and ever! And again I

say, how glorious is the voice we hear from heaven, proclaiming in our ears, glory, and salvation, and honor, and immortality, and eternal life; kingdoms, principalities, and powers! (D&C 128:19, 22–23)

In our day, as a professor at Brigham Young University, Jeffrey R. Holland wrote:

The life of Christ is a precious jewel that flashes in the flame of the sunlight and blinds our eyes with its rays. The prophets have, in reverence and holy appreciation, sought to speak of it, to praise him for the love and glory he displays. Some of the titles we hear often—Savior, Redeemer, Messiah; others we recognize less well—Dayspring, Ahman, Bishop of our Souls. He is the Mediator, the Advocate, the Author and Finisher of our Faith. He is Wonderful, Counselor, the Mighty God, the Everlasting Father. He is the Holiest of All, the Lion of Judah, the Mighty One of Jacob. He is the Man of Sorrows, the Horn of Salvation. He is Eternal and Everlasting. He is the Son of Man. He is the Bright and Morning Star. The list is only representative of another list that is only representative. What he is goes on forever, flashing in the sun.[1]

## Feelings beyond Words

We are grateful to read such expressions about our Savior. Our hearts are lifted and our spirits strengthened when others reach such heights of verbal expression in testimony.

But sometimes feelings reach far beyond the ability of words to express. This is the experience Ammon had when he said to his brethren: "My joy is full, yea, my heart is brim with joy, and I will rejoice in my God. . . . Therefore, let us glory, yea, we will glory in the Lord; yea, we will rejoice, for our joy is full; yea, we will praise our God forever. Behold, who can glory too much in the Lord? Yea, who can say too much of his great power, and of his mercy, and of his long-suffering towards the children of men? Behold, I say unto you, I cannot say the smallest part which I feel" (Alma 26:11, 16).

After the Nephites heard Jesus pray, it was written: "No tongue can speak, neither can there be written by any man, neither can the hearts of men conceive so great and marvelous things as we both saw and heard Jesus speak; and no one can conceive of the joy which filled our souls at the time we heard him pray for us unto the Father" (3 Ne. 17:17).

There are truths so glorious and there are feelings so deep that they go beyond expression. At such times, simplicity sometimes reaches more deeply than eloquence.

Nephi wrote in simplicity: "I glory in plainness; I glory in truth; I glory in my Jesus, for he hath redeemed my soul from hell" (2 Ne. 33:6).

Alma the Younger cried out in simplicity: "O Jesus, thou Son of God, have mercy on me, who am in the gall of bitterness, and am encircled about by the everlasting chains of death" (Alma 36:18).

The wife of King Lamoni pleaded in simplicity: "O blessed Jesus, who has saved me from an awful hell! O blessed God, have mercy on this people!" (Alma 19:29).

Paul wrote to the Galatians in simplicity: "Christ liveth in me: and the life which I now live in the flesh I live by the faith of the Son of God, who loved me, and gave himself for me" (Gal. 2:20).

Joseph Smith wrote in his diary in simplicity: "O, how marvelous are thy works, O Lord, and I thank thee for thy mercy unto me, thy servant. O Lord, save me in thy kingdom for Christ's sake."[2]

President Gordon B. Hinckley testified in simplicity: "He is the Savior and the Redeemer of the world. . . . I love Him. I speak His name in reverence and wonder. I worship Him as I worship His Father, in spirit and in truth. I thank Him and kneel before His wounded feet and hands and side, amazed at the love He offers me."[3]

## THE MEANING OF THE ATONEMENT

It is wonderful to see the multitude of witnesses that the Lord has given of the atonement of Jesus Christ. We can see him and his work in all the works of his hands; we can see the atonement clearly in the teachings and stories of the scriptures; we acknowledge truths about

Christ and his mighty offering in "things which are temporal, and things which are spiritual; things which are in the heavens above, and things which are on the earth, and things which are in the earth, and things which are under the earth, . . . all things bear record of [him]" (Moses 6:63).

But as we increase our understanding of types and shadows, we must also increase our understanding of the meaning and purpose of the atonement. It is not simply an interesting part of the gospel. It is the foundation. It is the hub of the wheel. It is the engine of the car. It is the root of the tree. Because of the atonement, the gospel has meaning and power.

Jesus Christ is the Author and Finisher of our salvation. He is the vine, the manna, the bread of life, the pillar of fire, the light of the world, the tree of life and its fruit, and the source of living water. His love and the atonement that stems from it are the most desirable above all things. His physical light and water are absolutely essential for the life and growth of every living thing on the earth. His spiritual light and water are equally essential to our spiritual and emotional life and growth. And all the ways in which he blesses us are made possible because of his atoning sacrifice.

As we come unto him with a submissive, obedient, broken heart—

He will cleanse us of sin.

He will change our hearts so we no longer have disposition to sin; he will help to change our character, our dispositions, our thoughts and feelings from those of natural men and women to Saints—men and women of God.

He will act as the Father of our spiritual rebirth.

He will heal our heartsickness, our emotional pain; he will calm our troubled hearts and minds; he will give comfort and blessing in the midst of turmoil and difficulty. He not only listens and understands, but he also has power to help.

He will guide our every step, giving us answers to many questions in prayer and leading us by the promptings of the Holy Ghost.

He will grant us the spiritual gifts he desires to give to everyone: peace, revelation, pure love, and joy.

He will grant us his greater spiritual gifts, culminating in the blessing of his presence.

He will bring us to eternal life (see Gal. 5:22–25; Mosiah 3:5–9; 14:3–7).

To the thousand testimonies and witnesses in this book, we add our own, in simplicity: With all our beings we know that Jesus is the Christ. We know that in his perfect love and mighty power he died for us. We know that he knows us and loves us personally and individually. We know that in him and through him, we receive blessings beyond measure—and that, as we continue in righteous covenant with the Father, we will, through Christ, eventually be lifted up to glory and everlasting life.

# FROM RANSOM TO MEDIATOR: ATONEMENT WORDS AND MEANINGS

THE PROPHETS USE DIFFERENT WORDS TO describe the atonement. These include *redemption, reconciliation, mediation, salvation, propitiation, ransom, atonement,* and *intercession.* Some of these words are related to other words that are derived from the same root. For instance, *redemption* is linked to *redeem* and *Redeemer,* and *salvation* is associated with *save* and *Savior.* Each of the atonement-related words evokes a particular understanding, feeling, or meaning to those who read the prophets' words. Each casts a beautiful light on Jesus Christ and his extraordinary and magnificent atonement.

Some of these words are difficult to comprehend, however, especially since they are not part of our daily speech; and we who study the prophets' words may not fully appreciate certain aspects of the atonement and how it blesses our lives because we do not fully understand the meaning of one or more of these significant words. For this reason, this appendix will briefly examine the meaning of some atonement-related words. Many other words that pertain to the atonement, including *repentance, forgiveness, sacrifice, infinite,* and *ordinance,* have been dealt with previously in this book.

## ATONEMENT (ENGLISH AT-ONE-MENT)

The English words *atonement, atone, atoned, atoneth,* or *atoning* collectively are found in the Pearl of Great Price (2 times), the Doctrine and Covenants (3 times), the Book of Mormon (39 times), the New Testament (1 time), and the Old Testament (80 times, but the Hebrew word *kpr* underlying the English word *atonement* appears 102 times). Each of these attestations adds to our understanding of the meaning, purpose, or significance of Jesus' atoning sacrifice.

The word *atonement* is a Middle English word that consists of three components—the preposition *at,* the number *one,* and the suffix *-ment.* During the Middle Ages, *one* sometimes served as a verb. For example, *to one, oned,* and *oneing* were all verbs that meant to unite or to make one. These verbs have fallen out of usage in modern times. The suffix *-ment,* which means "the state or condition of something," is still used in today's English, often added to verbs to make nouns. For example, enjoy*ment* is the state or condition of enjoying, amaze*ment* is the state of being amazed, and measure*ment* is the state of measuring (compare also improve*ment,* excite*ment,* treat*ment,* settle*ment,* and many others). Early English Bibles used the word *onement* to mean the state of being at one. In biblical usage, *onement* evolved into *at onement*[1] and then into *atonement,* a word that is used prominently today in English Bibles and religious writings regarding Jesus' divine sacrifice.

The English *atonement* and related words—*atone, atoned, atoneth, atoning*—specifically refer to the state or condition of becoming one with God. "*Atonement,*" explains Elder Boyd K. Packer, "is really three words: *At-one-ment,* meaning to set at one, one with God."[2] And Elder Jeffrey R. Holland explains: "The literal meaning of the word 'atonement' is self-evident: at-one-ment, the act of unifying or bringing together what has been separated and estranged. The atonement of Jesus Christ was indispensable because of the separating transgression, or fall, of Adam, which brought . . . both the physical and the spiritual death."[3]

There is more to the meaning of atonement, however, than becoming *at one* with God. As President Joseph Fielding Smith taught: "We often hear the word *atonement* defined as being 'at-one-ment' with God.

That is a very small part of it. In fact, *the great majority of mankind never becomes one with God, although they receive the atonement.* . . . We do not all become 'at one' with God, if we mean that we are brought back again and given the fulness of life which is promised to those who keep the commandments of God and become sons and daughters of God."[4] At-one-ment, then, suggests the ultimate blessing of the atonement; but there are many additional blessings that fall short of the ultimate. The Hebrew *kpr* sheds more light on the meaning of atonement (see chapters 3 and 6).

## Redeem, Redemption, and Redeemer

The English word *redeem,* derived from the Latin *redimere* (*re,* "back" or "again"; *emere,* "buy") means to "buy back; free . . . by payment; free by paying ransom."[5] *Redeem* is associated with the words *redeemer* and *redemption.* A redeemer is one who redeems, or buys back, freeing by payment; and redemption is the act of buying back or freeing by payment. In the scriptures, *redeem, redeemer,* and *redemption* are sometimes used in texts that describe legal situations. Here are four examples:

1. If a poverty-stricken Israelite sells his home or property to pay debts, his redeemer kinsman may redeem it (or buy it back) for the seller (Lev. 25:25–34; cf. Lev. 27; Jer. 32:6–7, wherein Jeremiah redeems his uncle's field).

2. If a poverty-stricken Israelite sells himself to become a servant or slave to pay a debt, a blood relative may redeem him or purchase him back to set him free (Lev. 25:39–55).

3. If a person accidentally or inadvertently kills another person, he flees for his life to one of six established Israelite cities called "cities of refuge." Meanwhile, one of the slain person's kin, called a "redeemer of blood" (which is a better Hebrew translation of the King James Version "revenger of blood"), pursues the manslayer with the intent to kill him, and this with the empowerment of the Mosaic law. If the manslayer reaches a city of refuge before the redeemer of blood overtakes him, he can live safely in the city of refuge (Num. 35; Deut. 19; Josh. 20).

4. The story of Ruth touches on legal arrangements involving redemption, or buying back (on Boaz and redemption, see chapter 6).

Each of these four examples has symbolic meanings that teach us about Jesus Christ, who is our Redeemer. For instance, example 2 above regarding the redeemer who buys back his poor relative who became a debt slave symbolizes Jesus Christ, who buys us back from being slaves to sin. The redeemer who buys back his poor relative pays with money, but the Redeemer who buys us back from being slaves to sin pays with his own blood.

Much more significant than the legal ramifications of *redeem* and *redemption* is the spiritual significance of *redeem*. This is because Jesus Christ himself is our great and all-powerful Redeemer. He is empowered to redeem us because of his own death and resurrection (Hel. 14:16–17)—he has "purchased [us] with his own blood" (Acts 20:28; cf. Ps. 74:2). The scriptures clearly testify of the incredible powers of Jesus, the Redeemer—he redeems us from hell (2 Ne. 33:6), from our sins and transgressions (Mosiah 15:12; Alma 5:21), from evil (Gen. 48:16), from physical death (Hosea 13:14), from violence and destruction (Ps. 72:14; 103:4), from spiritual death (Hel. 14:16), and from our enemies (Ps. 106:10; 107:2; Mic. 4:10). The Redeemer also redeems us from the fall, which brings us back to our "infant state, innocent before God" (D&C 93:38). As the Redeemer, the Lord also serves as our Advocate who pleads our cause. Israel's "Redeemer is strong; the Lord of hosts is his name: he shall throughly plead their cause" (Jer. 50:34; Prov. 23:11; Lam. 3:58).

Alma set forth the incalculable benefits of being redeemed by Jesus: "I have repented of my sins, and have been *redeemed* of the Lord; behold I am born of the Spirit. And the Lord said unto me: Marvel not that all mankind, yea, men and women, all nations, kindreds, tongues and people, must be born again; yea, born of God, changed from their carnal and fallen state, to a state of righteousness, being *redeemed* of God, becoming his sons and daughters. . . . My soul hath been *redeemed* from the gall of bitterness and bonds of iniquity. I was in the darkest abyss; but now I behold the marvelous light of God. My soul was racked with eternal torment; but I am snatched, and my soul is pained no more" (Mosiah 27:24–25, 29; emphasis added).

## SAVIOR

The terms *Savior, salvation,* and *save* are interrelated. *Savior* and *salvation* are derived from the Latin *salvare,* meaning "to save." The dictionary entry for the verb *save* includes the meaning "to rescue somebody or something from harm or danger."[6] This meaning is used in the Bible to refer to Christ's disciples who feared that they were going to drown: "And when [Jesus] was entered into a ship, his disciples followed him. And, behold, there arose a great tempest in the sea, insomuch that the ship was covered with the waves: but he was asleep. And his disciples came to him, and awoke him, saying, Lord, *save us:* we perish" (Matt. 8:23–25; emphasis added). The scriptures include numerous other examples of the verb *save* having reference to temporal safety (for example, Matt. 14:30; Mark 3:4; Acts 27:31, 43).

The scriptures also use the verb *save* in various spiritual ways: through the power of the resurrection, Jesus saves us from physical death; he also saves us from spiritual death, wherein we are separated from God's presence because of our sins. Matthew wrote regarding Mary, "And she shall bring forth a son, and thou shalt call his name Jesus: for he shall *save* his people from their sins" (Matt. 1:21; emphasis added). In view of the fact that Jesus saves us from sin and death, he is called our Savior. The Lord himself revealed to Isaiah, "I am . . . the Holy One of Israel, thy Savior" (Isa. 43:3) and to Joseph Smith, "I am Jesus Christ, the Savior" (D&C 43:34). Jesus Christ alone is the Savior; no one else has the authority or the entitlement to possess that responsibility. "Beside me there is no Savior" (Isa. 43:11; Mosiah 3:17; 5:8; D&C 18:23), the Lord revealed.

Elder David B. Haight provides this summary: "We learn from divine statements and truths contained in the scriptures of two great missions of the Master. The first was to atone and ransom mankind from the effects of the fall of Adam, as part of the plan accepted in the Grand Council in Heaven. *He is our Redeemer.* And he is also our Savior, for the Father sent his Son to be the Savior of the world and to bring salvation to all—to 'all who believe in his name.' 'To save that which was lost'—to save people from their sins—this is his second mission."[7]

## RECONCILIATION

The verb *reconcile,* related to the noun *reconciliation,* means "to bring again into friendly relations or agreement."[8] Reconciliation in the scriptures refers to people who are alienated from one another but who may reunite into positive relationships. Examples are an estranged wife and husband (1 Cor. 7:11) or a transgressing Church member (D&C 42:88; 46:4).

Reconciliation also refers to Jesus Christ's atoning work on behalf of all of us who have alienated ourselves from God through our iniquities. It is only through Jesus Christ that we can be reconciled to our Father. Jacob instructed his audience, "Wherefore, . . . be reconciled unto [God] through the atonement of Christ, his Only Begotten Son" (Jacob 4:11). Paul wrote regarding "the ministry of reconciliation" and made it clear that we may be reconciled to God through Jesus Christ: "And all things are of God, who hath reconciled us to himself by Jesus Christ, and hath given to us the ministry of reconciliation; to wit, that God was in Christ, reconciling the world unto himself, not imputing their trespasses unto them; and hath committed unto us the word of reconciliation" (2 Cor. 5:18–19). That Jesus' sacrifice is central to the doctrine of reconciliation is apparent by the following statement: "We were reconciled to God by the death of his Son" (Rom. 5:10).

Reconciliation to God is a commandment emphasized in the Book of Mormon: "reconcile yourselves to the will of God" (2 Ne. 10:24); "be reconciled to God" (2 Ne. 25:23). After we are reconciled to God, we are instructed to remember that "it is only in and through the grace of God that ye are saved" (2 Ne. 10:24; 25:23).

An understanding of the Latin root of *reconciliation* provides greater insights into the atonement. "*Reconciliation* comes from Latin roots *re,* meaning 'again'; *con,* meaning 'with'; and *sella,* meaning 'seat.' *Reconciliation,* therefore, literally means 'to sit again with.'"[9]

*Reconciliation* is related to the terms *conciliatory, conciliate, council,* and others. The word *council,* for instance has connections to reconciliation. It was during a premortal *council* that the Savior was chosen and the plan of salvation made. The Prophet Joseph Smith taught, "At the first organization in heaven we were all present, and saw the Savior chosen and appointed and the plan of salvation made, and we sanctioned it."[10] A central duty of members of the *Council* of the Twelve is to preach Jesus Christ and his gospel (1 Ne. 13:24; D&C 18:26–28; 27:12). And church *councils* on the stake and ward levels sometimes deal with repentant members who are working to re*concile* themselves to God.

## MEDIATOR

A *mediator* (from the Latin *medius,* "mid" or "middle"[11]) is one who comes between two sides to settle a dispute, or one who helps two sides reach an agreement and achieve reconciliation. Words related to mediator include *intermediary, intermediate, mediation,* and *mediate.* In modern times a mediator functions in social, economic, and political realms to settle disputes between parties; such a mediator may function in an official or unofficial capacity.

In the spiritual realm, our sins and uncleanness separate us from God, and we therefore need Jesus to be an intermediary to help us achieve at-one-ment with God. It is Jesus who stands and mediates our case before God. "For there is one God, and one mediator between God and men, the man Christ Jesus" (1 Tim. 2:5). Jesus himself taught in plain words: "No man cometh unto the Father, but by me" (John 14:6). Jesus is not at all similar to a commonplace go-between or mediator, of course; rather, he is the "great Mediator" (2 Ne. 2:27–28), "the mediator of a better covenant" (Heb. 8:6), and "the mediator of the new covenant" (Heb. 12:24; D&C 76:69; 107:19).

Only Jesus is authorized to serve as the great Mediator, and this is because he shed "his own blood" (D&C 76:69) and gave his life ("by means of death," Heb. 9:15). A number of extraordinary blessings are available to us because Jesus is the Mediator. For example, we "are free to choose liberty and eternal life, through the great Mediator of all men," or we may "choose captivity and death, according to the captivity and power of the devil" (2 Ne. 2:27). Another significant blessing pertains to the fact that we may be "made perfect through Jesus the mediator of the new covenant, who wrought out this perfect atonement through the shedding of his own blood" (D&C 76:69). A third blessing is identified in Jesus' great Intercessory Prayer to the Father, wherein he stated, "For their sakes I sanctify myself, that they also might be sanctified through the truth. . . . That they all may be one; as thou, Father, art in me, and I in thee, that they also may be one in us" (John 17:19, 21).

## PROPITIATION

*Propitiation* (related to the verb *to propitiate* or to "render propitious. . . favorable")[12] is used only three times in the scriptures, wherein it is stated that Jesus Christ is the "propitiation for our sins" (1 John 2:2; 4:10; cf. Rom. 3:25, where the King James Version has "propitiation" but the footnote reads "mercy seat"). As our *propitiation,* Jesus is the means whereby we who are sinners may obtain favor or grace before God. Some modern translations of the Bible prefer to use the words *atoning sacrifice* rather than *propitiation;* hence the New International Version of 1 John 2:2 reads that Jesus is the "atoning sacrifice for our sins."

## RANSOM

*Ransom* refers to "the redemption of a prisoner, slave, or kidnapped person, of captured goods, etc., for a price" and "the sum or price paid or demanded."[13] In ancient times, ransoms were paid to free prisoners, slaves, and others. Captain Moroni, for example, retained Lamanite prisoners to serve as a ransom in exchange for Nephite prisoners (Alma 52:8). With certain capital punishment cases under the law of Moses, the one sentenced to death could pay a ransom to save his life (Ex. 21:29–30). Also under the same law, the Lord commanded Moses that every man of Israel pay atonement money as "a ransom for his soul unto the Lord" and "to make an atonement for your souls." This ransom money protected the persons paying the money from having "plague among them"; it was also used to support "the service of the tabernacle" (Ex. 30:12, 16).

In another setting, *ransom* refers to Jesus Christ's atoning sacrifice, wherein he paid an astonishing price to free us from death and sin: the terrible sufferings in the Garden of Gethsemane and on the cross, culminating in the final price of his own life. Jesus Christ set us free when he spilled his precious blood. He testified that he "came not to be ministered unto, but to minister, and to give his life a ransom for many" (Matt. 20:28; see also 1 Tim. 2:6). Peter explained, "Forasmuch as ye know that ye were not redeemed with corruptible things, as silver and gold. . . . But with the precious blood of Christ, as of a lamb without blemish and without spot" (1 Pet. 1:18–19).

Jesus' ransom frees us from two conspicuous aspects of mortality—death and sin. Death is an unavoidable part of life. We are conscious of it as others pass away due to diseases, wars, accidents, and natural causes, and at some point each of us must experience death. Jesus paid the ransom to free us from death and its associated horrors. The Lord revealed, "I will ransom them from the power of the grave; I will redeem them from death: O death, I will be thy plagues; O grave, I will be thy destruction" (Hosea 13:14).

Just as death is unavoidable in mortality, so is sin. All of us, save Jesus only, have personally experienced sin (Rom. 6:23); and each of us is aware of the great sins, in terms of magnitude as well as quantity, committed by Heavenly Father's children in mortality. Jesus' divine sacrifice served as a ransom for our sins. Although we were "sold under sin" (Rom. 7:14), the Lord paid the price to set us free. "Ye are bought with a price," Paul wrote, "therefore glorify God in your body, and in your spirit, which are God's" (1 Cor. 6:20; cf. 1 Cor. 7:23).

President Joseph Fielding Smith summarized the meaning of Jesus Christ's ransom: "What did Christ do? He ransomed us. He restored us. He brought us back through his atonement, through the shedding of his blood. He paid the price, as Paul says. He rescued us from captivity and bondage. That is what ransomed means. He liberated us from death. He paid the price that death required; and we, through his redemption, were recovered by the payment of the shedding of his blood."[14] And Elder Bruce R. McConkie wrote clearly that "immortality is the ransom from temporal death; eternal life is the ransom from spiritual death. Both come by the grace of God. One comes as a free gift; the other is earned by obedience to the laws and ordinances of the gospel."[15]

## INTERCESSION

The verb *intercede* (from Latin *inter,* "between" and "in between," and *cedere,* "go")[16] means to intervene or come between two persons or parties with the goal of reconciling differences. Intercede is related to the words *intercessor, intercessory,* and *intercession.* In antiquity, individuals were intercessors for others in both temporal and spiritual matters (Jer. 7:16; 27:18; 36:25). Paul, for example, exhorted Christian believers to make "supplications, prayers, intercessions, and giving of thanks" for kings, authorities, and all men (1 Tim. 2:1–2). The prophets used *intercession* in significant ways when they taught that Jesus made intercession "for all the children of men" (2 Ne. 2:9; Mosiah 15:8; Rom. 8:26–27, 34; 11:2) through the power of the atonement, coming between us and our Father, from whom we have separated ourselves because of our sins.

Abinadi shows how the doctrine of intercession works. After Jesus was "crucified, and slain," he had "power to make intercession for the children of men—Having ascended into heaven, having the bowels of mercy; being filled with compassion towards the children of men; standing betwixt them and justice; having broken the bands of death, taken upon himself their iniquity and their transgressions, having redeemed them, and satisfied the demands of justice" (Mosiah 15:7–9). Jesus, because of his perfect compassion and mercy for us, took upon himself our sins. By doing so, he stood "betwixt [us] and justice."

Elder McConkie summarized just how the law of intercession impacts us: "Why is it that judgments are withheld and mercies are poured out—because of the Son? The answer is clear: He intercedes on man's behalf, advocating his cause in the courts above. 'He . . . made intercession for the transgressors.' (Isa. 53:12.) In the atonement that he wrought, he paid the penalty for the sins of men, on conditions of repentance, so that all might escape the judgments decreed for disobedience. In the same way and for the same reason, mercy replaces the justice that otherwise would impose the decreed judgments. Such is the law of intercession, a law that is valid and operative because of the atonement."[17]

# SATAN'S ATTEMPTS TO IMITATE THE ATONEMENT

To INCREASE THE NUMBER OF HIS OWN followers, and also to attempt to thwart God's divine plan of happiness, Satan throughout the ages has imitated the things of God. For example, during the Old Testament period Satan at times established false religions that were counterfeits to God's true religion. These false religions, which often belonged to the Israelites' neighboring nations, attracted many of the children of Israel because they appeared to be true religious systems. Satan's imitations included false and apostate temples with altars, corrupt priests, counterfeit sacred vestments, unholy sacrificial offerings, and more. His imitations also included false and apostate prophets, scripture-like texts, and doctrines, teachings, and laws that appeared to be hallowed. Satan's imitations of true religion also appealed to the carnal desires of humankind, and the imitations included things like temple prostitutes, the portrayal of unclothed idols with emphasis on body parts, and numerous other things that appealed to human sexual desires, greed, and power.

Beyond the false religions that belonged to different periods of the Old Testament, John in the book of Revelation listed a number of counterfeits that Satan has established in the past or will establish in the last days. Not all of these counterfeits apply directly to the atonement, but all are part of the overall pattern of Satan's attempts to deceive. These include the following examples (all references are to Revelation)[1]:

| God's Truths and Doctrines | Satan's Counterfeits |
|---|---|
| Seal of God (7:2–3) | Mark of the beast (13:16) |
| Christ, "Faithful and True Witness" (3:14) | Satan, deceitful serpent (12:9) |
| Virgin (the Church) | Harlot (Babylon) |
| Hosts of heaven, 100 million (5:11) | Armies of earth, 200 million (9:16) |
| Four angels of heaven (7:1) | Four angels of the abyss (9:14) |
| New Jerusalem | Babylon |
| Four living creatures in heaven (4:6) | Beasts of the earth |
| Temple in heaven | Great abyss |
| Number seven | Number 666 |
| Michael and his angels (12:7) | Satan and his angels (12:7) |
| Church of God | Church of the devil |
| Lamb of God (5:6, 12) | Beast with two horns like a lamb (13:11–13) |
| Christ was, is, and will be (1:4, 8) | "Beast that was, and is not, and yet is" (17:8) |
| Mark in forehead (7:3; 9:4; 14:1; 19:12; 20:4; 22:4) | Name on forehead (13:16–17; 14:9; 17:5) |
| Woman (12:1), bride, Lamb's wife (21:9) | Mother of harlots (17:5) |
| Righteous kings and priests (1:6) | Kings of the earth (18:9) |
| Heavenly harpers (14:2) | Worldly harpers and musicians (18:22) |
| White and pure linen of Lamb's wife (19:8) | Fine linen, purple, silk, scarlet, and riches of the worldly (18:12, 16) |
| Angels worship God day and night (7:15) | Satan accuses the Saints "day and night" (12:10) |

| God's Truths and Doctrines | Satan's Counterfeits |
| --- | --- |
| Slain Lamb (5:6, 12) | Wounded beast (13:3) |
| "Many crowns" of Jesus (19:12) | Ten crowns of the beast (13:1) |
| God gives power to two prophets (11:3) | Dragon gives power to the beast (13:2) |
| 144,000 virgins (14:3–4) | Those who consort with the mother of harlots and commit fornication (17:2, 5) |
| Colors associated with high priest | Colors associated with mother of harlots[2] |
| The bitter cup that Jesus drank | Golden cup of whore (17:4) |

There are many other examples of Satan's counterfeits in the world today—the fortune teller's crystal ball imitates the Urim and Thummin, false prophets mimic the Lord's prophets, false temples are copies of God's temples, clairvoyants impersonate God's seers, scripture-like texts imitate the revealed word of God, and lust and illicit sex are forgeries for true and eternal love. The devil makes counterfeits of anything that is "virtuous, lovely, or of good report or praiseworthy" (A of F 1:13), including gospel ordinances such as baptism and the Lord's sacrament, true worship, inspired music, prayer, the sanctity of marriage, feelings from the Holy Ghost, and much more.

Satan imitates gifts of the Spirit as well, including healing the sick, speaking in tongues, and appearing as an angel of light. Elder James E. Talmage wrote, "It may serve the dark purposes of Satan to play upon the human sense of goodness, even to the extent of healing the body."[3] The Prophet Joseph Smith explained, "The gift of tongues is so often made use of by Satan to deceive the Saints."[4] He added: "Again it may be asked, how it was that they could speak in tongues if they were of the devil! We would answer that they could be made to speak in another tongue, as well as their own, as they were under the control of that spirit, and the devil can tempt the Hottentot, the Turk, the Jew, or any other nation; and if these men were under the influence of his spirit, they of course could speak Hebrew, Latin, Greek, Italian, Dutch, or any other language that the devil knew."[5] The Prophet also taught, "The devil may appear as an angel of light."[6]

## Satan Produces Counterfeits for the Atonement

Inasmuch as the atonement of Jesus Christ is a core doctrine that affects all of God's children throughout all of his creations, Satan has worked over the ages to produce counterfeits to the atonement. Revelation 13 includes several such counterfeits.

This chapter refers to two beasts—earth's kingdoms, kings, or world powers (see JST Rev. 13:1).[7] The first beast has "ten crowns" (Rev. 13:1) on his head, imitating Jesus Christ, who has "many crowns" on his head and who is the "King of Kings, and Lord of Lords" (Rev. 19:12, 16). The dragon gave the first beast power and "great authority" (Rev. 13:2), mimicking the power and authority of Jesus Christ. The beast was "wounded to death; and his deadly wound was healed: and all the world wondered after the beast" (Rev. 13:3). This imitates Jesus, who was wounded and died in the great atoning sacrifice; and just as the world will wonder after the beast, many of earth's inhabitants marvel at Jesus Christ. The weapon that wounded the beast to death was none other than a sword (Rev. 13:14), which recalls the spear that pierced Jesus' side while he was on the cross. Just as the beast "did live" again after he was wounded to death (Rev. 13:14), so did Jesus live again after his sacrifice. The world "worshipped the dragon which gave power unto the beast: and they worshipped the beast" (Rev. 13:4), just as we worship the Father and the Son. This first beast is "scarlet colored" (Rev. 17:3; note also that the dragon, or Satan, is a "great red dragon," Rev. 12:3, 9), imitating Jesus' atoning blood and his red vestments at his Second Coming. The woman who sits upon the first beast has a "golden cup in her hand full of abominations and filthiness of her fornication" (Rev. 17:4), a counterfeit of the bitter cup that Jesus Christ drank during the atonement (Matt. 26:39; 3 Ne. 11:11; D&C 19:18).

How do we as disciples of Christ discern these counterfeits? John provided a number of clues. First, this beast is closely linked to blasphemy—"the name of blasphemy" is on his head, and he speaks blasphemies against God and against those who dwell in heaven (Rev. 13:1, 5–6). Second, he is a warmonger and makes war against the Saints (Rev. 13:4, 7). Third, his power is short-lived (Rev. 13:5), especially compared to God's eternal and infinite power.

The book of Revelation also mentions a second beast that imitates Jesus Christ and his atonement. It comes "out of the earth" (Rev. 13:11), imitating Jesus Christ, who came out of the earth at his resurrection; it has "two horns like a lamb" (Rev. 13:11), imitating Jesus, the Lamb of God who gave himself as a sacrifice (Rev. 5:6, 12). This beast "exerciseth all . . . power"—more power, in fact, than the first beast (Rev. 13:12), attempting to imitate Christ's infinite and eternal power. This second beast also "causeth the earth and them which dwell therein to worship the first beast" (Rev. 13:12), imitating Christ's desire that all worship the Father. The beast "doeth great wonders" (Rev. 13:13), imitating Christ's powers and miracles. One of his miracles is making "fire come down from heaven on the earth in the sight of men" (Rev. 13:13), imitating God's control over fire (Gen. 19:24; Ex. 13:21; 19:18; Dan. 3:25, and others) and all of earth's elements.

The second beast has "power to give life" (Rev. 13:15), imitating Christ's power to give life. The second beast causes people "to receive a mark in their right hand, or in their foreheads" (Rev. 13:16; 14:9; 17:5). This practice is counterfeit to the Saints' use of the right hand while making covenants with God; it also imitates the sealing of God's servants "in their foreheads" (Rev. 7:3; 9:4; 14:1; 19:12; 20:4; 22:4). The number of the beast, 666, imitates the number seven, which is associated with perfection and completion.

Other counterfeits have occurred historically, such as when Satan prompted the people of Abraham's time to take "unto themselves the washing of children, and the blood of sprinkling; and [to say] that the blood of the righteous Abel was shed for sins" (JST Gen. 17:6–7). Both the blood of sprinkling and the idea that Abel's blood was shed for sins are corrupt teachings, inspired by the devil. False prophets who wear "sheep's clothing" are also imitating Jesus Christ, who is the Lamb of

God. Jesus warned, "Beware of false prophets, which come to you in sheep's clothing, but inwardly they are ravening wolves" (Matt. 7:15).

False ordinances and religious creeds about God the Father, his Son, Jesus Christ, and the Holy Ghost are counterfeits to revealed truths. The false ordinances and creeds pretend to give people access to the blessings of the atonement but instead provide a false sense of security and thereby keep them from the truth.

How do we avoid the deception of Satan's counterfeits? King Benjamin taught that there are no other *means,* no other *conditions,* no other *names,* and no other *way* by which we may obtain salvation than through Jesus Christ's name and atonement:

"I say unto you, if ye have come to a knowledge of the goodness of God, and his matchless power, and his wisdom, and his patience, and his long-suffering towards the children of men; and also, the atonement which has been prepared from the foundation of the world, that thereby salvation might come to him that should put his trust in the Lord, and should be diligent in keeping his commandments, and continue in the faith even unto the end of his life, I mean the life of his mortal body— I say, that this is the man who receiveth salvation, through the atonement which was prepared from the foundation of the world for all mankind. . . . And this is the *means* whereby salvation cometh. And there is none other salvation save this which hath been spoken of; neither are there any *conditions* whereby man can be saved except the conditions which I have told you" (Mosiah 4:6–8; emphasis added).

Also, "there shall be no other *name* given nor any other *way* nor means whereby salvation can come unto the children of men, only in and through the name of Christ" (Mosiah 3:17; emphasis added; see also Mosiah 4:8; 5:8; Hel. 5:9). We must, therefore, conclude that the only way we can discern and withstand the counterfeits of Satan is through faith and obedience to our Savior, Jesus Christ.

# NOTES

## INTRODUCTION
### THE ATONEMENT, HINGE POINT OF GOD'S PLAN

1. Smith, *Teachings*, 121.
2. Romney, "Atonement of the Savior," 34.
3. McConkie, "Three Pillars of Eternity," 3.
4. Taylor, *Mediation and Atonement*, 123.
5. Nibley, *Approaching Zion*, 603.
6. Kimball, *Circles of Exaltation*, 8.
7. Scott, "To Establish a Secure Foundation for Life," 4–5.

## CHAPTER 1
### FROM FONT TO TEMPLE: MODERN ORDINANCES AND THE ATONEMENT

1. Packer, "Accomplishing the Mission of the Church"; see also Ballard, *Counseling with Our Councils*, 124.
2. Smith, *Teachings*, 367, 308.
3. Madsen, "Jesus, the Very Thought of Thee," 311.
4. Tvedtnes, "Symbolism of the Sacrament."
5. Widtsoe, "Temple Worship," 56.
6. Widtsoe, "Temple Worship," 63.
7. Skinner, *Temple Worship*, 47, 53.
8. Hanks, "Christ Manifested to His People," 18–23.
9. Read, "Jesus Christ, Types and Shadows of," in Ludlow et al., *Encyclopedia of Mormonism*, 2:745.
10. Richards, in Conference Report, April 1916, 53–54.

## CHAPTER 2
### FROM WATER CLEANSINGS TO THE VEIL:
### ANCIENT ORDINANCES AND THE ATONEMENT

1. McConkie, *Promised Messiah*, 28.
2. Nelson, "Personal Preparation for Temple Blessings," 32.

3. Livingstone, *Anatomy of the Sacred,* 98; Durkheim, "Elementary Forms of the Religious Life," 57.
4. It is difficult to ascertain who first coined the phrase "gestures of approach." Certainly it is now a common expression used by many. See, for example, Eliade, *Patterns in Comparative Religion,* 370–71, and Bokser, "Approaching Sacred Space," 279–80, 299.
5. The concept of the holy as being "wholly other" was introduced by Otto, *Idea of the Holy,* 25–30.
6. William W. Phelps, *Times and Seasons* 5 (Jan. 1, 1845): 758.
7. For various scriptural passages that deal with the laying on of hands, see LDS Topical Guide, "Hands, Laying on of," 196–97.
8. Durham, *Exodus,* 385. The subject of sacral priestly vestments is discussed on pages 384–90.
9. Nibley, *When the Lights Went Out,* 46–47; n. 78, "The resurrection itself is conceived as the putting on of a new garment."
10. Koehler and Baumgartner, *Hebrew and Aramaic Lexicon of the Old Testament,* 2:493–95; Douglas, "Atonement in Leviticus," 117–18.
11. See LDS Bible Dictionary, "Priests," 753.
12. Botterweck and Ringgren, *Theological Dictionary of the Old Testament,* 7:295.

## CHAPTER 3
### PRIESTS AND PURITY: THE LAW OF MOSES

1. LDS Bible Dictionary, "Sacrifices," 766.
2. Commenting on Exodus 29:37, Propp writes, "Anything touching the Altar absorbs sanctity, even a pot or garment" (*Exodus 19–40,* 470).
3. Although the word *atonement* is not mentioned in this passage (Lev. 13:47–59; 14:54–57), it is certainly implied; in addition, the passage is set in the context of several other chapters that pertain to the atonement.
4. Douglas, "Atonement in Leviticus," 117–18.
5. "There were apparently several types of leprosy, and the word is used in the Bible to designate other sicknesses or diseases" (LDS Bible Dictionary, "Leprosy," 724).
6. LDS Bible Dictionary, "Leper," 724.
7. Habershon, *Study of the Types,* 79.
8. Douglas, "Atonement in Leviticus," 124.
9. The rituals also included anointing and sprinkling of blood and oil, sacrificial offerings (lamb, doves, pigeons), sevenfold sprinkling, hyssop (a symbol of purification, Ps. 51:7; Num. 19:6, 18–20; Heb. 9:19–22), and the priest anointing the subject's right ear, thumb, and toe (Lev. 14:14).
10. Douglas, "Atonement in Leviticus," 117–18.

## CHAPTER 4
### PIERCED BREAD AND BLOOD: THE LAW OF SACRIFICE

1. Smith, *Teachings,* 58.
2. Smith, *Answers to Gospel Questions,* 1:188.
3. Jukes, *Law of the Offerings,* 44–45; emphasis in original.
4. LDS Bible Dictionary, "Sacrifices," 766.
5. See Topical Guide, "Excommunication," 130.

6. Kimball, "Jesus of Nazareth," 6.
7. Brown, Driver, and Briggs, *Hebrew and English Lexicon of the Old Testament*, 319.
8. John Taylor, *Deseret News Semi-Weekly*, Jan. 5, 1873, 760.
9. From the Hebrew adjective *katit*, "beaten," and the verb *ttk*, "to beat, crush by beating." Brown, Driver, and Briggs, *Hebrew and English Lexicon of the Old Testament*, 510.
10. Brown, Driver, and Briggs, *Hebrew and English Lexicon of the Old Testament*, 510.
11. Kimball, "Jesus of Nazareth," 5.
12. Ricks, "Law of Sacrifice," 25; emphasis in original.
13. Smith, *Doctrines of Salvation*, 1:126.
14. Douglas, "Atonement in Leviticus," 126.
15. Lund, in Conference Report, April 1912, 12.
16. Taylor, *Mediation and Atonement*, 135.
17. Smith, *Teachings*, 58.
18. Smith, *History of the Church*, 2:15; see also Heb. 9:22; Alma 5:21.
19. Personal correspondence with James Rose, MD, FAAP, Family Practitioner, and Cordell Bott, MD, FACP, Hematology/Oncology, May 19, 2008. Original in possession of Donald W. Parry.
20. Ibid.
21. Ibid.
22. Ibid.
23. Ibid.
24. Ibid.
25. Ibid.

## CHAPTER 5
### FEASTS, FASTS, AND FESTIVALS: HOLY DAYS ANTICIPATE JESUS' ATONEMENT

1. See also McConkie's comparison of the Passover with Jesus' sacrifice in *Promised Messiah*, 428–31.
2. McConkie, *Promised Messiah*, 435.

## CHAPER 6
### FROM ADAM TO JONAH: PEOPLE AS TYPES AND SHADOWS

1. McConkie, *Promised Messiah*, 451. Although in this passage Elder McConkie referred to "high priests of the Melchizedek Priesthood," his statement regarding "living, walking, breathing Messianic prophecies" could just as easily refer to all those who were types and shadows.
2. Holland, *Christ and the New Covenant*, 137.
3. Skinner, *Prophets, Priests, and Kings*, 8. In this excellent work, Skinner provides an in-depth treatment of Adam, Abel, Enoch, Noah, Melchizedek, Abraham, Isaac, Samuel, David, Elijah, and others who were types of Jesus Christ.
4. Holland, *Christ and the New Covenant*, 171–73. Elder Holland lists several ways that Abinadi served as a type and shadow of Jesus Christ.
5. Holland, *Trusting Jesus*, 58.
6. Joseph Smith, as quoted by Zebedee Coltrin in Smith, *Encyclopedia of Joseph Smith's Teachings*, 18.

7. For God as a *help*, see Ex. 18:2–4; Deut. 33:7, 26, 29; Ps. 20:1–2; 33:19–20; 70:1–2, 5; 89:19; 115:9–11; 121:1–2; 124:8; Hosea 13:9.

8. The meaning of *'ezer* in Daniel 11:34, with the Niphal verb and the impersonal subject, is ambiguous.

9. Smith, *Teachings,* 58.

10. Parts of this and the previous paragraph have been adapted from McConkie and Parry, *A Guide to Scriptural Symbols,* 71–72. For additional parallels between the life of Joseph and the life of Jesus, see McConkie, *Gospel Symbolism,* 30–36, and Skinner, *Prophets, Priests, and Kings,* 45–54.

11. Holland, *Christ and the New Covenant,* 137.

12. Brown, Driver, and Briggs, *Hebrew and English Lexicon of the Old Testament,* 602.

13. McConkie and Parry, *Guide to Scriptural Symbols,* 162–64.

14. Orson Pratt, *Journal of Discourses,* 2:342.

15. Packer, "Mediator," 56.

16. McConkie and Parry, *Guide to Scriptural Symbols,* 84.

17. McConkie, *Doctrinal New Testament Commentary,* 1:278.

## CHAPTER 7
### FROM NOAH'S ARK TO ABIGAIL'S OFFERING: SCRIPTURAL STORIES AND EVENTS THAT TESTIFY OF CHRIST

1. McConkie, *Promised Messiah,* 453; emphasis added.

## CHAPTER 8
### TOUCH AND TESTIMONY: SCRIPTURAL PATTERNS OF THE ATONEMENT

1. Matthew 1:5 mentions Rahab (or Rachab) as one of the female ancestors of Christ, although it is possible that this was a different Rahab. See Ludlow, *Companion to Your Study of the Old Testament,* 202; Rasmussen, *A Latter-day Saint Commentary on the Old Testament,* 196.

2. Benson, "Keeping Christ in Christmas," 4.

3. Macdonald, *Miracles of Our Lord,* 88–89.

4. The superscripts in this paragraph differentiate some of the men in the Book of Mormon who shared the same name. Nephi[1], for example, refers to the first Nephi we meet in the book. These superscripts correspond to those found in the index to the Book of Mormon (1981 edition).

## CHAPTER 9
### FROM THE LOST SHEEP TO THE UNMERCIFUL SERVANT: PARABLES OF THE ATONEMENT

1. For further background and insight into the parables discussed in this chapter, see Parry and Parry, *Understanding the Parables of Jesus Christ.*

2. Hafen, *Broken Heart,* 60.

3. Hinckley, *Be Thou an Example,* 51.

4. Hunter, *Teachings,* 33.

## CHAPTER 10
### ANGELS' FOOD, SCARLET, AND ALMONDS: THINGS THAT BEAR WITNESS OF CHIRST

1. Taylor, *Mediation and Atonement,* 123.
2. Bullinger, *Number in Scripture,* 266.
3. For additional reading on manna as a symbol of Jesus, see McConkie, *Promised Messiah,* 397–99.
4. Note that parts of the following temple components are adapted from McConkie and Parry, *Guide to Scriptural Symbols,* 13–14, 66, 76, 82–83, 94, 100, 105.
5. Brown, Driver, and Briggs, *Hebrew and English Lexicon of the Old Testament,* 1052.
6. Maxwell, *Even As I Am,* 120.
7. Durham, *Exodus,* 385. The author discusses the subject of sacral priestly vestments on pages 384–90.
8. McConkie and Parry, *Guide to Scriptural Symbols,* 47.

## CHAPTER 11
### THE LION AND THE LAMB: THE ATONEMENT SYMBOLISM OF ANIMALS

1. Taylor, *Mediation and Atonement,* 146; emphasis added.
2. Heber C. Kimball, *Journal of Discourses,* 5:137.
3. Smith, *History of the Church,* 5:343–44.
4. Fee and Stuart, *How to Read the Bible for All It's Worth,* 177–78.
5. Fee and Stuart, *How to Read the Bible for All It's Worth,* 177–78.
6. Parry and Parry, *Understanding the Book of Revelation,* 69.
7. For the bronze serpent as a type of Jesus, see McConkie, *Promised Messiah,* 399–402. For the serpent as a type of Jesus, see Skinner, "Savior, Satan, and Serpent," 359–84.

## CHAPTER 12
### FROM STONES TO STARS: THE TESTIMONY OF EARTH AND SKY

1. Eyring, *Faith of a Scientist,* 126; emphasis added.
2. Read, "All Things Testify of Him," 7.
3. For other references to Christ as the source of living water, see Ps. 42:1–2; 63:1; 110:3; Isa. 55:1–3; Rev. 21:6; 22:17; Alma 5:34; 42:26–27.
4. See McConkie and Parry, *Guide to Scriptural Symbols,* 104.
5. Madsen, "Olive Press," 57.
6. See Parry and Parry, *Understanding the Parables of Jesus Christ.*
7. Nibley, *Approaching Zion,* 603.
8. See "Venus," www.wikipedia.org; http://kepler.nasa.gov/ed/pdf/Morning-Evening Star.pdf.
9. Hinckley, "We Testify of Jesus Christ," 7.
10. Nibley, *Old Testament and Related Studies,* 37–39.
11. Nibley, *Enoch the Prophet,* 49.
12. "Eudoxus-of-Cnidus," http://www.britannica.com.
13. For early studies of the relationship of the gospel to the constellations, see Rolleston, *Mazzaroth;* Seiss, *Gospel in the Stars;* Bullinger, *Witness of the Stars.* For the point of view of an LDS astronomer, see John P. Pratt, "Enoch's Constellations Testify of Christ"; "The Constellations Testify of Christ"; and "What Every Mormon Should Know about Astronomy." Pratt's arguments are admittedly speculative, but they do provide a fascinating perspective that might have some validity.

## CHAPTER 13
### THE MAN OF SORROWS: PROPHECIES OF CHRIST'S MORTAL MINISTRY AND ATONEMENT

1. For various prophecies regarding Jesus Christ, see McConkie, *Promised Messiah,* 22–97.
2. Smith, *Teachings,* 121.

## CHAPTER 14
### WALKING ON WATER AND OTHER MIRACLES: WITNESSES OF ATONING POWER

1. Hunter, "Reading the Scriptures," 65.
2. Satterfield, "I Am the Bread of Life."
3. Valletta, "True Bread of Life," 9.
4. Lee, "Truly All Things Testify of Him," 108–9.
5. Lee, "Truly All Things Testify of Him," 111.

## CHAPTER 15
### SON OF GOD, SON OF MAN: A LIFE OF CONTRADICTIONS

1. Smith, *Lectures on Faith,* 5:2.
2. See LDS edition of the Bible, Heb. 12:3, n. 3a.
3. Parley P. Pratt, "Jesus, Once of Humble Birth," *Hymns,* no. 196.
4. Bunker, "Ultimate Paradox," 10; a number of the contrasts in the table in this chapter were suggested by this address.
5. Maxwell, "Irony," 63–64.

## CHAPTER 16
### DRINKING THE BITTER CUP: GETHSEMANE

1. Phillips Brooks, "O Little Town of Bethlehem," *Hymns,* no. 208.
2. Smith, *Dictionary of the Bible,* 54.
3. Since the Kidron is a wadi, water does not flow down it year round. However, inasmuch as John called it a "brook" (John 18:1), it's clear that it held running water when Jesus crossed it. Further, when Alfred Edersheim visited the Holy Land at Passover in preparation for his book, he found that the brook had "swelled into a winter torrent" (*Life and Times of Jesus the Messiah,* 2:533; see also Ball, "Gethsemane," 146).
4. Parry, "Garden of Eden," 126–27. For further discussion of the characteristics of the temples of the ancient Near East, see Lundquist, "The Common Temple Ideology of the Ancient Near East," 83–118.
5. Madsen, "Olive Press," 57; emphasis added.
6. Skinner, *Gethsemane,* 117–18.
7. Parry, Parry, and Peterson, *Understanding Isaiah,* 554–55.
8. Brigham Young, *Journal of Discourses,* 3:206.
9. Murphy-O'Connor, "What Really Happened at Gethsemane," 36.
10. Skinner, *Gethsemane,* 58.
11. Taylor, *Mediation and Atonement,* 146–47.
12. Talmage, *Jesus the Christ,* 613.
13. Romney, in Conference Report, October 1953, 35; emphasis added.
14. Maxwell, "Willing to Submit," 73; paragraphing altered.

15. Holland, *Christ and the New Covenant*, 92, 223–24.
16. Robinson, *Believing Christ*, 122–23.
17. Whitney, *Saturday Night Thoughts*, 152.
18. Packer, "Atonement, Agency, Accountability," 69.
19. Talmage, *Jesus the Christ*, 613.
20. Taylor, *Mediation and Atonement*, 147.
21. Packer, "Atonement, Agency, Accountability," 69.
22. Talmage, *Jesus the Christ*, 613.
23. Talmage, *Jesus the Christ*, 613–14.
24. Haight, "The Sacrament—and the Sacrifice," 60.
25. For a powerful modern witness of Christ's solitary offering, see Jeffrey R. Holland, "None Were with Him," *Ensign*, May 2009, 86–88.
26. Matthews, "The Atonement of Jesus Christ," 190. Also see Skinner, *Gethsemane*, 72–73, where he writes of Jesus, "The things he had to experience included spiritual death, the withdrawal of the Father and the removal of his immediate influence (which experience later returned to the Savior as he hung on the cross)—in truth, the atmosphere of hell itself."
27. The Joseph Smith Translation clarifies that this specific verse applies to Melchizedek. However, since the passage is designed to show that Melchizedek was a powerful type of Christ, it seems justifiable to apply these words to Christ, which is one possible reading of the King James Version (see Holzapfel, "Early Accounts of the Story," 411, note 18).
28. Placide Cappeau, trans. John Sullivan Dwight, "O Holy Night," http://www.hymnsand carolsofchristmas.com/Hymns_and_Carols/o_holy_night.htm.

## CHAPTER 17
### THE CRUEL CROSS: THE CRUCIFIXION

1. Ballard, *Sermons and Missionary Services*, 152–55.
2. Skinner, *Golgotha*, 17.
3. McConkie, "Purifying Power of Gethsemane," 9. This detail about the arrest of Jesus is not found in the Gospel accounts and must therefore be ascribed to the prophetic understanding of one whom we sustained as prophet, seer, and revelator.
4. This council may have been the Sanhedrin, although it is impossible to know for certain; there were a number of ruling councils in Jerusalem in the time of Jesus. See Skinner, *Golgotha*, 38–39.
5. Talmage, *Jesus the Christ*, 626.
6. Kimball, "Jesus of Nazareth," 5–6.
7. Farrar, *Life of Christ*, quoted in McConkie, *Doctrinal New Testament Commentary*, 1:816.
8. Quoted in McConkie, *Doctrinal New Testament Commentary*, 1:814.
9. Smith, *Teachings*, 309.
10. Skinner, *Golgotha*, 148.
11. Jackson, "Crucifixion," 332.
12. Skinner, *Golgotha*, 148; see also Talmage, *Jesus the Christ*, 661.
13. This incident is sometimes conflated with an earlier one that occurred immediately before Jesus was placed on the cross. There Jesus was offered "wine mingled with myrrh: but he received it not" (Mark 15:23). Matthew records this same earlier incident, but

"wine" there is mistranslated as "vinegar" (Matt. 27:34). For a discussion of the two times Jesus was offered liquid, see Jackson, "Crucifixion," 324–25, 330.

14. McConkie, *Mortal Messiah*, 4:232, n. 22.
15. Taylor, *Mediation and Atonement*, 148–49.
16. Holland, "Teaching, Preaching, Healing," 42.
17. Holland, "I Stand All Amazed," 68.
18. McConkie, "Purifying Power of Gethsemane," 11.
19. Hinckley, "Symbol of Christ," 93.

## CHAPTER 18
### "HANDLE ME AND SEE": THE RESURRECTION

1. The atonement performed in the Garden of Gethsemane, which was a necessary prerequisite of Christ's resurrection, was the greatest *private* manifestation of God's power since the creation of the earth.
2. Holland, *Christ and the New Covenant*, 238.
3. Hinckley, "Empty Tomb Bore Testimony," 66.
4. Young, *Discourses of Brigham Young*, 374.
5. Penrose, "The First-Born, the Resurrection, and the Life," 754.
6. Lee, *Ye Are the Light of the World*, 260.
7. Penrose, "The First-Born, the Resurrection, and the Life," 754.
8. McConkie, *Mormon Doctrine*, 711–12.
9. The superscripts in this paragraph differentiate some of the men in the Book of Mormon who shared the same name. Nephi[1], for example, refers to the first Nephi we meet in the book. These superscripts correspond to those found in the index to the Book of Mormon (1981 edition).
10. Nephi[3] is the third Nephi referenced in the Book of Mormon. The superscript corresponds to that found in the index to the Book of Mormon (1981 edition).
11. Holland, *Christ and the New Covenant*, 244.

## CHAPTER 19
### THE LIMITLESS ATONEMENT: ITS MAGNITUDE, POWER, AND SCOPE

1. Smith, *Millennial Star*, 4:49–55; *Times and Seasons* 4 (Feb. 1, 1843): 82–85.
2. McConkie, "Christ and the Creation," 10.
3. Smith, *Answers to Gospel Questions*, 2:133.
4. Nelson, *Perfection Pending*, 167.
5. Smith, *Doctrines of Salvation*, 1:138.
6. Smith, *Doctrines of Salvation*, 1:74.
7. Parley P. Pratt, *Journal of Discourses*, 3:315.
8. Young, *Discourses of Brigham Young*, 21.
9. Smith, *History of the Church*, 5:343.
10. See discussion in Parry and Parry, *Understanding the Book of Revelation*, 73.
11. Smith, *Words of Joseph Smith*, 190; capitalization and punctuation standardized.
12. Young, *Discourses of Brigham Young*, 388.
13. Brigham Young, *Journal of Discourses*, 3:315–16.
14. Young, *Discourses of Brigham Young*, 27.
15. Nelson, "Standards of the Lord's Standard-Bearers," 6.

16. Smith, *Teachings,* 181.
17. There is, of course, a sin that is unforgivable, but to commit that sin we must purposely and knowingly choose to reject the atonement (see, for example, D&C 76:31–38).
18. Packer, "The Brilliant Morning of Forgiveness," 20.
19. Maxwell, "Willing to Submit," 73.
20. Faust, *Reach Up for the Light,* 132.
21. Hinckley, *Teachings of Gordon B. Hinckley,* 28.

## CHAPTER 20
### ALL THIS FOR ME? PARTAKING OF CHRIST'S MARVELOUS GRACE

1. *True to the Faith,* 78; emphasis added.
2. Robert Robinson, "Come, Thou Fount of Every Blessing," http://www.cyberhymnal.org/htm/c/o/comethou.htm.
3. *True to the Faith,* 78.
4. LDS Bible Dictionary, "Grace," 697.
5. Faust, "The Supernal Gift of the Atonement," 13.
6. Maxwell, *"Not My Will, But Thine,"* 51.
7. Robert Keen, "How Firm a Foundation," *Hymns,* no. 85.
8. Hafen, *Broken Heart,* 20.
9. Hafen and Hafen, *Belonging Heart,* 153.
10. Millet, *By Grace Are We Saved,* 19, 86.
11. Henry F. Lyte, "Abide with Me," *Hymns,* no. 166.
12. Benson, *Teachings of Ezra Taft Benson,* 372; emphasis added.
13. Hinckley, "If Thou Art Faithful," 91; emphasis added.
14. Eyring, "Rise to Your Call," 76–78.
15. McConkie, *Seeking the Spirit,* 57.
16. Featherstone, *Incomparable Christ,* 11–12.
17. Hafen, "Restored Doctrine of the Atonement," 12.
18. Packer, "Brilliant Morning of Forgiveness," 19–20.
19. Scott, "Jesus Christ, Our Redeemer," 54.
20. Thomas, *Selected Writings,* 189–90; emphasis in original.
21. Bednar, "Clean Hands and a Pure Heart," 82; emphasis in original.

## CHAPTER 21
### THE UNIQUENESS OF CHRIST: ATTRIBUTES AND
### CHARACTERISTICS OF THE REDEEMER

1. See, for example, Smith, *Teachings,* 220; Petersen, "Creator and Savior," 63; Holland, *Christ and the New Covenant,* 25; Matthews, *Behold the Messiah,* 74; Skinner, "Jacob: Keeper of Covenants," 52.
2. Since this book focuses on the many witnesses of Christ, it is valuable to note that the mythology of many cultures can be included as an unwitting witness of the Savior. The truth about God and his plan was revealed to Adam and passed from father to son through the generations. But over the millennia, particularly in times and places of apostasy, the truth became corrupted. For instance, a number of mythological stories tell of God fathering a mortal son who then did mighty works on earth. Other stories recount the heroic exploits of sons of God who saved their people, often at the sacrifice of their own

lives. For instance, in Norse mythology Odin, the chief god, gained essential knowledge by hanging himself as a sacrifice on the World Tree, Yggdrasill. The Hindu *Rig-Veda* (10:80) tells us that the Primal Man, the ruler and source of all, allowed himself to be sacrificed so that all else could come into existence. The Greeks and Romans, the Egyptians, the Aztecs, and others all had myths of a god being sacrificed, all of which were perversions and corruptions of the revealed truth from God about his own Son, Jesus Christ. Some stories then pointedly tell us of the resurrection of the hero after his death.

3. Maxwell, "O, How Great the Plan of Our God," in *Neal A. Maxwell Quote Book*, 37.
4. Holland, "Teaching, Preaching, Healing," 42; emphasis in original.

## CHAPTER 22
### LOVE, POWER, AND SACRIFICE: KEYS TO THE ATONEMENT

1. Benson, "Jesus Christ: Our Savior and Redeemer," 6–7; emphasis in original.
2. Benson, "Jesus Christ: Our Savior and Redeemer," 6; emphasis in original.
3. Benson, *Come unto Christ*, 7.
4. Hunter, "He Is Risen," 16–17.

## CHAPTER 23
### FOREVER LOST: CALAMITOUS CONSEQUENCES WITHOUT THE ATONEMENT

1. McConkie, "The Atonement," 1.
2. Maxwell, "All Hell Is Moved," 7.
3. Smith, *Doctrines of Salvation*, 1:126–27.
4. Smith, *Answers to Gospel Questions*, 2:138.
5. Romney, in Conference Report, October 1953, 34–35.
6. Young, *Discourses of Brigham Young*, 27.
7. Webster, *American Dictionary of the English Language*, "Lost."
8. LDS Bible Dictionary, "Abaddon," 600. The Hebrew root of Abaddon (*abad*) also denotes "destruction."

## CHAPTER 24
### MAKING IT OURS: PERSONALIZING THE ATONEMENT

1. Skinner, *Prophets, Priests, and Kings*, 136–37.
2. Whitney, *Through Memory's Halls*, 82–83.

## CHAPTER 25
### "I CANNOT SAY THE SMALLEST PART": AN APPRECIATION FOR THE ATONEMENT

1. Holland, *However Long and Hard the Road*, 24.
2. Smith, *Personal Writings of Joseph Smith*, 21; spelling and punctuation are standardized.
3. Hinckley, "The Father, Son, and Holy Ghost," 51.

## APPENDIX 1
### FROM RANSOM TO MEDIATOR: ATONEMENT WORDS AND MEANINGS

1. For the early history of "onement" and "at onement," see *Oxford English Dictionary*, "atonement." English *at-one-ment* can be traced to the sixteenth century, first appearing as "at onement" (Bromiley, *International Standard Bible Encyclopedia*, 1:352).

2. Packer, "Atonement, Agency, Accountability," 69; emphasis in original.

3. Holland, "Atonement of Jesus Christ," 1:83.

4. Smith, *Doctrines of Salvation,* 1:125; *Church News,* Mar. 9, 1935, 6.

5. Onions, *Oxford Dictionary of English Etymology,* "redeem," 748.

6. *Encarta World English Dictionary,* "save," 1595.

7. Haight, "Uttermost Part of the Earth," 165; emphasis in original.

8. Onions, *Oxford Dictionary of English Etymology,* "reconcile," 747.

9. Nelson, "Atonement," 34; see also Nibley, *Approaching Zion,* 556, 559.

10. Smith, *Teachings,* 181; see also Abraham 3:22–28; Topical Guide, "Council in Heaven," 77.

11. Onions, *Oxford Dictionary of English Etymology,* "mediate," 566.

12. Onions, *Oxford Dictionary of English Etymology,* "propitiate," 716.

13. *Random House Webster's Unabridged Dictionary,* "ransom," 1600.

14. Smith, *Doctrines of Salvation,* 1:124.

15. McConkie, *New Witness for the Articles of Faith,* 152.

16. Onions, *Oxford Dictionary of English Etymology,* "intercede," 480.

17. McConkie, *Promised Messiah,* 329.

## APPENDIX 2
### SATAN'S ATTEMPTS TO IMITATE THE ATONEMENT

1. Adapted from Parry and Parry, *Understanding the Book of Revelation,* 312–14.

2. Parry and Parry, *Understanding the Book of Revelation,* 221–22.

3. Talmage, *Articles of Faith,* 232.

4. Smith, *History of the Church,* 2:141.

5. Smith, *History of the Church,* 4:579; see also 3:392.

6. Smith, *History of the Church,* 3:392.

7. See Parry and Parry, *Understanding the Book of Revelation,* 162–77.

# SOURCES

Ball, Terry B. "Gethsemane." In *From the Last Supper through the Resurrection.* Edited by Richard Neitzel Holzapfel and Thomas A. Wayment. Salt Lake City: Deseret Book, 2003.

Ballard, Melvin J. *Sermons and Missionary Services of Melvin Joseph Ballard.* Compiled by Bryant S. Hinckley. Salt Lake City: Deseret Book, 1949.

Ballard, M. Russell. *Counseling with Our Councils.* Salt Lake City: Deseret Book, 1997.

Bednar, David A. "Clean Hands and a Pure Heart." *Ensign,* November 2007, 80–83.

Benson, Ezra Taft. *Come unto Christ.* Salt Lake City: Deseret Book, 1983.

———. "Jesus Christ: Our Savior and Redeemer." *Ensign,* November 1983, 6–8.

———. "Keeping Christ in Christmas." *Ensign,* December 1993, 2–5.

———. *The Teachings of Ezra Taft Benson.* Salt Lake City: Bookcraft, 1988.

Bokser, Baruch M. "Approaching Sacred Space." *Harvard Theological Review* 78, nos. 3–4 (1985): 279–80, 299.

Botterweck, G. Johannes, and Helmer Ringgren. *Theological Dictionary of the Old Testament.* 15 vols. Grand Rapids, Mich.: Eerdmans, 1974–2007.

Bromiley, Geoffrey W., ed. *The International Standard Bible Encyclopedia.* 4 vols. Grand Rapids, Mich.: Eerdmans, 1979–88.

Brown, Francis, S. R. Driver, and Charles A. Briggs. *A Hebrew and English Lexicon of the Old Testament.* Translated by Edward Robinson. Oxford: Clarendon Press, 1977.

Bullinger, Ethelbert W. *Number in Scripture.* Grand Rapids, Mich.: Kregel, 1967.

———. *The Witness of the Stars.* London, n.p., 1893.

Bunker, Gary L. "The Ultimate Paradox." Brigham Young University Speeches of the Year, Provo, Utah, 1994, Address delivered 1 March 1994. Available at http://speeches.byu.edu.

Cappeau, Placide. "O Holy Night," translated by John Sullivan Dwight. Available at http://www.hymnsandcarolsofchristmas.com/Hymns_and_Carols/o_holy_night.htm

*Church News.* Salt Lake City, 1931–present.

Conference Reports of The Church of Jesus Christ of Latter-day Saints. Salt Lake City: The Church of Jesus Christ of Latter-day Saints, 1898–present.

*Deseret News Semi-Weekly.* Salt Lake City, 1865–1922.

Douglas, Mary. "Atonement in Leviticus." *Jewish Studies Quarterly* 1 (1993–94): 109–30.

Durham, John I. *Exodus*. Vol. 3 of *Word Biblical Commentary*. Waco, Texas: Word Books, 1987.

Durkheim, Émile. "The Elementary Forms of the Religious Life." In *Reader in Comparative Religion. An Anthropological Approach*. Edited by William A. Lessa and Evon Z. Vogt, 56–65. 2d ed. New York: Harper and Row, 1965.

Edersheim, Alfred. *The Life and Times of Jesus the Messiah*. 2 vols. Grand Rapids, Mich.: Eerdmans, 1950.

Eliade, Mircea. *Patterns in Comparative Religion*. Translated by Rosemary Sheed. New York: New American Library, 1958.

*Encarta World English Dictionary*. New York: St. Martin's Press, 1999.

*Ensign*. Salt Lake City: The Church of Jesus Christ of Latter-day Saints, 1971–.

Eyring, Henry. *Faith of a Scientist*. Salt Lake City: Bookcraft, 1967.

Eyring, Henry B. "Rise to Your Call." *Ensign*, November 2002, 75–78.

Farrar, Frederic W. *The Life of Christ*. Portland, Oreg.: Fountain Publications, 1980.

Faust, James E. *Reach Up for the Light*. Salt Lake City: Deseret Book, 1990.

———. "The Supernal Gift of the Atonement." *Ensign*, November 1988, 12–14.

Featherstone, Vaughn J. *The Incomparable Christ: Our Master and Model*. Salt Lake City: Deseret Book, 1995.

Fee, Gordon D., and Douglas Stuart. *How to Read the Bible for All It's Worth*. Grand Rapids, Mich.: Zondervan, 2003.

Habershon, Ada R. *The Study of the Types*. Grand Rapids, Mich.: Kregel, 1997.

Hafen, Bruce C. *The Broken Heart: Applying the Atonement to Life's Experience*. Salt Lake City: Deseret Book, 1989.

———. "The Restored Doctrine of the Atonement." *Ensign*, December 1993, 6–13.

Hafen, Bruce C., and Marie K. Hafen. *The Belonging Heart: The Atonement and Relationships with God and Family*. Salt Lake City: Deseret Book, 1994.

Haight, David B. "The Sacrament—and the Sacrifice." *Ensign*, November 1989, 59–61.

———. "The Uttermost Part of the Earth." In *Brigham Young University Speeches of the Year, 1978*, 165–70. Provo, Utah: Brigham Young University Press, 1979.

Hanks, Marion D. "Christ Manifested to His People." In *Temples of the Ancient World: Ritual and Symbolism*. Edited by Donald W. Parry. Salt Lake City and Provo: Deseret Book and FARMS, 1994.

Hinckley, Gordon B. *Be Thou an Example*. Salt Lake City: Deseret Book, 1981.

———. "The Empty Tomb Bore Testimony." *Ensign*, May 1988, 65–68.

———. "The Father, Son, and Holy Ghost." *Ensign*, November 1986, 49–51.

———. "If Thou Art Faithful." *Ensign*, November 1984, 89–92.

———. "In These Three I Believe," *Ensign*, July 2006, 2-8.

———. "The Symbol of Christ." *Ensign*, May 1975, 92–94.

———. *Teachings of Gordon B. Hinckley*. Salt Lake City: Deseret Book, 1997.

———. "We Testify of Jesus Christ." *Ensign*, March 2008, 4–7.

Holland, Jeffrey R. "Atonement of Jesus Christ." In *Encyclopedia of Mormonism*. Edited by Daniel H. Ludlow. 5 vols. New York: Macmillan, 1992.

———. *Christ and the New Covenant: The Messianic Message of the Book of Mormon*. Salt Lake City: Deseret Book, 1997.

———. *However Long and Hard the Road*. Salt Lake City: Deseret Book, 1985.

———. "I Stand All Amazed." *Ensign*, August 1986, 68–73.

———. "None Were with Him." *Ensign*, May 2009, 86–88.

———. "Teaching, Preaching, Healing." *Ensign*, January 2003, 32–42.

————. *Trusting Jesus.* Salt Lake City: Deseret Book, 2003.

————. "Whom Say Ye That I Am?" *Ensign,* September 1974, 6–11.

Holy Bible. Authorized King James Version. Salt Lake City: The Church of Jesus Christ of Latter-day Saints, 1979.

Holzapfel, Richard Neitzel. "Early Accounts of the Story." In *From the Last Supper through the Resurrection: The Savior's Final Hours.* Edited by Richard Neitzel Holzapfel and Thomas A. Wayment, 401–21. Salt Lake City: Deseret Book, 2003.

Hunter, Howard W. "He Is Risen." *Ensign,* May 1988, 16–17.

————. "Reading the Scriptures." *Ensign,* November 1979, 64–65.

————. *Teachings of Howard W. Hunter.* Edited by Clyde J. Williams. Salt Lake City: Bookcraft, 1998.

*Hymns of The Church of Jesus Christ of Latter-day Saints.* Salt Lake City: The Church of Jesus Christ of Latter-day Saints, 1985.

Jackson, Kent P. "The Crucifixion." In *From the Last Supper through the Resurrection: The Savior's Final Hours.* Edited by Richard Neitzel Holzapfel and Thomas A. Wayment. Salt Lake City: Deseret Book, 2003.

*Journal of Discourses.* 26 vols. London: Latter-day Saints' Book Depot, 1854–86.

Jukes, Andrew. *The Law of the Offerings.* Grand Rapids, Mich: Kregel, 1966.

Kimball, Spencer W. "Circles of Exaltation." Address to religious educators, Brigham Young University, Provo, Utah, 28 June 1968, 1–8.

————. "Jesus of Nazareth." *Ensign,* December 1984, 2–7.

Koehler, Ludwig, and Walter Baumgartner. *The Hebrew and Aramaic Lexicon of the Old Testament.* 5 vols. Leiden, The Netherlands: E. J. Brill, 1995.

Lee, Harold B. *Ye Are the Light of the World: Selected Sermons and Writings of Harold B. Lee.* Salt Lake City: Deseret Book, 1974.

Lee, Robert England. "Truly All Things Testify of Him." In *Lord of the Gospels: The 1990 Sperry Symposium on the New Testament.* Edited by Bruce A. Van Orden and Brent L. Top, 99–111. Salt Lake City: Deseret Book, 1991.

Livingstone, James C. *Anatomy of the Sacred.* New York: Macmillan, 1989.

Ludlow, Daniel H. *A Companion to Your Study of the Old Testament.* Salt Lake City: Deseret Book, 1981.

Ludlow, Daniel H., et al., ed. *Encyclopedia of Mormonism.* 5 vols. New York: Macmillan, 1992.

Lund, Anthon H. In Conference Report, April 1912, 10–13.

Lundquist, John M. "The Common Temple Ideology of the Ancient Near East." In *The Temple in Antiquity: Ancient Records and Modern Perspectives.* Edited by Truman G. Madsen, 83–118. Provo, Utah: BYU Religious Studies Center, 1984.

Macdonald, George. *The Miracles of Our Lord.* London: Strahan & Co., 1870. Available at http://books.google.com.

Madsen, Ann N. "Jesus, the Very Thought of Thee." In *Every Good Thing: Talks from the 1997 BYU Women's Conference.* Edited by Dawn Hall Anderson, Susette Fletcher Green, and Dlora Hall Dalton, 301–17. Salt Lake City: Deseret Book, 1998.

Madsen, Truman G. "The Olive Press." *Ensign,* December 1982, 57–62.

Matthews, Robert J. "The Atonement of Jesus Christ: 2 Nephi 9." In *The Book of Mormon: Second Nephi: The Doctrinal Structure. Papers from the Third Annual Book of Mormon Symposium.* Edited by Monte S. Nyman and Charles D. Tate Jr., 179–99. Provo, Utah: BYU Religious Studies Center, 1989.

————. *Behold the Messiah.* Salt Lake City: Bookcraft, 1994.

Maxwell, Neal A. "All Hell Is Moved." Brigham Young University Speeches of the Year, Provo, Utah, 8 November 1977. Available at http://speeches.byu.edu.

———. *Even As I Am.* Salt Lake City: Deseret Book, 1982.

———. "Irony: The Crust on the Bread of Adversity." *Ensign,* May 1989, 62–64.

———. *"Not My Will, But Thine."* Salt Lake City: Bookcraft, 1998.

———. "O, How Great the Plan of Our God." Church Educational System Fireside, February 3, 1995. In *The Neal A. Maxwell Quote Book.* Edited by Cory H. Maxwell. Salt Lake City: Bookcraft, 1997.

———. "Willing to Submit." *Ensign,* May 1985, 70–73.

McConkie, Bruce R. *The Atonement.* Brigham Young University Speeches of the Year. Provo, Utah, 6 May 1953.

———. "Christ and the Creation." *Ensign,* June 1982, 9–15.

———. *Doctrinal New Testament Commentary.* 3 vols. Salt Lake City: Bookcraft, 1965–73.

———. *Mormon Doctrine.* 2d ed. Salt Lake City: Bookcraft, 1966.

———. *The Mortal Messiah.* 4 vols. Salt Lake City: Deseret Book, 1979–81.

———. *A New Witness for the Articles of Faith.* Salt Lake City: Deseret Book, 1985.

———. *The Promised Messiah: The First Coming of Christ.* Salt Lake City: Deseret Book, 1978.

———. "The Purifying Power of Gethsemane." *Ensign,* May 1985, 9–11.

———. "The Three Pillars of Eternity." Brigham Young University Speeches of the Year, Provo, Utah, 17 February 1981. Available at http://speeches.byu.edu.

McConkie, Joseph Fielding. *Gospel Symbolism.* Salt Lake City: Bookcraft, 1985.

———. *Seeking the Spirit.* Salt Lake City: Deseret Book, 1978.

McConkie, Joseph Fielding, and Donald W. Parry. *A Guide to Scriptural Symbols.* Salt Lake City: Bookcraft, 1990.

*Millennial Star.* 1840–1970.

Millet, Robert L. *By Grace Are We Saved.* Salt Lake City: Bookcraft, 1989.

Murphy-O'Connor, Jerome. "What Really Happened at Gethsemane." *Bible Review* 14 (April 1998): 28–39, 52.

Nelson, Russell M. "The Atonement." *Ensign,* November 1996, 33–36.

———. *Perfection Pending, and Other Favorite Discourses.* Salt Lake City: Deseret Book, 1998.

———. "Personal Preparation for Temple Blessings." *Ensign,* May 2001, 32–35.

———. "Standards of the Lord's Standard-Bearers." *Ensign,* August 1991, 5–11.

Nibley, Hugh. *Approaching Zion.* Salt Lake City and Provo: Deseret Book and FARMS, 1989.

———. *Enoch the Prophet.* Salt Lake City and Provo: Deseret Book and FARMS, 1986.

———. *Old Testament and Related Studies.* Salt Lake City and Provo: Deseret Book and FARMS, 1986.

———. *When the Lights Went Out.* Provo, Utah: FARMS, 2001.

Onions, C. T., ed. *The Oxford Dictionary of English Etymology.* Oxford: Clarendon Press, 1966.

Otto, Rudolph. *The Idea of the Holy.* London: Oxford University Press, 1936.

*Oxford English Dictionary.* 2d ed. 20 vols. New York: Oxford University Press, 1989.

Packer, Boyd K. Address given in the videoconference "Accomplishing the Mission of the Church." Broadcast, 28 June 1987.

———. "Atonement, Agency, Accountability." *Ensign,* May 1988, 69–72.

———. "The Brilliant Morning of Forgiveness." *Ensign,* November 1995, 18–21.

———. "The Mediator." *Ensign,* May 1977, 54–56.

Parry, Donald W. "Garden of Eden: Prototype Sanctuary." In *Temples of the Ancient World: Ritual and Symbolism.* Edited by Donald W. Parry. Salt Lake City and Provo: Deseret Book and FARMS, 1994.

Parry, Donald W., Jay A. Parry, and Tina M. Peterson. *Understanding Isaiah.* Salt Lake City: Deseret Book, 1998.

Parry, Jay A., and Donald W. Parry. *Understanding the Book of Revelation.* Salt Lake City: Deseret Book, 1998.

———. *Understanding the Parables of Jesus Christ.* Salt Lake City: Deseret Book, 2006.

Penrose, Charles W. "The First-Born, the Resurrection, and the Life." *Improvement Era* 22 (July 1919): 747–55.

Petersen, Mark E. "Creator and Savior." *Ensign,* May 1983, 63–65.

Phelps, William W. "The Answer." In *Times and Seasons* v. 5 (1 January 1845): 757–61. Available at http://www.centerplace.org/history/ts/v5n24.htm.

Pratt, John P. "The Constellations Testify of Christ," http://www.meridianmagazine.com.

———. "Enoch's Constellations Testify of Christ," http://www.meridianmagazine.com.

———. "What Every Mormon Should Know about Astronomy," http://www.meridian magazine.com.

Propp, William H. C. *The Anchor Bible: Exodus 19–40: A New Translation with Introduction and Commentary.* New York: Doubleday, 2006.

*Random House Webster's Unabridged Dictionary.* Edited by Wendalyn R. Nichols et al. 2d ed. New York: Random House, 1998.

Rasmussen, Ellis T. *A Latter-day Saint Commentary on the Old Testament.* Salt Lake City: Deseret Book, 1993.

Read, Lenet Hadley. "All Things Testify of Him: Understanding Symbolism in the Scriptures." *Ensign,* January 1981, 5–7.

———. "Jesus Christ, Types and Shadows of." In *Encyclopedia of Mormonism,* edited by Daniel H. Ludlow. New York: Macmillan, 1992.

Richards, George F. In Conference Report, April 1916, 51–55.

Ricks, Stephen D. "The Law of Sacrifice." *Ensign,* June 1998, 24–29.

Robinson, Robert. "Come Thou Fount of Every Blessing." Available at http://www.cyber hymnal.org/htm/c/o/comethou/.htm.

Robinson, Stephen E. *Believing Christ: The Parable of the Bicycle and Other Good News.* Salt Lake City: Deseret Book, 1992.

Rolleston, Frances. *Mazzaroth; or, The Constellations.* London: Rivingtons, 1862.

Romney, Marion G. "The Atonement of the Savior." *Improvement Era* 56 (December 1953): 942–43.

———. In Conference Report, October 1953, 34–37.

Satterfield, Bruce. "I Am the Bread of Life," http://www.meridianmagazine.com/gospel doctrine/nt/070313nt12.html.

Scott, Richard G. "To Establish a Secure Foundation for Life." Brigham Young University Speeches of the Year, Provo, Utah, 18 March 2008. Available at http://speeches. byu.edu.

———. "Jesus Christ, Our Redeemer." *Ensign,* May 1997, 53–59.

Seiss, Joseph A. *The Gospel in the Stars.* Philadelphia: Claxton, 1882.

Skinner, Andrew C. *Gethsemane.* Salt Lake City: Deseret Book, 2002.

———. *Golgotha.* Salt Lake City: Deseret Book, 2004.

———. "Jacob: Keeper of Covenants." *Ensign,* March 1998, 50–55.

———. *Prophets, Priests, and Kings: Old Testament Figures Who Symbolize Christ.* Salt Lake: Deseret Book, 2005.

———. "Savior, Satan, and Serpent: The Duality of a Symbol in the Scriptures." In *The Disciple As Scholar: Essays on Scripture and the Ancient World in Honor of Richard Lloyd Anderson.* Edited by Stephen D. Ricks et al., 359–84. Provo, Utah: FARMS and BYU, 2000.

———. *Temple Worship.* Salt Lake City: Deseret Book, 2007.

Smith, Joseph. *Encyclopedia of Joseph Smith's Teachings.* Edited by Larry E. Dahl and Donald Q. Cannon. Salt Lake City: Bookcraft, 1997.

———. *History of The Church of Jesus Christ of Latter-day Saints.* Edited by B. H. Roberts. 2d ed. rev. 7 vols. Salt Lake City: The Church of Jesus Christ of Latter-day Saints, 1932–51.

———. *Lectures on Faith.* Salt Lake City: Deseret Book, 1985.

———. *The Personal Writings of Joseph Smith.* Compiled and edited by Dean C. Jessee. Salt Lake City: Deseret Book, 1984.

———. *Teachings of the Prophet Joseph Smith.* Selected by Joseph Fielding Smith. Salt Lake City: Deseret Book, 1976.

———. *The Words of Joseph Smith.* Compiled and edited by Andrew F. Ehat and Lyndon W. Cook. Orem, Utah: Grandin Book, 1991.

Smith, Joseph Fielding. *Answers to Gospel Questions.* 5 vols. Salt Lake City: Deseret Book, 1957–66.

———. *Doctrines of Salvation.* Compiled by Bruce R. McConkie. 3 vols. in 1. Salt Lake City: Bookcraft, 1999.

———. *Salvation Universal.* Salt Lake City: Genealogical Society of Utah, 1920.

Smith, William. *A Dictionary of the Bible.* London: John Murray, 1863.

Talmage, James E. *Articles of Faith.* Salt Lake City: The Church of Jesus Christ of Latter-day Saints, 1950.

———. *Jesus the Christ.* Salt Lake City: Deseret Book, 1916.

Taylor, John. "Discourse." *Deseret News Semi-Weekly,* 5 January 1873, 760.

———. *Mediation and Atonement.* 1882. Reprint, Salt Lake City: Stevens & Wallis, 1950.

Thomas, M. Catherine. *Selected Writings of M. Catherine Thomas.* Salt Lake City: Deseret Book, 2000.

*Times and Seasons.* Nauvoo, Illinois, 1839–46.

*True to the Faith: A Gospel Reference.* Salt Lake City: The Church of Jesus Christ of Latter-day Saints, 2004.

Tvedtnes, John A. "Symbolism of the Sacrament," www.meridianmagazine.com/gospel-doctrine/nt/070530nt23sf.html.

Valletta, Thomas R. "The True Bread of Life." *Ensign,* March 1999, 6–13.

Webster, Noah. *American Dictionary of the English Language.* New York: S. Converse, 1828. Reprint, San Francisco: Foundation for American Christian Education, 1980.

Whitney, Orson F. *Saturday Night Thoughts.* Salt Lake City: Deseret News, 1921.

———. *Through Memory's Halls: The Life Story of Orson F. Whitney.* Independence, Mo.: Press of Zion's Printing and Publishing Co., 1930.

Widtsoe, John A. "Temple Worship." *Utah Genealogical and Historical Magazine* 12 (April 1921): 49–64.

Young, Brigham. *Discourses of Brigham Young.* Selected by John A. Widtsoe. Salt Lake City: Deseret Book, 1943.

# INDEX

Aaron, rod of, 127, 259–60
Abel, 59, 77–78, 348–49
Abigail, 94–96
Abilities, magnified, 287–88
Abinadi, 72
Ablutions, 22–23, 126
Abraham, 78–79, 222–23, 226
Adam: learns to give animal sacrifices, 9; commanded to give animal sacrifice, 48, 210; as type of Christ, 76–77; as shadow of resurrection, 260
Alma the Younger, 217, 320–21
Almond tree, 127, 134
Altar: atonement for, 37; of incense, 125–26; sacrificial, 126; horns of, 126, 136; stones and, 153
Angel(s): sacred clothing of, 28–29; blood of Jesus Christ as protection from destroying, 63, 64–65
Animals: commandment to sacrifice, 48; slaughter of, 50; female, 141–45; as sacrifice of value, 146; clean and unclean, 146–48; atonement typified by sacrifice of, 210; used for clothing, 231; covered by atonement, 271–72. *See also* Sacrificial animals
Apostasy, 102
Aquarius, 166
Aries, 166
Ark, 88–91
Ark of the covenant, 236
Arrest, 224–26
Atonement: importance of, 1–2; symbols,

shadows, and witnesses of, 2–4; deepening understanding of, 5–6; ordinances and, 7–11, 20, 21–22; temple and, 18–20; blood as essential component of, 59–63; feasts focusing on, 64, 69–70; fall and, 76–77; provides protection, 88–89; parables teach of, 113–14; colors associated with, 130–33; prophecies on, 173–77; preparations and events preceding, 200–207; symbols at offering, 207–21; on cross, 243; receiving gift of, 250–52; covers many worlds and inhabitants, 268–69; perfect, 278; lifting power of, 291–93; love, power, and sacrifice as elements of, 301–3; consequences without, 312–13; accepting, 319–24; bringing, into our hearts, 325–26; gratitude for, 327–29; understanding meaning of, 329–31; words used to describe, 333–43; definition of term, 334–35; Satan attempts to imitate, 344–49. *See also* Day of Atonement; Infinite atonement
Auriga, 166
Ax, 93–94

Ballard, Melvin J., 222–23
Baptism: symbols in, 14–15; flood parallels, 89–90; as shadow of Jesus Christ, 134; of Jesus Christ, 259; for children, 272–73
Barabbas, 230–31
Barren women, 103–4, 298

369